MARITIME DOMINION
AND THE TRIUMPH OF THE FREE WORLD

MARITIME DOMINION
AND THE TRIUMPH OF THE FREE WORLD

Naval Campaigns that Shaped
the Modern World 1852–2001

PETER PADFIELD

THE OVERLOOK PRESS
New York

This edition first published in hardcover in the United States in 2010 by

The Overlook Press, Peter Mayer Publishers, Inc.
141 Wooster Street
New York, NY 10012
www.overlookpress.com
For bulk and special sales, please contact sales@overlookny.com

Cataloging-in-Publication Data is available from the Library of Congress

Manufactured in the United States of America
FIRST EDITION
2 4 6 8 10 9 7 5 3 1
ISBN 978-1-59020-332-3

For Guy and Fiona

Contents

Illustrations

The author and publishers would like to thank the following for permission to reproduce illustrations: Plates 1 and 2, National Portrait Gallery, London; 3, 4, 13, 14, 25, 26 and 27, Private Collection; 5, 6, 7, 9, 10, 15, 28, 29, 30, 35, 36, 37, 38, 39, 40 and 41, US Navy; 8, © Corbis; 11, 12, 17, 19 and 31, Getty Images; 16, PA Photos; 18, 20, 21, 22, 23 and 24, Imperial War Museum, London; 32 and 33, Bundesarchiv Koblenz; 34, US National Archives

Maps and Diagrams

Acknowledgements

A S EVER, JANE, my wife, provided extensive support and encouragement throughout the writing of this book; and our son, Guy, gave
excellent counsel and practical assistance.

Professor Jon Tetsuro Sumida was generous with time and help on
the subject he has illuminated so brilliantly, gunnery fire control in the
Dreadnought era, as well as on many other topics. I have been unable to
do full justice to his insights within the tight framework of this book, but
for those wishing to pursue the argument his key works are listed in the
Bibliography. They provide superb examples of how determined investigation and lateral thinking can prevail over deliberate obfuscation of
official records – and goodness knows there has been enough of that. I
have benefited equally from Professor Nicholas Lambert's penetrating
interpretations of this era of radical change at the British Admiralty, and
am grateful for permission to quote from his 'Strategic Command and
Control for Maneuver Warfare', published in the *Journal of Military
History*.

I have been particularly fortunate that Robin Jessup, who produced the
maps and battle diagrams for both previous volumes in this maritime trilogy, was able to employ his talent for clarity in this final volume; and I am
indebted to Ian Paten for his meticulous copy-editing and Caroline
Westmore for smoothing the book's path through production. I am grateful to my *Mayflower II* shipmate, David Thorpe, for the loan of books and
much practical help, as also to John and Sara Symes for encouragement
and the loan of books.

I thank the following publishers, authors, translators and editors for
permission to quote from their books: Cambridge University Press for John
G. Röhl (trans. Terence F. Cole), *The Kaiser and His Court*; Weidenfeld &
Nicolson, an imprint of the Orion Publishing group, for Sebastian Haffner
(trans. Oliver Pretzel), *Defying Hitler*; W. W. Norton for E. O. Wilson, *The
Creation*; John Murray for Margaret MacMillan, *Peacemakers*; Hodder &

Stoughton, an imprint of Hachette Livre (UK), for C. V. Usborne, *Blast and Counterblast*, and W. S. Chalmers, *The Life and Letters of David, Earl Beatty*; Sidgwick & Jackson, an imprint of Pan Macmillan, for Julian Thompson, *The War at Sea 1914–1918*.

If there is anyone I have overlooked, I apologize.

Introduction

WE SPOILED CHILDREN of the Enlightenment are heading for a shock of scarcely imaginable proportions. We are for the squeeze between an inexorably increasing world population and the demand for economic growth to support stable societies in the West and to lift the poorest from poverty in the developing giants, India and China particularly. We are in Thomas Malthus territory; but in the 210 years since Malthus argued that increase of population will always tend to outrun growth of production we have consumed so many of the earth's resources that it seems our very survival as a species is at stake. At the least we will learn, contrary to Genesis, 1:28, that God did not create earth's bounty solely for our enjoyment. What the future holds in war, famine or pestilence to restore some balance is uncertain; some thoughts will be found at the end of this volume. In the meantime here is the story of the Western maritime trading system that has brought us to this pass.

It is the final volume in a trilogy begun with *Maritime Supremacy and the Opening of the Western Mind*. That book described the Dutch republic rising to maritime trading and financial dominance in the seventeenth century, and Great Britain overtaking her in the eighteenth century, both at the expense of their larger, more populous rival, France. The second volume, *Maritime Power and the Struggle for Freedom*, charted the epic final rounds of the contest between Britain and France, and Britain's emergence in the nineteenth century as supreme trading, financial and industrial world power.

At the heart of both volumes was the opposition between 'maritime' and 'territorial' power as embodied in contrasting types of government and society. Both supreme maritime powers, the Dutch and the British, evolved similar governing forms: characterized as 'merchant government', or government by merchants for merchants, these were unique among states of any consequence since they could survive only in countries enjoying both access to major sea trading routes and natural barriers against land attack –

I

in the Dutch case a web of waterways and low land which could be flooded, in the British case the English Channel. Without such natural defences merchant cities fell prey to neighbouring territorial powers. But secure behind their moats, the merchants of Amsterdam and London and other Dutch and British port cities amassed wealth from sea trade and used it to build political power, which they wielded through consultative assemblies to curb the prerogatives of the executive head of state, particularly in matters of finance and taxes.

Territorial powers, on the other hand, concerned with the defence or extension of their land borders and the suppression of separatist tendencies within provinces acquired by conquest or dynastic marriage, were dominated by warrior elites whose compulsions provided a very different governing form. All powers were concentrated in the person of the ruler and transmitted through his appointed ministers, a professional bureaucracy and provincial proconsuls; the aim was to harmonize all regions under a system of uniform regulation and harness the full strength of the people. If local or national consultative assemblies existed they had been drained of meaningful authority. Taxation and expenditure were the prerogative of the ruler and were directed by his ministers, accountable to him alone. There was no public audit, nor usually a proper government audit. When required extra finance was raised by extraordinary levies – masked often as 'voluntary patriotic contributions' – levies on conquered populations, the sale of public offices, or loans from financiers secured on the credit of the ruler.

Here the maritime powers had a crucial advantage. Transparency in all matters of taxation and expenditure combined with the security of private wealth from arbitrary levies had led to the development of sophisticated financial institutions and, crucially, long-term borrowing. A large part of the extraordinary costs of war was met in this way, spreading the burden to future generations. And since the borrowing formed a 'national debt' guaranteed in the representative assembly of the nation, it commanded the confidence of the moneyed interest at home and abroad and allowed the maritime powers to borrow at substantially lower rates of interest than territorial powers whose credit was tied to the reputation of the ruler. Finance was always the sinews of war; and since the great wars of the seventeenth and eighteenth centuries were essentially armed struggles to extend or defend overseas markets it is appropriate that they were decided largely on margins of interest. It is scarcely too much to say that for the maritime powers war was a business venture, their ever-increasing national debt the debentures for capital necessarily laid out to extend their markets.

Cheaper borrowing was not the only factor in the success of the maritime powers: the ability of states enjoying ascendancy at sea to draw resources from all over the world and in war deny this possibility to the enemy was equally important. Finally, Britain's triumph over Napoleonic France demonstrated beyond doubt that trade was superior to conquest for the creation of national wealth. This was the vital factor. Plunder was inevitably a diminishing asset, while trade generated both wealth and mutual relationships; indeed, the nineteenth-century philosopher, John Stuart Mill, celebrated it as 'one of the greatest instruments not only of civilisation in the narrowest, but of improvements in culture in the widest sense'.[1]

Brilliant trading city-states shine throughout history, but it was the coalition of trading wealth in nation-states of the size and natural defensive capacity of the Dutch republic and Great Britain which enabled the trading ethic to gain ascendancy over the martial and spread around the world. And it was this global expansion of trade, stimulating industry, which for the first time in world history produced 'intensive' growth: a rise in average income per head rather than simple economic expansion benefiting elites only.[2] Capitalism and popular consumerism were developed to high levels in the seventeenth-century Dutch republic, but it was Great Britain in the nineteenth century which brought these dominant features of the modern West to fruition; as Niall Ferguson has argued, 'the world we know today is in large measure the product of Britain's age of empire'.[3]

If this is so for global trade and finance and armed power it is also true in socio-cultural terms. The essence of the merchant ethic was freedom. The Dutch republic in the seventeenth century and Great Britain in the eighteenth century stood out from Continental powers as beacons of intellectual and religious freedoms. Since both were centres of printing and publishing, they were viewed in Continental courts that maintained strict control of information and ideas as founts of subversion, as they were. The seismic uprising known as the French Revolution was prepared by ideas that found first expression in the maritime powers.

Within the maritime powers, meanwhile, freedom worked to undermine received ideas and class values and shape a more mobile, enterprising and entrepreneurial society than was possible under the authoritarian regimes of territorial powers. It was the hierarchical rigidity of the French social order and the lack of representative institutions which ensured that the financial difficulties of the French Crown in 1788 touched off revolution; evolution was impossible. By contrast, the fine balancing of authority in the governance of the maritime powers and the democratic influences of commerce and popularly elected institutions positively encouraged change and adaptation. It was not simply trading wealth or naval force which ensured the triumph of maritime over territorial power; it was the fusion of trading, financial, naval, constitutional and social strengths, each growing from and feeding the others to create a virtuous ascending spiral that carried all before it.

During the period covered by this final volume the United States picked up from Great Britain the baton of maritime and world supremacy, while Germany and Russia replaced France as expressions of territorial power and extreme martial values. Both were humbled. So, too, was Japan, an island nation rather like Britain yet imbued with the territorial ethic. The question is whether the opposition of 'merchant' and 'territorial' power as described in the previous volumes holds good for this period despite anomalies like Japan; if so, whether it is likely to continue as a universal principle of indefinite duration, or whether, as seems more likely, pollution, damage to ecosystems and depletion of essential natural resources resulting from the success of the global trading system will force radical change which alters the power equations.

This volume begins with Great Britain as the world's only superpower, still grounded in the Christian faith and convinced of an earthly mission to civilize the world.

I

The British Empire

———•———

GREAT BRITAIN'S NINETEENTH-CENTURY empire is subject to constant reinterpretation. For those who created and served it, interpretation was hardly necessary: Britain was the fount of moral and material progress, the empire a vehicle for civilizing the world. It was an inspiring conceit; yet it had a solid basis: by replacing human energy with inanimate power sources Britain's Industrial Revolution was transforming the terms of existence, and expectations. Steam railways and steamships were opening hitherto remote parts of the world; cheap manufactures were clothing and equipping mass consumers in all regions touched by British trade. Britons themselves were materially better off by reason of the productivity gained by machines.

The intellectual foundations were as secure. They were based largely on the economic theories of Adam Smith. In his seminal work on *The Wealth of Nations*, published in 1776,[1] Smith had deplored the high prices and inefficiences created by national monopolies and protective tariffs on imports, and argued for 'natural liberty' for men and nations to pursue their own interests free of artificial constraints on trade or labour. One of his earliest converts had been William Pitt, the younger, Prime Minister from 1783. Pitt had begun reducing customs duties but was prevented from continuing by the outbreak of the French Revolutionary War and the consequent need for increased government revenues.

Pitt also supported abolition of the slave trade. Adam Smith had argued against slave labour on economic grounds, but for the leaders of the British abolitionist movement and their mass supporters it was purely a moral issue, and there is no doubt Pitt viewed it as such. He died in 1806. The following year, by coincidence, both the British Parliament and the US Congress had outlawed the slave trade on grounds of moral conviction against powerful vested interests and their own countries' economic self-interest. British abolitionists expected other nations to follow their lead. When this did not happen Britain took it upon herself to force them to do so. It was an extraordinary project, unique in recorded history, since it was driven, like Britain's own renunciation, by philanthropy, not economics. A French historian described it as 'global moralism'.[2] So it was. It had little connection with rational foreign policy – however much French politicians and journalists ascribed it to the British desire to rule the world – and was attended by increasing costs, diplomatic, financial and in health and lives aboard the warships that were dispatched from 1808 to patrol the slaving coasts of West Africa.[3]

The United States was unable to take the same high line. The economy of the southern states, particularly their chief exports of cotton and tobacco, was inextricably bound up with the institution of slavery; many northern shipowners and financiers were linked to the plantation economy. As a result virtually no provision was made for enforcing abolition in the United States, and American ships continued the trade illegally. Moreover, such was the sensitivity of the US government to British naval boarding parties searching their ships that the United States' ensign became a pre-ferred flag of immunity for slavers of all nations. The French government was equally sensitive to British claims to the right of search, and their position had been upheld by the Admiralty Court in London.

Successive British governments had reacted to the difficulties by increasing their efforts with states that could be coerced, particularly Portugal and Spain and their New World dependencies, Brazil and Cuba. Foremost in the campaign were Pitt's protégés, Lord Castlereagh and George Canning. Both had served in wartime governments and believed, like Pitt, that in leading the coalitions than defeated Napoleon, Britain had saved Europe from tyranny. Both assumed continuing British leadership and held that Britain herself provided the model for Europe and the world. 'Let us hope for the interests of mankind', Canning said in 1830, 'that all nations will endeavour to introduce that vital spirit, that germ of strength which has enabled so small a country to make such extraordinary exertions to save itself, and to deal out salvation to the world.'[4]

It was in this mind that he and another of Pitt's disciples, William Huskisson, had set out to complete their former chief's work by reducing tariffs on imports and modifying the Navigation Laws imposed in the seventeenth century to protect British shipping and assure a reservoir of sailors by reserving imports to British ships or ships of the country of origin. The aim was to increase the volume of international trade by freeing it from restrictions, and create on scientific economic principles a global division of labour in which countries produced only those goods for which they were best suited by climate and resources.

There were several areas where the British commitment to free trade and the abolition of slavery either clashed or merited the charges of hypocrisy that they received regularly from France. A large proportion of the textile manufactures Britain exported worldwide under the terms of free trade were made from slave-grown cotton from the southern United States; similarly, sugar, coffee and cotton from the slave-worked plantations of Brazil were handled, processed and sold on by British firms, as was Cuban sugar and tobacco, also produced by slaves. When in 1846 Parliament reduced duties on imported sugar in the cause of free trade, anti-slavery societies raised an outcry, demanding the reintroduction of duties on at least the 'blood-stained sugars' of Brazil and Cuba.[5]

Lord Palmerston, Foreign Secretary for long periods in the 1830s and 1840s, succeeded in closing down the major market for African slaves in Brazil. He was a passionate abolitionist and pursued his aims with a mixture of diplomatic and financial pressure, monetary inducements and naval force – on the latter commenting that such 'half-civilised governments all require a dressing down every eight or ten years'. Naval action in flagrant violation of Brazilian sovereignty provided the catalyst for his success, but the deeper cause was the penetration of the Brazilian economy by British finance. Since declaring independence from Portugal in 1822 the country had been developed with the aid of British trade and loans, and it was the need to maintain commercial relations and credit with the City of London which underlay Brazil's conversion.

Near the close of his life Palmerston looked back on the ending of the Brazilian slave trade as the achievement which gave him 'the greatest and purest pleasure'.[6] It was appropriate. He had not ended transatlantic slaving altogether, nor the institution of slavery, which continued in the southern United States until the Civil War and the Spanish colonies of Cuba and Puerto Rico until almost the end of the century – and far beyond in Africa itself – but he had achieved a decisive shift in perspectives. After mid-century the Atlantic trade was an anomaly, its days clearly numbered.

Palmerston's was a principled objection driven by passion. Yet the crusade he, his Cabinet colleagues and their predecessors had sustained was intimately connected with a desire to establish legitimate commerce in Africa and South America; this, in turn, formed part of the drive to extend free trade and with it British commercial and financial norms around the world. P. J. Cain and A. G. Hopkins, economists of British imperialism, have described this as 'the world's first comprehensive development programme'.[7] It involved exporting the liberal values of individual freedoms and property rights guaranteed by law, free markets and fiscal and financial disciplines and carried with it a strong Christianizing and 'civilizing' mission. It was an attempt, again to quote Cain and Hopkins, 'to reshape the world in Britain's image'.

Before mid-century industrialists had been the main supporters and beneficiaries of the drive to free trade. Leading figures in the City of London had not subscribed, believing the increase in imports that would result from cutting tariffs would lead to a drain of gold to pay for them.[8] Despite the realization of their fears in 1846 when Corn Laws designed to protect British farmers and landowners from foreign competition were repealed and wheat from abroad flooded into the country, the momentum to free trade was irresistible; and from 1849 to 1854 the remaining Navigation Laws were abolished. It had been a bitter struggle. Opponents of the legislation charged the government with abandoning the defence of the nation as shipowners forecast the collapse of the merchant marine, rightly regarded as nursery and reserve of sailors for the Royal Navy in time of war. In truth the shipping industry had been sapped by protection and needed the prick of competition: in those international trades that had not been reserved to British ships, Americans ruled, their reputation such that British skippers aped the Yankee manner, even adopting a nasal American twang to increase their authority.[9]

The collapse of the last redoubts of protectionism in foodstuffs and merchant shipping had coincided with the discovery of gold in California (1849) and Australia (1851), and with radical improvements in transport and communications as railways and steamship routes were extended and tele-graph cables laid under the sea. The result was a prodigious expansion of international trade and capital flows and the flowering of what David Kynaston, historian of the City of London, has called 'the nearest we would ever come to a fully liberal [international], free trading system'.[10]

London was the hub, the entrepôt and financial-commercial mediator for the world. Comparisons with seventeenth-century Amsterdam are compelling: like the River Ij then, the Thames was crowded with shipping and its banks were lined with warehouses filled with commodities from every region of the world. Adjoining streets were hazed with smoke and the scents and smells of a maze of finishing, refining and manufacturing workshops interspersed with wholesale and auction rooms and brokers' offices extending to the financial quarter of the City around the Bank of England in Threadneedle Street. The Bank was the pivot of the system, as the Exchange Bank of Amsterdam had been two centuries before, and for the same reason: it guaranteed the exchange value of the currency.

Specifically the Bank maintained the British pound sterling on the 'Gold Standard', equivalent in value to a fixed weight of gold. The mechanism was largely self-regulating. Charged by law with holding sufficient bullion to back note issues, the Bank responded to movements of gold in or out of the country as a result of trading imbalances by adjusting its interest rate, only occasionally intervening directly in the bullion market. Since the Bank guaranteed to exchange its notes for the equivalent in gold and there were no barriers to the movement of gold out of Britain, traders anywhere in the world had the assurance that settlements made in sterling cheques or bills of exchange drawn on London were literally as good as gold. In consequence sterling had become the major international trading currency, even when there was no commercial link with Great Britain.

With the international primacy of sterling, London finance houses had evolved an unrivalled market in short-term commercial credit. Thus sterling bills of exchange which were 'accepted' – in effect guaranteed – by merchant banks specializing in 'acceptance' business were readily saleable in the London bill market at a discount off face value. The system lubricated trade worldwide; as it was put in a parliamentary committee report in 1858, 'A man in Boston [USA] cannot buy a cargo of tea in Canton without getting a credit from Messrs Matheson or Messrs Baring'[11] – both London houses. And for this reason many foreign merchants preferred to operate from London itself.

The more spectacular role of London's leading merchant banks was the issue of long-term loans to foreign governments. Here Rothschild was the major force, largely because the London house was allied with houses run by family members in Paris, Frankfurt, Vienna and Naples. Niall Ferguson, latest biographer of this extraordinary clan, suggests that the five houses operated in effect as 'component parts of a multinational bank'.[12] The father of the London bank, Nathan Rothschild, and his main rival, Alexander Baring, had been instrumental in stabilizing Europe after the devastation of Napoleon's wars. Baring had given essential financial support for the British-style constitutional monarchy imposed on France after Waterloo; Rothschild had inaugurated loans for foreign governments designed to be as attractive to investors in the London market as British stock; they were usually more attractive since they carried a higher interest than British government bonds. He achieved this by arranging for interest to be paid in sterling in London, cutting out exchange rate risks, and most significantly by insisting on more certain security than the word of a sovereign, hitherto the only backing for international lending.

By linking loans to constitutional reform, and subsequently to fiscal discipline, the Rothschilds, Baring and others had become powerful instruments of the drive to reshape the world in Britain's image, even more potent perhaps than the Royal Navy, whose worldwide demonstrations of British reach and strength were more immediately obvious. In truth the City and the navy were interdependent; the aura of invincibility the navy had won in the French wars provided the ultimate security for sterling's gold standard.

British finance had wrought a similar transformation in the less developed regions outside Europe. The newly emerged states of Latin America were formally independent but so permeated with British commerce and capital, so constrained by the need to maintain credit in the City of London, that they were in effect dependencies – as Brazil's abrupt renunciation of the slave trade had demonstrated.[13] The formal empire, India, Canada, Australia and New Zealand, was no less dependent on development funds from the City; a Canadian historian would later acknowledge the role played by City investment for canal and railway construction, the lumber and grain trades, mines and industries in preserving Canada from a takeover by her powerful southern neighbour.[14] Even that neighbour, the United States, relied heavily on the London capital market for the canal and railway projects it was stretching across the continent.

To contemporaries, the great financiers, particularly the greatest of all, the Rothschilds, appeared to wield such power that they could dictate peace or war between nations. Niall Ferguson suggests their influence was actually limited to underwriting peace once it had been made and supporting legitimate regimes against subversion.[15] The poet and radical socialist Heinrich Heine, who came from a merchant background, saw financiers themselves as subversives, destroying the old aristocracies based on landholding. He charged James Rothschild, dominant in the Paris capital market, which almost equalled London in the issue of foreign loans, with 'raising the system of state bonds to supreme power, thereby mobilising property and income and at the same time endowing money with the previous privileges of the land'.[16]

The British landholding aristocracy, too, had been permeated by merchant money and values, and for rather longer than their French counterparts; an alliance between the British landholding elite and the merchant interest had resulted in Britain being governed from at least the 'Glorious Revolution' of 1688/89 as a merchant state. Similarly in the nineteenth century, particularly the second half, the merchant bankers who built fortunes on London's financial pre-eminence were received smoothly into the country houses and gentlemen's clubs of the ruling groups, where power was mediated. Absorbing the style of the aristocracy and building great country houses themselves, where they entertained lavishly and hunted and shot, it was their necessities, not the industrialists', whose wealth was small by comparison, which influenced national policy,[17] just as the conditions they imposed on foreign creditors were the prime instruments in the project to anglicize the world and make it safe for British trade and capital. All in the City were by mid-century committed free traders. Their anxieties on that score had dissolved in the rising tide of internationalism and prosperity following the end of protection.[18]

From mid-century it was interest on foreign loans and investments, together with receipts from the financial, insurance, shipping and legal services associated with the City's international trading role – so-called 'invisible' earnings – which made up for increasing deficits on visible trade and pushed Britain's overall trade balance into credit.

This new order in which the City of London and its professional services provided the motor of economic expansion and much of the dynamic behind foreign policy has been characterized by Cain and Hopkins as 'gentlemanly capitalism'. The dominant financiers moving in the ruling circles of the aristocracy mutated: Rothschild's heir, 'Natty', became 1st Baron Rothschild, Baring's heirs the Barons Ashburton, Northbrook, Revelstoke and Cromer.

The investors, bondholders, merchants and men who ran the City's institutions servicing international capital and commerce also adopted the aristocratic code and sent their sons to public schools to mix with and be educated as English gentlemen.[19] Thus the new wealthy middle-class entrants to the historically porous ranks of gentlemen were moulded in religious observance, the classics, self-reliance, loyalty and team games: cricket, the Rugby schoolmaster told Tom Brown, 'merges the individual in the eleven; he doesn't play that he may win, but that his side may win'.[20]

Dynamic cultures require a creed. The code of the Christian gentleman was an inspiring one. Married to the scientific liberalism of Adam Smith and his followers and the revelations of extreme 'Manchester School' economists that nations which traded with each other were less likely to fight one another, hence free trade was the path to universal peace, it was irresistible. The practical value was confirmed by recent history and observation. The British had irrefutably, in the words of the historian Lord Macaulay, 'carried the means of locomotion and correspondence, every mechanical art, every manufacture, everything that promotes the convenience of life, to a perfection which our ancestors would have thought magical',[21] while the state of the country was such that a politician in the 1860s could legitimately comment: 'Is not property safe? Is not every man able to say what he likes? Can you not walk from one end of England to the other in perfect security? I ask you whether, the world over or in past history, there is anything like it? Nothing.'[22]

Overseas the Royal Navy guaranteed similar security. The captain of a steam gunboat ordered at mid-century to the Italian coast off Rome to protect British interests wrote home, 'You cannot imagine the effect of a British man of war . . . my presence at Rome kept the city tranquil, though my ship was 50 miles off.'[23] He reflected in his private journal: 'English influence still carries the day, and a word of advice from us will do anything. How glorious is the title of "Englishman" – and yet we are not loved. How is it? Is it our national conceit; or self-confident and supercilious bearing – the consciousness of superiority we show? Or is it jealousy?'[24]

Heinrich Heine could have supplied one answer: '*die ächtbritische Beschränkheit*' – the genuine British narrow-mindedness, or philistinism.[25] Heine hated the British for their impermeability to ideas. The poet and social philosopher Matthew Arnold, who fought all his life against this philistinism, laid the cause in history:

> In truth, the English . . . great as is the liberty which they have secured for themselves, have in all their changes proceeded . . . by the rule of thumb; what was intolerably inconvenient to them they have suppressed, and as they have suppressed it, not because it was irrational, but because it was practically inconvenient, they have seldom in suppressing it appealed to reason, but always, if possible, to some precedent, or form, or letter, which served as a convenient instrument for their purpose, and which saved them from the necessity of appealing to general principles. They have thus become, in a certain sense, of all people the most inaccessible to ideas and the most impatient of them . . .[26]

He absolved Edmund Burke – an Irishman – from the charge; he believed Burke great 'because, almost alone in England, he brings thought to bear upon politics, he saturates politics with thought'.[27] Burke was, of course, the political prophet who had predicted the failure of the French Revolution entirely from first principles, because it was attempting a wholesale restructuring of society on abstract theory. He believed in the organic development of society, rights defined by precedent and duty, liberty as 'an entailed inheritance derived to us from our forefathers and to be transmitted to our posterity',[28] not in political systems attempting to manufacture desired outcomes from reason.[29]

Yet the empirical order he extolled was not so much an essentially British system, rather a merchant organism which had found in London the safest, most nourishing locus for growth. Adopting and adapting the habits and institutions it found, it naturally assumed a British complexion, although its most powerful exponents were often of immigrant stock: the Rothschilds descended from a Frankfurt ghetto, the Barings from north German Protestant origins, the Queen from a Hanoverian dynasty, her consort, Prince Albert, from the German state of Saxe Coburg Gotha.

A subordinate branch of the system flourished in New York, where it had been planted by the Dutch in the seventeenth century – New Amsterdam as it then was. This Dutch-British offspring was now over-running North America. Another vigorous offshoot of the system had taken root in Paris.

Whether termed international capitalism, free market economics, economic liberalism or imperialism, in the second half of the nineteenth century the system was reshaping the world; and since its epicentre was London, much of the world came to look British. At bottom it was concerned solely with acquisition and financial gain; it led in all less developed regions of the world to the ruthless exploitation or suppression of materially weaker peoples and defenceless animal species, and similar exploitation in British and European industrial cities. It is a mistake, however, to reduce it to a simple economic imperative: it was served by the higher intellectual and moral values touched on here and was demonstrably constructive, not destructive in the manner of warrior power systems; it developed world-wide transport and communication infrastructures and raised industries that lifted material living standards, just as they had in Britain, and spread the concept of individual freedom guaranteed by property rights; indeed, Niall Ferguson has argued that 'the idea of liberty' was the most distinctive feature of the British Empire, which set it apart from its European rivals.[30]

The British perceived the obviously beneficent effects of the system as a sign of the value of their civilizing mission, and of their own value – even racial superiority – as did the Americans driving their branch of the system across the continent to the west coast. They were human; and presumption, as Montaigne observed, 'is our [human] natural and original disease'.[31] More than that, they had a human need to make the everyday more meaningful by investing it with high moral or intellectual purpose. For the British of the ruling and middling classes there were the obligations of the gentlemanly code; for the Americans settling former Indian wilderness the ideals of liberty and democracy.

Economists of Adam Smith's persuasion, statesmen and pragmatic bankers and dealers in the City of London were clear that increased international trade and loans, and the consequent intermeshing of economies worldwide, must lead to international peace, at least among great powers. This was sadly reminiscent of the high expectations at the beginning of the French Revolution of 1789. As then, the aspirations of intellectuals and practical men alike were to come up against the irrationality of the world. For the British the lesson would take longer; their dominion would extend throughout the century until they ruled directly almost a quarter of the world's population inhabiting a quarter of the earth's land surface, and of course the oceans that connected them. Early the next century they were to come up against a personification of the folly at the heart of power, the German Kaiser Wilhelm II.

2

The Russian (Crimean) War, 1854

WILLIAM GLADSTONE, CHANCELLOR of the Exchequer in the administration formed by Lord Aberdeen in 1853, was the embodiment of all aspirations for free trade, fiscal probity and rigorous economy that distinguished British nineteenth-century governments. Similarly, he personified the moral and religious fervour that possessed large swathes of the upper and middle classes. The established Church of England was, as he described it, 'the pole star' of his existence;[1] in its service, as a humbling duty, he devoted much extra-parliamentary time and energy to rescuing 'fallen women'. He founded houses of refuge funded with his own money and undertook personal missionary work in the area of west London bounded by Piccadilly, Soho and the Thames Embankment, walking the streets at night and engaging prostitutes in conversation about the state of their soul. In the words of a biographer, 'all his life . . . he did his best to reconcile a nineteenth-century political career with the Gospel and example of his Saviour'.[2]

In his first budget in 1853 he removed duties altogether from a wide range of commodities and reduced them further on others. The consequent loss of customs revenue obliged him to retain income tax, first imposed as an emergency wartime measure, but he regarded it as an immoral charge tempting politicians to extravagance, and proposed successive reductions in the rate until it could be abolished completely.

Britain was now virtually a free trade nation, yet relations between the great powers hardly supported the school of economists predicting an era of universal peace following the expansion of international trade. One factor that caused the British government anxiety throughout the century was Russia's southward expansion. The great land empire of the tsars spreading by conquest and absorption was the antithesis of Britain's sea trading empire and its chief rival for world power. It was of particular concern to British generals that Russia should not gain a foothold in the Ottoman Empire stretching around the eastern Mediterranean across the overland routes to India.

Britain also had a commercial stake in the Ottoman Empire. A free trade treaty Palmerston had concluded with Ottoman Turkey in 1838 contained provisions designed to modernize the Byzantine institutions of that state after the British model, since when trade had increased, providing Lancashire cotton goods with a substantial outlet and the British Exchequer with a trade surplus, although the hoped-for institutional reforms had proved disappointing.

France had comparable strategic-commercial interests in the country. Her policy was driven by the Emperor Napoleon III, a nephew of Napoleon Bonaparte, who had seized power in the crumbling second Republic on a promise to restore the nation to its former imperial glory. His forward policy had led to a bizarre dispute with Tsar Nicholas I of Russia over custody of Christian shrines within the Ottoman Empire. Nicholas, as Father of the Eastern Orthodox Church, escalated the controversy by declaring a virtual protectorate over all Christians in the Ottoman Balkan states and seeking Austrian support to remove these territories from the Ottoman Sultan and secure joint control of the straits leading into the Mediterranean, the Bosphorus and Dardanelles. This sounded the alarm in Britain. By 1853, as Gladstone delivered his economical budget, Lord Aberdeen found himself being drawn by France into war with Russia on behalf of the Ottoman Sultan Abdülmecid I. Like Gladstone, he was horrified.

His too obvious disinclination to intervene encouraged Nicholas, who sent troops into Ottoman territories at the mouth of the Danube – modern Rumania. Turkey declared war. Aberdeen still hoped desperately for a diplomatic solution, but in November a Russian squadron of six sail-of-the-line armed with shell guns annihilated a Turkish squadron in Sinope Bay on the southern shore of the Black Sea – the first hostile as opposed to experimental demonstration of the devastating effect of explosive shells on timber ships. It seemed to vindicate anxieties about the Tsar's designs on Constantinople held by a section of the Cabinet led by Palmerston. The time for diplomacy had passed. The public and the City of London certainly believed so, and Napoleon III seized the opportunity to call on the British government to join him in an ultimatum to Russia. Aberdeen bowed to the pressure. He believed in his heart that going to war for the Turks would be 'an act of insanity . . . utterly disgraceful to all of us concerned',[3] but found himself committed to cooperation with the historic enemy to protect Ottoman Turkey against Russia. On Christmas Eve orders went out for the British and French Mediterranean fleets to enter the Black Sea.

Both powers declared war on Russia on 27 March 1854 and the following month signed a treaty of alliance to which Sultan Abdülmecid subscribed. Gladstone had already doubled the rate of income tax in anticipation of the costs of war. Now he raised a loan on Exchequer bonds. 'War! War! War!' he wrote to his wife. 'I fear it will swallow up everything good and useful.'[4]

Britain's immediate aims were to secure the Dardanelles and Constantinople. Beyond this, the First Lord of the Admiralty, Sir James Graham, saw the goal as the destruction of Russia's Black Sea fleet and its base, Sebastopol: 'the eye tooth of the Bear must be drawn; and 'til his fleet and naval arsenal in the Black Sea are destroyed there is no safety for Constantinople, no security for the peace of Europe'[5] – a somewhat maritime-centred view since Russia's empire had been forged by her army; her navy was scarcely more than an appendage. Napoleon III backed the project and an allied expeditionary force was gathered for the purpose.

The other theatre where Russia was vulnerable to the Western allies was the Baltic. Here Graham assembled a powerful fleet under Vice-Admiral Sir Charles Napier to enter when the ice broke. The cabinet, however, was hopelessly divided on aims. A group of hawks led by Palmerston wanted to roll back Nicholas's empire on all fronts, and proposed enlisting Sweden with the prospect of her recovering Finland from Russia, liberating Russia's Baltic provinces and re-establishing Poland as a barrier between Russia and Germany. Aberdeen, Gladstone and the majority meant to limit the war to the protection of the Sultan's domains; consequently the Baltic campaign was left without a focus and without sufficient troops for meaningful action ashore. And since the Russian Baltic fleet was much inferior to Napier's fleet, it refused to emerge from the protection of its bases. Napier could find no more important target for his magnificent command than a Russian fort complex under construction at Bomarsund in the Aaland Islands commanding the entrance to the Gulf of Bothnia.

He had been provided by the Admiralty Hydrographic Department with two shallow-draught paddle steamers equipped as survey vessels and manned by surveying officers. The senior, Captain Bartholmew Sulivan, had learned his craft as second lieutenant in HMS *Beagle* on her voyage of exploration around South America and the Galapagos Islands with Charles Darwin aboard as naturalist. He now spent two weeks charting and buoying an intricate passage through the Aaland Islands to allow Napier's great ships to approach the forts without coming under fire from the guns commanding the main anchorage; subsequently he led five steam ships-of-the-line through the marked channel. At times the ends of the ships' yards

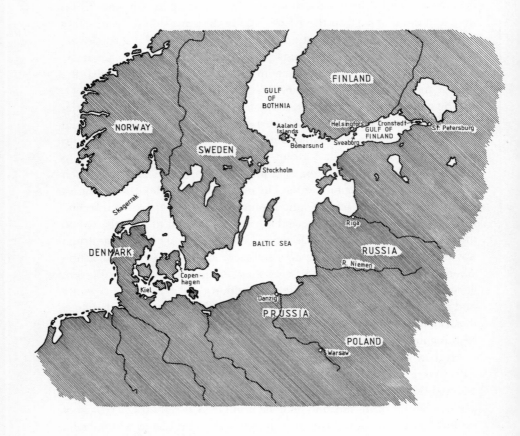

Baltic

almost brushed the branches of trees ashore, but he brought the vessels into positions some 2,000 yards from the main fortress. Heavy cannon were then landed, swayed on to specially constructed timber sleds and each hauled by 150 to 200 men over fields and up and down rock escarpments, played on by the ships' bands, to form a breaching battery only 400 yards from the fortress walls. Sulivan, meanwhile, piloted steam vessels carrying French troops to landing beaches he had identified on either flank.

As a result of Sulivan's skill and the extraordinary exertions of the ships' companies, it took just four days of bombardment to compel the surrender of the forts. Over two thousand prisoners were taken and more than two hundred guns, at the cost of few casualties apart from hundreds of French victims of cholera. The ruined walls of the fort and cannon cast with the Russian eagle can still be seen at Bomarsund. The strategic results were negligible. The real success of the Baltic campaign was the commercial blockade and destruction of merchant ships, property and stores carried out by smaller warships Napier detached for the purpose. Nonetheless, Russia continued to receive arms, ammunition and supplies through or from Prussia; the British government could do nothing about this without driving Prussia into the Russian camp.

In the southern campaign, meanwhile, Prussian and Austrian hostility to Nicholas's Balkan ambitions had resulted in the withdrawal of Russian troops from the western shores of the Black Sea, removing the threat to Constantinople and allowing the Anglo-French force to concentrate on the destruction of the Russian Black Sea fleet and its base at Sebastopol on the Crimean peninsula. Over fifty thousand British and French troops in about equal numbers, with horses and guns, were landed unopposed some thirty miles north of the base in mid-September. Marching south, they drove the Russians from a defensive position on the River Alma, then bypassed Sebastopol to seize the small harbour of Balaclava just to the south to serve as a supply port. The commander of the Russian fleet wanted to sail and give battle to the Allied fleet outside, but was ordered instead to sink his ships across the harbour entrance and send their guns and men to the landward defences.

The Allies mounted a combined naval bombardment and land assault on the base fortifications on 17 October, but were repulsed, after which, as the weather deteriorated, they settled in for a siege. This was to last throughout the winter and to be immortalized through the reports of the world's first war correspondent, William Howard Russell of *The Times* of London, as an epitome of logistical and medical incompetence and suffering.

The shortcomings of the British army were in a sense, as Paul Kennedy has pointed out, consequences of the country's unique strengths of small

The Black Sea and Ottoman Empire

government, reliance on a dominant navy and suspicion of a standing army at home as a danger to individual liberty.[6] They were also caused by the closed, club-like – or amateur – oligarchy of army officers and the strict economy applied to government spending in the belief that the country's real strength lay in expanding trade and industry and that this was best achieved in Adam Smith's terms by allowing individuals maximum use of their own income and savings unrestrained by taxes or official interference. The resultant striving for economy had seen the departments responsible for the provisioning and health of the British army cut to mere skeletons.

In Britain feelings of shame and rage aroused by Russell's reports, and thunderous leading articles by the editor of *The Times* on the basis of private information supplied by Russell, led to a public outcry, subscriptions for the troops and the dispatch of Florence Nightingale to organize the hospital at Scutari on the Bosphorus. The British commander-in-chief of the Black Sea fleet and Napier were both scapegoated for the failure to meet public expectations of great victories over the Russians, and relieved of their commands. Still public criticism of the conduct of the war continued and the government fell. Palmerston succeeded Aberdeen and replaced Graham at the Admiralty with Sir Charles Wood.

As Prime Minister, Palmerston retained all his larger war aims, but kept them largely to himself for fear of alarming his ministers. He recognized, nonetheless, that the capture of Sebastopol was the essential first stage and made no changes to the strategy already prepared under Graham; this was to force the narrows into the Sea of Azov above the Crimea and cut Russian supply lines to the peninsula. For the Baltic campaign Graham had turned to Captain Sulivan for advice on the reduction of the Russian naval bases and set in hand a building programme of shallow-draught gunboats and mortar vessels able to work close inshore to bombard the fortifications.

Rear Admiral Sir Richard Dundas was appointed to command the Baltic fleet in 1855 and provided with an even more splendid force than his predecessor, composed entirely of steam vessels; the previous year's campaign had shown how impossible it was to manoeuvre steamships and sailing ships together.

In most essentials the ships-of-the-line heading the fleet were little changed from those that fought at Trafalgar; they were larger but still mounted broadside guns on two or three decks and spread square sails on three masts; the most modern had been designed and built with steam engines driving a screw propeller, others had been converted to auxiliary screw propulsion. The cruisers for reconnaissance and everyday blockade work had steam engines driving screws or paddle wheels; and there was a flotilla of over fifty shallow-draught gunboats, mortar vessels and floating batteries ordered expressly for an assault on the Russian naval bases. These joined in June shortly after a small French squadron, also including mortar vessels. Yet Dundas was provided with virtually no troops. Sulivan had suggested that a minimum of forty thousand troops would be needed for combined operations against the main Russian fleet bases, Cronstadt and Sveaborg,[7] but without a Swedish alliance and with Palmerston's strategy focused on the Crimea, none could be sent.

Dundas re-established a commercial blockade in April directly the ice cleared; his cruisers seized or destroyed enemy shipping, stores and coastal telegraph posts and batteries unopposed by the Russian fleet, which again remained inside its fortified bases. He knew, of course, that very much more was expected of him. Sulivan had been sent out again with the fleet, and he lost no time in boarding his survey vessel, *Merlin*, to reconnoitre Cronstadt. He found the enemy fleet sheltering in the inner basins, block ships moored across the entrance, underwater obstructions in the approach channels and extensive works under construction for defence against an Allied landing. He concluded in his subsequent report to the Admiralty, 'no serious attack appears to me to be practicable with the means at my disposal'.[8] He then conferred with the French admiral and they decided on a purely naval attack on the secondary base at Sveaborg. Preparations went ahead through July and August. As with the assault on Bomarsund, Sulivan played the key role, in charge of surveying and sounding operations, buoying dangerous shoals and marking the positions to be taken by each mortar vessel and gunboat. He also ensured that the approach channels were cleared of mines, referred to by Dundas in his reports as 'explosive machines which have recently been introduced by the enemy'.[9] The concept of towing or drifting explosive charges in floating containers on to enemy warships dated back to the American War of Independence. The moored mines the Russians were now using to guard the approaches to their fleet bases represented a new concept; they were detonated chemically on contact by sulphuric acid contained in a glass tube.

Sulivan's plan, copied to all vessels taking part, positioned altogether thirty mortars mounted in vessels or on rock islets in an arc with a radius of 3,300 yards from the fortifications and employed gunboats armed with heavy guns from the ships-of-the-line to steam back and forth along buoyed channels between the mortars and the forts to shield them from enemy fire. After preliminary ranging shots, Dundas began the bombardment soon after seven on the morning of 9 August. By ten o'clock fires had broken out in buildings and forts, and ammunition explosions followed. The Russian fire slackened. In the evening the boats of the fleet went in firing Congreve rockets, which added to the conflagration. Several mortar boats worked nearer their targets in the dark, and next morning the bombardment recommenced, continuing through the 10th and concluding again with rockets in the evening. By this time Dundas had reports of mortars cracking, and after consulting the French admiral, he called off the action on the morning of the 11th.

The French admiral's report, written off Sveaborg on the 11th, described the base under bombardment as having had 'the appearance of a vast, fiery furnace'; and continued: 'The fire, which still continues its ravages, has destroyed nearly the whole place and consumed storehouses, magazines, barracks, different government establishments, and a great quantity of stores for the arsenal . . .'[10]

Many of the inhabitants of Helsingfors, fearing their homes would be the next targets, had fled in panic into the countryside with their possessions, but Dundas decided against carrying the war to the now defenceless city, and the bombardment of Sveaborg was the only major action by his fleet. Astonishingly, it had not cost a single allied life, and only sixteen men were wounded, none seriously. The Russians lost 55 dead, 199 wounded, according to the governor's report; locals questioned by Dundas's interpreter laughed in scorn at such low figures. All expressed the warmest gratitude for the admiral's forbearance in not destroying Helsingfors.

The commercial blockade was continued until ice again prevented navigation. As in the previous year's campaign, this had done immense damage to Russian trade. Moreover, as *The Times* correspondent with the fleet reported: 'Our presence has obliged the Emperor [the Tsar] to maintain in a state of inactivity an enormous army . . . along the coasts of Bothnia and Finland, while the food, clothes, luxuries, and all manufactures of countries more civilised than his own . . . have been rigidly withheld from approaching his shores . . . His mercantile marine has ceased to exist . . .'[11]

Meanwhile, in the Black Sea campaign that year the Allies carried out their most successful operations: the port of Kertch, which commanded the narrows leading into the Sea of Azov, was taken by amphibious assault, after which steam-powered gunboats entered the enclosed sea, destroyed Russian shipping, bombarded granaries, storehouses and official buildings and sent parties ashore to complete the disruption of the supply lines to the Russian army in the Crimea; this led to the fall of Sebastopol in September.

The last act of the season was the capture of five sand and stone works comprising Fort Kinburn, commanding the gulf leading from the mouths of the Bug and Dnieper rivers in the north-western corner of the Black Sea opposite Odessa. Strategically the action was of minor importance, but in historic terms it hastened an inevitable revolution in warship design, for the bombardment was spearheaded by three French floating batteries, *Dévastation, Lavé* and *Tonnant*, built to the instructions of Napoleon III with iron plates 4½ inches thick bolted over timber hulls. These came into action against the Kinburn forts on the morning of 17 October at ranges of between 900 and 1,200 yards and made good practice for over three hours before Allied ships-of-the-line joined in. The forts surrendered an hour and a half later. The point noted by naval officers was that the iron armour of the floating batteries, although struck by over a hundred Russian projectiles, had not been penetrated. A total of twenty-eight casualties had all been caused by shot or splinters entering through gun ports or imperfectly protected hatches.[12]

The earlier destruction of the Turkish frigate squadron under Russian shell fire in Sinope Bay and the Kinburn demonstration of the resistance of iron armour – proved before in test conditions – spelled the end of the unarmoured ship-of-the-line. Napoleon III drew this conclusion and ordered a committee of naval architects and a naval historian to report on future construction policy. Out of their deliberations came the specifications for a new type of single-gun-deck vessel mounting rifled shell guns and protected by iron armour impermeable to existing ordnance, rigged with masts and sails for cruising and equipped with a steam engine driving a screw propeller for high speed in action – the 'weather gage' of the days of fighting sail. These were translated by Napoleon's new Directeur du matériel, Dupuy de Lôme, into the *Gloire* and two sister ships laid down in early 1858. De Lôme declared that one of these armoured frigates in the midst of an enemy fleet of timber ships would be like a lion among a flock of sheep.[13]

The British Admiralty had to respond. Naval supremacy was the indispensable condition for the security of the nation and empire. No one supposed the present alliance with France had ended the historic rivalry; the Board could never lose sight of the need to match capital shipbuilding in the other naval powers, France, Russia and the United States, and the response to the French armoured frigates was emphatic. Taking advantage of Britain's industrial primacy, particularly her lead in the construction of iron merchant ships, and borrowing heavily from the lines of merchant 'clippers' racing opium or tea to and from China, the Admiralty Chief

Constructor, Isaac Watts, designed a superb class of warship as superior to the *Gloire* and her sisters as these were to conventional timber ships-of-the-line. Yacht-like in appearance with a sharp bow and long, sweet run to a counter stern, perhaps the most beautiful class of warship ever built, they were faster under steam or sail and more heavily armed than the French 'ironclad' frigates and were recognized immediately as the new type of capital ship. Construction of conventional ships-of-the-line was halted immediately. The lead ship of the class, HMS *Warrior*, can be viewed today at Portsmouth restored to her Victorian condition, even to the sailors' kit and mess tins and the silver set for the captain's dining table, a spur to the imagination more vivid than any description.

The action at Kinburn which may be said to have begun the leapfrogging competition in warship design that was to gather pace through the century was the closing act of the Russian War. The commercial blockades of both Baltic and Black seas had destroyed the greater, maritime part of Russia's export trade;[14] the City of London, while assuring the servicing of existing Russian debt, had refused to issue new Russian loans,[15] and to pay for the war the tsarist government borrowed heavily on Berlin and Amsterdam capital markets and printed paper money; this led to inflation and the collapse of the rouble. By January 1856 it was clear that continuing the war must bankrupt the state. Moreover, Dundas's destruction of the fortifications of Sveaborg had demonstrated that Cronstadt and St Petersburg itself were vulnerable to an Allied fleet and expeditionary force in the coming campaigning season. It was known the Allies were planning such an assault.

Nicholas I had died early in 1855. The new Tsar, Alexander II, capitulated. In the peace signed in Paris in March 1856 Russia agreed to the neutralization of the Black Sea and Danube basin; neither she nor Turkey would maintain a fleet or anything larger than patrol vessels for police work in the Black Sea, and the fortifications and naval installations of Sebastopol would be razed. This fell short of Palmerston's wider aims of reducing Russia everywhere, but did meet the government's original goal of preserving the Ottoman Empire and preventing Russian penetration into the eastern Mediterranean and Levant.

Before the representatives of the powers left Paris talks were held on the laws of war at sea, during which the British Foreign Secretary, Lord Clarendon, with the full support of Palmerston, appeared to give away one of Britain's fundamental maritime claims, the right of belligerents to seize non-contraband goods from neutral ships. By signing the final 'Declaration of Paris', he seemed to bow to the Continental view that the nationality of a merchant vessel covered her cargo, so undermining the strategy of commercial blockade through which Britain had weakened her enemies' economies over centuries, particularly that of France. It seemed an extraordinary renunciation then, and has to historians since. There was, however, a large measure of guile in Clarendon's position. Firstly, the Declaration also abolished privateering, which had caused British shipowners and merchants great losses in previous wars and was likely to become more effective when conducted by steamers. Second, Clarendon knew that the United States, a trade rival and potential enemy bordering the British Canadian colonies, would not agree to outlaw privateering; indeed, the American government did not sign the Declaration. Consequently a traditional commercial blockade could still be used against her in war – as it could be used against any enemy such as France or Russia which broke the terms of the agreement by sending out privately commissioned ships to prey on commerce. Palmerston saw Britain's signature on the Declaration as both a significant gesture towards neutral opinion and a positive safeguard for the country's merchant shipping in any future war, and considered it a diplomatic coup.[16]

Others who welcomed it were 'Manchester School' economists and free trade politicians who believed that with growing international trade and prosperity universal peace would surely follow.

3

The Indian Mutiny, 1857

THE GREAT PARADOX of the British Empire was its exotic centrepiece, India. Here the original web of trading outposts of the East India Company connected by sea routes dominated by the Royal Navy, the very essence of maritime empire, had coalesced into a land power dominating the subcontinent. It had never been planned, but was the cumulative result of a host of local tactical decisions made in response to real or supposed threats to the company's operations, or opportunities for greater profit. The East India Company, acting as agent for the British Crown, now governed some two-thirds of the country directly and was recognized as paramount power by the remaining third of notionally independent princely states – an astonishing outcome for what had begun as a trading venture.

The Company's armies attached to the three presidencies of Bengal, Madras and Bombay were composed largely of Indian soldiers – sepoys – recruited from the traditional warrior classes of the populace, whose loyalty was retained by regular wages and pensions, the high status uniformed fighting men were traditionally accorded in India, and above all perhaps by the paternal leadership of British officers. At the core of the armies, providing a decisive moral edge over the forces of local princes and confederacies, were regiments of British troops. These were comparatively few in number, giving a ratio of approximately one European to five Indian soldiers in 1857,[1] but they formed, in the words of a recent historian of the British Raj, 'quite literally the cutting edge of empire'.[2]

As the leaven in the Company's armies they were equally critical for the maintenance of British rule, but in this role their proportionately small numbers constituted a danger: should the sepoys become disaffected and band together the British regiments might be overwhelmed, and by early 1857 there were clear signs of sepoy dissatisfaction. Underlying grievances over pay and conditions, the deeper causes lay in fears about recruitment policy and British attempts to anglicize aspects of Indian culture, which seemed to strike at the sepoys' caste and religious identity.

Anglicization was, of course, intrinsic to Britain's post-Napoleonic drive to confer the benefits of her unique civilization on less enlightened races. Christian missionaries saw their duty as bringing the followers of Hindu idols to Jesus, while a system of education inaugurated in 1835 aimed to liberate Indians from superstition and misgovernment by creating a class of Indian 'English in tastes, in opinions, in morals, and in intellect',[3] which would support a British style of rational administration, law, economics and intellectual and social behaviour in the subcontinent.

Sepoy anxieties on these counts were exacerbated by rumours that the cartridges for a new Enfield rifle to be issued in place of their existing smooth-bore muskets were greased with beef or pork fat. The cow was sacred to Hindus; pork was forbidden to Muslims. Army authorities attempted to quell unrest by stating that cartridges would be issued ungreased for sepoys to apply whatever grease they wished. The dispute was then moved to the cartridge paper, said to be manufactured with improper materials. Whoever the conspirators behind this campaign of disinformation, they were assisted by a growing divide between British officers of Indian regiments and their sepoys. The recent improvements in communications with the home country had led to British communities forming around cantonments and hill stations; and officers who in earlier times might have taken Indian mistresses or wives, so gaining insights into their sepoys' lives and beliefs, increasingly mixed with and married their own kind, to the detriment of relations with their men.

Mutiny erupted at the beginning of the hot season on 10 May 1857 among Indian regiments at Meerut, a military station 30 miles north-east of Delhi, former Mogul capital of India, which soon became the focus of rebellion. The British authorities used the telegraph to alert threatened outposts before rebel emissaries could reach them, and to call up reinforcements. British regiments were transported by steamship from Madras, Burma and Ceylon to Calcutta to march up the trunk road to Delhi. An expeditionary force en route for China was diverted to India by urgent telegraph messages, and troops and naval brigades were sent from Malta, Hong Kong, Cape Town and Mauritius.

Besides the advantage of the telegraph and steamships for rapid troop concentration, the British had the edge in the field: the new Enfield rifle with which most British regiments were equipped had over twice the effective range of the sepoys' smooth-bore musket. Equally crucial for the survival of British India was the quality of the leaders on the ground. Despite failures in imagination before the rebellion, afterwards key senior officers, civil and military, reacted with intelligence, resource, extreme daring and ruthlessness, especially in the most threatened area of the Punjab. It is significant that these men joined absolute belief in Britain's civilizing mission to usually fervent faith in God. Theirs was an Old Testament reading of the Scriptures, however; from the beginning they fought terror with terror.

Atrocities were committed on both sides. Mutinous sepoys captured in the north-west frontier region and sentenced to death were shot from the mouths of cannon. Severed arms tied to gun wheels were the only visible remains when the smoke cleared, although some onlookers were spattered with blood and fragments of flesh. One of the defining images of the Mutiny, this fearful deterrent needs explanation: it was used by the Moguls before the British, and, as Saul David puts it, 'was regarded by Indian troops as an instantaneous and honourable "soldiers' death" and infinitely preferable to hanging'.[4] For their part, mutineers slaughtered women and children in garrison communities. In retribution British troops resorted to summary mass hangings and the wholesale burning of villages. Barbarity was one side of the coin, heroism and resolution the other, and it was these high virtues displayed by officers and men which saved British India, particularly in the opening months when the revolt might have spread beyond the central provinces of northern India. No significant independent ruler joined the rebellion, however, and many Indian irregulars, chiefly Punjabis and Sikhs, fought on the British side. Nonetheless, it was not until July 1859 that the British felt able to declare a 'State of Peace'.

By this date the London government had brought the rule of the East India Company to an end. The India Act of August 1858 vested authority over the subcontinent in a Secretary of State for India, a new member of the government answerable to Parliament in Westminster, while in India the Company's Governor General was transformed into the Viceroy representing the Crown. Queen Victoria became Empress of India. Subsequently the Indian army was reformed to such good effect that it was to serve for almost a century as guarantor of Britain's hold on the subcontinent, which in turn guaranteed Britain's eastern empire. The Royal Navy guarded the oceanic supply lines and secured the home country, but it was the Indian army, acting as a reservoir to boost Britain's minute standing army, that provided essential support in policing the empire.[5] To adapt an economic metaphor, Britain achieved an extraordinarily high military gearing from the British regiments deployed in India.

If India was the paradox at the heart of Britain's trading empire, 'gunboat diplomacy' was the contradiction that empowered her liberal trading policy.

The so-called 'Opium Wars' are notorious examples. Caused by Chinese attempts to prevent the import of opium grown and processed in India under the monopoly control of the East India Company, they were at a more fundamental level an expression of the frustration of Western traders with a Chinese government bureaucracy ideologically opposed to commerce. British victory in the first Opium War of 1839 had forced China to open five 'treaty ports' to British merchants and to cede the island of Hong Kong to Britain.[6] This had become an emporium for British trade and opium smuggling and a base for naval operations against pirate fleets endemic to the China seas. Subsequently China had concluded treaties with France and the United States granting their merchants similar trading rights at certain ports.

Profits in the illegal opium trade to China were extraordinarily high. Captains who survived the hazards of pirates, Chinese customs vessels and typhoons made quick fortunes and retired – several, it seems, to follow their fathers into holy orders or the legal profession.[7] Their ships were 'clippers' evolved from the fast schooners of Baltimore with a sharp entrance, raked masts and clouds of upper sails and stunsails to augment the plain sails whenever the weather allowed. They were armed with cannon and provided with 40-foot-long oars which could be run out of the gun ports when the ship lay becalmed and at risk of capture. Meeting Chinese smugglers in lonely creeks, they exchanged their high-value freight for silver, usually in the form of Mexican dollars. In this way the East India Company, which provided the opium cake, gained the silver needed for its legitimate trades in tea and other Chinese wares.

With free trade and the abolition of the Navigation Laws in 1849 large, ship-rigged US clippers of 500 tons upwards, which were making astonishing passages bringing China tea to New York, penetrated the London market. British shipbuilders responded with their own style of clipper, and from the early 1850s British and American captains vied each season to race the first China tea to London, the start of a brief flowering of design and hard-driving sailing skills before steamers won the contest in the 1870s.

The American involvement in China was such that from 1853 US warships worked with British squadrons against the pirates infesting the coasts and islands. Constant friction with Chinese officialdom remained a factor affecting all Western traders, and in 1856 this flared into open hostilities when officials boarded a Hong Kong merchantman, the *Arrow*, and allegedly lowered her British ensign. The Americans and the French were drawn into this conflict, which became known as the *Arrow* or Second Opium War. While opium smuggling was an important contributory factor, it was more about upholding Western privileges; and as in India the deeper cause lay in the tides of Western commercial expansion coming up against the opposing values of a deeply conservative territorial/agricultural nation in which trade was officially despised. It was about the Westernization of the Orient.

The Chinese war junks and their obsolete weapons were no match for the steam-powered gun vessels and gunboats and naval brigades armed with field guns and rifles deployed by the Western powers; and although the British expeditionary force to China had to be diverted to India on the outbreak of the Mutiny, the final result was never in doubt. In the summer of 1860, after an Anglo-French force, including Indian army regiments, had pressed up the Peiho river to the capital, Peking, sacked the city and burned the exquisite summer palace of the emperor, the Chinese government accepted Western terms. Ten new ports were opened to foreign trade and residence, subjects of the signatory powers were allowed to travel anywhere in China, missionaries permitted to propagate the Christian faith, and the import of opium was legalized. Known in Chinese historiography as one of the 'Unequal Treaties', the Peking Convention heralded the break-up of the Chinese empire to external force and internal rebellion. France had begun to carve out territory in Cochin China, Russia in the northern maritime provinces, and other European powers vied with Britain and the United States for trading spheres.

The offlying island empire of Japan was under similar pressure. The ruling Tokugawa Shogunate had deliberately closed off contact with Western traders, missionaries and all foreigners in the early seventeenth century[8] and the country had retained an essentially feudal structure over the following 200 years of isolation. The United States was the first power to break in. A naval squadron under Commodore Matthew C. Perry sailed into Tokyo Bay in July 1853 with a demand from the US President to open trade relations. The government was thrown into crisis, split between conservatives who wanted to preserve Japan's seclusion and realists who knew they were militarily so far inferior to the Western nations that they could not resist. The realists proved right. When Perry returned in February 1854 the government acceded to the American demand for a trade treaty; and over the next two years Britain, Russia and Holland signed similar treaties. Before the end of the decade foreigners had taken up residence and set up businesses at the main ports.[9] The modernization of Japan had begun.

Free traders may have dreamed of universal peace, but in the eastern seas the concept was imposed by gunboats.

4

The American Civil War, 1861

A S THE TIDE of Western commerce broke down the walls of the great Eastern civilizations and flooded in, undermining their foundations, elsewhere in wilderness areas in Australasia and North America Western settlers continued to advance into the domains of less materially endowed peoples. Aborigines in Australia, Maoris in New Zealand and native American tribes found themselves progressively deprived of land by unequal purchase backed by guns, and decimated by Western diseases against which they had no immunity. The cultural divide between these peoples and those who took their inheritance was expressed by the chief of the Duwanish Indians when asked to sell tribal land in Washington State in 1855: 'We do not own the freshness of the air or the sparkle of the water. How can you buy them from us?' And he closed with a reflection on the lack of quiet in white men's cities.[1]

New York, financial capital and powerhouse of American expansion, might have served as an extreme model for the Duwanish reproach. Enjoying a superb harbour for oceanic shipping and canal and rail links with the interior, the city was the major trading emporium and manufacturing centre of the country, as well as chief point of entry each year for thousands of European immigrants escaping famine, unemployment or repression in their homelands, chiefly Irish, German and English. Many stayed in the metropolis. They existed on the peripheries with the unskilled and free black workers in overcrowded and insanitary tenement blocks or shanty homes constructed of scavenged timbers, barrel staves and flattened tin cans, alongside domestic animals reared for local markets, particularly pigs, which roamed the streets rootling out garbage but leaving their own malodorous contribution of waste. Disease, pauperism, hopelessness, radical politics, drunkenness, crime – and, particularly among young female immigrants, insanity – bred in these festering slums and spilled out, threatening the health and safety of respectable citizens and the super-rich alike.

At the other end of the scale, members of the plutocracy who had inherited or made fortunes in the rapidly expanding US economy lived in style along Fifth Avenue and around Madison Square, employing staffs of servants and enjoying every convenience of the industrial age, hot running water, baths, central heating and water closets in place of outside privies and chamber pots. Like the merchants of Amsterdam at the height of that city's prosperity in the seventeenth century, many had abandoned republican simplicity for ostentatious display with increasingly ornate mansions and showy carriages with liveried footmen.

New York was little different from London or other British industrial cities and growing cities in the northern United States in these respects, although its problems were exacerbated by the annual flood of poor immigrants and the sheer pace of industrial expansion driven by railroad construction to open up and exploit the agricultural products of the Midwest. More recently gold had been discovered on the west coast; the resulting sudden flood of specie had not only stimulated the economy, but encouraged foreign investors to buy US railway and government bonds. Practically all foreign investment came through New York.[2]

As North American arm of the financial system transforming the world, New York City served the plantation economies of the southern states of the Union with banking, shipping and brokering facilities for their staple products of cotton, tobacco and rice. All were produced with slave labour; indeed, the institution of slavery defined the South. To the north of the line dividing Maryland from Pennsylvania or farther west above the 'Missouri Compromise' line of 1820 slavery was illegal. It was the most immediately obvious difference between the northern and southern halves of the Union, but the effects on the two societies were as profound. The North was, like New York City, commercial, entrepreneurial, increasingly industrial and driven by profit, and on the part of rural settlers by the desire to prosper by their own efforts. The South, by contrast, based on landholding and slave-owning values, was static or even backward looking, fearing change that might allow commerce or industry to upset the traditional orders of society. While the overriding desire of northerners was to make money, the southern slave-owning elites were concerned primarily with personal honour, chivalry and style.[3] It could be said that they lived for the moment, graciously, while northerners invested, or speculated, for the future. Thus the two halves of the United States exemplified the opposing power systems designated in these volumes as 'maritime' and 'territorial'; the South even had the military traditions and reverence for the profession of arms inherent in classic territorial powers.

The Union had been born in compromise between free and slave states. As it spread westward by settlement, purchase and more recently by the

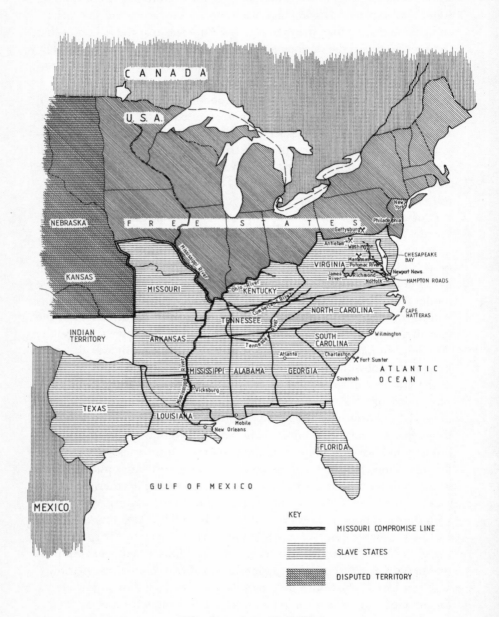

The American Civil War

conquest of Mexico, the compromise had been extended across the continent, new free states north of the line matched by new slave states in the South. This had been a political necessity for the southerners. Their aggregate population was half that of the North – nearer a quarter if slaves were excluded – but since each state had equal representation in the US Senate the South had been able to block or delay legislation against its interests passed in the lower House of Representatives, where membership was based on numbers of citizens.

It had become increasingly obvious to both sides that the two radically opposed systems could not be reconciled within one nation. It was not simply the moral abhorrence of slavery felt by 'abolitionists' in the North, or the sense that it was outdated and had been outlawed by modern nations; it was the sheer impossibility of managing slave and wage labour within the same economic framework. Moreover, the plantation crops produced in the South sold in international markets, hence required free trade, whereas northern manufacturers sought tariff barriers to protect their young industries from foreign, chiefly British, competition, and reserve the potentially vast continental market to themselves. They envisaged the integration of the market with transcontinental railroads and a centralized economy. The ideology was at hand to support them: expressed most succinctly in 1845, it was the 'manifest destiny' of the United States to spread over the continent allotted to it by Providence.[4] They were agents of Providence, and they had grown weary of southern obstruction in the Senate.

The confrontation came to a head in 1854 with a proposal to admit the new territories of Kansas and Nebraska to the Union. They were north of the 'Missouri Compromise' line and should, therefore, have been admitted as free states, yet the Bill before Congress left their status to be determined by the vote of their residents. The possibility of slavery extending north of the line caused outrage and bloodshed in the territories, and led to the formation of a new political grouping, the Republican Party, dedicated to preventing the further spread of slavery. The Manhattan commercial community was potential chief beneficiary of the party's aims, but it was too involved in southern trade; New York financiers had extended too much credit on the security of plantation slaves; agents, brokers, shipbuilders and shipowners made too much profit in the marketing and distribution of southern plantation crops to be able to contemplate a serious rupture with the South, let alone the end of slavery as an institution.

While it appears paradoxical that those who stood to benefit most from the Republican Party's vision of an integrated federal economy should be the party's fiercest opponents, the exigencies of trade and credit had always predisposed merchants to compromise with rather than fight commercial partners of a different nationality, religion or polity. Commerce recognized no barriers; hence the 'Manchester School' prediction of universal peace to be brought about by internationalizing trade. What free traders failed to recognize was that subjective political drives might prove stronger than the objective demands of profit, political differences override commercial necessity.

So it would prove in America. A rogue element in the shape of a deranged northern abolitionist named John Brown precipitated events. In October 1859 he led a raid on a federal arsenal at Harper's Ferry on the Potomac river some fifty miles north-west of Washington, seizing the armoury and taking sixty hostages from the local community. His aim was to encourage escaped slaves to join him and form an 'army of emancipation' to liberate other slaves. Instead, he found himself surrounded by militiamen and was captured next day by a party of US Marines.

News of his manic exploit and subsequent trial sent shudders of alarm through the South, always sensitive on issues of slave revolt. Northern abolitionists applauded him, and when the inevitable verdict of guilty of murder, slave insurrection and treason was delivered and he was hanged they raised him to immortality as a martyr, further proof in southern eyes of the depth of northern hostility. Talk of secession spread.

In such an atmosphere of distrust, early the following summer, 1860, Abraham Lincoln, a self-educated lawyer from poor immigrant stock, was nominated by the Republican Party as their presidential candidate. Although revolted by slavery, he was no abolitionist. He wanted to contain the practice within its own boundaries rather than attack it, believing it would eventually wither. His prime concerns were individual freedoms and the core value of the US Constitution that the people were capable of governing themselves. It was a difficult balancing act, nonetheless, for he believed the government 'could not endure permanently half slave and half free' and predicted it would eventually become 'all one thing or all the other'.[5]

During the presidential election campaign later that year business leaders in New York City set out to convince their employees that a Lincoln victory would lead to depression and unemployment as southerners withdrew their custom. They succeeded, but elsewhere in the North Lincoln polled sufficient votes to win the contest by a clear margin. Five days later, on 20 December, delegates to a specially convened session of the South Carolina legislature voted to leave the Union; they were followed within weeks by six other southern states and in February 1861, before Lincoln's inauguration as President in March, representatives of the seceding states drew up a provisional constitution for the Confederate States of America and elected a provisional President, Jefferson Davis. One of the first acts of Davis's government was to declare a tariff war on the North by announcing that from April duties on imports through southern ports would be reduced to half the rate imposed by the federal government. Faced with the prospect of southerners stealing their entrepôt trade and international connections, besides reneging on debts owed to northern banks and merchants, the mood in New York business circles changed from appeasement to open belligerence. Finally Lincoln had full support from the captains of American finance and industry.

Hostilities began in April 1861 over the issue of federal forts within the seceding southern states. The Confederate government could not permit armed United States garrisons within their territory now that they had left the Union; Lincoln's government could not permit the surrender of its garrisons to rebels. When the US commander of Fort Sumter in the harbour of Charleston, South Carolina, refused Confederate demands to yield, the guns of other harbour batteries were ordered to open fire to compel him. Lincoln declared an insurrection; the simmering conflict between the opposing systems which had bedevilled the Union from its beginning broke out in open war.

There was little realization on either side of the horrors to come. Lincoln called for 75,000 volunteers to serve for three months to put down the rebellion. Patriotic fervour swept the North, not least New York City, whose business leaders set up and partly funded a Union Defence Committee to purchase arms, ships and supplies and provide for the families of volunteers away on war service. Among the many units raised in the city and dispatched south to defend Washington from the rebels was the 7th Regiment, comprising young bankers, merchants and professional men. Meanwhile the Confederacy was joined by four more southern states, bringing the total to eleven. The enthusiasm for their cause was equally fierce. In New Orleans William Howard Russell of *The Times* of London, observing 'resolute, quick, angry faces' about him, sensed 'the South will never yield to the North unless as a nation which is beaten beneath the feet of a victorious enemy'.[6] It was a prophetic judgement.

Neither belligerent was prepared for war. The US army was minute by European standards, so too the navy with only forty-two commissioned ships. Yet in terms of potential there was only one possible victor provided outside powers remained aloof. Finance, ever the sinews of war, was predominantly in northern hands; so was the trade and industry on which financial strength rested. The North had by far the major share of coal, iron, manufacturing and shipbuilding capacity, which could be turned to war production, and rail and water communications for the supply of its forces, and of course it had overwhelmingly the larger population.

The South's major asset was cotton. Exports would pay for the ships and arms the rebels were unable to manufacture themselves in sufficient quantities. Lincoln's first strategic decision was to order a blockade of southern ports to prevent cotton leaving and arms entering. The navy was plainly inadequate for the task, but the rebel government shortly placed its own embargo on the export of cotton with the aim of bringing pressure particularly on the British government to recognize the Confederacy. British manufacturers had, however, accumulated stocks and opened new sources of supply in Egypt and India, and although thousands of British textile workers lost their jobs, the main effect of the embargo was to cripple the Confederate economy.

It did not move the British government. The Prime Minister was Palmerston, now seventy-six. He considered that a permanent division of the United States would be in Britain's interest, since the southern or Confederate states 'would afford a valuable and extensive market for British manufacturers'.[7] On slavery, the abomination that had informed Palmerston's whole career, he held the North as accountable as the South: the trade had been carried on for years under the shelter of the US flag. While holding these views in private, in public he steered a neutral course between the belligerents.

At the beginning of hostilities Lincoln had convened the chiefs of the two armed services as a strategy board; they had advised gaining control of the Mississippi and so pinioning the main block of southern states between that great river and the blockaded Gulf of Mexico and Atlantic coasts, cutting off supplies and squeezing the life out of the rebellion – popularly named the 'Anaconda' plan. Lincoln had not been convinced, nor would it have been politically possible to have followed such a studied policy: the press and public were demanding an immediate march on the Confederate capital, Richmond, only 120 miles south of Washington, and expected rapid victory.

Lincoln ordered such an advance by the Union army defending Washington, but it was met by the main Confederate force based at Manassas and routed at the Battle of Bull Run in July. Lincoln now drew up a strategy to utilize the Union's advantage in numbers by attacking with superior forces 'at *different* points at the *same* time'[8]. As developed over the following months, the plan incorporated an advance down the Mississippi and an amphibious attack on New Orleans at the mouth of that river, together with separate invasions along the rivers Ohio, Cumberland and Tennessee, while the main Army of the Potomac at Washington under a new general, George B. McClennan, prepared another advance on Richmond, this time by way of Chesapeake Bay, the James river and the Virginia 'peninsula', in order to make use of the North's naval superiority. Meanwhile, amphibious expeditions seized havens on the coasts of North and South Carolina as bases for the naval blockade.

The Confederate government, lacking the warships or shipbuilding capacity of the North, had to rely at the start on licensing privateers, but they sent a former US naval officer to Britain to procure fast steamships which could be armed for the war on trade in more distant seas. And arguing that 'Inequality in numbers [of warships] may be compensated by invulnerability',[9] they began converting a captured US steam frigate, *Merrimack*, into an ironclad. Her side timbers were cut down to the waterline and a casemate or battery was built on the lower hull over some two-thirds of her length, sloping inwards at about 45 degrees; it was constructed of 20 inches of pine overlaid with 4 inches of oak with two layers of 2-inch-thick plates rolled out from railroad irons bolted on top. Pierced all round with fourteen gun ports, it was to house ten guns, six 9-inch smooth-bore cannon and four 6- or 7-inch rifled shell guns. A single funnel protruded from the top; all masts were removed. A cast-iron ram was attached at the bow of the lower hull.[10]

Reports during construction of this impregnable ironclad caused the Union government increasing alarm. With the ships and shipyards at their disposal they might have responded in kind; instead Lincoln was persuaded by a Swedish engineer named John Ericsson to adopt a revolutionary design he had been promoting for years. It was a bold, even rash, decision, since the concept was quite untested. It consisted in essence of a revolving armoured turret in the shape of a cylinder mounted on a wide armoured deck whose sides dropped below the waterline to protect a timber hull containing steam machinery for turning a single-screw propeller. The turret, constructed of eight layers of 1-inch iron plating, was 20 feet in diameter and 9 feet high and was to house two 11-inch-calibre smooth-bore cannon firing solid shot. The inch-thick iron deck on which it turned floated only 2 feet above the water; the 5-inch-thick iron sides extended from the deck 3 feet below the water.

Launched from the Continental Ironworks on New York City's Greenpoint waterfront on 30 January 1862 – expected to sink by a good proportion of the watching crowds – she was the first of three projected Union ironclads. She was named *Monitor* after claims by Ericsson that she would prove 'a severe monitor' to the rebel leaders.[11] He also predicted some alarm in London. The British Admiralty was supremely indifferent. The *Monitor* and the converted *Merrimack*, renamed *Virginia*, were unfit for the open sea, and neither was a match in speed, endurance or firepower for the British *Warrior* or the French *Gloire* classes, which both predated them. Their impact on history was confined to the duel they were destined to fight.

The *Virginia*, formerly *Merrimack*, was completed towards the end of February 1862 and worked up with a raw crew under Captain Franklin Buchanan, a US Naval officer who had resigned his command to join the rebel states. Her very presence at the mouth of the James river had already caused the Union General McClennan of the Army of the Potomac to postpone his advance upriver towards Richmond in case she should emerge and cause havoc with his unarmoured ships.[12] On 8 March his fears were confirmed. Buchanan took the *Virginia* out and across Hampton Roads towards a line of Union warships anchored off Newport News. The ships and batteries opened up as she approached, but any shots hitting her sloping casemate simply bounced off. Buchanan closed and sank a sloop by ramming. The others weighed and made off, but the heavy frigate, *Congress*, ran aground, and Buchanan, positioning himself off her stern, poured in fire which set her ablaze and forced her to strike.

That evening the *Monitor* arrived in the roads. The *Virginia*'s crew made her out by the light of the burning frigate. She had departed New York two days before and had barely survived a rising sea on the second day. Water had gushed down under the turret like a waterfall despite all her crew could do, and twice it had seemed she must sink. Despite her presence, the *Virginia* sallied out the next day, 9 March. Command had devolved on Lieutenant Catesby Jones as Buchanan had been wounded in the previous action. Jones steered for another Union frigate which had run aground seeking escape. The *Monitor* intervened and a ponderous gunnery duel ensued during which neither succeeded in penetrating the other's armour at the closest ranges. This was followed by an equally indecisive ramming contest. Finally, after some four hours, watched by soldiers from both sides lining opposite shores, the two strange craft drew apart to make repairs. Each had sustained over twenty hits[13] but no vital damage and, despite casualties caused by fragments entering the gun ports, no one had been killed. Tactically it was a draw. Strategically, the *Monitor* had prevented the rebels gaining a spectacular triumph by routing the Union blockade. Nonetheless, the *Virginia* had not been eliminated and the threat she still posed caused McClennan to abandon his move up the James river; instead he transferred his force to the north side of the Virginia peninsula, where his advance was slowed by creeks, marsh and not least by his own extreme caution.

Neither ironclad survived long. The Confederates abandoned Norfolk in order to reinforce their army defending Richmond, and burned the *Virginia* rather than allow her capture by Union forces. Later that year the *Monitor* was swamped by heavy seas off Cape Hatteras and went down with sixteen of her crew. By that time she had spawned many armoured vessels of varying sizes in her own image for the Union blockade and river campaigns; none was truly ocean-going.

Meanwhile, in the Mississippi campaign Union forces operating with a naval component of extemporized armoured and unarmoured gunboats captured key forts on the Tennessee and Cumberland rivers and pushed down the Mississippi, while Union warships under Flag Officer David G. Farragut took New Orleans at the mouth of that great river. By midsummer the whole of the Mississippi apart from a short stretch on the lower reaches was in Union hands. Communications between the eastern and western Confederacy were all but severed, and with the capture of Norfolk and New Orleans the rebels had lost their major shipbuilding centres.

In the defence of Richmond they had, however, discovered a commander of genius, General Robert E. Lee. In September Lee took the war to the North, invading Maryland and threatening Washington, until held by the Union army under McClellan at Antietam Creek near the village of Sharpsburg. According to one British observer of this ferocious battle every tree on the battlefield was left 'full of bullets and bits of shell'.[14] An extreme example of the industrialized fighting that had marked the war from the start, it left 8,000 dead or mortally wounded and 15,000 severely wounded, the highest casualty toll of any twenty-four hours in American history. Afterwards Lee withdrew his force across the Potomac into Virginia. McClellan failed to pursue, but Lincoln took the opportunity provided by the boost to Union morale to move the war on to a higher moral plane, proclaiming the emancipation of slaves in Confederate states. This signalled a new war aim, the abolition of slavery, and transformed Union armies into forces of liberation. By appealing to liberal sentiment in Britain and France it also removed any remaining Confederate hope that either power would recognize or aid them. In this sense Antietam represented a major turning point in the war.

The following summer, 1863, Union forces took the last remaining strongholds on the Mississippi, cutting the agricultural western states of the Confederacy completely from the eastern states. Simultaneously Lee's tactical touch deserted him. Advancing against the centre of the Union Army of the Potomac outside Gettysburg, his men suffered terrible losses, and he was forced to retire into Virginia.

The twin defeats in east and west ended any possibility of military victory for the Confederacy. For the Union the war aims were defined by Lincoln when he came to dedicate the military cemetery at Gettysburg four months later. Far wider than either reunification or the abolition of slavery, they were nothing less than the survival of the American model of democracy:

> Four score and seven years ago our fathers brought forth on the continent a new nation, conceived in Liberty, and dedicated to the proposition that all men are created equal.
> '. . . It is . . . for us to be here dedicated to the great task remaining before us . . . that we here highly resolve that these dead shall not have died in vain – that this nation under God, shall have a new birth of freedom – and that government of the people, for the people, by the people, shall not perish from the earth.[15]

These simple phrases would achieve immortality and provide a beacon for future generations of Americans.

Beneath the lofty ideals were, of course, the people, neither perfect, nor entirely of one mind. Both political parties, Republicans and Democrats, were split on the abolition of slavery, which seemed to many an attack on established custom and the rights of property and no justification for the appalling sacrifice of life in the war. Free blacks were already regarded by white working people in the North as a threat to their jobs and wage levels; even Lincoln espoused voluntary emigration for blacks.

The boom induced by war production, facilitated by issues of greenbacks and interest-bearing bonds, had led to hugely increased stock market activity, raising Wall Street, New York, into a world position second only to the City of London in volume of transactions. At the same time the national debt, rising by the day, tied Union financiers, businessmen and bondholders, large and small, into the war effort[16] and drew the Union into that 'military-fiscal' conjuncture of rising costs of war met by rising government borrowing and rising taxes to fund the borrowing which had distinguished both the Dutch republic and Great Britain during their ascents to world power in the seventeenth and eighteenth centuries. Equally, the necessities of war had meant a substantial transfer of powers, fiscal and executive, from individual states to the federal government.

In spring 1864 Lincoln at last found the military leaders and command structure for his strategy of confronting the rebel states 'with superior forces at *different* points at the *same* time'.[17] He appointed General Ulysses S. Grant to overall command of Union armies under his own direction as commander-in-chief; and while Grant advanced on Richmond, his subordinate, General William T. Sherman, in command of Union forces in the west, laid siege to the railroad junction and manufacturing centre of Atlanta, Georgia. At sea, meanwhile, the Union navy seized one after another of the remaining ports through which the Confederates received supplies from overseas.

In August Farragut, now a rear admiral, confirmed the reputation he had won at New Orleans and on the Mississippi by capturing the heavily fortified port of Mobile, Alabama. His squadron comprised four ironclad descendants of the *Monitor* and fourteen conventional timber warships, including his flagship, *Hartford*. Forming the ironclads in the van, he followed with the timber ships lashed in pairs in case they should strike one of the moored mines, known as torpedoes, with which the narrow entrance channel was strewn. The decisive moment came when his leading monitor detonated a mine and sank. Surveying the action from high in the *Hartford*'s rigging, Farragut called down, 'Damn the torpedoes! Full speed ahead!',[18] an order that entered legend since, although the *Hartford* bumped several torpedoes on the way in, they did not explode, and his ships entered without further loss. His monitors then engaged the Confederate flagship, an ironclad descendant of the *Virginia*, and forced her to strike.

Early in September Atlanta fell and Sherman began scything a path of destruction through Georgia designed deliberately to break civilian will. The twin victories lifted Lincoln's credit, and in presidential elections that November he was returned to complete the task he had begun, so removing the Confederates' last, faint hope of a compromise settlement with a less convinced federalist. Still-bitter fighting continued until April 1865, when Lee was forced to abandon Richmond. With his capital in Union hands he at last bowed to the inevitable and agreed terms allowing the remnants of his now hungry and dispirited army to lay down their arms and return to their homes with a promise not to continue the struggle.

Perceptions of the American Civil War are dominated by the land campaigns with their enormous casualty figures and the photographs of the dead lying with bent limbs haphazardly where they fell, images that conveyed the shocking reality of the battlefield to civilians on both sides as no artists' impressions could have done before. Yet the result was determined not by armies but by the financial-commercial and industrial dominance of the North, particularly New York City, and the ascendancy of the US over the Confederate navy. From the beginning the campaigns of the Army of the Potomac had been based on the transport of troops and supplies by sea and river, while the Confederate army under Lee had moved inland to draw the enemy from the sea – thereby allowing the Union to establish bases along the coasts from which to maintain the naval blockade. During the final campaign against Lee in 1864/65 Grant kept his rear positioned on coastal rivers to secure his supply lines. Meanwhile the Union naval blockade had grown ever tighter and the eventual elimination of the blockade-running ports by assault from the sea had cut the Confederacy from all outside support.

The costs of the war had pushed US national debt up from just under $65 million at the start to $2,755 million at the end.[19] Yet the northern economy was booming and well able to service the debt. By contrast the Confederate economy was ruined, the currency worthless, plantations and the transport infrastructure over large areas destroyed, poverty and disease widespread, families broken by the loss of their menfolk. As northern financiers and businessmen moved in to buy properties and businesses at knockdown prices with gold, southern bitterness grew, and the North had to impose military government to oversee the return of the rebel states to the Union. Lincoln was not at the helm. While attending the theatre in Washington on the evening of 14 April, two days after the formal surrender of Lee's army, he had been shot in the back of the head by a fanatical southerner, and had died the next day.

The most obvious outcome of Lincoln's leadership during the war was the abolition of slavery within the United States – incorporated in the Constitution as the Thirteenth Amendment. This hastened the end of the remaining transatlantic slave trade to the Spanish dependencies of Cuba and Puerto Rico, which had continued despite the British, other European and US naval patrols on the West African coast, among other reasons because the American squadron was too small and British warships were not permitted to search vessels flying the US flag. But in September 1861 Lincoln's Secretary of State had told the British ambassador in Washington that the United States was willing to relinquish its objection to Royal Navy searches of US ships; and further, 'the fitting out of vessels designed for the Slave Trade will no longer be permitted in New York'.[20] No doubt Lincoln was influenced by the need for good relations with Great Britain to prevent Palmerston recognizing the rebel states. The climbdown nevertheless astonished British ministers, who lost no time in agreeing a treaty, signed in 1862, giving each country's warships the right to search the other's merchant vessels in the Atlantic, and by a later protocol off East Africa. Since US warships were withdrawn from the African coast to blockade the southern states, the Royal Navy was able to act alone, and did so with vigour.

The final suppression of the trade, however, was triggered by abolitionists in Spain. In May 1865 a spokesman for their cause in the Spanish assembly, the Cortes, pointed out that since the war in the United States had ended, slavery on the whole continent could be regarded as finished.[21] The following year a Bill for the suppression of the trade was passed in the Cortes, and became law in 1867; by 1870 the Atlantic trade had virtually ceased.[22] Over the following two decades the institution of slavery itself collapsed in its last strongholds in Cuba and Brazil.[23]

The shutting down of the Atlantic slave trade after more than 350 years was a triumph of liberal morality as expressed through the political institutions in the northern United States and Great Britain, a particular triumph for post-Napoleonic War British ministers, Palmerston especially, and for the Royal Navy's West African squadron. The final pressure that broke both the trade and Western slavery itself came from Lincoln. Yet freeing slaves did not bring about equality between all Americans: prejudice remained and blacks were to suffer segregation, humiliation and actual violence for many generations.

The historic victors of the war were the northern barons of finance, commerce and industry – and the Republican Party, which expressed their integrationist aims. The other victor in the war was freedom. The very essence of the merchant ethic, the gold thread running through all merchant empires in history, freedom was powerfully embedded in the commercial drive of the northern United States. Freedom was also Lincoln's core belief. The hope he had expressed at Gettysburg for 'a new birth of freedom' had been realized, and with it his overriding desire that 'government of the people, by the people, for the people, shall not perish from the earth'.[24] This was the true legacy of his war leadership.

5

Pax Britannica

FOR THE MAINTENANCE of her world empire Britain depended crucially on the primacy of her industrial base, particularly marine
engineering and iron shipbuilding; and successive Admiralty Chief
Constructors ensured that the Royal Navy kept a clear lead in warship
design over France, the only near rival. Otherwise British naval supremacy
was maintained by habit and default. The habit was to match the number
of first-line warships to those in the next two largest navies, those of
France and Russia, combined, while maintaining sufficient cruisers and
gunboats on distant stations to protect trade from local threats. In moral
terms the habit was sustained by a legend of invincibility won over the preceding century, culminating at Trafalgar. In this sense the assumption of
British naval mastery almost precluded analysis. Foreign navies accepted it;
British Admiralty Boards confined themselves to practical considerations of
the amount of money they had been granted in the annual naval estimates
and the number and types of ships under construction in rival navies.

A similar aversion to conceptual thought affected Parliament. Debates
centred on economy. Gladstone, the most influential Chancellor of the
Exchequer of the age, cut costs ruthlessly in order to reduce taxation,
which, he believed, acted in restraint of trade. Convinced that the true
wealth of a nation was the product of private thrift and industry, both
moral qualities, he saw public and indeed private extravagance as moral
evils, and pruned with religious fervour.[1]

Paring naval expenditure was matched by retrenchment in the shore
establishments of the worldwide chain of bases on which overall command
rested. That other powers allowed Britain to hold her empire and rule the
seas at minimal cost was due in part to their concentration on pressing
internal affairs or the ambitions of neighbours, and more importantly, perhaps, to Britain's enlightened trade policies. By opening up home and
empire markets to all comers and stimulating international trade, Britain
had removed a major cause of the continuous warfare that had distinguished the former era of mercantilism when trade, colonies and shipping

had been tied to the mother country, and made it unlikely that resentment at British maritime dominion would be sufficient to raise a hostile coalition against her. Cooperation with the overseas warships of other trading powers against local threats was more usual.

Yet the 'Pax Britannica', as it came to be known, was not a prescription for world peace. There had been a period immediately after Napoleon's defeat in 1815 when British ministers had been able to use naval and financial pressure to preserve the great-power balance in Europe, but this ended with the resurrection of the French empire under Napoleon III in 1852. Napoleon had broken the post-war settlement by allying with Britain against Russia in the Crimean War, and he subsequently played a leading role in the unification of Italy by allying with Piedmont to expel Austria from her Italian possessions. Britain's powerlessness to influence Continental events was shown up more cruelly in three sharp wars through which, from 1864 to 1870, Bismarck unified the German states under Prussian domination, and broke Napoleon.

The 'Pax Britannica' applied only on the oceans and in the colonial and trading spheres. Even here there were areas that were not entirely secured by naval control: one was Canada, which shared a long land border with the United States and was potentially vulnerable to influence or takeover by its expansionist southern neighbour; more important was India, which appeared vulnerable to Russian armies pushing eastwards of the Caspian Sea towards Afghanistan. The Middle East was another region through which India could be threatened, hence Britain's support for the Ottoman Empire. But apart from these potential threats from Continental powers, Britain's widely scattered maritime empire remained inviolable while the Royal Navy maintained control of the seas, as it did throughout the nineteenth century. In this sense Pax Britannica had meaning.

The queen at the centre of the imperial chessboard was the Mediterranean fleet based at Malta. With sparkling paintwork alow and aloft, crews drilled to spectacular levels of skill in timed, competitive evolutions, the battle fleet provided the pomp and if necessary during political crises the demonstration of British might. Meanwhile the everyday tasks of empire were carried out by cruisers and gunboats on overseas stations: North America and the West Indies, South America (East Coast), Pacific, Cape of Good Hope and West Coast of Africa, East Indies, China, Australia. It was these ships which upheld the traders' and settlers' law, mounting expeditions to punish African chiefs for crimes against European life or property in their domains, enforcing treaties with Arab sheikhs enlisted to help guard the approaches to India, landing naval brigades to reinforce troops on the north-west frontier of the subcontinent, put down risings in Burma or fight Maoris disputing land claims in New Zealand, chasing pirates in the China seas and Indonesian archipelago or slaving dhows on the coast of East Africa.

The Atlantic slave trade had been virtually closed by the end of the 1860s but the traffic in Africans from the interior to the rivers and creeks of the east coast, thence by Arab dhow in the south-west monsoon to the main slave market on Zanzibar island or direct to the Red Sea or Persian Gulf to supply plantation and household slaves and concubines to the elites of the Levant, continued; slavery was rooted in the culture. The conditions in which the slaves were transported were quite as vile as they had been in the Atlantic trade, the effects of overcrowding and carelessness rather than calculated cruelty. The crews of the corvettes and gunboats charged with catching slavers were moved more by compassion and the affront to decency and by the excitement of the chase than by the small amounts of 'head money' they would receive for each slave released. One officer wrote: 'The bluejacket [sailor] is *very* gentle to the negro slave newly liberated, there is no amount of inconvenience he does not cheerfully submit to in their behalf . . . I should say the poor creatures never had . . . such gentle treatment as they received at the hands of our English seamen.'[2]

The other liberal goal to which the Admiralty had committed the service was charting the seas and coasts of the world for the benefit of sailors of all nationalities. Teams of specialist officers, usually armed to beat off native attack, worked their way painstakingly along unexplored coasts and up estuaries recording the line of the shore and landmarks by triangulation from beacons previously moored at sea, taking soundings, noting the nature of the seabed, rocks, shoals and drying heights for incorporation in an Admiralty chart of the area which would afterwards be published by the Hydrographic Department for worldwide sale. In addition the department published *Sailing Directions* and *Light Lists*, *Tide Tables* and regular *Notices to Mariners* to update the charted information. Surveys of the deep oceans were conducted largely in preparation for laying telegraph cables, which before the end of the century linked all main cities and bases of the empire with London, adding significantly to Britain's maritime control.

The momentous, unforeseen by-product of Admiralty surveying was the theory of evolution by natural selection. The young Charles Darwin had been appointed naturalist – unpaid – on the survey vessel HMS *Beagle* in 1831 and had remained with her during her subsequent five-year voyage to South America, thence into the Pacific and home around the world. While her officers were engaged surveying he had spent long periods ashore collecting specimens of fossils, animals, birds and insects. At the Galapagos Islands in the Pacific he was struck by the variety of unique species distinct from their mainland relatives, each adapted to the habitat of a different island. On return home he addressed himself systematically to 'the species problem', and found the key he was searching for when reading *An Essay on the Principle of Population*, published in 1798, in which the economist Thomas Malthus argued that population growth would always tend to outrun food supply. The consequent 'struggle for existence' formed the core of Darwin's theory, published in 1859 as *On the Origin of Species by Natural Selection*. The premise was that individuals in a species varied and those individuals whose characteristics gave them advantages in the struggle for existence had the best chance of surviving and procreating. 'On the other hand, we may feel sure that any variation in the least degree injurious would be rigidly destroyed. This preservation of favourable variations and the rejection of injurious variations, I call Natural Selection.'[3]

With this insight into a mechanism for evolution Darwin revolutionized man's concept of the world, fatally undermining literal belief in the biblical account of creation and showing that all living things, including man, are subject to natural laws. It is worth noting that, by contrast with earlier scientists such as Galileo who had upset the world view of their day, Darwin was neither censored nor punished. He was opposed by many, but both he and Alfred Russel Wallace, who reached the same conclusion on natural selection at the same time, and coined the explanatory phrase 'survival of the fittest', were feted, honoured and supported, a striking demonstration of the liberal values of British society. The cosmic intellectual revolution these two effected was, like the liberal reception it received, the product of a maritime nation. The sea has ever induced imagination and discovery. It may be asked whether Darwin or Wallace would have come to their pivotal conclusions had they never strayed out of England.

In everyday life Britain's most significant contribution to the world and certainly to the empire during this period was the export of rule-based sports. Cricket was the first. It had been carried to the colonies by the military at least as early as the 1820s; in Australia the first game is recorded in 1826 in Hyde Park, Sydney.[4] But it was through the second half of the century that games evolved and codified chiefly in English public schools and universities were adopted around the empire. Football, both 'soccer' and rugby, spread most widely among settlers and indigenous peoples alike; warships fielded teams to play local sides wherever they called.

Other games requiring greater expenditure were confined largely to the higher social ranks: polo, which the British found in India and adopted enthusiastically, rackets, its later variant, squash rackets, fives, lawn tennis, billiards and its later variant, snooker, said to have been invented by officers on leave in Ootacamund, the hot-weather hill resort of the Madras presidency. Yet cricket was the game that above all defined the empire. It encapsulated the code of the gentleman which inspired the British upper and middle classes as they sought to bring order, justice and godliness to the disparate peoples they ruled. Cricket was an analogy for life; it required patience, self-control, good humour and philosophical acceptance of mutability; the umpire's decision was final, no matter how perverse, to be accepted with good grace. The 'muscular Christians' who went out from British universities to spread the Gospel used cricket as an enjoyable introduction to the religious life and a moral substitute for the tribal warfare, cannibalism or headhunting traditions of their flocks. Of the three Anglican bishops of the Pacific diocese of Melanesia during the second half of the nineteenth century, the first and third were first-class cricketers, one of whom had played for his county against visiting Australians; the second was a Cambridge rowing blue, but also a mighty hitter of the ball. At the Mission College on Norfolk Island was a pine which used to be pointed out as the tree over which Bishop Selwyn had hit a six.[5]

Cricket was played in the United States, but not widely, possibly because of its English roots, and in the 1850s it was comprehensively overtaken by baseball, an adaptation of the equally ancient English game of rounders. The rules of baseball had been developed in the 1840s by a group of New York business and professional men and clerks who started playing in a vacant lot off Madison Avenue and formed the Knickerbocker Baseball Club.[6] Other clubs followed in the city and surrounding conurbations with a mainly middle-class membership, and in 1858, only twelve years after the Knickerbockers laid down the code, a National Association of Base Ball Players was founded as ruling body for 125 clubs established in Manhattan, Brooklyn, Long Island and New Jersey. As in finance, commerce, manufacturing industry and so much else, New York City led the way in the formation of a national game. Played by soldiers in the Civil War, baseball became so popular it was subsequently able to support professional leagues which spread continent-wide.

British overseas policy changed markedly from the 1880s. The change was foreshadowed in the previous decade when the Conservatives were returned to power under a prime minister, Benjamin Disraeli, resolved to pursue a more vigorous policy than the former Liberal government under

Gladstone, especially against threats to India posed by Russian expansion in central Asia and the Middle East.

The symbol of Disraeli's imperialism that was to have the most profound effect on his successors was the purchase of a controlling interest in the Suez Canal. The canal connecting the Mediterranean across the isthmus of Suez with the Red Sea, thence the Indian Ocean, had been one of Napoleon III's prestige projects, and had been completed in 1869 by the French engineer Ferdinand de Lesseps, financed largely by French investors. Since it reduced the distance from London to Bombay via the Cape of Good Hope by some 4,400 miles and the distance to Hong Kong by 3,300 miles it had been of huge benefit to British steamship companies, which had become its principal users. In November 1875 Disraeli discovered that the Pasha of Egypt was heavily in debt and negotiating with two French groups to sell his 44 per cent holding of Canal Company shares. Making use of a long-standing personal and financial relationship with the Rothschild banking family, Disraeli applied for an immediate loan of £4 million to buy the shares. Rothschilds made a lightning decision to advance the money, and the deal was done under the noses of the French. The following February Parliament debated the purchase.

For Gladstone, words were seldom strong enough to express the revulsion he felt at Disraeli's opportunism and populist imperialism. He predicted during the Commons debate that financial control of the Suez Canal would lead ultimately to political control. That he himself was to bring this about is the supreme irony of British nineteenth-century history. Equally, it is the clearest indication of the deep economic tides on which even the most dominant statesmen are borne.

For Egypt was not only perceived as the hinge of the eastern empire, Britain was her major financial and commercial partner, taking 80 per cent of Egyptian exports – mainly raw cotton – and providing 44 per cent of the country's imports;[7] over 80 per cent of traffic through the Suez Canal flew the British ensign,[8] and British investors held the largest share of Egyptian government bonds and loans raised for harbour and railway projects. Rigorous financial disciplines imposed by both British and French bondholders on the Egyptian government led to nationalist unrest culminating in September 1881 when a Colonel Arabi of the Egyptian army led a coup directed primarily at lifting European financial control. Disraeli had fallen by this time. Gladstone was back in power. It is interesting that 37 per cent of his personal portfolio of securities was invested in Egyptian stock,[9] but scarcely relevant to his actions since the British financial and strategic commitment to Egypt was absolute. The Admiralty was concerned particularly with the safety of the Suez Canal. Detailed preparations were made for naval brigades and marines from both the Mediterranean and East Indies fleets and reinforcements from home to occupy the main towns along the canal, Port Said, Ismailia and Suez, and sufficient ships were assembled at both ends to patrol the length of the waterway; orders even extended to the dispatch of water distillation plant and bullet-proof shields for machine-gun crews of the patrolling vessels. Recent research suggests, however, that what really exercised Gladstone were threats by Arabi to repudiate Egypt's foreign debts.

At first he tried to induce the European powers to intervene in concert; when this failed a joint Anglo-French naval demonstration was planned, but the French, anxious at the last moment that Bismarck might somehow spring a surprise while their focus was on the eastern Mediterranean, ordered their ships home, leaving the British battle fleet alone off Alexandria. Arabi then began strengthening the forts commanding the harbour. This was enough for Gladstone; he had instructions wired to the commander-in-chief to send in an ultimatum to cease all work on the forts within twelve hours. Arabi ignored it, and at daybreak on 11 July 1882 the ships, which had taken up positions for bombarding the forts and were cleared for action, opened fire. Gladstone explained afterwards to the House of Commons that he had no option; this was surely true. After the other powers and the French turned their backs he either had to act alone or allow Arabi to subvert the financial disciplines on which trade and development and Britain's own world position ultimately rested. Whether or not the traffic through the Suez Canal was threatened by Arabi, the City of London was. Through the spring Lord Nathaniel 'Natty' Rothschild was reported to have been paying daily visits to the Foreign Office, 'helping to create a climate in which occupation [of Egypt] appeared the only answer'.[10]

The bombardment of the forts at Alexandria was the first and only action undertaken by a British ironclad fleet. The vessels were of heterogenous design, illustrating the conflicting demands imposed by ever-increasing gun size and penetrative power within an Admiralty policy of keeping individual ship size and cost to a minimum. The largest and latest was the *Inflexible* of 11,900 tons displacement, commanded by Captain 'Jackie' Fisher, a formidable officer marked out for the highest positions in the service. She mounted four 81-ton rifled muzzle-loading guns in two turrets trained by hydraulic machinery. Altogether the fleet mounted forty-three heavy-rifled muzzle-loaders on any one side; the opposing forts mounted forty-one, together with over two hundred obsolete smooth-bore guns whose projectiles could not penetrate armour. Nonetheless, had Arabi's men been skilled gunners they would have enjoyed the traditional advantages of forts over ships: their fire could be ranged on to the comparatively large targets by observing the waterspouts raised by the fall of shot, whereas ships' officers stationed aloft to spot where their projectiles landed against the dun shore had a more difficult task and a far smaller target; usually only a direct hit on a gun or its embrasure would knock it out. Arabi lacked skilled gunners, however. Nor did he have mines, torpedoes or torpedo boats. The British guns' crews, stripped to the waist as in the old days, were allowed practically undisturbed practice.

It was a bright summer's morning. The black hulls of the ships, glistening white upperworks and yellow funnels and masts shrouded with white smoke rising from the guns, were reflected in a flat sea barely ruffled by a light offshore breeze. They were not ideal conditions: the mechanical gear for elevating most guns was so slow and clumsy that gun captains were trained to fire as their ship rolled the sights on target, and at least one ship's captain had parties of men moving from side to side across the deck to produce an artificial roll. Nonetheless, the volume of fire from the fleet, the constant whine of approaching shells interspersed every five minutes or so with the rumble of the *Inflexible*'s great projectiles tearing the air 'with a noise like that of a distant train',[11] explosions and occasional direct hits that wiped out a gun and its crew sapped the defenders' morale, and by afternoon Arabi's men had begun abandoning their positions. The forts were deserted after dark.

The Egyptians suffered some 550 casualties, the British 5 killed, 28 wounded. All ships remained fully battle-worthy; no armour had been pierced.[12] A storm prevented action next day, but parties of sailors and marines were landed on the 13th to occupy the forts and bring order to the town beyond, where the populace were venting their rage at the assault by looting, burning buildings and slaughtering any Europeans they found. The situation was soon brought under control, yet Arabi and his army remained at large in the interior and defiant. Gladstone, who had envisaged a limited punitive action by the navy, found instead that he had boosted Arabi and the nationalists. He was compelled to order a full-scale invasion by the army; France again refused to cooperate. A 17,000-strong force was landed at Port Said in August under the command of General Sir Garnet Wolseley, hero of retributive expeditions throughout the empire. Joined by naval brigades with additional artillery and Gatling guns, he advanced on Arabi's far larger force entrenched some thirty miles to the west at Tel el Kebir and achieving surprise after a night march destroyed it with superior fire power.[13] Five days later he was in Cairo.

Having occupied Egypt – most reluctantly so far as Gladstone was concerned – the British had little choice but to stay for a while to restore order.
Sir Evelyn Baring of the banking family was sent out as Consul General
with plenipotentiary powers to reform the government and place the country's finances on a sound footing prior to evacuating British forces. Quickly
deciding that reform was incompatible with evacuation, he settled in for the
long term, attaching British advisers trained in India to key government
ministries and running the country on strict, Gladstonian principles of
economy under the nominal rule of the Khedive. British ministers repeatedly assured other powers that the occupation was only temporary, but
the troops remained and Sir Evelyn, raised to the peerage as Lord Cromer,
continued to control the country as a 'Veiled Protectorate', in the phrase of
the time, as did his successors after he retired the following century. The
British did not leave Egypt until after the Second World War.

The occupation of Egypt upset the delicate balancing act whereby British
diplomacy and free trade policies prevented dangerous combinations against
her. The liberal, humanitarian mask had fallen away, revealing naked self-
interest, so it was perceived, especially in France, which had her own
colonial ambitions in Africa. She and Russia drew closer together and
increased their naval building programmes to curb Britain's overweening
power, while seeking territorial compensation where they could. At the
same time Bismarck asserted Germany's claims to overseas possessions.
Italy, Spain, Portugal and Belgium joined the drive to stake out parts of
Africa for themselves and Britain was drawn southwards from Egypt into
the Sudan, Uganda and British East Africa, and northwards from her possessions at the southern tip of Africa into Bechuanaland and Rhodesia.
Within a decade the continent was a patchwork of European colonies.

Despite Britain's vastly increased territorial holdings, two Boer republics,
Transvaal and the Orange Free State, succeeded in retaining independence
outside British possessions in southern Africa. Created by 'Afrikaner'
descendants of original Dutch, German and Huguenot settlers who had
trekked northwards out of British jurisdiction rather than submit to the
legislation outlawing slavery in the empire, they had been annexed during
Disraeli's premiership, but had rebelled and broken free when Gladstone
came to power. Since then gold had been discovered in the Transvaal hills
called Witwatersrand. Capital, largely British, had flowed in to develop
mining, and through the 1890s the 'Rand overtook Russia, Australia
and California to become the largest single source of gold production in
the world.[14]

In these altered circumstances Britain could no longer afford Boer independence. As with Egypt in 1882 she had a major financial and commercial stake in southern Africa; again like Egypt with the canal, the Cape was a strategic hinge of the eastern empire and the whole system of oceanic control. Yet the vast gold reserves of the 'Rand made it certain that the Transvaal would become the real fulcrum of the region; it was even possible, as the Under-Secretary for the Colonies suggested to the Prime Minister, Lord Salisbury, that a United States of South Africa could emerge, controlled from the Boer capital, Pretoria. The British government's initial attempts to block such a calamitous prospect relied on private enterprise: Cecil Rhodes, who had made a multi-million fortune from diamond mines close to the Orange Free State, was granted a Royal Charter to form a British South Africa Company. The same thing had been done earlier in East Africa; it was curiously reminiscent of the Crown–private partnerships Elizabeth I had used for piracy and colonization, or the great East- and West-India Companies with which the Dutch had founded their overseas empire in the seventeenth century. Like them, Rhodes's company was granted sovereign powers to make treaties and acquire, distribute and administer territory. Rhodes was an entrepreneur on the grandest scale and a romantic, believing passionately that the English-speaking peoples had attained the highest degree of civilization and it was his God-given mission to extend British influence. He aimed to destabilize the Boer government, but a colleague, Dr Leander Jameson, ruined the scheme with a premature armed incursion.

With Rhodes discredited, the Secretary for the Colonies, Joseph Chamberlain, who had been fully apprised of Jameson's attempt, and was fortunate to survive the repercussions, turned to more direct measures. His chosen instrument was Sir Alfred Milner, like Rhodes a passionate advocate of imperial unity and British 'race patriotism', as he called it,[15] and unlike Rhodes absolutely reliable. He had colonial experience in Egypt, a first-class brain, patience, austere self-control and an implacable will. Chamberlain sent him to the Cape in 1897 as High Commissioner for South Africa and Lieutenant Governor of Cape Colony with the task of increasing the pressure on the Transvaal president, Paul Kruger, to extend the franchise to thousands of immigrant outsiders, many British, who had flocked to the 'Rand. The aim after political reform in Pretoria was to bring the Boer states, leavened by non-Afrikaner voters, into a British South African Confederation.

Milner believed that any concessions he might extract from Kruger would prove illusory, and conceived that he had been given a mandate to work up to a crisis with Pretoria.[16] This he did, assisted by collaborators in London, particularly the 'Rand gold financiers Julius Wernher and Alfred Beit, both Germans who had become British citizens and committed British imperialists, although their main aim in supporting Milner was to bring down 'outrageous' wage levels for African labourers in the mines.[17]

The historian of the City, David Kynaston, has considered whether there was also a connection between London's role as the world's only free gold market 'and the perceived need to ensure in the long term a regular supply of gold from south Africa'. The City's paramount position in the world rested on the pound sterling pegged to the price of gold. 'South Africa meant gold, gold had become the very pivot of the City's existence, and to deny the connection surely goes against the grain.'[18] 'Natty' Rothschild, however, was one City mogul who worked consistently to prevent war.

Milner's masterstroke in working up to a crisis came on 30 August 1899 when he assured Chamberlain that the only way to bring Kruger to heel without war was to send a strong expeditionary force to South Africa to face down the Boers; he and his allies knew that this was the very thing that would provoke war. Salisbury's cabinet was persuaded. Salisbury himself was not; yet he recognized that the alternative was to allow supremacy in southern Africa to pass inevitably to Pretoria, and that was unimaginable. He told his Secretary for War, 'We have to act upon a moral field prepared for us by him [Milner] and his jingo supporters.'[19] Cables exchanged between the War Office and overseas commands located 10,000 men available from British regiments in India, Egypt, Malta and Crete, and these were embarked on troopships for Africa. The news reached Pretoria on 9 September. The Boers might have struck immediately with overwhelming numerical superiority over British forces in the region, but hoped fighting might still be avoided, and it was not until 9 October that an ultimatum was handed to the British, to expire on the 11th. Milner had achieved the war he knew to be necessary; it was his good fortune that the majority of troopships had by this time arrived with reinforcements.

In Britain the war was greeted with enthusiasm, not least in the City. At the Guildhall the following week rousing choruses of the National Anthem, 'Rule Britannia', 'Soldiers of the Queen' and other patriotic songs were accompanied by waving Union Jacks and Royal Standards for a rapturous hour before the Lord Mayor gave the first address in support of government policy.[20] The mood darkened in December and the stock market fell as the Boers inflicted a series of reverses on British forces. But their mobile, sharpshooting tactics could not prevail against the weight of an army corps dispatched from Britain in the wake of the initial reinforcements from the empire. Nor could Kruger hope for succour from the great powers. Despite rabid Anglophobia in European capitals, the Royal Navy held the ring, isolating the conflict and blockading the coast to prevent arms and ammunition from reaching the Boers. Meanwhile the white dominions, Canada, Australia and New Zealand, were swept up in a surge of feeling for the mother country and sent contingents to join the British forces in South Africa. The number of colonial volunteers eventually reached 29,000.[21]

After one more terrible reverse in the new year, 1900, Field Marshal Lord Roberts, former commander-in-chief in India, took command of the British army and advanced up the line of the railway into the Transvaal, entering Pretoria in June. The Boers continued fighting as guerrillas, but Roberts regarded the war as virtually won and, turning over command to his chief of staff, Lord Kitchener, returned home. To combat the guerrilla tactics Kitchener took the war to the entire Boer people, burning farms, seizing horses and cattle and incarcerating families, women and children in 'concentration camps' to deprive the fighting men of means of survival. Conditions in these hastily constructed camps soon became a scandal in Britain and Europe. Meagre rations, inadequate water and sanitary arrangements, overcrowding and disease killed many more than the fighting, and children were in the majority.[22]

Milner had opposed the policy from the beginning. The plan he proposed, first to Roberts before he left, then to Kitchener, was to recolonize the two states gradually by securing administratively and economically crucial areas such as the 'Rand, resuming production in the mines, and progressively expanding the protected areas.[23] Finally the government came down on his side. The results of reversing the strategy were surprising: when Kitchener ordered his commanders not to bring women and children into the camps it was found they faced even crueller hardships and were exposed to assault by the native Africans roused by Boer attacks on their fellows aiding the British.

Caught between Kitchener's commanders and the indigenous people, and with their farming families unprotected, the Boer leaders at last admitted defeat. On 31 May 1902 at Vereeniging on the Vaal river border between the Transvaal and Orange Free State they signed away the independence of both republics subject to a promise of internal self-government in the future. Milner had won time to anglicize the former republics. In 1906, when the promise given at Vereeniging was fulfilled and both states were granted self-government as Crown colonies within the empire, the former Boer commando leaders, Jan Smuts and Louis Botha, were voted into power. Yet the final irony was that both former enemies had in the meantime mutated into empire loyalists, and the Union of South Africa, which was inaugurated in May 1910 under Botha's leadership, was to prove as staunch in support of Britain as the older white dominions.

The Boer War exemplified the new face of British imperialism. Gone were the assumptions of universal free trade and minimal territorial intervention – apart from India and the white dominions – when Palmerston and Gladstone had run the empire and the Royal Navy which protected them all on a shoestring. The war cost over £200 million, raised by borrowing and doubling the rate of income tax; 22,000 British and colonial soldiers had died in action or as a result of disease; thousands more had been wounded. Moreover, the manner in which the war was fought, particularly the deaths of so many Boer women and children in the camps, had swelled support for Liberal opponents of the war and caused a curious dichotomy among the British: huge pride in the empire, distaste in many quarters for 'imperialism'.

There have been many interpretations of this sea change: it has been ascribed to a search for export markets, Britain in competition with newly industrialized nations for markets in the undeveloped world.[24] In this view Britain was an ageing power in relative industrial decline struggling to hold her own against aggressive younger rivals. The explanation has been challenged by P. J. Cain and A. G. Hopkins, who have pointed out that Egypt and South Africa were and remained throughout the imperial epoch the most important regions in Africa, beside which the territories gobbled up by France, Germany and other European powers were marginal; they ask how, if Britain were in decline, she had 'begun and ended partition [of Africa] as the dominant foreign power'.[25] The same argument applies in the grand strategic context: the Suez Canal and the Simonstown naval base at the Cape were crucial for global command. Britain held on to both.

After the partition of Africa the British overseas empire remained, as before, the largest in history: it covered a quarter of the earth's surface and embraced a quarter of the world's population. Moreover, British finance permeated the globe; Britain was by far the largest creditor nation with twice as much capital invested abroad as her nearest rival, France.[26] The South American states of Argentina, Chile and Uruguay were so dominated by British capital and services they have been termed 'honorary colonies'. The income this investment generated was practically equal to an annual negative balance on Britain's visible trade in goods, some £150 million in the period after 1900. Other 'invisible' earnings, chiefly from shipping and business and financial services, brought the overall balance of payments into credit by some £130 million a year.[27] It can scarcely be doubted that the need to preserve the rule of law and financial discipline in regions where capital was threatened was the prime driving force behind the new imperialism, particularly as the financial masters of the City and leaders of the institutions servicing international commerce and capital had entered the ranks of the governing class. From this perspective, as Cain and Hopkins assert, 'Britain was an advancing not a retreating power'.[28]

This was evident at sea. Britain had the largest shipbuilding and shipping industries; by 1913 she owned 18.7 million tons of merchant shipping, 40 per cent of total world tonnage; and while her share had fallen from 60 per cent in the 1880s, it was over three times the tonnage of her nearest rivals, the United States and Germany.[29] Her maritime lead and resolve to maintain it were demonstrated most clearly in the fighting navy. A Select Committee on Naval Estimates had reported in 1889 that in view of 'Britain's unique dependence on sea supplies' the navy was inadequately funded, for 'The command of the sea once being lost it would not require the landing of a single soldier upon her shores to bring her to an ignominious capitulation'.[30]

Following the committee's recommendations, a Naval Defence Act was passed the same year formalizing the 'Two Power Standard' of parity with the next two naval powers, France and Russia, which had guided Admiralty policy since 1815, and allocating the unprecedented sum of £21.5 million to add seventy vessels to the fleet over the next five years, among them forty-two cruisers and ten battleships. But it was in design as much as numbers that Britain demonstrated ascendancy. The battleships of the *Royal Sovereign* and subsequent classes built under a new Director of Naval Construction, William White, emerged, as it were, from the chrysalis of the experimental years as mature capital units. In the balance struck between guns, armour, speed and sea-keeping ability they were the finest warships of the day, tangible expressions of a theory of battle-fleet command by ocean-going ships able to dictate gun action outside torpedo or ramming range, and majestic symbols of naval power.

6

Aspirant Navies: the United States

THE OCEANIC SUPREMACY with which Britain advanced into the twentieth century concealed the serious apprehensions of her leaders. She had lost industrial primacy; the use of steam power for manufacturing and transport had spread to countries in Europe and outside; the United States and Germany had outstripped her in steel production and led the way in newer technologies based on chemicals and electricity. Both had erected tariff barriers to protect their industries; both were searching for export markets and encroaching steadily on her share of world trade.[1] The United States, knit by continental railroads into a huge domestic market, had become the world's foremost economy; the volume of transactions on the Wall Street stock exchange approached that in the City of London, although London remained the fulcrum of global finance.

Relative industrial decline and Britain's perceived inability to compete against states with greater population and resources had led Joseph Chamberlain to advocate bringing the dominions into closer unity as 'Greater Britain'.[2] In 1902 he proposed erecting a tariff wall around the empire combined with preferential duties within. The white dominions rejected federal union – they had only recently gained financial and constitutional independence – while tariff reform was opposed by free-traders and even split his own party. Eventually 'imperial preference' received the *coup de grâce* when put to the people in a general election in 1905, for Britain was a net importer of foodstuffs and raising duties on foreign imports would increase food prices.

Chamberlain's approach had academic support in the works of Sir Halford Mackinder, pioneer of 'geopolitics', an attempt to marry science and the humanities by relating political history to geography. In *Britain and the British Seas*, published in 1902, Mackinder argued that the recent rapid growth of other countries behind protective tariffs made it questionable 'whether Britain can much longer defend her trade by keeping the "open door" to her own and certain neutral markets'.[3]

He went farther two years later, arguing in a paper for the Royal

Geographical Society that transcontinental railways were shifting the strategic balance away from maritime powers towards great land powers, away from colonial annexation towards internal industrial concentration, and suggesting that future historians would date the end of the 'Columbian epoch' of maritime exploration and expansion to 'soon after the year 1900'.[4] He predicted that the future lay with 'that vast area of Euro-Asia which is inaccessible to ships, but in antiquity lay open to the horse-riding nomads, and is today about to be covered by a network of railways',[5] indicating the huge stretch of Eurasian landmass embracing Russia and central Asia from the Ukraine and Persia through Turkestan and Mongolia almost to the Pacific coast, terming it variously 'the pivot region of the world's politics' and 'the heartland'. It was over three times the size of the United States and the potential in terms of population, wheat, cotton, fuel and mineral production was 'so incalculably great, that it is inevitable that a vast economic world, more or less apart, will there develop inaccessible to oceanic commerce';[6] and he drew the breathtaking conclusion: 'The oversetting of the balance of power in favour of the pivot state . . . would permit the use of vast continental resources for fleet-building, and the empire of the world would then be in sight.'[7]

Mackinder's vision of the decline of maritime relative to territorial power was remarkable not least for its appearance soon after the most influential paeans to maritime power ever penned: the volumes by the US navy captain Alfred Thayer Mahan beginning with *The Influence of Sea Power upon History, 1660–1783*, published in 1890, and *The Influence of Sea Power upon the French Revolution and Empire, 1793–1812*, published in 1892. Although the volumes were confined to the period of Britain's naval triumphs over France and Spain during her ascent to world power, Mahan claimed that the strategic principles he had teased out were immutable, 'remaining the same, in cause and effect from age to age', belonging 'as it were to the Order of Nature'.[8] The message was reassuring for naval officers, suggesting after the confusions of rapid technological change that the battle fleet remained the arbiter of naval power, and a strategy of blockade and engaging the enemy fleet wherever possible, as practised consistently by the British in the great Anglo-French wars, would always defeat an enemy intent on husbanding the fleet for specific tasks or engaging in cruiser warfare against trade, as the French had done.

In the broader field of geopolitics the message seemed particularly relevant as Mahan practically equated 'sea power' with world power; at the least he sought to show that 'command of the seas' had proved historically superior to land power, and would continue to be so. Statesmen of the industrial nations seeking overseas markets and spheres of influence in the shadow of Britain's global empire may not have needed this confirmation, but Mahan provided stimulus and intellectual justification for increased naval building programmes.

The results increased the concerns of British ministers. Whereas in the early 1880s Britain had almost as many capital ships as the rest of the world combined, by the turn of the century naval building by all industrial nations had reduced her share of capital ships to two-thirds of the rest of the world.[9] She still possessed overwhelmingly the largest battle fleet and maintained the 'two-power' standard comfortably against France and Russia combined, but most worryingly two of the new battle-fleet powers, the United States and Japan, were outside Europe, hence could not be contained while the Royal Navy concentrated against her potential European enemies.

The British government met the situation by conciliating the Americans and allying with Japan. They were fortunate that the once brittle relationship with the United States had warmed, particularly in naval matters; indeed, the US service, which had been deprived of funds and allowed to wither after the Civil War, had been revived during the 1880s with the aid of technical data passed on freely by the Royal Navy.[10] One striking example occurred in Hong Kong in early 1901 when Captain Percy Scott, commanding HMS *Terrible*, initiated Lieutenant William Sims of USS *Kentucky* into aiming methods and training devices he had introduced in his ship. These had enabled his guns' crews to break all records in the annual Prize Firing competition and would over the following years revolutionize gunnery accuracy throughout the Royal Navy. Sims attempted to have Scott's methods adopted in the US service, finally succeeding when he secured the personal backing of the President, Theodore Roosevelt.[11]

Roosevelt had long been a strenuous supporter of the navy. He had read Mahan's first volume in two days when it appeared, and enthused over it. He believed, like the historian, Frederick J. Turner, that since the United States' westward drive had ended at the Pacific coast, the expansion that had been the main fact of American life since the first settlers landed could only be continued overseas. This fitted the teachings of Mahan, who stressed that Britain's wealth and influence derived from the 'three interlocking rings' of sea power, namely colonies, maritime trade and battle-fleet command of the seas. Roosevelt, who was representative of powerful forces within the American commercial-financial community, had resolved that the United States should follow a similar path:

... if we are to hold our own in the struggle for naval and commercial supremacy, we must build up our power within our own borders. We must build the isthmian [Panama] canal, and we must grasp the points of vantage which will enable us to have our say in deciding the destiny of the oceans of the East and West.[12]

The United States had acquired 'points of vantage' in 1898 as a consequence of war with Spain fought ostensibly in support of Cuban rebels seeking to free their island from Spanish colonial rule. The deeper causes lay in the assertiveness of American economic power and the strategic importance of the Caribbean, particularly for the anticipated 'isthmian' canal, which would allow US warships rapid transit between the Atlantic and the Pacific. Moreover, the United States claimed moral authority in the western hemisphere: under a doctrine proclaimed by President James Monroe in 1823 European powers had been warned against attempts to oppress or control any nation in the Americas. Cuba was a Spanish colony, hence exempt from US interference, but Spain was represented in the public prints as a brutal oppressor. Roosevelt, who had been Assistant Secretary of the Navy at this time, was a strong advocate of the isthmian canal project and at the forefront of calls for war.

Hostilities were precipitated by an explosion which destroyed the US cruiser *Maine* in Havana harbour with the loss of 260 men. It was attributed to a Spanish mine, but why and how Spain should have contrived to blow up a US warship on a goodwill visit to calm US inhabitants in the city has never been explained. In all probability it was a spontaneous explosion of unstable ammunition, as occurred in several navies during these years.[13] Roosevelt resigned his post immediately war was declared on 24 April and, suiting action to his tough words, recruited a volunteer cavalry brigade for service in Cuba.

The war was decided by naval force after the precepts of Mahan, who had been appointed to the Naval War Board formed to direct strategy. The first strike was in the Spanish Philippines. The US Asiatic squadron of four modern cruisers and two gunboats under Commodore George Dewey sailed from Hong Kong to Manila Bay, where an older, less well-trained Spanish cruiser squadron lay behind the protection of shore batteries. Passing these in darkness without sustaining a hit, Dewey proceeded in line ahead, disregarding possible mines, and opened fire at 5,000 yards, closing steadily in a series of countermarches to 2,000 yards, where superior American equipment and training decided the action. By midday the Spanish squadron had been annihilated.

In the Caribbean the strategy adopted by the War Board was to block-ade Spanish forces in Cuba while supplying the rebels. Nevertheless, a Spanish squadron of four cruisers and three destroyers under Admiral Pascual Cervera crossed the Atlantic and succeeded in entering the harbour of Santiago at the east of the island. It was a futile gesture. The US main fleet comprising three first-class battleships, one smaller battleship and two armoured cruisers seized the excellent anchorage of Guantánamo Bay 40 miles along the coast and blocked him in; after which US troops, includ-ing Roosevelt's volunteers, were landed nearer Santiago to flush the Spanish squadron out. Cervera received orders from Madrid to break away, and did so on the morning of 3 July, leading a doomed charge with panache.[14] The American battleships waiting off the entrance closed to get within torpedo range, but Cervera turned and ran westward. Commodore W. S. Schley, in temporary command of the US fleet, chased, opening fire with turret and starboard guns and gradually bringing the range down inside 1,600 yards, when the Spanish vessels, overwhelmed by the weight of American fire and wreathed in smoke from flames breaking out from shell holes and gun ports and rising up the masts, peeled out of line and ran themselves aground. For the captain of the *Iowa*, latest and largest of the US battleships, it was a 'magnificent sad sight to see these beautiful ships in their death agonies';[15] below, his ship's decks echoed with the yells and cheers of the men.

Cervera's heroic attempt marked the last gasp of the Spanish Empire, so long in decline. With the US navy in command in the Caribbean and South China Sea nothing could prevent American forces occupying Santiago, Puerto Rico and Manila. Spain capitulated and in the subsequent peace treaty[16] transferred the Philippines to the United States for $20 mil-lion, together with the mid-Pacific island of Guam and Puerto Rico in the Caribbean, and renounced her claim to Cuba, which became in fact if not in name an American protectorate. The United States had already acquired rights to bases at Pearl Harbor on the Hawaiian island of Oahu and Pago-Pago in the Samoan group in the western Pacific; with the acquisition of the former Spanish colonies coinciding with an agreement the same year to annex Hawaii as a state of the Union she completed the transformation from a hemispheric to a world power, indeed a colonial power in the Old World mould justified with Old World moralism.

As Vice-President and President in 1901 Roosevelt never tired of assert-ing that the United States' mission as a materially advanced, expanding power was to bring civilization to barbaric states and peoples. Rejecting voices raised against ruling other peoples as incompatible with the principles of American democracy, he called on his fellow countrymen in essence to take up the white man's burden. By doing their duty in the Philippines Americans would not only add to their nation's renown and benefit the inhabitants of those islands, but would above all play their part in 'the great work of uplifting mankind'.[17] He explained on another occasion, 'every expansion of a great civilised power means a victory for law, order and righteousness'.[18]

With acquisitions in the western Pacific, the question of an isthmian canal across Panama had become even more urgent for the US navy, and Roosevelt pursued the project with energy. When negotiations with Colombia for construction and ownership rights in its territory of Panama collapsed he supported a revolution in Panama which succeeded in gaining independence. The new Panamanian government then granted the United States the building and operating rights it required with full control over an adjacent 'Canal Zone' across the isthmus. Construction began in 1904. Formidable physical difficulties and unhealthy swamps breeding mosquitoes that spread yellow fever and malaria through the workforce slowed operations, and it was not until August 1914 that the canal opened, a triumph of will and preventive sanitation and medicine as much as a heroic feat of engineering.

Roosevelt, meanwhile, had been elected President for a second term in his own right (1904). Taking naval affairs under his wing, he oversaw a great expansion of the battle fleet and established bases in the Caribbean at Guantánamo Bay and the island of Culebra off Puerto Rico. He also issued a 'Corollary' to the Monroe Doctrine designed to prevent European powers intervening in the Americas to recover debts or impose fiscal discipline; the United States itself would guarantee that states in the western hemisphere would meet their international financial obligations. It was more significant in practice than the original doctrine, whose enforcement had relied on the Royal Navy. The new US navy had the power to impose compliance.

7

Aspirant Navies: Imperial Japan

———•———

SOON AFTER THE informal accord with the United States Britain was forced to adjust her position in eastern waters, where Russia and France, seeking territory at the expense of the dying Chinese empire, were expanding their fleets. The Royal Navy could not match their combined strength in the east without reducing its battle squadrons in the Mediterranean and home waters to dangerous levels;[1] the Admiralty recommended an alliance with Japan to add her naval strength to that of the British China squadron.

Japan was the newest naval power. Since being forcibly opened to external trade by Commodore Perry's mission in 1854[2] she had undergone a revolution as decisive in setting a permanent new course for the nation as England's 'Glorious Revolution' of 1688, yet taking her in diametrically the opposite direction. The reason appears to be that, unlike England's merchant community, Japanese merchants failed or declined to set limits on the executive. Those who fashioned the Japanese revolution in 1867 and ended the Tokugawa Shogunate were samurai raised in the warrior code known as bushido; their success took Japan along the path of the warrior.

The merchants' failure is hard to explain. They were the lowest of the legal classes or estates into which Tokugawa Japan had been divided, the samurai at the top; yet during the two centuries of the country's isolation from the outside world the economy had expanded greatly[3] and the merchants had been the beneficiaries. The pace of growth and innovation had been slowed by lack of foreign competition and foreign models, and by government regulations imposed to preserve the feudal order unchanged; consequently production remained pre-industrial. Notwithstanding, agricultural output had almost doubled in the period, the population had grown by 45 per cent,[4] the number of towns with populations over 5,000 had increased to more than 160 and the larger towns had expanded hugely: the Tokugawa Shogun's capital, Edo – later Tokyo – had grown into a city of over a million. Osaka was not far behind. These were all symptoms of a flourishing internal trade in food, textiles of all kinds and domestic goods and handicrafts, many of exquisite taste and finish. The merchants who controlled this nationwide market and financed the cottage industries which, as in pre-industrial Britain and France, extended into rural areas dominated economic life and amassed wealth, in some cases great fortunes.

The samurai, by contrast, had been denied their role as warriors since there had been no serious wars during the period of national seclusion. They had become bureaucrats administering the system of repressive laws and checks instituted by the first Tokugawa shoguns, which with a thousand rules of custom, obligation and etiquette had preserved internal stability and the feudal order for such an extraordinarily long time – at the cost of much individual freedom, social mobility and significant technological progress. The samurai retained their noble status at the top of society but had only their stipends as office-holders to support them and had become poorer relatively as the economy had grown and the merchants prospered. Many samurai borrowed from merchant-financiers to support the style expected of their rank and fell into chronic debt; some, like impoverished aristocrats throughout history, sacrificed their contempt for trade and tapped into merchant wealth through marriage. In general the two orders arrived at an uneasy mutual dependency: samurai needed merchants for their economic power; merchants needed samurai administrators who monopolized civil power. The memoirs of a Russian officer taken prisoner and confined on Hokkaido for three years from 1811 to 1813 illustrate aspects of the relationship:

> The merchants have not the right to bear arms; but though their profession is not respected, their wealth is . . . The Japanese told us that their officers of state and men of rank behaved themselves outwardly with great haughtiness to the merchants, but in private, are very familiar with the rich merchants and are often under great obligations to them.[5]

He added that the laws in Japan, although rigorously enforced, were often 'outweighed by the influence of gold',[6] and he compared the commercial spirit of the Japanese people to that of the English. This was reflected in the arts, literature and amusements, which expressed a vigorous urban, even bourgeois, culture far removed from the austere certainties of the samurai; indeed, a significant theme in drama was the conflict between individual desire and feudal loyalty.[7]

It is a puzzle: the merchants were masters of both the Japanese economy and the intellectual and artistic life of the great conurbations, yet they never sought to translate financial ascendancy into political power; they may have done so on a personal basis, but never as a class to impose merchant imperatives on the country. To all appearances they resigned themselves to social humiliation in return for the security of the established order whose real burdens were laid on the peasantry. Merchants lived in varying degrees of ease or luxury while peasant farmers were squeezed between feudal taxes and rising prices to the very margin of existence, ever on the edge of starvation. The merchants who drove the system in tandem with the samurai bureaucracy were complicit. Perhaps they had little reason to desire change. Perhaps they had been conditioned by 250 years of the Tokugawa regime to accept their second-class status and the hauteur of the samurai as belonging to the unchanging order of things. On the other hand they lacked any national consultative institution such as the English had had in Parliament through which to generate change. And the principal object-ive of the Tokugawa secret state police network was to snuff out any hint of rebellion.

At all events, after Japan had been opened to Western trade the revela-tion of how backward and defenceless the country had become during the centuries of isolation caused a crisis of confidence, and disaffected samurai from peripheral south-western domains seized power in the name of the imperial dynasty, which had been reduced under the Tokugawas to a purely ceremonial role. The coup is known as the 'Meiji Restoration' since the seventeen-year-old youth who had recently succeeded to the imperial throne took the name Meiji at his coronation in 1868.

The young samurai who invoked his authority to refashion the state were dedicated to reversing Tokugawa isolation. They aimed to make Japan strong by adopting the technologies and institutions of the powers that had humiliated their country and were carving up China between them; to which end they swept out the feudal land and caste system, in theory opening all occupations to all men, and introducing a nationwide school system that over time converted possibility into reality, releasing a flood of talent from all former classes of society and producing a general level of education far superior to anything in other Eastern countries.

After initial guidance from United States' educationists the school system was transformed into an instrument for passing on the values and aims of the ruling samurai. All school systems tend to transmit the prevail-ing national ethos; the samurai appear to have taken this to the extreme. Western values were excluded deliberately because of the danger, so it was put in an Imperial Decree of 1879, 'that in the end our people will forget the great principles governing the relation between ruler and subject, and father and son'.[8] What this meant in practice was that schools were run like military institutions, often with military officers in charge, and pupils were indoctrinated with the military virtues of absolute obedience and loyalty to the state and the person of the Emperor, who was held sacred. Thus emperor worship, a prime component of the traditional Japanese *Shinto* belief system which was elevated into the state religion during this period, was inculcated from an early age, together with nationalistic pride, at the expense of individual expression or creative thinking. Combined with conscription for military service, this had the desired effect of creating a warrior nation whose young were imbued with the idea that to die for the Emperor was the most glorious service they could render their country.[9]

Industrialization was driven by the Meiji government with the same object: to make Japan strong and able to compete with the Western powers. Delegations were sent abroad to study Western steel-founding, engineering, armaments and shipbuilding works, and foreign engineers and craftsmen were recruited to set up and supervise these industries in Japan. The government financed the projects partly with revenues from a land tax, partly with loans from the merchant-financiers who had accumulated wealth in the former regime, striking testimony to the prosperity built up under the Tokugawas. Foreign managers were also recruited to mechanize textile, paper-making and other light industries. The combination of Western technology and cheap Japanese labour brought ready export earnings for consumer products and the government sold these profitable enterprises to its merchant-financier partners, several of whom, such as Mitsui, Mitsubishi and Sumitomo, grew into corporate giants. At the same time the government retained control of strategic industries like ship-building, armaments and railways.[10]

Such exposure to the West inevitably allowed in liberal, democratic and socialist notions, which were seized upon for their novelty or political potential by factions opposed to the ruling elite. They were quite incompatible with the centralized, bureaucratic administration the samurai oligarchy had fashioned to make the country strong, but by 1881 a movement for popular rights had gained so much ground that the government felt it necessary to promise a constitution and a national assembly. Again, delegations were sent abroad, this time to study European political systems. The outcome, however, had already been decided in the inner circle of government. It was to be the Prussian model fashioned by Bismarck to keep all threads of power in his own hands[11] – nominally on behalf of his sovereign – not the British model, where power was exercised through a popularly elected house. By this date the British franchise extended to males throughout the middle and artisan classes.

Again, it appears that Japanese merchants missed an opportunity to curb the power of the executive. No important groupings of city merchants or industrialists supported the movement for democratic rights. The leaders of the popular movement were chiefly disaffected samurai who formed a Liberal Party (*Jiyuto*) as a vehicle for organized opposition to the ruling oligarchy, not from democratic conviction, which was foreign to them. Smaller merchants and rural landlords participated, but the real impulse came from the peasantry and urban poor seeking a say, particularly in the taxes they suffered. The government clamped down on popular demonstrations and gagged the press while appearing to bow to the demands for an elected assembly.

The constitution was gifted to the nation by the Emperor in 1889. It embedded the leadership of the ruling oligarchy by placing the Emperor above and outside the framework of laws. He was supreme commander of the armed forces and appointed government ministers to act in his name and initiate legislation in a national assembly or Diet (*Gikai*) comprising an upper House of Peers for a new nobility and a House of Representatives elected by males over twenty-five who paid a certain level of tax. The Diet had no say in the composition of the government or the functions of the bureaucracy; its chief role was to assent to legislation proposed by ministers.[12] It was a mere token attached to the centralized structure; and since the tax qualification limited the electorate to just over 1 per cent of the population it was in practice responsive only to the aims of the ruling elite.

These aims had already been realized to an astonishing degree: all major Japanese cities had been linked by telegraph and over 1,400 miles of railways had been laid by 1890; heavy industry and shipbuilding had been developed, a substantial merchant marine built up by the same methods of government subsidy and protection, and the armed services had been equipped with modern ships and weapons, their personnel imprinted with the warrior virtues. Officers were inspired by the samurai code, bushido, demanding martial spirit, simplicity, self-sacrifice and absolute loyalty to the Emperor, scorning luxury, even pleasure, as corrupting influences. The men were trained with a similar spartan devotion and imbued with fanatic nationalism.

Having achieved the goal of forging a strong nation with the aid of Western technology, it is not surprising that Japan's ruling oligarchy began a Western pattern of imperial acquisition. Whether this was the logical next stage in securing independence from the powers pressing in on China or whether it was the first stage in a project for overseas conquest are probably not meaningful alternatives. It is more realistic to see Japan's decision to join the nations competing for territory and influence around the carcass of the Chinese empire as inevitable once she felt she had the armed strength to do so.[13] She had already extended into island groups to the east (the Bonins), south (Ryukyus) and north (Kuriles); now she challenged China for dominance over Korea, a strategic target from before her centuries of isolation.

She provoked war with China in 1894. Her aims were to seize the Liaotung peninsula north-west of Korea, commanding the Korean peninsula and the Yellow Sea and northern Chinese commercial ports, and to take the Chinese island of Formosa (Taiwan) as a naval base adjacent to the trade routes of the China Sea. Japanese troops were landed in north-west Korea, and when the Chinese hastened reinforcements to the area by sea under escort of their battle fleet the Japanese fleet intervened.

The action took place on 17 September 1894 off the mouth of the River Yalu. The day was bright and windless. The Chinese fleet comprised two obsolescent battleships built in 1881/82 as smaller versions of the British *Inflexible*, three even smaller ironclads and five obsolescent cruisers, all beautifully lacquered and gilded but poorly maintained. The administration was corrupt and some shells for the battleships' heavy guns were filled with sand instead of bursting charges. The tactics employed by the Chinese admiral Ting Ju-ch'ang belonged to the same era as his ships, when the idea of dealing the enemy a mortal blow by ramming had been ascendant. Ting gave his captains instructions to fight in pairs, bows on to the enemy if possible, and to follow his movements, and steamed towards the Japanese at 6 knots in line abreast, his two battleships at the centre of the line.[14]

The Japanese had followed the Royal Navy by readopting the single line of battle allowing all broadside guns clear arcs of fire as in the days of sail. The Japanese admiral, Sukenori Ito, lacked any battleships but had seven fast, modern cruisers armed for broadside fire with the latest quick-firing (QF) 6-inch or 4.7-inch guns developed to repel torpedo boat attack. The Chinese had no quick-firers. Three of Ito's cruisers had been built in Britain, two in France and two in the Japanese naval yard at Yokosuka, one to the British, one to the French design. Ito formed his fleet in line with the latest, British-built *Yoshino*, capable of 23 knots, in the lead, followed by the three other cruisers of British design as a fast division. He followed in the *Matsushima* leading a main division of the three French-designed ships and four smaller, older vessels that would have been better left behind.

The sea was glassy calm. As the *Yoshino* approached within 3 miles of the Chinese centre, Admiral Ting's battleships opened fire. The shells plunged harmlessly into the water. Ito did not reply but, spotting that the cruisers on Ting's right were weaker, he ordered an alteration across the Chinese advance, then wheeled around Ting's right wing, opening fire at the same time at about 3,000 yards. Ting altered to starboard to meet the attack. His ships turned in pairs to conform, becoming hopelessly confused just as the Japanese fire, short at first, moved up among them. The battle was decided by the Japanese QF guns and the intensive training of their crews. It was calculated later that all told the Japanese guns were capable of firing 185 rounds in ten minutes against a Chinese fleet total or 33 rounds in ten minutes.[15]

Nonetheless, the Chinese battleships' armour was not pierced. They remained afloat, their heavy guns still active, and one succeeded in putting a 12-inch shell into the *Matsushima*'s battery, detonating the ammunition supply, wiping out the guns' crews and starting fires that forced the flagship to retire. Earlier, two of the smaller, older Japanese cruisers had been forced out of the action by hits from 12-inch shells. Four Chinese ships were destroyed by gunfire, however, one sank after a collision, and after four hours' fighting, with sunset approaching, Ting retired to Port Arthur, leaving the Japanese fleet in effective control of the sea.

On land Japanese troops proved their superiority with the same combination of modern weapons, training and fanatic spirit. They crossed the Yalu, descended on the Liaotung peninsula and advanced towards Port Arthur. Admiral Ting withdrew his surviving ships to Weihaiwei on the opposite peninsula, but Japanese torpedo boats penetrated the obsolete defences and sank his flagship. He committed suicide. Port Arthur had already fallen. Weihaiwei surrendered in February 1895 and, with the Japanese in full control of the sea and both peninsulas, China sued for peace. At the Treaty of Shimonoseki in April Japan gained all her war aims, the Liaotung peninsula, Formosa and the adjoining Pescadores islands, the independence of Korea from Chinese suzerainty, the opening of four Chinese ports to Japanese trade and an indemnity estimated as 50 per cent greater than the costs of the war.

The settlement was unwelcome to the powers, particularly Russia, whose Pacific base at Vladivostok was now surrounded by Japanese or Japanese-controlled territory and at the mercy of a blockade. Joined by her partner, France, and by Germany in expansionist mood, she forced Japan to relinquish the Liaotung peninsula in return for a further payment. She and France then arranged a loan to China to pay the debt, as a reward for which she was granted a concession to take the trans-Siberian railway across Manchuria to Vladivostok. Subsequently she was also ceded Port Arthur as a base for her Pacific fleet and granted a further concession to run a railway from the port up the length of the Liaotung peninsula as a southern extension of the trans-Siberian line.

These advances heightened tension in the region and forced Japan into the orbit of Britain and the United States, both of whom sought to preserve China and her markets for the trade of all nations. They also raised a formidable future enemy. For the immediate response of the Japanese government was to double the size of the army to 600,000 men and expand and transform the fleet by ordering 12-inch gun battleships, armoured cruisers and other warships, chiefly from Britain. In turn, Russia increased her Pacific fleet. It was this regional competition which persuaded the British Admiralty that it could no longer match Franco-Russian strength in the region, and to propose enlisting Japanese aid with a local alliance.[16]

Japan seized the chance. Besides the prestige of allying with the world's greatest sea power, she could pursue her strategic and commercial goals in Korea and Manchuria with assurance that she could not again be pushed aside by the Franco-Russian axis. The Anglo-Japanese treaty was signed on 30 January 1902, by which time the Japanese navy was headed by five scaled-down versions of the latest British battleships of the *Royal Sovereign* and successor classes. Under the terms, if either signatory were at war with a third party the other would remain neutral, but if the third party were joined by an ally then the other signatory would join in with its partner. The agreement affirmed Korean 'independence', but recognized Japan's special interest 'politically as well as commercially and industrially in Korea'.[17]

For Britain, the Japanese alliance and the understanding with the United States in the western hemisphere guaranteed continued naval ascendancy. For Japan the alliance confirmed her status among the world powers and served as a springboard for the next stage of her expansion.

8

Aspirant Navies: Imperial Germany

A S THE ROYAL Navy came to terms with the need for allies in the western and eastern hemispheres the most dangerous threat to its
hegemony was growing in the shipyards of Germany, the most dynamic
industrial and commercial power in Europe. Since the formation of the
new Reich in 1871 from the separate German states Prussia had led to victory against France the population had grown by almost 40 per cent and
was approaching 60 million, against under 40 million in France, where the
rate of increase had been a bare 3 per cent.[1] German industry had made
equally spectacular gains. In iron and steel production Germany had over-
taken Great Britain and her output was four times that of France.[2] She led
the way in the new chemical and electrical industries and her total manufacturing output had risen to 13 per cent of world production, fast catching
Britain, whose share had fallen to 18 per cent. The United States, now the
largest industrial power, had 23 per cent of total world manufacture; France
had fallen back from a position ahead of Germany in 1871 to a mere 7 per
cent of world output.[3]

While static in material and power terms by comparison with the
German Reich, France had experienced a remarkable artistic flowering in
the wake of defeat in 1871. In painting, Claude Monet and Pierre Renoir
had initiated an 'impressionist' school seeking to capture the moment
through the effects of light. Claude Debussy inspired impressionism in
music; and in poetry, literature and all the arts Paris had become a magnet
for those wishing to be original and change the world. Vienna experienced
a similar burst of artistic creativity at this time. Hitherto periods of resur-
gence in the arts had been linked to the merchant wealth of city-states
or maritime powers. In Paris and Vienna the phenomenon evidently
depended on bondholder or *rentier* money.

Meanwhile, French intellectuals, pursuing abstraction, sought to explain
the changed relationship with Germany as the result of opposing principles,
France embodying lightness of spirit, wit, imagination, artistic grace,
Germany as the quintessence of soulless modernity where all emphasis was

on industry, technology and mechanical efficiency; and arguing that whereas France had developed organically as a nation, the separate German states had been annexed by Prussia, 'victims of internal conquest as brutally subjugating as the external conquest of France'.[4] Prussia with its militaristic foundations and habits of obedience was the real enemy, the anti-France that Britain had been historically. Prussians, in the words of Ernest Renan, were 'men of iron . . . whom our century has seen with terror emerge from the entrails of the ancient Germanic world'.[5]

However much this analysis glossed brutal aspects of France's earlier history and the terror she had visited on all Europe during the Revolutionary and Napoleonic wars, the characterization of Prussia as a regressive, militaristic state with dangerous ambitions was echoed by observers in Britain. Rudyard Kipling was not the first, but as early as 1897 he had foreseen war with Germany.[6] In his allegorical poem 'The Rowers' in 1902 he was more explicit: after the ordeal of the Boer War, the British now had to exert themselves against 'the Goth and the shameless Hun'.[7]

By this date conviction of Germany's aggressive intent had spread to sections of the British press and government and service departments. The Admiralty had most reason for concern since a German fleet-building programme begun in 1898 was quite evidently aimed against the Royal Navy. The battleships had a limited cruising radius and cramped accommodation that made them unsuitable for action outside the North Sea. After a visit to Wilhelmshaven and Kiel in August 1902, the Parliamentary Undersecretary wrote: 'Against England alone is such a weapon as the modern German Navy necessary; against England, unless all available evidence and all probability combine to mislead, that weapon is being prepared.'[8]

The director of naval intelligence, a noted naval historian, commented on the paper, 'We shall have to fight for command of the North Sea as we did in the Dutch Wars of the seventeenth century.'[9] Now that the German naval archives are available it is clear that the conclusions drawn at the Admiralty were correct: the new German navy was from its inception aimed at Great Britain. It has become equally clear that the driving force behind the fleet was the Kaiser, Wilhelm II.[10]

Wilhelm was the son of Queen Victoria's daughter 'Vicky', an eager, clever woman who had imbibed all the earnestly liberal views of her father, Victoria's consort, Prince Albert, and transmitted them to her husband, Crown Prince Friedrich of Prussia, making him the great hope for German liberals. In the event, by the time he ascended the throne he was terminally ill, and he reigned for little more than three months.

Wilhelm, who succeeded him in 1888, represented the opposite of everything he and 'Vicky' had stood for.

Wilhelm's birth had been protracted. In the struggle to deliver him the
nerves to his left shoulder, arm and hand had been torn from his spinal
column, leaving him with a permanently crippled arm, uncertain balance
and a rightward tilt to his head and neck. It is possible he also suffered brain
damage from temporary suffocation.[11] As a boy he had been unable to run
as fast as others or climb or ride a horse and had been subjected to experimental cures by machines to stretch his muscles, electrical treatments and
special baths. To teach him to ride his tutor denied him stirrups and
remounted him when he fell off. His mother wondered whether in consequence of his afflictions and the 'tortures' he was put through by the
doctors she spoiled him, for he flew into a passion whenever he didn't wish
to do anything; and she noted when he was seven his inclination to be
'selfish, domineering and proud'.[12]

From school, whose pupils failed to dent his vanity, he had been sent to
Bonn University, thence into the First Regiment of Guards at Potsdam,
traditional training ground for Prussian kings. By the time he emerged
from this monarchical and nationalist stronghold his arrogance, rudeness
and obvious contempt for the ideals his parents had tried to instil were past
his mother's bearing: instead of the cultivated and intellectual son she had
wanted was a melodramatic braggart without depth of mind living in a fantasy of Teutonic knighthood.[13] Bismarck manipulated him shamelessly for
his own ends to isolate his parents and their liberal circle.

Bismarck did not long survive Wilhelm's accession. The constitution
devised to concentrate all power in his own hands as Chancellor depended
on the fiction that it was the sovereign who governed through his ministers, who merely modulated (*redigiert*) and executed his orders.[14] This was
the device the Japanese samurai oligarchy borrowed to preserve their own
power derived from the Emperor. Through it Bismarck had been able to
exercise near-dictatorial authority, at the same time preserving the Prussian
monarchical and military-bureaucratic order through a period of rapid
industrialization and consequent social change. Friedrich Engels compared
the system to 'Bonapartist semi-dictatorship', and commented that this was
the norm when there was no 'bourgeois' oligarchy, as there was in
England, to manage the state and society in its own commercial-financial
interests.[15]

After his ascent to the throne Wilhelm transformed Bismarck's fiction of
the sovereign ruling into reality: as put by John Röhl, he forged 'a genuinely monarchical regime in which the Kaiser and his Court rather than

the Chancellor and 'his men' exercised political power and decision-making authority'.[16] Bismarck was an early victim: there could not be two autocrats governing the Reich. In 1890 he was forced to resign. Thereafter Wilhelm, who had supreme military and naval command and the right to appoint and dismiss ministers and officials in Prussia and the Reich, fashioned a system that has been termed 'personal rule' since he was virtually free from parliamentary control. The lower house, the Reichstag, whose members were elected by male suffrage, was like its later Japanese copy a debating chamber whose functions were limited to passing or amending legislation and expenditure proposed by ministers. In theory it could deny approval. In practice there were so many political parties represented, each with its own interests, that a skilful Chancellor could nearly always fashion a majority for his policy. The Reichstag could not initiate legislation, nor of course influence the composition of the government, since all ministers were Wilhelm's appointees. The upper house, the Bundesrat, represented the different states within the Reich, but Bismarck had ensured that Prussia, the largest state, had the decisive voting weight; and Wilhelm was King of Prussia. Meanwhile both armed services lay outside the civil constitution in all matters except budgetary overview; so did foreign policy and the decision to go to war. These were Wilhelm's prerogatives.

Wilhelm discharged his momentous responsibilities with the aid of three personal secretariats or *Kabinette*, civil, military and naval, and ministers and courtiers whom he trusted. There was no coordinating apparatus, only his own mind. Since he was incapable of sustained application and subject to whim, envy, rage, flattery and the impressions left by his latest articulate adviser, this was a grotesquely inappropriate instrument, incapable of maintaining a steady perspective.

Whether a more rational sovereign or system of government might have avoided catastrophe is questionable:[17] it has been a theme of these volumes that individuals, however highly placed, cannot bear the weight of responsibility often laid upon them. For the Reich Wilhelm inherited was inherently unstable. The real power behind the throne was the Prussian army, so feared by the French, which had used Bismarck as its instrument of genius to forge the empire and create a constitution stifling liberalism or democracy. The military enjoyed the prestige of their victories and set the tone in the Reich. Wilhelm sought to embody their values in his person, adopting a harsh public face, always wearing uniform, referring in speeches to his 'mailed fist' or 'shining armour'. His *Kabinett* chiefs and most ministers and advisers came from this same east Prussian nobility, the Junkers, who provided the army officer cadres and higher civil servants for the state. Ernest Renan described them as emerging from the entrails of the ancient Germanic world:[18] they were indeed a pre-industrial elite whose stiff standards were far from the commercial values of much of the modern Germany, and they resented the wealth of the new class of industrialists, merchants and shipowners who posed a threat to their hold on power. While they aimed for military hegemony on the continent, the merchants and industrialists had their sights on the markets of the world.

Both groups were threatened by radical socialism. Institutionalized in the Social Democratic Party (SPD), it had taken root in slum tenements in the industrial quarters of Berlin and the mining and steel-making districts of the Ruhr and the shipyards and docks of Hamburg and Bremen. Its prophets were Karl Marx and Friedrich Engels, its goals the elimination of private property, nationalization of the means of production and distribution, and the abolition of national borders. It was anti-militarist, anti-monarchical and campaigned against wealth and privilege in the bitter language of class hatred. It was the reverse image of the Junker power-state it sought to replace, similarly absolutist in its convictions, and its members had the same instincts for discipline and individual subordination to the needs of the whole.

The answer to the deep schisms in society emerged as a consensus among Wilhelm's most influential advisers during the 1890s: namely an expansionist or adventurous foreign policy whose achievements abroad would be used to inspire a national spirit at home and so prise the workers from the SPD and line them up with the bourgeoisie behind their Kaiser. It was termed *Weltpolitik*, world policy. It answered the needs of industry and commerce and nationalist pressure groups calling for German influence in the world commensurate with her economic power; and it was perfectly suited to Wilhelm's own ambitions. These had swollen since he had rid himself of Bismarck and fashioned his own ruling cabal: he was convinced it was his mission to lead Germany to world power as successor to Great Britain. And since Britain possessed so much of the overseas world and lay across all German exits to the oceans this required a navy able to challenge the British navy. Wilhelm was, in any case, a true believer in Mahan and obsessed with navies and all that concerned them. As early as 1895 the German Foreign Minister had confided to his diary that Wilhelm had 'nothing but the navy in his head'.[19] By the following year a great fleet plan had been drawn up in the naval *Kabinett*.

The man chosen to pilot this plan through the Reichstag was Rear Admiral Alfred von Tirpitz. Wilhelm appointed him Minister for the

Reich Navy Office in June 1897. At the same time he appointed Prince Bernhard von Bülow as Foreign Minister. These were the key executives for *Weltpolitik*, Tirpitz to build the battle fleet, Bülow to steer the Reich through the 'danger zone' when the British divined what was afoot but before Tirpitz's fleet was strong enough to resist a pre-emptive attack. All were aware of the Royal Navy's preventive attack on Copenhagen and seizure of the Danish fleet in 1807. All subscribed to a 'Social Darwinist' view of history whereby in the constant struggle between civilizations the fittest nations and empires prevailed over the less fit. All assumed that the future lay with the vigorous young Reich, not the older world empire. Disciples of the Prussian prophet-historian Heinrich von Treitschke, who had helped to convince generations of students and officials and officers of the armed services that Prussia was the sword destined to spread Germany's high culture through the world,[20] they accepted armed conflict as the mainspring of history. Bülow believed that Britain and Russia were bound to go to war through rivalry in Asia, and directed his efforts to encouraging such a conflict.[21] If that brought France in on Russia's side, the fleet Tirpitz was to build would give Germany decisive leverage. Ultimately, Bülow believed, his task was to destroy Britain's world position in order for Germany to inherit.[22] This was the purpose Tirpitz saw for his fleet. In his first memorandum to Wilhelm in June 1897 he pointed out: 'For Germany the most dangerous enemy at the present time is England . . . Our fleet must be so constructed that it can unfold its highest battle function between Heligoland and the Thames . . .'[23]

As he expressed it later, 'The lever of our world policy was the North Sea.'[24] This was Britain's weak point. With her main battle strength in the Mediterranean to meet the Franco-Russian threat, and other squadrons around the world to protect her trade and possessions, she would be unable to meet the new threat in home waters without leaving herself vulnerable elsewhere. Neither he nor Bülow could envisage the European situation changing so radically as to bring Britain into the Franco-Russian orbit. Yet France already felt threatened by Germany's strength and Bülow's projected overseas policy was bound to increase her anxiety. Above all, as Tirpitz's fleet grew it would exert increasing 'leverage' on Britain to move towards France. This was the lesson of European history. Wilhelm had the most powerful army in Europe; by building a fleet to rival the world's greatest navy he would be perceived as a new Louis XIV or Napoleon seeking universal hegemony. Of course, he was. In 1900 the Austro-Hungarian ambassador in Berlin reported to Vienna: 'The leading German statesmen, and above all Kaiser Wilhelm, have looked into the distant future and are striving to make Germany's already swiftly-growing position as a world power into a dominating one, reckoning hereby upon becoming the genial successor to England . . .'[25]

Tirpitz's internal political goal was no less far reaching: it was to remove the naval budget from the Reichstag's purview, so placing the fleet entirely in Wilhelm's hands beyond interference by representative politicians.[26] To this end Tirpitz proposed a construction and replacement programme fixed by law. He argued it on the need to provide continuity of work for the shipbuilding and armaments firms and attempted to make it more palatable by the modesty of his initial demands: two homogeneous squadrons of eight battleships and one fleet flagship, seventeen capital units in all, each to be replaced automatically after twenty-five years. He maintained that such a fleet would provide an effective defensive force.

He had already set up a News and Propaganda Department to disseminate articles and news stories to the press to educate the mass of the people, who had no concept of sea power, to the benefits a navy would confer on Germany. His natural support came from the representatives of the industrial, commercial and professional classes who stood to gain directly from the construction programme and the enhancement of Germany's position in the world. The conservative elite opposed him; their gaze was focused on the continent, the army and their estates, and in order to obtain their grudging support he had to commit the government to higher tariffs on imported grain. The Social Democrats and other radical parties were irredeemably hostile and the issue came down to whether he could convince the leader of the Centre Party, the political wing of the Roman Catholic Church, which would hold the balance in the Reichstag. Tirpitz impressed him with the economic case for ensuring system and regularity in orders and assured him the Centre Party would obtain its reward in future legislation.

So he succeeded in pushing the fleet Bill through the Reichstag. The Centre Party appeared to accept his argument that a programme bound by law was limited by law. Socialists were not fooled, as their leader, August Bebel, made clear: 'There is, especially on the Right side of the House, a large group of fanatical Anglophobes made up of men who want to pick a fight with England and who would rather fight today than tomorrow.'[27]

The Bill became law in spring 1898. Remarkably Wilhelm's chief minister, the Reich Chancellor, was bitterly opposed to the whole fleet concept, regarding it as one of Wilhelm's personal aberrations, a view that has been endorsed by historians: John Röhl, in his study of Wilhelm's reign, finds the conclusion that Wilhelm was 'originator and co-author of the "Tirpitz Plan"[28] inescapable'.

The following year Wilhelm and Tirpitz decided to double the size of the fleet to four squadrons with a supplementary naval law, or *Novelle*, an extraordinarily bold move since, of course, the initial programme and budget had been represented as limited by law. By this date Tirpitz had an additional publicity organ, the Navy League, founded and financed by the great Krupp steel and armaments firm, which also contributed to his Navy Press Office funds. The outbreak of Britain's war against the Boers and Germany's impotence to influence events provided perfect material for the propagandists, and Tirpitz launched his *Novelle* in the Reichstag on a wave of inspired Anglophobia. Again, he made the case for legal establishment on the grounds that the shipbuilding and armaments industries needed a steady flow of work to justify their capital investment.

Nonetheless, the increase in numbers of battleships was so remarkable so soon after the original fleet law that he had to provide an explanation. He did so by arguing that to protect her overseas trade and colonies Germany needed a battle fleet 'so strong that even for the adversary with the greatest sea power a war against it would involve such dangers as to imperil her position in the world'.[29] It came to be known as the 'Risk Fleet' theory, and was utterly specious. Tirpitz had no intention of coming off second best on the day.[30] His explanation appeared to satisfy the deputies, however, who divided along the same lines as before, the Centre Party holding the balance. The party's heartland covered the wine-growing regions of the south and west; they were promised a tariff on imported wines, and the Bill passed.

The fleet to be provided by the 1900 *Novelle* was far from Tirpitz's final goal; it was but a step on the way to what he defined as an 'Iron Budget' or '*Marineaeternat*' to be reached when he had sixty battleships each with a statutory lifespan of twenty years, hence a self-perpetuating 'building tempo' of three big ships a year established by law and beyond interference by the people's representatives in the Reichstag. This was the breathtaking vision he and Wilhelm shared. Externally, of course, both intended supplanting Britain as supreme world power.

The foreign policy assumptions on which the plan was based began to collapse almost at once. First, Britain's informal understanding with the United States navy[31] and formal treaty with Japan[32] safeguarded her position in the western and eastern hemispheres, allowing her to concentrate her battle strength in European waters. Next, the impossible happened. The French government, as alarmed as the British by Wilhelm's battleships as they slid down the ways, agreed to settle all differences with Britain around the world. An entente between the two powers was signed in April 1904.

Later the same year, on the ninety-ninth anniversary of the Battle of Trafalgar, an inspirational leader arrived at the British Admiralty as First Sea Lord armed with a scheme to jolt the Royal Navy from complacency induced by a century of unquestioned supremacy and reposition it in the context of the entente with France and the threat from Germany. Admiral Sir John 'Jackie' Fisher was a revolutionary with an irreverent, flexible mind salted with combatant quotations from the Old Testament. He intended to preserve the ascendancy of the Royal Navy not by massing more battleships but by reshaping the fleet in the light of technological possibility; indeed, the core of the scheme was the elimination of conventional battleships. He aimed to supplant them with torpedo craft, both surface and submersible (submarine), for the defence of home and overseas bases and the blockade of enemy coasts, and large, fast, lightly armoured cruisers mounting a uniform armament of heavy guns – later christened 'battlecruisers' – to protect overseas trade.[33] Heavily armoured battleships would then have no purpose. Their slow speed in comparison with the lightly armoured battlecruisers would prevent them closing the latter, which would be able to hit them with their heavy guns outside the battleships' own effective range. He based this on very recent British developments in long-range gunnery fire control. Why enemy powers should not develop equally effective methods of long-range fire was a question he did not address.[34]

Fortunately for Britain he was not allowed to eliminate battleships. Instead, he inaugurated a new type which incorporated most of the features of his projected armoured cruisers. The prototype was HMS *Dreadnought*, laid down in 1905. Instead of the contemporary battleship's four heavy guns in turrets and a range of intermediate calibres between, she mounted a heavy battery of ten 12-inch guns and no secondary battery, only light quick-firers to repel torpedo boats; instead of reciprocating engines she was fitted with turbines that gave her a cruiser speed of 21 knots, some 3 knots more than contemporary battleships. With her greater speed and weight of fire and advantages in long-range accuracy gained from the uniform trajectory of her shells, she rendered existing battleships outdated and served as a model for all subsequent classes of battleship throughout the world, which took the generic name of 'dreadnoughts'.[35]

The new ship caused a sensation worldwide, but Fisher remained committed to battlecruisers. He had a class of three laid down with a uniform armament of 12-inch guns like the *Dreadnought*, but with considerably thinner armour protection and more powerful turbines to drive them at 25 knots. Although their primary purpose was commerce protection their 12-inch guns fitted them for use as a fast auxiliary battle squadron in a fleet action, as Fisher envisaged.[36] They were termed dreadnought battle-cruisers and in future comparisons of fleet strength were counted alongside battleships.

News of the *Dreadnought*'s unique features caught Tirpitz and his constructors unprepared. They were working on a battleship class with powerful secondary batteries and conventional speed which could not stand comparison with Fisher's masterpiece.[37] All work was stopped for two years while the essentials of the British design were probed for incorporation in plans for a new class. Even this was inferior. There was only one firm in Germany capable of building large marine turbines; Tirpitz wanted these for his cruisers so the new battleships had to have reciprocating engines that gave less speed and required considerably more maintenance. They also required more space and forced an inefficient distribution of turrets for a uniform heavy battery of 11-inch guns, a smaller calibre than the *Dreadnought*'s, but compensated by thicker armour capable in theory of resisting the heavier British shells. The resulting class was larger than previous German classes and too large for the Kiel Canal. In order to allow them safe passage between the North Sea and the Baltic without exposure to a pre-emptive British strike in the open sea, Tirpitz was forced to have work started on deepening the canal and enlarging the locks, a bonus for Fisher, which caused him continual delight.

Fisher's qualitative advance doomed Tirpitz's budgetary calculations and with them the whole policy of internal harmony that *Weltpolitik* was designed to promote. Against such an opponent resolved to preserve British naval supremacy he could only strive to respond with ever larger, more powerful classes of ship in an armaments race whose increasing costs must lead to rising taxes and borrowing, so alienating both socialists and land-holding elites.[38] His foreign policy goal also lay in ruins. Britain had already settled her differences with France. The new Liberal Foreign Secretary, Sir Edward Grey, made a similar agreement with Russia one of his first priorities: 'An *Entente* between Russia, France and ourselves would be absolutely secure. If it is necessary to check Germany it could then be done.'[39] An Anglo-Russian Convention agreeing spheres of influence in Asia was signed in 1907.

Had Germany been governed rationally Tirpitz would have been removed or forced to rethink his goals. But the fleet was an extension of Wilhelm's ego, and he clung to Tirpitz even as the Reich was forced farther and farther into internal and external deadlock.

9

Tsushima, 1905

———•———

THE CONTEST BETWEEN Russia and Japan for control of Korea and Manchuria came to a head in early 1904. It had the appearance of a struggle between a great territorial empire and an emerging maritime power, yet Japan showed none of the characteristics of maritime power as defined in these volumes, every symptom of territorial power. Her ruling oligarchy was imbued with traditional warrior values which had been spread through the nation by the schools system. Merchant values were absent: there were no constitutional checks on government; the Diet was a token assembly without real powers. The Emperor in whose name the samurai oligarchy ruled was seen as the embodiment of the state and venerated as father of the people with divine attributes, much as in Russia the Tsar was revered as the patriarch; like the Tsar, the Emperor held the key position at the apex of an implacably authoritarian structure.

There were many other similarities between the two nations: in both the state had forced rapid industrialization based on steel production, railways and armaments in order to gain parity with the advanced Western powers. Government loans raised for the purpose had been serviced in both nations partly by squeezing labourers on the land into poverty by taxation, suppressing protest brutally. While the Japanese centralized bureaucracy was undoubtedly more efficient than its Russian counterpart, and a larger proportion of the Japanese people was literate, the fundamental aims of both governments were the same: industrial expansion and political order at home, colonial acquisition abroad.

Tsar Nicholas II aspired to an empire extending from Europe to the Pacific. As proposed by his most effective finance minister, Count Sergei Witte, this resembled Halford Mackinder's (later) concept of a Eurasian 'heartland'[1] served by railways to exploit the mineral resources and commercial opportunities of the vast area across the top of Asia from the Black Sea to the Sea of Japan. Witte had calculated that the trans-Siberian railway could carry raw materials and merchandise between the Far East and Europe in half the time ships took for the voyage, and would thereby

84

undercut the basis of particularly British maritime power. With an autonomous industrial and military empire of such extent, the Tsar would dominate Europe, Asia and the world. In this respect Witte's vision coincided precisely with Mackinder's.

For Japan it held the greatest danger. The army General Staff proposed the annexation of Korea and parts of northern China and Manchuria both as a buffer against Russian expansion and to secure raw materials essential for Japanese industry. By 1903 Russia's increasingly threatening posture had caused civilian ministers to overcome caution and adopt an army proposal for a pre-emptive strike before the completion of the trans-Siberian railway. It was a huge risk. Against the vastly more populous Russian empire with an army a million strong and over twice that number of reservists, the Japanese mobilization potential was some 600,000 men; while the Russian Pacific fleet headed by seven battleships all completed within the past decade was on paper the equal of the entire Japanese navy, headed by six battleships. In heavy armoured cruisers and light cruisers for reconnaissance and sea control the Japanese were stronger, but naval doctrine decreed that the issue would be decided by the battle fleets.

The first task of the Japanese navy, therefore, was to reduce Russian battleship strength to ensure safe passage for troop transports to the mainland. They struck on the night of 7/8 February 1904. Destroyers covered by the battle fleet under Admiral Heihachiro Togo attacked the Russian battle fleet anchored in Port Arthur. There was no prior declaration of war, although the Russians had ample notice of Japanese preparations from their naval attaché in Tokyo.[2] Torpedo nets had been rigged and two destroyers detailed to patrol the harbour entrance. These confused the Japanese attackers and only two battleships, including the flagship *Tsarevich* and a cruiser, were hit at bow and stern beyond the extremities of their nets. They were damaged but not mortally. This was sufficient for immediate Japanese aims. Both sides declared war on the 10th, and Togo returned with the fleet to blockade and mine the entrance to Port Arthur, while Japanese troops were landed at Inchon on the west coast of Korea.

Togo was of samurai stock from the Satsuma clan of south-western Kyushu. His first action experience at the age of sixteen had been serving stone-shotted cannon in a fort at Kagoshima under punitive bombardment by a Royal Naval squadron. That was in 1863. No doubt the British squadron made an impression on him. Another Japanese youth who witnessed the bombardment wrote later, 'The squadron was very magnificent, a war vessel is indeed a brave object . . . I felt this so much that I determined to enter the Navy and devote the whole of my life to its service.'[3] Togo did

The Far East and Pacific

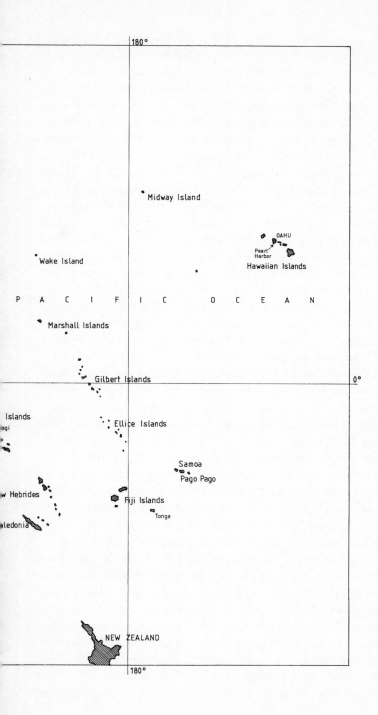

180°

• Midway Island

◦ OAHU

Pearl
Harbor

Hawaiian Islands

• Wake Island

P   A   C   I   F   I   C   O   C   E   A   N

◦ Marshall Islands

Gilbert Islands   0°

Islands

agi

Ellice Islands

Samoa
Pago Pago

w Hebrides

Fiji Islands

Tonga

aledonia

NEW ZEALAND

180°

this after the Meiji restoration. Selected to study in England but apparently lacking sufficient command of English and too old at twenty-four to enter the Royal Naval College at Dartmouth, he had been entered as a cadet in HMS *Worcester*, a training establishment on the Thames primarily for merchant service officers. He completed the three-year course, and after returning to Japan rose rapidly through the ranks. By the time of the Sino-Japanese war in 1894 he had been a captain for two years. He participated in the annihilation of the Chinese fleet off the Yalu in command of a British-built cruiser, and was promoted to flag rank the following year. In 1904 he was appointed commander-in-chief of the Japanese Combined Fleet.

In contrast to Togo and his senior officers, few Russian officers had first-hand battle experience, none of recent naval action. Flag officers and captains had been trained in sail and, unlike the Japanese, had not engaged positively with the mechanization of ships and weapons during the recent expansion of the fleet.[4] The service reflected the autocratic nature of the tsarist regime; senior officers seem to have compensated for lack of technological knowledge with arbitrary decisiveness and great rages. Combined with illiteracy among ordinary sailors and their treatment as menials incapable of independent thought, it resulted in a service ill prepared for modern war. Their allies, the French, were aware of this and feared that if they combined their own naval forces with a Russian fleet its 'cumbersome mass could do nothing but weigh down and paralyse our own'.[5]

After the failure to prevent Japanese destroyers entering Port Arthur a new commander-in-chief, Admiral Stepan Makarov, was appointed to the Pacific Squadron. The son of a bosun, he was one of very few from an inferior social background to have broken into the officer caste. He was also, by all accounts, exceptional in his attitude to technology and his ability to enthuse his men. Unfortunately for Russia his flagship struck a mine while on a seagoing exercise and he was lost with most of the ship's company. He was succeeded by Admiral Wilhelm Witgeft, who lacked his spirit.

In May the first Japanese army in Korea crossed the Yalu river and a second army was landed on the Liaotung peninsula and began advancing on Port Arthur. Although two of Togo's battleships were lost to Russian mines the same month and repairs were completed on the damaged Russian ships, Witgeft did not go out and seek to exploit his sudden numerical advantage of six battleships to four. It was not until 10 August, after Japanese troops had reached the outskirts of the base and their field guns were lobbing shells over the surrounding hills into the harbour, that he left on the orders of the Russian Eastern Commander to make a run for Vladivostok.

Seeing him come out, Togo led his blockading force south-easterly to draw him seawards, then turned to close. In both squadrons the command-ing admirals took the lead with their flagships. Togo and his staff gathered on the exposed deck of the pilot house above the bridge of the *Mikasa*; Witgeft and his staff crowded in the armoured conning tower of the *Tsarevich*. Togo faced the more critical decisions. He had four 12-inch-gun battleships and four modern cruisers armed with 8-inch and 6-inch QF guns against four Russian battleships with 12-inch guns, two with 10-inch guns, and three cruisers. To exploit his advantage in the QF guns of his cruisers he needed to close well inside the effective range of the enemy's heavy pieces. Yet his four battleships were Japan's first and only line of sea defence. He could scarcely afford to lose one. The Russians, on the other hand, could transfer battleships from their Baltic or Black Sea fleets. In the event he seemed to compromise, steering to cross ahead of Witgeft, so bringing on a manoeuvring contest, but keeping well outside what was regarded with the primitive aiming apparatus of the day as decisive range, generally passing and paralleling outside 7,000 yards. The range for the annual 'prize-firing' competition in the Royal Navy was 1,500 yards, and it was only in 1905 that 'battle practice' ranges of 5,000 yards were introduced.

At the start Togo's battleships concentrated on the *Tsarevich*. Ranges for the guns were taken in both fleets by British Barr & Stroud rangefinders with a base length of 4 feet 6 inches. This was insufficient to give accurate readings at the distances at which fire was opened and the first Japanese heavy shells fell short. In the *Tsarevich* the junior navigating officer, Lieutenant D. Daragan, was stationed above the conning tower taking ranges to the *Mikasa* with a Barr & Stroud and passing them by electric telegraph to the gun turrets.

> I had a splendid view over the whole situation. The first projectiles from *Mikasa* came very short, ricocheted, flew over us and fell somewhere behind our ships. The ricochet-flying projectiles flew very slowly, turned in the air and made such a noise which reminded [me of] the flight of big birds. At least during five minutes I was sure that these are birds frightened by the Japanese firing. Only after the first hits I understood what it was.[6]

The Russians, with their preponderance of heavy guns firing shells with flatter trajectories, hence with a greater effective range than those of lighter pieces, should have had a 6:4 advantage at the comparatively long ranges Togo maintained, and they probably did. A British naval observer aboard the Japanese battleship *Asahi* believed their fire was the more accur-ate,[7] and his description of the Japanese fire control arrangements suggests they were inferior to those on the Russian flagship:

All ranges were taken from a Barr & Stroud rangefinder placed on the fore pilot house. The captain named the object to the officer at the instrument, who ascertained the range, and gave object and range to an assistant, who passed them by speaking trumpet to the fore superstructure, whence they were forwarded, again by trumpet to the after superstructure. From these two stations voice tubes carried the orders to the batteries . . .[8]

He ascribed poor practice from the Japanese heavy pieces to over-reliance on ranges passed from the rangefinders; when the range closed later in the battle and secondary batteries opened, drowning out the repeating hands with their speaking trumpets and ending any semblance of control, he noticed a marked improvement in accuracy.[9] It is evident that neither Japanese instruments nor marksmanship matched the men's diligent training and fanatic commitment. Consequently the battle continued down a long day, mainly on parallel courses, with Witgeft steering southerly for the Korean Strait. Of the two flagships, the *Mikasa* probably took the worse punishment; by late afternoon she had received about twelve direct hits, her after turret was out of action, she was taking in water from holes and shaken plates in her side, and her bridge party had been decimated by a shell explosion. Togo narrowly escaped with his life. The *Tsarevich* had taken approximately the same number of hits. The leads to Lieutenant Daragan's range transmitter had been cut and he was reduced, like the Japanese, to shouting ranges by megaphone to the captain of the forward 12-inch guns, who stood outside the door of his turret to receive them.

The battle was decided by chance. At 5.40 p.m. a Japanese 12-inch shell struck the sea just short of the *Tsarevich* and, flying upwards, hit her conning tower under the mushroom-like projection of the armoured roof, where it burst and showered metal splinters through the observation slits. Daragan dashed down from his post immediately above to find a scene of carnage: Witgeft, the ship's captain, two other officers and two signalmen were dead or mortally wounded. Almost at the same instant, but coincidentally, the flagship began turning to port towards the enemy. She made a complete circle before it was found that a valve had been displaced in the steering engine right aft in the tiller flat. Directly it was repaired the ship answered her helm again.[10]

By this time the Russian line was in disorder. The *Tsarevich*'s next astern had followed her towards the enemy, but when the flagship's turn began taking her back towards the Russian line and she found she was on her own, she too turned back; after which the second-in-command evidently panicked and signalling 'Follow me!' steered north-westerly, back for Port Arthur. The other battleships and some of the lighter craft followed. The *Tsarevich* did not. The first gunnery officer assumed command and took the flagship southwards, intending to escape into the Pacific, steam around Japan and make Vladivostok by the La Perouse Strait north of Hokkaido. A few cruisers and destroyers also made off southwards.

Togo, meanwhile, headed north-westerly after the bulk of the squadron making for Port Arthur and, at last sensing his opportunity, pressed in to 4,000 yards where his secondary batteries and the cruisers' QF guns soon established a potentially decisive advantage. It was too late. The light was fading and as darkness fell he called off the chase. No ships on either side were lost in this protracted engagement, yet it was an undoubted strategic victory for Japan. The Port Arthur ships, having returned to base, became sitting targets for Japanese field guns from the surrounding heights and were all eventually destroyed. The *Tsarevich*, meanwhile, put in to the German naval station at Tsingchau for coal, but the authorities refused permission and interned her until the end of the war. Other escaping warships were interned in different ports on the Chinese coast.

Russian troops were already on their way to the Far East via the still-incomplete trans-Siberian railway, and after the rout of the Port Arthur ships the Russian government took the decision to send the Baltic fleet east. It was a bold move, born of desperation. Britain would not permit passage of the Suez Canal so the ships were routed around Africa; and since Russia lacked overseas coaling bases a contract was made with the Hamburg-Amerika Line to provide colliers along the way. The subsequent epic had many of the elements of the voyage of the Spanish Armada in 1588 and a similarly tragic end. The naval officer selected as a latter-day Duke of Medina Sidonia was a fifty-six-year-old gunnery specialist in the Tsar's retinue, Vice-Admiral Zinovy Petrovich Rozhestvensky.

Rozhestvensky had seen action during the Russo-Turkish war of 1877 aboard an auxiliary cruiser that had escaped from a Turkish ironclad by out-running her. He had been decorated and promoted captain. A large man with a short, square-cut beard, grave expression and 'piercing black eyes which seemed to indicate a dauntless will',[11] he drove the supply and fitting out of his fleet with fierce energy. His martial leadership was to prove less effective.

The fleet, headed by four impressive modern battleships, *Suvoroff*, the flagship, *Alexander III*, *Borodino* and *Oryol*, each mounting four 12-inch guns, twelve 6-inch and forty-two anti-torpedo-boat QF guns, was

reviewed by the Tsar in Reval Roads on 9 October, and sailed the following morning. A halt was made for coaling at the northern tip of Denmark,
but the operation was cut short and the order given to prepare for immediate departure. This bred the rumour that Japanese destroyers were on
their way to surprise them, and as they steamed down the Skagerrak and
into the North Sea that night ships' companies were at action stations,
lookouts nervy as they tried to pierce the darkness.

The ships were equipped for signalling by wireless telegraphy, a very
recent innovation developed by the Italian Gugliemo Marconi in collaboration with the chief engineer of the British Post Office. The Royal Navy
had placed its first large contract for Marconi wireless equipment in 1899,
by which date a Russian physicist, Aleksandr Popov, who had read
Marconi's patent, had produced an apparatus enabling the Russian service
to send messages over 30 miles.

It seems probable that the first use of wireless in action conditions – or
what were thought to be action conditions – occurred during the passage
of Rozhestvensky's fleet down the North Sea on the night of 21/22
October 1904. The repair ship attached to the fleet was steaming independently ahead of the battleship division when she used her transmitter to
report torpedo boats. Rozhestvensky reacted by ordering his division to
prepare for torpedo boat attack. Later, fog closed in, magnifying the perceived Japanese threat from the darkness, and as they neared the fishing
grounds of the Dogger Bank after midnight coloured flares appeared
through the murk. Immediately the flagship's searchlight and QF guns'
crews broke into action. The following battleships also opened fire. The
darkness was split with gunflashes and searching beams of light. Aboard the
Oryol men panicked; gunners fired at random, sailors seized life jackets or
cork mattresses to keep themselves afloat when their ship was torpedoed,
and discipline collapsed throughout the division.[12] It took some twelve
minutes before order was restored and a ceasefire enforced, by which time
four Hull trawlers were ablaze, another was listing and sinking and the
chaplain of a cruiser flanking the battleship division was dying of wounds
received from the guns of the *Oryol*. Rozhestvensky, who could not have
failed to realize the mistake, lacked the presence of mind to order the
boats to rescue the stricken fishermen.

Any prestige the Russian navy retained was lost. For several days there
was a serious prospect of war resulting from the incident, and after
Rozhestvensky made his next coaling stop at Vigo in northern Spain he
was joined by a squadron of British cruisers which escorted him in increasingly provocative fashion as far as the Canary Islands.[13] By then diplomatic

relations had been restored and the British government gave permission for a small detachment of ships to proceed through the Suez Canal. The main body carried on around West Africa to Dakar, where German colliers were waiting, thence into the Gulf of Guinea to restore bunkers again off the Gaboon estuary. So they continued down the African coast in a series of short passages, rounding the Cape of Good Hope in December and steering north-easterly for Madagascar. Reaching the French island at the end of the month, they learned that Port Arthur had fallen and the squadron they had been sent to join had been annihilated. Profound depression seized all hands.[14]

Spirits revived briefly when they were reunited with the Suez Canal detachment in the anchorage of Nosi Bé on the north-western coast of the island. They waited there for over two months as Rozhestvensky received orders not to continue until a third squadron being fitted out in the Baltic joined his flag. More coal and provisions were taken aboard, boilers were cleaned, machinery overhauled and ships' companies exercised in anti-torpedo-boat work, minelaying and target practice. Although the battleships' guns were fitted with the latest telescopic sights – which the Port Arthur squadron had lacked – marksmanship and station-keeping proved lamentable. After each exercise Rozhestvensky issued an order of the day bringing attention to the poor performance of commanders and guns' crews, but it had little effect. Soon target practice was discontinued, not because shooting had improved but because no spare rounds had been provided and Rozhestvensky did not want to fire off all his ammunition before the decisive battle.

Meanwhile in Russia news of the disasters to their forces by land and sea had sparked uprisings. The motive for the government's blatant forward policy in the east had been, at least in part, to damp down social unrest with a successful foreign war.[15] Victory over a minor oriental nation had seemed certain. Subsequent demonstrations of the superiority of the Japanese armed forces had produced the opposite effect, confirming dissatisfaction with the inept and corrupt regime and bringing students and workers out in often violent demonstrations. On 22 January 1905 a mass march of workers in St Petersburg to present a petition for reform to the Tsar in the Winter Palace was fired on and charged by cavalry. Huge losses were inflicted. Reports of this and other strikes and protests throughout Russia in newspapers reaching the fleet in Nosi Bé undermined the men's morale in a more profound way than their previous apprehensions of being led to inevitable defeat, and even tested the loyalty of officers.

Whether Rozhestvensky appreciated the depth of the men's despair is doubtful. He was aware of increasingly frequent breaches of discipline in the fleet, but it is a feature of autocratic regimes that reports on the way up the chain are adjusted to conform with the inclinations at the top. According to the secretary to the admiral's general staff, Rozhestvensky 'never left the *Suvoroff* except to administer reprimands. Nor did he summon the rear admirals and captains to the flagship. He neither asked their advice nor discussed any problems with them'.[16] His techniques of leadership were limited to criticism, uncontrollable rages and public abuse, even for senior officers who ventured aboard his flagship. His chief of staff was a particular target for humiliation. Before reporting to the admiral he would ask the duty orderly what mood the great man was in; if bad, he would postpone his report.

The ships finally weighed to cross the Indian Ocean in March. By this time local French newspapers were reporting the opening phases of the Japanese army's assault on the city of Mukden (Shen-yang), one-time capital of the Manchus and more recently seat of Russian imperial power. It was evident from the accounts that the Japanese had the upper hand, evident to everyone in Rozhestvensky's fleet as it set out on the penultimate leg of its odyssey that it was Russia's last and forlorn hope.

Five stops were made for coaling in the open ocean. Steam pinnaces towed boats laden with sacks filled from the holds of colliers to the ships' sides, where they were hoisted aboard and tipped down chutes, raising clouds of acrid dust; when the bunkers were full the coal was distributed along the mess decks. 'We were continually inhaling coal dust, until our lungs were choked. Our teeth were gritty with it. We swallowed it with our food. It blocked the pores of our skin. We slept upon heaps of coal which occupied our usual resting place between decks . . .'[17]

After frequent unscheduled stops for engine breakdowns the fleet reached the Straits of Malacca in just under three weeks. As they passed Singapore, the Russian consul came out in a launch with news that the Japanese fleet had been sighted recently and was waiting for them at Labuan on the west coast of Borneo. Ships cleared for action. Wooden furniture and fitments were stowed below or thrown overboard. It was a false report. There were alarms but no sign of the enemy as they steamed up the South China Sea to Camranh Bay, French Indochina, where they anchored to take on more coal and provisions.

Early in their passage across the Indian Ocean Mukden had fallen to the Japanese. The reputation of Russian arms was at a nadir. The French, their allies, bowed to Japanese pressure and expelled them from Camranh after barely a week, but a few hours steaming up the coast brought them to another bay where they sheltered awaiting the approach of the reinforcements from the Baltic. These made wireless contact on 8 May and joined the following day, a small, obsolescent battleship, *Nicholas I*, flying the flag of Rear Admiral Nebogatoff, followed by three equally outdated coast defence ironclads, an ancient armoured cruiser, transports, a second repair ship and a second hospital ship, together more of an encumbrance than a useful fighting addition.

After the new ships had taken on coal and made machinery repairs Rozhestvensky led the whole force north-eastwards on the final leg. Officers speculated on whether he intended taking the direct route through the Korean Strait into the Sea of Japan or rounding the Japanese islands to enter by the northern La Perouse Strait. He gave no hint. On 23 May, after leaving the island of Formosa (Taiwan) astern, the fleet stopped to take on yet more coal from accompanying colliers and Rozhestvensky issued instructions for the coming battle: on sighting the enemy the main division of four modern battleships was to 'proceed to the attack', supported by the older ironclads and cruisers, which could act independently if circumstances allowed. 'If no signal is made, the battleships must follow the flagship, concentrating their fire on the enemy's flagship or leading vessel.'[18]

It was a follow-your-leader order, yet Rozhestvensky could hardly be more specific. He was encumbered by vessels that could make no more than 9 knots and the Japanese would have an advantage in speed which would allow them to dictate the terms of the coming battle. Besides the speed handicap, most of, perhaps all, the Russian battleships were now so overloaded with coal and provisions that their main 10-inch armour belts were completely submerged. The waterlines of the four modern ships on which the fighting power of the fleet rested were protected by only 6 inches of armour at mid-length, thinning to 2½ inches towards bow and stern. To add to these weaknesses, when Rozhestvensky dismissed his colliers for the last time and steamed towards Japan he failed to spread his cruisers far enough ahead to provide advance information on the enemy. Disposing the fleet in two fighting columns abreast with destroyers and transports between them and the hospital ships astern, he steamed blindly towards his fate.

Togo awaited him in the Korean Strait. Aware that his ships' gunnery against the Port Arthur fleet had been largely ineffective until the closing stage at shorter ranges, he had driven forward improvements in training and materiel. The detonators for the shells had been modified to render them less sensitive so that they would deliver the greater part of the explosion inside rather than outside enemy plating. The telescopic sights of the 6-inch guns had been replaced by vastly superior instruments manufactured by J. Hicks of Hatton Garden, London; voice pipes had been fitted to replace speaking trumpets for the transmission of ranges from rangefinders to turrets; and training devices originated by Captain Percy Scott in the Royal Navy had been introduced to improve the hand-eye coordination of gunners, notably the 'Dotter', which accustomed gun-layers to keeping their sights on target throughout the rolling motion of their ship.[19] The British naval attaché with the Japanese fleet had reported: 'Every day, weather permitting, one or two ships carry out target practice, and aiming rifle practice at targets towed by steamboats is going on all day long . . .'[20]

At first light on 27 May a Japanese cruiser sighted the Russian fleet formed in its two columns steaming towards the eastern passage of the Korean Strait between the island of Tsushima and the southern island of Japan, Kyushu, and reported by wireless to Togo. Some two hours later another Japanese cruiser found the Russians and held contact from just beyond effective gun range, sending continual wireless reports; soon other Japanese scouts joined on the opposite flank. Rozhestvensky took no action to drive them off or jam their reports and made no attempt to mislead them by altering course. His chief concern, it seemed, was to celebrate the anniversary of the coronation of the Tsar and Tsarina: St Andrew's flags were hoisted throughout the fleet and bugles called all hands to thanksgiving services. His actions suggest that, notwithstanding his criticisms of his guns' crews at Nosi Bé, he believed he could mark the Tsar's anniversary with a victory over Togo's fleet and force his way through to Vladivostok.

Togo in the *Mikasa* led his fleet westerly to cut him off. Despite a bright sun overhead and a strong south-westerly wind lacing the sea with streaks of foam, mist banks hung over the water, at times hiding even the rear ships of his own line from view. By 1.30 p.m. he judged from his cruisers' reports that he had crossed ahead of Rozhestvensky's track and altered to south-south-west. Minutes later the Russians showed up on his starboard bow. He had already decided to fight with the wind astern and, hoisting battle flags, he hauled round to north-west to give himself space to pass ahead, then turn back to close from the Russian's port side. Now directly ahead, he could see down the enemy lines, Rozhestvensky's four modern battleships leading the starboard column with their dark upperworks and tall yellow funnels glistening in the sun, dwarfing the other heterogenous units into insignificance.[21] He turned west, then south-west, before heading due south towards the enemy, flying a flag signal reminiscent of Nelson's at Trafalgar: it was the centenary year of that legendary victory.

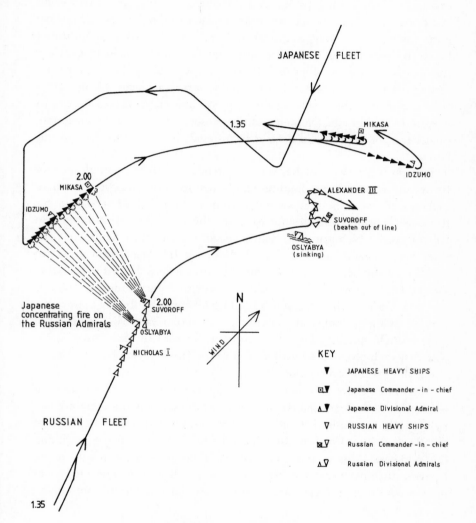

JAPANESE / FLEET

1.35

MIKASA

IDZUMO

2.00
MIKASA

IDZUMO

ALEXANDER III

SUVOROFF
(beaten out of line)

OSLYABYA
(sinking)

Japanese
concentrating fire on
the Russian Admirals

2.00
SUVOROFF

OSLYABYA

NICHOLAS I

N

WIND

KEY

▼ JAPANESE HEAVY SHIPS

▣▼ Japanese Commander – in – chief

△▼ Japanese Divisional Admiral

▽ RUSSIAN HEAVY SHIPS

▨▽ Russian Commander – in – chief

△▽ Russian Divisional Admirals

RUSSIAN / FLEET

1.35

Tsushima, 27 May 1905

'THE FATE OF OUR EMPIRE HANGS ON THIS ONE ACTION. YOU WILL ALL EXERT YOURSELVES AND DO YOUR UTMOST.'[22]

The Japanese line was organized in two divisions of heavy ships, the first division of four battleships and two armoured cruisers mounting 8-inch and 6-inch QF guns, the second of six similar armoured cruisers. In heavy guns he was decisively outnumbered. His four battleships mounted between them sixteen 12-inch pieces, equalling the number in the four modern Russian battleships, but Rozhestvensky's older ships mounted a further ten 12-inch, fourteen 10-inch and four 9-inch pieces. There was no such disparity in the smaller calibres. Togo's best tactic, therefore, was to press in to within effective range of his cruisers' batteries and concentrate on sections of the Russian fleet; it seems evident he had decided on this course.

It is probable that Rozhestvensky intended to fight in single line of battle, and when he saw Togo moving across towards his port side where Nebogatoff's weak division was stationed he had no choice but to order his starboard division of battleships to move ahead of the port column. He failed to order Nebogatoff to reduce speed; consequently, while his flagship, *Suvoroff*, and his next astern, *Alexander III*, successfully took up positions at the head of the line, the ships astern were thrown into confusion as they manoeuvred to avoid collision with the incoming vessels.[23] It was a basic error. The *Mikasa* was heading for him and shortly before two o'clock, with the range at something over 7,000 yards, he opened fire with a single ranging shot, then with his forward-turret 12-inch guns. The first shell dropped 20 yards astern of the Japanese flagship and subsequent shots were equally close.[24]

Togo might have continued on his opposite course to concentrate on the weak and disorganized Russian rear; instead he took the extraordinarily bold decision to lead round 180 degrees to port and attack the head of the Russian line. Captain Pakenham, British observer in the battleship following the *Mikasa*, reported that the Russians concentrated on the Japanese turning point and every shot was well aimed. The range was now down to under 6,000 yards (3 miles). Pakenham's report continued:

> It was interesting to see each [Japanese] ship approach and run through this warm spot which all were lucky enough to do without serious injury. This commencement was made notable by the close shooting of the Russians. Shells were falling alongside the Japanese ships, throwing heavy bodies of water on to their decks . . . but no larger projectiles seemed to get home.[25]

Togo was extremely fortunate during this critical period when his lead-ing ships were turning, masking the fire of those following to the turning point, but by shortly after two o'clock he had completed the movement without serious damage and was steaming on an almost parallel course, converging slightly on the Russians, his first division concentrating all fire on Rozhestvensky's flagship, *Suvoroff*, which was hidden at times behind high columns of shell splashes and smoke. Rozhestvensky played into his hands by altering two points to port – towards him – allowing him to draw ahead and, with his greater speed, threaten to cross the Russian track. Seeing his error, Rozhestvensky turned away four points to bring all broad-side guns back in bearing. For Pakenham: 'This was the scenic part of the battle . . . Two long lines of ships were firing at one another vigorously, damages were still conjectural, and the fate of the day seemed to hang on every shot . . .'[26]

Ships disappeared from time to time in mists and streaming smoke, and it was seldom, if ever, that either side saw the enemy fleet as a whole, only their gun flashes through the murk.[27] As the greater speed of the Japanese fleet again took Togo ahead of the Russian van he turned to starboard to close the range. Rozhestvensky bore away again, but subsequently made a sharp alteration to port to pass astern of the Japanese line. Togo replied by wheeling 180 degrees to port, all his first division together, to close from the other direction, still concentrating on the leading Russians as they appeared from the haze.

The *Suvoroff* had by now taken heavy punishment. Flames and smoke issued from holes torn in her sides and superstructure, her after 12-inch turret was disabled by a heavy shell, half her other guns were out of action and she was holed about the waterline. In the armoured conning tower Rozhestvensky and his staff and signalmen crouched or knelt below the level of the observation slits to avoid flying metal splinters from outside explosions. The admiral was powerless to control his fleet: the wireless aerial and signal halyards had been shot away, the signal flags consumed by flames. In any case he could see little of the enemy. Even his ability to lead by example was taken from him when a shell burst close to the conning tower, killing the helmsman and wounding others, for as in the battle of 10 August the previous year the steering broke down and the flagship turned out of control. She was followed briefly by the *Alexander III* until her cap-tain realized the *Suvoroff* was incapacitated and resumed the former northerly course.

By this time the leader of the Russian second division, the older battle-ship *Oslyabya*, had sunk. She had been the target of concentrated fire from

Togo's cruisers and had been struck early in the engagement by two 8-inch shells which had penetrated below the waterline – since the main armour belt had been submerged by overloading. A subsequent hail of high-explosive shells had set her upperworks ablaze as she settled by the head and heeled over.

With the *Suvoroff* beaten from the line, the Japanese battleship division concentrated on the new leader, *Alexander III*, or, as she disappeared intermittently in the mist, on the following *Borodino* or *Oryol*, whose guns replied resolutely, although with less accuracy than at the start. Below, their sickbays filled with casualties from exposed positions on deck. Surgeons and assistants with hands, arms, faces, beards and once-white overalls smeared with blood worked with instruments little changed since the days of sail. A high proportion of the wounded were torn by shell splinters, others burned in explosions, some so severely as to be unrecognizable. Assistants dressed minor wounds, splinted broken limbs and administered morphine to those in great pain, while the most serious cases were stretchered to the surgeons' operating tables. Shattered limbs were sawn through, the raw wound swabbed with iodine and flaps of flesh sewn together over the stump. Elsewhere, amid groans and cries, priests knelt by the dying, hearing their confessions and administering the last sacrament.[28]

At around three in the afternoon firing died away briefly as the fleets lost each other in mist, but broke out again some minutes later as the *Alexander III* appeared on Togo's port bow, heading northwards and on fire. She was met by a storm of shell which forced her away; the ships following turned in different directions as Togo closed the range. Shortly afterwards the *Suvoroff* on her own and steering unsteadily with the aid of port and starboard engines materialized close astern of the Japanese battleship division and received the concentrated fire of the whole line at ranges coming down to scarcely over 1,000 yards. 'Shells seemed to rain down on us without pause. Steel plates and parts of our superstructure were blown to pieces . . . the high temperature of the explosions spread a kind of liquid fire which smothered everything, further enhancing the terrifying effects of the shells.'[29]

Pakenham watched the destruction:

> The forward funnel was gone and a raging fire had consumed the space between the other and the after barbette [turret] – in spite of which she continued in action . . . Flames had crept to the stern and the dense smoke emitted was being rolled horizontally away by the wind. Less than half the ship can have been habitable, yet she fought on.[30]

Rozhestvensky had quit the conning tower. He and only three other survivors had been forced out by fires on the bridge which threatened to suffocate them with smoke or roast them inside the metal cylinder. They had made their way down the ladder to the central control position where a lieutenant was directing the ship's course. From there the admiral, bleeding and possibly concussed from a blow to his forehead, wandered alone through the bowels of the ship, determined to find his way up to a gun position. Eventually he succeeded in entering one of the few undamaged 6-inch turrets on the starboard side.

Togo's tactic of using his greater fleet speed to press in constantly across the Russian line of advance while concentrating fire on the van had resulted not only in the elimination of Rozhestvensky's flagship as an effective fighting unit, but utter confusion in the Russian line. The Japanese ships had not escaped damage, the *Mikasa* in particular, but all were fully under command, keeping perfect station and responding to signals as if on exercises. Togo had released the commander of his cruisers to act independently and both divisions now wheeled separately around the Russians, firing whenever the gunners saw a target through the haze. To Pakenham, it appeared that 'every ship in the Baltic fleet that was still able to move had got into a sort of pool, in which they were circling or standing to and fro aimlessly'.[31]

Later in the afternoon mist closed in on the fleets and firing again ceased. The Russians made another attempt to break through north-westwards to Vladivostok behind a new leader, the battleship *Borodino*, but Togo discovered them and, overhauling from their starboard quarter again, concentrated on their van, forcing the *Alexander III* out of the line, on fire and heeling from water taken in through numerous shell holes and shaken plates. Her list increased until the sea came in through the ports for her anti-torpedo boat guns and took her farther over and down. Of Rozhestvensky's four first-class battleships only two were left, *Borodino* and *Oryol*. Soon after seven, when the sun had disappeared in haze above the horizon, a 12-inch shell hit the *Borodino* close by her forward 6-inch turret, bursting and igniting the ammunition train. A great column of smoke, ruddied by flames, shot up to the height of her funnel tops, and flames shortly reached the forward magazine. 'While all were watching, the unfortunate ship disappeared, her departure only marked by a roar, not greatly louder than that of the explosion of one of her own shell. At one moment the ship was there; the next she had gone, that was all . . .'[32]

This shocking incident marked the close of the main battle. Sporadic firing continued astern, but Togo ceased fire and steamed on ahead, spreading his division in a line of observation in case the few Russian war-ships at Vladivostok had come out to support their comrades. Meanwhile he sent in his torpedo boats. These found the burning *Suvoroff*,and although she fought them off with her starboard 12-pounders they closed from the port side and hit her with three torpedoes, which caused her to fill and sink. Rozhestvensky and his surviving staff had been taken off in a Russian destroyer earlier.

Other Japanese night attacks accounted for two older battleships and a coast defence ironclad. Since one older battleship had been destroyed by Japanese cruisers during the daylight action, the Russian battle line the following morning comprised just four ships, the obsolete *Nicholas I*, flying the flag of Rear Admiral Nebogatoff, the *Oryol*, listing and so damaged she retained barely half her fighting strength, and two coast defence ironclads. Nebogatoff assumed from the absence of Rozhestvensky's flagship that command had devolved on him, and when Japanese cruisers appeared, followed by Togo's entire fleet in fighting trim, he knew his alternatives were to yield or face annihilation. Convening a hurried council of war, he proposed surrender rather than a useless sacrifice of lives. Most of the council agreed, whereupon the orders were given to hoist the signal for surrender, strike the colours and raise the Japanese flag.[33]

Tsushima was one of the most decisive naval battles ever fought, in strategic and material terms probably the most conclusive. Only one light cruiser made a dash for Vladivostok and succeeded in escaping. Otherwise the Second Pacific Squadron had ceased to exist, Russia had been wiped from the list of major naval powers and Japan had complete control of sea communications with her victorious army in Manchuria. The Russian government could not send sufficient troop reinforcements and supplies to stabilize the situation by the incomplete, single-track trans-Siberian railway and, beset at home by revolutionaries spurred on by the military disasters, had no option but to seek terms. The Japanese were by this time close to bankruptcy and equally ready to agree peace. Theodore Roosevelt mediated. Engaged in building up the US navy as a power-political factor in the world, and sensitive to Japan's growing dominance in East Asia, he sought a balance of power in the region.

The peace conference was convened at Portsmouth, New Hampshire, in August. In the resulting treaty, signed in September, Japan gained Port Arthur, the Liaotung peninsula and the southern extension of the trans-Siberian railway, together with the southern half of Sakhalin Island, and recognition as the dominant power in Korea. The rest of Manchuria was restored to China, but Russia retained her dominance there.

Victory at Tsushima was won by superior gunnery at decisive range. There were many contributory factors: the intensive training the Japanese had undergone and the improved telescopic sights and modified shell detonators which had rendered the incendiary properties of the high explosive more devastating. Pakenham reported that the battle had hinged on the tremendous incendiary effects of the Japanese shells. To this he added that the Japanese had learned from the battle of 10 August to husband the nervous energy of their gun-layers, who had fired only when a target was clearly in view and within effective range. The Russians, on the other hand, had been too profligate with their shooting.[34]

As for Togo's tactics, although none of the British observers remarked on it, there were echoes of Nelson's unorthodox approach at Trafalgar in this centenary year. Togo was confronted, as Nelson had been, by a numerically more powerful but less rigorously trained fleet, and risked a manoeuvre of considerable danger within effective range of the enemy guns in order to concentrate each of his two divisions on the flagships of the enemy – as Nelson had done. As at Trafalgar, this created confusion in the enemy fleet; and, like Nelson, he had allowed independence to his second division – the lee column in Nelson's case. Togo was an admirer of Nelson and his signalled exhortation to his fleet was a conscious emulation of Nelson's 'England expects . . .'[35]

The victory made Togo a hero in Britain as well as Japan, and the following year he was invited to London to receive the Order of Merit, an almost unprecedented honour for a foreigner. Five years later he donated the battle flag of the *Mikasa* to his former training ship, HMS *Worcester.* In 2005 the flag was loaned on a permanent basis to the administrators of the Togo Shrine in Tokyo, where it was used as centrepiece in the centenary celebration of the Battle of the Sea of Japan.[36]

Tsushima and the other stunning victories of Japanese arms gave further stimulus to Japanese armaments conglomerates and related strategic industries; even more significant was the boost the successful war gave to the government's expansionist policy. Japan's 'special interest' in Korea had been asserted in the Anglo-Japanese Naval Treaty – renewed in 1905 – and in the peace treaty of Portsmouth. In 1910 she annexed the whole country without discernible protest from other powers, and began the ruthless exploitation of its resources and people, suppressing opposition with a brutal police regime.[37] The following year the naval treaty with Great Britain was again renewed.

10

Long-range Gunnery

———•———

THE GUNNERY FIRE control developments in the Royal Navy, which persuaded Fisher he could build battlecruisers sacrificing armour for high speed since they would be able to hit outside the range at which an enemy could hit them, originated with an inventive genius named Arthur Pollen. He was not a naval officer. After Oxford University, he had started out as a barrister, financing himself by writing for the *Westminster Gazette* on art, literature, music and drama. After marrying the daughter of the chairman of the British Linotype Company, he transformed himself into a businessman and technician, becoming both managing director of Linotype and an innovator associated with twenty-nine patents for the printing machinery the company manufactured.[1] However, the crucial experience that was to give his life a new and compelling direction occurred in 1900, less than two years after he joined Linotype. On holiday in Malta, he was invited by a cousin in the Mediterranean fleet to witness practice firings aboard a cruiser. The Boer War was then at its height and by coincidence Pollen went aboard the cruiser with a copy of *The Times* carrying a report of naval 4.7-inch guns at Ladysmith silencing Boer artillery 5 miles distant. In consequence he was astonished when the practice firings he witnessed at sea were carried out against a target towed on a parallel course under a mile away. When he expressed surprise at the disparity between the accuracy the guns were capable of at a great range ashore and the very short range at which they were fired at sea he was told this was due to lack of an effective rangefinder.

He returned from holiday fired with an ambition to bring science to bear on naval gunnery. What excited him was the complex mathematical problem of hitting a moving and possibly turning target at long range from a moving and possibly turning ship. This required more than accurate rangefinding and sight setting; prediction of the target's future position was necessary, since over 5 miles a shell took some thirty seconds to reach its target and during this time a ship might move a distance of almost half a mile. Pollen realized that the only way to predict a target ship's future position was to plot her past movement relative to the firing ship and project this forward – although even this could not meet the case of a ship that altered course during the time the shell was in the air; no tracking device could. He therefore set himself the task of designing instruments to measure a target's range and bearing at the same instant and plot the observations on paper moving at a speed representing the firing ship's forward motion; second, to devise a machine to integrate the information provided by this continuous 'true plot' for transmission to the gun positions as gun range and deflection (aim-off).

Defining the problem was very much easier than producing the necessary instruments or convincing naval officers of the value of the idea; for from the start he worked with and entirely for the Royal Navy, intent on giving the British service a decisive lead over all comers in long-range gunnery. The most rooted objection from naval officers, which appeared to be supported by centuries of British naval history, was that battles would and should be fought at decisive range, where the skill and discipline of British guns' crews would tell, not at long range, where hitting was a matter of chance. Added to this it was believed that precision instruments could be deranged by the concussions of battle and that any centralized system for aiming the guns would be counterproductive since errors in the system would affect all guns, whereas with individual gun-layers errors from some would be compensated by hits from others. The reports from the British observers with the Japanese fleet during the Russo-Japanese War seemed to bear this out. Few hits were made at long range and it was only when Togo pressed in to 5,000 yards and Japanese fire control collapsed that their fire began to tell.[2]

By this date, 1905, the gunnery renaissance in the Royal Navy ignited by Percy Scott had taken hold. Scott himself had been appointed Inspector of Target Practice, a new post Fisher had created for him, and was introducing a spirit of extreme rivalry between ships and squadrons in annual gun-layers' and 'battle practice' competitions, the former at very short range, the latter at ranges from 4,000 to 8,000 yards[3] – still well inside 5 miles. Since conditions had to be the same for all ships these trials became rule-dominated tests of individual marksmanship and speed of fire within a known framework far removed from the likely realities of battle; indeed, the 'long-range' battle practice target was until 1907 stationary. Gun range and deflection were found by observing – 'spotting' – the fall of shot in a salvo and correcting the elevation or training of the pieces until the target was 'straddled', some shells short, some over.

To Pollen it was self-evident that in real action against a real enemy at long range moving on courses and at speeds that could only be estimated, spotting would give no better results than chance, since applying corrections to guns without knowing the precise movement of the target ship between one salvo and the next was pure guesswork. For scientific gunnery the speed and course of the target ship had to be established relative to the firing ship; if these were found with sufficient accuracy the enemy could be rendered in effect a stationary target for the firing ship, when spotting corrections would bring the guns on target. Although his approach was dismissed by the majority of officers with whom he discussed the problem – chiefly on the plausible grounds alluded to earlier – he was supported by a significant number of intelligent gunnery specialists, including Percy Scott, who besides promoting gun-layer accuracy was also working against the grain of service orthodoxy to introduce director firing. His director system complemented Pollen's work since it involved the control of all guns from a single position aloft.

Pollen was so certain of his concept and so determined to bring it to fruition that he resigned as managing director of Linotype at the end of 1905 and, with the assistance of a brilliant design engineer named Harold Isherwood, whom he took with him, devoted himself to developing the necessary instruments in collaboration with the Admiralty. He had an ally in Fisher. The Director of Naval Ordnance, Captain John Jellicoe, who, unlike Fisher, understood the complex mathematics of the problem, was another ally, and by September 1906 Pollen had reached agreement with the Admiralty that he would be paid for rights in his system and royalties on instruments should trials prove them viable; he, for his part, would preserve the system's secrecy, assign all patents to the British government and not apply for foreign patents.

It should be noted that Pollen was heralding a revolution, not only in gunnery but, as he recognized and asserted repeatedly, in tactics, naval architecture and building policy. Instead of the current orthodoxy of seeking action at 'decisive' range, his system demanded keeping outside the range at which an enemy could hit – for he assumed that the Royal Navy would be able to preserve the long-range hitting advantage provided by his system for at least five years before any foreign navy caught up. This implied building faster ships able to dictate the range at which an action was fought, mounting larger-calibre guns whose shells would have a flatter trajectory at long range, and having more horizontal armour to resist shells plunging from a high angle.[4] It also meant spending on research and development.

Instead, over the following years his ambition to make long-range gunnery a reality was repeatedly set back. First, Jellicoe received a seagoing appointment and was succeeded as Director of Naval Ordnance by Captain

Reginald Bacon, who was not a gunnery specialist and took the prevailing view that complex fire control instruments would be less reliable in action than simple, manually-operated devices. As assistant, Bacon chose an ambitious gunnery officer, Lieutenant Frederic Dreyer, who had made a reputation by using Percy Scott's methods in his last ship to gain first place for her in the firing competitions for three years in succession. Dreyer knew of Pollen's fire control system. Pollen had explained it to him and a group of officers and shown them plans of his proposed automatic plotter, gyroscopic rangefinder mounting and integrating mechanism or 'Clock' to generate range from rates of change of range. Dreyer, misunderstanding the complexity of the problem, had devised a mechanism for plotting ranges manually on a strip of moving paper to obtain the rate of change, and later added a separate bearing plot to obtain rates of change for both range and bearing, the two components of hitting.

When Pollen's first instruments were ready for sea trials towards the end of 1907 Bacon chose Admiral Sir Arthur Wilson to conduct them and, since Wilson was not a gunnery specialist, sent Dreyer as his technical assistant. Dreyer was convinced that his own system of plotting rates of change was the more practical and told Pollen before the trials he intended to 'crab' him.[5] Between them, Wilson and Dreyer did just that, running the tests under such easy conditions with such modest changes of range that they were able to judge Dreyer's plotting 'vastly superior'.[6] Pollen had considered Dreyer's method of plotting rates of change of range and bearing at an early stage and dismissed it, since in most cases it resulted not in straight lines but in curves with constantly changing inflection, which made it impossible to project them with sufficient accuracy to ascertain future rates while the shells were in the air – particularly when ships were approaching each other at speed.

Pollen requested a retrial, but was rejected. Determined to complete the task he had set himself, he formed a company named Argo to secure finance and appealed over Bacon's head to the First Lord of the Admiralty for further trials. These took place late in 1909 and so impressed the captain of the trials cruiser that he proposed an additional feature to fit the system for battle – as opposed to the benign conditions of battle practice. Pollen was astonished to find a demand for *increased* complexity from a naval officer, and wrote to a backer:

> The great change in our plotting system which we have funked all these years on the grounds that it was an extra complication, he with his eye for sea fighting, insists on as a primary necessity; it is, of course, making the table

plot irrespective of helm – i.e. Our course is no longer a straight line . . . but is itself accurately plotted. This makes captain and Admiral free to manoeuvre as they please . . . No more bother about turns etc.[7]

Despite positive reports on the 1909 trials and further tests of Pollen's Argo gear in 1910, a new Director of Naval Ordnance, Captain Archibald Moore, again not a gunnery specialist, rejected the recommendations and told Pollen the Admiralty had decided that plotting in any form was impracticable.[8] Money was a factor as it had been from the start. Pollen's precision instruments and rights to their exclusive use were naturally far more expensive than the standard rangefinders and rate of change calculators in use.

There was also the Dreyer factor. Two weeks before telling Pollen that the Admiralty had discarded plotting, Moore ordered the adoption of Dreyer's system of plotting ranges and bearings. As he explained in a memo, this was 'to protect the Admiralty from any developments of Mr Pollen or others',[9] meaning, presumably, that by developing a fire control system within the service they would not in future have to submit to what he regarded as Pollen's outrageous financial demands.

In December that year, 1910, Dreyer was appointed to Jellicoe's flagship in the Atlantic fleet and began working with him on the fire control problem. From the collaboration there emerged the 'Dreyer Fire Control Table' manufactured for the Admiralty by an engineering company, Elliott Brothers. It was a skilfully machined realization of Dreyer's manual range and separate bearing plotting system incorporating drives to feed in wind force and spotting corrections, and employed no less than eight men on its operating handles.[10]

Pollen, meanwhile, pressed on with the development of his true course system to enable it to accommodate the plotting ship's own course alterations. The integrating mechanism he and Isherwood produced was a variable-speed range rate 'Clock' capable of transmitting the ranges it generated. Pollen supplied detailed plans and descriptions to the Admiralty Ordnance Department, whence they were passed to Dreyer; and engineers at Elliott Brothers adapted the principle to construct a similar variable speed 'Clock' for use on the Dreyer Fire Control Table.[11] It was not a direct copy and was in practice inferior to Pollen's Argo machine. By 1912, however, when Pollen submitted his instrument to sea trials in competition with Dreyer's, Jellicoe had convinced himself that Dreyer's system was as accurate as Pollen's for any conditions likely to arise in war.[12]

Jellicoe had, of course, been one of Pollen's early champions; he was a very able gunnery specialist and fully aware of the theoretical superiority of Pollen's true plotting system if ranges were long and changing rapidly – for instance, if one or both opposing fleets attempted to close quickly to decisive range. His belief that Dreyer's system was adequate for likely battle conditions could only have rested on the assumption that firing would not begin at long range, or alternatively that even with Pollen's system hits at long range would be so infrequent they would not affect the subsequent action at 'decisive' range. He knew that German dreadnoughts were designed for close-range action: they mounted heavy secondary batteries and fired both main and secondary guns at battle practices. Yet even in the future battleground, the North Sea, whose mists encouraged both sides to believe that ranges would be limited to some 11,000 yards,[13] there were many clear days when visibility was limitless.

That same year, the Inspector of Target Practice, Rear Admiral Richard Peirse, who was fighting to have Scott's directors fitted in the fleet, wrote to the First Sea Lord pointing out that, in addition to the concentrated broadsides achievable only with the director system, a means was required to place such broadsides on the enemy and keep them there; 'Pollen's apparatus is without any doubt whatever, the one best calculated to give us this'.[14] In an accompanying memorandum, he asserted that when the rate of change was large and rapidly varying owing to a steep approach, 'present methods of determining the rate amount to nothing better than guesswork'.[15]

It is remarkable that such an outstanding officer as Jellicoe failed to foresee the likely conditions of battle that so concerned Peirse, and consequently put his faith in a range-rate method of fire control Peirse deemed 'nothing better than guesswork'. Some of the probable answers have been touched on: the historic argument for battle at 'decisive' range, which seemed confirmed by Tsushima, the naval staff appreciation that the German fleet was designed for close action, the generally poor visibility in the North Sea. There were also technical considerations with which, as a former Director of Naval Ordnance, Jellicoe was very familiar: British armour-piercing shells could not be counted upon to penetrate heavy armour if they struck at over 30 degrees to a right angle, as they would if fired from long range.

There is also the 'Dreyer factor'. Dreyer was a strong personality with tremendous drive; it is possible that his single-minded promotion of his system, combined with the high standards to which he trained his gunnery teams for the artificial requirements of test firings, blinded Jellicoe to the inherent flaws in the system. Above all, the drive to orthodoxy in such a traditional, self-confident hierarchy as that of the Royal Navy cannot be overestimated. And undoubtedly naval orthodoxy required action at decisive range. It is not necessary, therefore, to attribute the rejection of Pollen's system to the strong professional relationship that had grown up between Jellicoe and Dreyer, or to service prejudice against an 'outsider' who was demanding large sums of money for his inventions – although the expense of adopting Pollen's Argo gear did weigh against him throughout his struggles with the Admiralty.

The most persuasive hypothesis to account for Jellicoe's swing in favour of Dreyer over Pollen has been put forward recently in a number of papers by Professor Jon T. Sumida.[16] Through analysis of Admiralty procurement policy, ship design and battle practices prior to the war, Sumida has been led to the startling conclusion that by 1912 the Admiralty, guided by Jellicoe, had devised a secret tactic of Nelsonic boldness not simply to defeat but to annihilate the German fleet in battle at their own (German) preferred medium to close range, and that concentration on this goal precluded further progress on long-range fire control – hence leading to the preference for Dreyer over Pollen.

Sumida's argument is this: by 1911 new hydraulic elevating and training machinery for the main armament of the Royal Navy's dreadnoughts had made it possible for gun-layers and trainers to employ 'continuous aim' throughout the rolling, pitching and yawing motions of their ship. This allowed more rapid fire when in independent gun-layer – as opposed to director – control since gun-layers did not have to wait for the ship's motion to bring their pieces on target. During the same period, as noted, Jellicoe and Dreyer were collaborating on the development of the Dreyer Fire Control Table employing separate range and bearing plots. From this emerged a system of plotting a number of ranges reported from different rangefinders dispersed at various positions in the ship, striking an average known as 'the mean rangefinder range of the moment' and feeding this into the range-rate Clock. If the range generated by the Clock subsequently fell out of step with the mean range from the plot, the Clock could instantly be 'tuned' to the observed range – which was not the case with Pollen's true course system – and set with a more appropriate rate of change of range. In battle practices, after one or two ranging shots or salvoes, ships would commence rapid independent fire with the gunsights set with the Clock-generated range, a method known as 'rangefinder control', which did not depend upon 'spotting' corrections. By eliminating the need to wait for the fall of the previous salvo or for the roll of the ship to bring the guns on target, 'rangefinder control' allowed the fastest possible rate of fire, limited only by the time it took to reload the pieces; and pro-vided the target was at medium to close range, inside 10,000 yards, moving in the same direction on a roughly parallel straight course, minimizing the rate of change of range, a hitting rate of 30 per cent or more could be and was achieved in practice.

In action this would be crushing. Improved armour-piercing shells for British 13.5-inch-gun dreadnoughts entering service in 1912 were almost 60 per cent heavier than the largest German 12-inch projectiles and were believed to be capable of penetrating the thickest German armour at 10,000 yards or less.[17] Early in 1913 gun calibre was increased to 15 inches for a new class of British battleship whose shells were double the weight of German 12-inch. Such huge projectiles delivered with the accuracy and rapidity possible with 'rangefinder control' would, it was assumed, over-come the more lightly gunned German ships in short time. Sumida has calculated that a 13.5-inch-gun dreadnought with a loading time for the guns of thirty-five seconds, achieving a 30 per cent accuracy rate – as in battle practices – would place twenty hits aggregating 35,000 lbs on its opponent in five minutes; a 15-inch-gun dreadnought would deliver over 38,000 lbs in the same period.[18] The enemy would be effectively knocked out before even his high-speed torpedoes could reach the British line, which, after the initial brief and violent cannonade, would be turned away by signal, all ships together, in time to avoid the underwater threat. Meanwhile enemy destroyers would be repulsed by light cruisers and destroyers deployed specifically to hold the ring for the battle-fleet action.

In December 1912 Jellicoe was appointed Second Sea Lord. He brought with him to the Admiralty the new tactical plan based on 'rangefinder con-trol', and evidently convinced the Board of its feasibility. Fisher had predicted that Jellicoe would be the new Nelson for the Battle of Armageddon in 1914. His tactical concept was Nelsonic, both in its emphasis on overwhelming firepower and in the element of surprise: the Germans would not expect acquiescence in the kind of medium- to close-range encounter for which they had designed their ships and battle tactics, but would anticipate the British using their superior fleet speed to hold them outside torpedo range.

Nelson, however, had known that nothing is certain in a sea battle, and the obvious problem with what Sumida terms Jellicoe's new 'technical-tactical synthesis' was that it required the German fleet to do precisely what was expected of it – to close rapidly to inside 8,000 yards and turn to a par-allel course to steam in the same direction as the British line. There was, in fact, every reason to believe it would. The design of the German heavy ships and intelligence reports on their tactical doctrine and the range at which they conducted firing practices pointed conclusively to their intention to fight at medium range where their heavier secondary batteries and torpedo armament could be expected to give them the edge.

The Admiralty surrounded gunnery and fire control with extreme secrecy in the years immediately before the war; and after the war had shown up shortcomings in British long-range gunnery, papers bearing on the Jellicoe–Dreyer 'synthesis' were weeded and the technical history manipulated in such a way as to expunge it from the record. Sumida has been able to find no documentary proof of its existence. The circumstantial evidence he has gathered, however, is sufficient to remove any reasonable doubt that Admiralty policy from at least 1912 to the opening months of the war was guided by preparation and training for medium- to short-range battle-fleet action designed to remove the German fleet from the strategic board.

Strong corroboration has appeared since first publication of this book, notably in Norman Friedman's *Naval Firepower: Battleship Guns and Gunnery in the Dreadnought Era*. Friedman has shown, inter alia, that Admiralty war-game rules for 1913 stipulated 12,000 yards as the maximum range for heavy guns. Even more compelling, perhaps, a Royal United Services Institute prize essay written by a serving officer in 1920 stated that before the outbreak of war fleet tactics were entirely dominated by the gun:

> The gunnery expert said under what conditions he could best hit the enemy, and the tactician adopted tactics which would provide these conditions. It was considered that to achieve success the fleet must, as far as possible, steer a steady course and the enemy must be brought within the comparatively short range of 10,000–12,000 yards.[19]

The final resolution in favour of Dreyer's Fire Control Table was made in December 1912 shortly after Jellicoe had joined the Board, and the same month the Admiralty ended its monopoly agreement with Pollen, allowing him to sell his system on the open market to foreign governments – although not the Argo Clock, since its dial revealed that the Royal Navy used rate plotting, and this was an official secret. With this decision the Admiralty not only rejected the one system with the potential to give the Royal Navy helm-free gunnery and the kind of dominance at long range it had exercised at close quarters in the French Revolutionary and Napoleonic wars, it allowed the sale of some essential fire control components to future enemies.[20]

It is worth noting that no other navy adopted either a plotting system for fire control or Percy Scott's director firing. In the German service a director sight was used to align all guns on target, but individual gun-layers still used telescopic sights set for the required elevation to follow the target through the roll of their ship. German fire control instruments were similar to those developed in the Royal Navy before the Dreyer Table: their *EU/SV Anzeiger* was equivalent to the Royal Navy's Dumaresq, a trigonometrical calculator named after its inventor, which when set with known and observed factors of own ship's course and speed and enemy range and bearing, and with estimates of enemy course and speed, provided the rates of change of range and bearing; alternatively it could be set with observed rates of change to provide truer estimates of enemy course and speed. The rates obtained were set on the *Entfernungs-Meldeuhr* – range-reporting 'Clock' – which performed the function of the standard Vickers 'Clock' in the Royal Navy, indicating the reducing or increasing range according to the rate of change with which it was set. Like the Vickers 'Clock' it lacked a variable-speed drive, and hence could not represent changing rates of change.[21]

Overall, the Royal Navy's director firing system and the larger calibre of its guns compared to those of German dreadnoughts, class for class, should have given British battleships decisive advantages in any prolonged fleet action, particularly in rolling weather. German gunnery officers had the edge in one respect, however: their rangefinders were over twice as long as those fitted in all but the very latest British capital ships. Since range was found by measurement of the small angular difference between observations of the target from either end of the instrument, the greater base length of German rangefinders gave greater discrimination at longer ranges. They also worked on a different optical principle. While British rangefinder operators had to align two half-images of the target, an upper and a lower half reflected into their eyepieces from the opposite ends of the instrument, their German counterparts received whole images reflected from both ends and had to focus them together as in normal vision. It was a subjective judgement against an objective alignment. The exactness required by the British system became a liability, however, if the ship were juddering at speed, and there is much evidence to suggest that the Germans found the range more rapidly in the initial stages of an action.[22]

II

Towards Armageddon

THE GROWTH OF Tirpitz's fleet and the inference drawn in London that Wilhelm II aimed like a latter-day Napoleon for European and world hegemony drew Britain inexorably towards full engagement on the Continent. The reality of the German threat, hence of this interpretation of the British retreat from isolation, has been questioned recently by a historian of formidable intellect and forensic skills;[1] it is nonetheless clear from the German archives that British apprehensions were well founded.

The first overt sign of the shift was the Franco-British entente of 1904. This was followed by informal military conversations,[2] and after a Liberal government took office in December 1905 the new Foreign Secretary, Sir Edward Grey, agreed to a French request for formal talks between the British and French General Staffs. These began in January 1906. Cabinet approval had not been sought; apart from Richard Haldane, Secretary of State for War, Cabinet ministers were not told, and even the Prime Minister, Herbert Asquith, was not informed of progress. Nonetheless, it was soon agreed by the British that in order to compensate for French numerical inferiority, in the event of a German attack a British expeditionary force 105,000 strong would be dispatched to operate in Belgium. The French were convinced, correctly, that a German assault would come through Belgium.

The commitment was not binding. The entente was not a military alliance and the General Staff had no authority to pledge the government to come to France's aid in a European war; the French were given no assurances that they would. Moreover, the Royal Navy, in the person of the First Sea Lord, the formidable 'Jackie' Fisher, was vehemently opposed to any commitment that would involve Britain's tiny regular army in a clash between mass conscript armies on the Continent. He held a traditional view of British strategy in which expeditionary forces were launched by the navy for unexpected peripheral 'descents' to draw off enemy troops from the main theatre; he had in mind particularly Heligoland, Schleswig-Holstein, Antwerp and a stretch of coast inside the Baltic only 90 miles from Berlin.[3] He refused to cooperate with the army plan to send troops to France, thence Belgium, and refused cooperation with the French navy, which was in a poor state at this time. He would not even agree to the preparation of common codes for communication or identification.

Hopelessly uncoordinated as British planning was at this stage, in retrospect the initial military conversations endorsed by Grey can be seen as the seeds of a revolution in British strategy out of which huge civilian and later conscript armies would emerge to fight on the slaughterfields of Europe, while the navy held the ring. This was foreseen by few, and was not inevitable. The navy contributed by failing until too late to create a thinking and planning staff, while the army produced as Director of Military Operations a passionate Francophile, General Sir Henry Wilson, who spent much of his leave reconnoitring the terrain and rail and road networks of Belgium with bicycle, maps and notebooks, afterwards working up detailed timetables for British troops to embark for particular French ports on specified days after mobilization to operate on the left flank of the French army.

The conflict between the opposing strategies of the two armed services was brought to a head during a Franco-German crisis in summer 1911 which threatened war. At a special meeting of the Committee of Imperial Defence (CID) called by the Prime Minister on 23 August and attended by selected members of the Cabinet, Fisher's successor, Admiral Sir Arthur Wilson, who, like Fisher, prided himself on keeping his war plans locked away in his head, failed to give a convincing account of naval strategy under modern conditions. Advocating a close blockade of the estuaries of the German rivers and the entrance to the Baltic, he was unable to demonstrate how such a traditional strategy could be maintained in the face of mine and submarine defences, long-range shore-based artillery and night torpedo attack. Nor could he satisfy his listeners on the feasibility of peripheral seaborne landings to draw off enemy troops from the main theatre, since the development of motorized road and rail transport had given the advantage to land defences.[4]

Admiral Wilson did not convince. By contrast General Sir Henry Wilson's plan to send six divisions of the British army across the Channel within days of the outbreak of war was precisely formulated and appeared to meet the commonsense military and political imperatives of restoring balance on the decisive front to prevent French defeat. Grey backed the plan. The previous month he had authorized Wilson to travel to Paris and with the Chief of the French General Staff sign an agreement to put it into effect if Britain should join France in a Continental war.[5] He still could not commit Britain to joining in. The Cabinet contained too many Liberal idealists, radicals and pacifists to agree to any military commitment. They were not informed of Wilson's agreement with the French staff, nor was the Admiralty. Both Cabinet and navy were deliberately outflanked.

It was a curious way of formulating imperial grand strategy. Speculation on the course of the world war had Grey, Haldane and Henry Wilson not been drawn into a Continental commitment by the French and their own fears of German ambition is idle: counterfactual argument produces expanding circles of conjecture. In the event the CID meeting of 23 August was decisive. Convinced by the army's case, Asquith sent Winston Churchill to the Admiralty as First Lord expressly to introduce a naval staff and bring naval planning into line with War Office thinking. As Home Secretary Churchill had been sceptical of the German threat, but during the crisis that summer the German government's intimidatory pressure on France had opened his eyes, and he responded to his move to the Admiralty with a high sense of mission. 'This is the big thing,' he told Asquith's daughter, 'the biggest thing that has ever come my way . . . I shall pour into it everything I've got.'[6]

He brought to the Admiralty boundless energy and self-confidence, an ever-enquiring mind, imagination, courage and a prevailing sense of the menace emanating from Kaiser Wilhelm's court.[7] He called upon Fisher in retirement as unofficial adviser. Fisher, who had lost none of his mental vigour, was delighted to be back at the centre of the struggle, and drawn to Churchill. 'He's a genius without doubt,' he told his friends, 'and he is brave, which is everything.'[8] Both he and Churchill anticipated war in autumn 1914 when the enlargement of the Kiel Canal would be complete, allowing the inland transfer of Tirpitz's dreadnoughts between the Baltic and the North Sea.

Feeling he was working against time, Churchill created a naval staff and set up a Naval War College at Portsmouth – later transferred to Greenwich – to train officers for the work. Among the most important strategic plans put forward by the new staff and adopted by the Admiralty Board before the outbreak of war was the replacement of 'close' blockade of the German coast, as outlined by Arthur Wilson, with 'distant' blockade of the North Sea exits, a southern line across the Strait of Dover, a northern line covering the gap between the Scottish coast and islands and Norway, with the Home Fleet based on Scapa Flow in the Orkneys.

His most dramatic initiatives were in the materiel sphere, guided by Fisher. Out of the collaboration came the formidable *Queen Elizabeth* class of fast battleships which almost realized Fisher's 'battlecruiser' ideal without, however, sacrificing heavy armour, still judged an unacceptable risk. With 15-inch guns and a speed of 25 knots achieved by switching to oil fuel – giving greater thermal efficiency than coal – they marked as daring an advance over existing dreadnoughts as the *Dreadnought* herself had over pre-dreadnoughts. Their huge projectiles carried over twice the bursting charge of 12-inch shells and had a flatter trajectory, giving them greater effective reach, since the smaller angle of descent reduced the significance of errors in range.

The change to oil fuel was particularly bold since Britain had practically inexhaustible supplies of the best steam coal in the world, but no domestic sources of oil. Within the empire, the Burmah Oil Company drew from wells in Burma and Assam and had a stake in oil rights in southern Persia; there in 1909 drillings produced copious flows. Encouraged by the Admiralty, Burmah formed the Anglo-Persian Oil Company – later British Petroleum – to exploit the discovery. A refinery was constructed on a mud island, Abadan, on the Shatt al-Arab waterway at the head of the Persian Gulf, and a pipeline laid across the desert from the wells some 130 miles to the north. Oil-fired destroyers and submarines were already in service in the Royal Navy, but it was this major development in southern Persia, which with the Gulf was a vital British sphere of interest between Russia and India and on the flank of the Suez-eastern shipping routes, which gave Churchill the confidence to commit the new class of capital ships to oil. The first shipment from the Abadan refinery passed through the Suez Canal en route for the Thames in November 1913, and in May 1914 Asquith's government bought a controlling interest in the Anglo-Persian Oil Company for £2.2 million, a transaction that has been compared to Disraeli's purchase of Suez Canal shares the previous century. Both illustrate how Britain's command at sea allowed her to pursue commercial objectives around the world which, in turn, increased her sea command. She was indeed an expanding, not a declining, empire.

Tirpitz could not follow Churchill into oil-fired dreadnoughts since he could not guarantee supplies in war. It scarcely affected him. He had a single goal before his eyes: the achievement of the *Marineaeternat* of sixty capital ships each with a statutory lifespan of twenty years to give a building tempo of three large ships a year fixed by law and thus removed from the control of the Reichstag. For this he was prepared to sacrifice ship size, speed and gunpower. In these respects the Royal Navy set the pace and he simply followed. His justification, supported by a 'historical' school of naval theorists led by A. T. Mahan, was that numbers, not superiority in individual ships, would prove decisive in battle.

It is difficult to penetrate Tirpitz's real views. He used so many specious arguments in his struggle for the fleet that he was known, admiringly, by his subordinates as 'the father of the lie'.[9] It is clear, however, that in his single-minded pursuit of numbers and building tempos, he not only disregarded the tactical advantages of speed and gunpower, hence size of capital ships, but also neglected the potential of submarines[10] and failed to foresee the possibility of the Royal Navy abandoning its traditional strategy of close blockade on which he based expectations of a decisive fleet battle in the southern North Sea. More seriously for Wilhelm's government, he refused to listen to those who saw that his fleet programme was rebounding disastrously on both the external and internal goals of *Weltpolitik*, limiting German more than British political freedom of action and widening the internal divisions the policy was supposed to heal.

When Britain followed her entente with France with a similar understanding with Russia, Bülow, Reich Chancellor since 1900, publicly branded the policy 'encirclement' (*Einkreisung*), 'the creation of a ring of powers around Germany to isolate and cripple her'.[11] Tirpitz used the consequent wave of hostility towards Britain to float another *Novelle* designed both to accelerate construction of capital ships over the years 1908 to 1911 and to take a vital step towards the *Marineaeternat* by reducing the lifespan of each from twenty-five to twenty years. The Reichstag passed the Bill in March 1908. For the British Admiralty, Foreign Office and much of the press the systematic increments in Tirpitz's programme confirmed his hostile intent. There could be no other explanation. The short-range battleships could not protect German overseas trade, nor would they be of use in a land war against France; indeed, they consumed huge funds that might have been expended on the army. Viscount Esher, a confidant of King Edward VII, Grey, Fisher and most of those in the highest circles of influence, wrote, 'Nothing can prevent a struggle for life [between Britain and Germany] except the certainty that attack would fail.'[12]

Fisher repeated to the King an earlier suggestion of his that the nascent German fleet be 'Copenhagened'.

'Fisher,' the King said after a moment, 'you must be mad.'[13]

The German ambassador in London, Count Metternich, reported the hardening attitude to Bülow, pointing out that whether Tirpitz's fleet was designed to attack Britain or was merely a potential threat, all England agreed on the danger: 'A defeat in the North Sea means the end of the British Empire. A lost battle on the continent is a long way from the end of Germany.'[14]

Both Grey and Lloyd George, Chancellor of the Exchequer, tried to persuade Metternich that Tirpitz's increase in building tempo was self-defeating since it would be matched by the Admiralty. Lloyd George stressed that if, on the other hand, both Germany and Britain could agree to cut their building programmes by one dreadnought a year it would transform the situation. When these conversations were reported to Wilhelm he erupted: Metternich should not listen to such 'measureless impertinence'; he should tell Grey and Lloyd George to 'go to hell'. He was 'too flabby';[15] and he sent Bülow a telegram describing how he had responded to the British request to stop or slow construction with the words, 'Then we shall fight, for it is a question of national honour and dignity.'[16] Bülow recognized that the time for negotiation was past; while Wilhelm refused to compromise on the fleet it would be impossible to separate Britain from her entente partners. As with the original Navy Law and the *Novelle* of 1900, which doubled fleet numbers, final responsibility for the 1908 *Novelle* and its consequences lay with Wilhelm. Tirpitz was merely the tool providing executive force and sophistical justifications.

Meanwhile the rising cost was exacerbating the strains within the Reich. In the federal constitution Bismarck had devised to preserve the power of the Prussian nobility, individual states controlled their own internal affairs and raised necessary revenue through direct taxes or loans. This placed the Reich government in Berlin, which was responsible for matters affecting all states such as foreign and defence policy, in competition with the individual states for tax and loans on the money market. Tirpitz's fleet was financed largely by borrowing;[17] and since the states had a virtual monopoly on direct taxation, the debt was serviced by raising taxes on imports and on consumption.[18] The resulting discontent played into the hands of the Social Democratic Party, precisely reversing the original aims of *Weltpolitik*. Yet proposals to impose direct taxes on wealth and property at the Reich level were resisted by both groups that had been brought together as a 'patriotic' bloc to support the government in the Reichstag, the landholding Conservatives and the commercial-industrial National Liberals. Moreover, the crisis exposed their essential differences, sending the Conservatives back to their traditional reliance on the army and distrust of the navy.[19]

There are echoes here of the political deadlock in eighteenth-century France before the Revolution: the government spending hugely on a fleet to challenge the British fleet but unable to reform the tax system against the resistance of the elites, thus unable to tap the wealth of the propertied classes as effectively as the British government, while ordinary people suffered rising prices for necessities. It was evident to most observers that

Tirpitz's fleet policy had backfired disastrously internally and externally; it also exposed the Reich's financial weakness compared to Great Britain.[20]

Britain not only had greater financial strength, but as an island empire she naturally spent a greater proportion of her total armed services budget on her navy than on her army, whereas in Germany, a Continental power, the positions were reversed[21] – as indeed they had been in pre-Revolutionary France. Thus for Tirpitz to approach British naval strength total Reich defence spending had to exceed that of Britain by an unattainable margin – given the reluctance of her propertied classes to contribute. Even more important, perhaps, British statesmen knew that their world position depended on the twin pillars of their navy and the City of London; each was dependent on the other; should either fall the empire would topple. They had to outbuild Tirpitz.[22] This was now apparent to most German politicians and men of affairs. Albert Ballin, head of the Hamburg-Amerika Line, and once an enthusiastic supporter of the fleet policy, saw that Britain would not and could not yield supremacy at sea, and the time had come to enter a sensible agreement with her. 'Otherwise', he wrote in July 1909, 'the life will certainly be knocked out of us, and in two years what will we have for this accelerated construction – a new financial crisis or a war?'[23]

For Bülow, both possibilities seemed very real, and he attempted to persuade both Tirpitz and Wilhelm of the necessity for a naval agreement. Both were affronted.[24] Rebuffed by his sovereign and with the parties comprising his 'patriotic' bloc in the Reichstag paralysed by the proposals on direct taxation, Bülow resigned. He was replaced as Chancellor by Theobald von Bethmann Hollweg, a Prussian with all the punctilious virtues of a civil servant, driven by loyalty to his Kaiser and his caste, but altogether lacking flair. Bülow had recommended him as 'a good plough horse'. It was an accurate assessment. Bethmann recognized that the relationship with Britain, hence the fleet question, lay at the root of the problems confronting him, but misread the situation, supposing that by accepting Lloyd George's previous suggestion of a mutual reduction in building tempo he could obtain a neutrality pact from Britain. When he proposed this it simply increased Grey's suspicion: Britain could hardly agree to remain neutral if Germany were at war on the Continent without rendering the French and Russian ententes meaningless. The inept proposals were soon dismissed – to Tirpitz's satisfaction. The construction race continued.

The following year Grey and the Admiralty had further direct confirmation of their fears. It came from August Bebel, Social Democrat leader in the Reichstag. Reduced to despair by the ever-rising costs of Tirpitz's programme and what he perceived as a drive to war by the Prussian leadership, anxious to awaken Britain to the danger she faced so that her liberal democracy would survive and triumph in the coming struggle with the forces of militarism and autocracy in his own country, he opened a clandestine correspondence with the British Foreign Office via the British consul general in Zurich to pass on secrets of the armaments programme gleaned from his membership of the Budget Committee of the Reichstag. He began:

> Though a Prussian myself by birth, I consider Prussia a frightful state [*schreck-licher Staat*] from which nothing but frightful things may be expected; this England is sure to experience sooner than most people think. To reform Prussia is impossible; it will remain the *Junkerstaat* it is at present, or go to pieces altogether. The Hohenzollerns too won't change . . .
>
> I cannot understand what the British government & people are about in letting Germany creeping up to them so closely in naval armaments. As a regular member of the Budget Commission I can assert that the German Naval Law of 1900 was directed against England & England alone . . .
>
> I am convinced we are on the eve of the most dreadful war Europe has ever seen. Things cannot go on as at present, the burden of military charges are crushing people & the Kaiser & the government are fully alive to the fact. Everything works for a great crisis in Germany . . .[25]

When Churchill introduced the naval estimates to the Commons on 18 March 1912 he made public a new standard of British naval strength as 60 per cent above Germany's fleet strength, then addressed a warning to Tirpitz over the heads of the MPs: for every ship Germany added to her naval law Britain would lay down two. He also made the converse clear: any reduction in German construction would be met by a fully proportional British reduction, and he suggested a building 'holiday' in 1913 when no great ships would be laid down by either side. 'The three ships that she [Germany] did not build would therefore automatically wipe out no less than five British potential super-dreadnoughts [*Queen Elizabeths*], and that is more than I expect them to hope to do in a brilliant naval action.'[26] The speech received great applause in the press. Esher wrote to say that in all his time in public life 'no speeches have been made as yours – so straight and so daringly truthful'.[27]

The only discernible effect on Wilhelm and Tirpitz was to reinforce their resolve not to have the size of their navy dictated by Britain. Tirpitz placed a *Novelle* before the Reichstag in April. The Conservatives and

National Liberals closed ranks against the Social Democratic and radical opposition and with the centre again sweetened with concessions to their views on tax and tariffs, the Bill passed and became law in May. Tirpitz had achieved his ambition. In little more than a decade the fleet specified in his programme had swollen from seventeen battleships to sixty-one capital units – dreadnought battleships and battlecruisers – each with a lifespan of twenty years, thus a perpetual building tempo of three great ships a year protected by law. The *Marineaeternat* had been reached. Whether this was his ultimate goal is doubtful.[28]

Meanwhile, in July Churchill had agreed to French requests for naval conversations to define areas of command and arrange common signals in case of war. Like Asquith, Grey and the entire Cabinet, Churchill was concerned that the talks should not lead to a binding political commitment or even furnish France with a moral claim to British aid if she were attacked by Germany[29] since this might encourage her to hazard war. But like the more detailed General Staff talks earlier, the Naval Staff talks were bound to give the impression that an obligation existed. In September France moved her northern squadron from Brest to join her Mediterranean fleet at Toulon, leaving her Channel and Atlantic coasts protected only by torpedo boats. Since Churchill had already brought the battleships of the British Mediterranean fleet back to home waters – leaving only a battlecruiser squadron at Malta – the effect was to place the defence of the Mediterranean against the Austrian and Italian fleets in French hands, leaving Britain to contain the German fleet in the North Sea and safeguard France's northern coasts. Wilhelm and Tirpitz assumed that the entente powers had concluded a secret naval agreement.

Later that year fighting broke out in the Balkans and it seemed that Austria-Hungary might be drawn in against Serbia, a client of Russia, so precipitating war between the great power blocs. Haldane issued a warning to Germany. Metternich had been recalled as ambassador for reporting constantly on the pernicious effect Tirpitz's fleet laws had on British opinion, and Haldane told his successor, Prince Lichnowsky, that in the event of the Balkan conflict spreading to the great powers, Britain would find it impossible to remain neutral; she had formed links with France and Russia to preserve the balance of power in Europe and no British government would be able to withstand pressure to join them.

Lichnowsky's report of the conversation tipped Wilhelm into a characteristic outburst. He filled the margins of the dispatch with crude objections: the balance of power was an 'idiocy' that would make England 'eternally into our enemy', and as if the veils had suddenly been lifted, 'the final struggle between the Slavs and Teutons will see the Anglo-Saxons on the side of the Slavs and Gauls'.[30] Repeating this formula in a note to his Foreign Minister, he instructed him to find allies wherever he could in south-eastern Europe and Turkey, and summoned the chief of his naval *Kabinett*, Admiral von Müller, together with Tirpitz and the chief of the Naval Staff and von Moltke, Chief of the Great General Staff of the army. Von Müller recorded in his diary the gist of what was said at the meeting, and there are three other accounts from officers who learned of the conference at second hand. All agree on the main points: Wilhelm opened with an account of Haldane telling Lichnowsky, no doubt at Grey's instigation, that Britain would unconditionally come to France's aid in a great-power war. Von Moltke then said he believed war unavoidable so 'the sooner [it came] the better',[31] at which Tirpitz said he would prefer a postponement for one and a half years until the enlargement of the Kiel Canal and a U-boat harbour and fortifications on Heligoland were completed. Moltke retorted that the navy would not be ready even then. One of the second-hand reports stated:

> The Kaiser agreed to a postponement only reluctantly. He told the War Minister the following day only that he should prepare a new large army Bill immediately. Tirpitz received the same order for the fleet . . .
>
> The Kaiser instructed the General Staff and the Naval Staff to work out an invasion of England in grand style. Meanwhile his diplomats are to seek allies everywhere . . .[32]

It is remarkable that the Balkan crisis that precipitated the First World War occurred in just under twenty months from the date of this meeting – within two months of the time Tirpitz had asked for to complete his preparations – and as remarkably about the time Fisher had always predicted for the Battle of Armageddon. Such precise timing was no doubt a coincidence, yet the accounts of the December 1912 meeting show that Wilhelm and his army staff deliberately set a course for war within a measurable time, their rationale or justification being that they needed to pre-empt French and particularly Russian army increases, which would leave the German army inferior. This is made even plainer by the policies resulting from the council. A Bill for the largest ever army increases in peacetime was prepared and passed the following year; the officially inspired press and other propaganda organs began a campaign to alert (or alarm) the German people to the danger they faced from the east, while the General Staff discarded the contingency planning for war in the east alone, leaving only one plan for Continental war, the 'Schlieffen Plan' to use the bulk of the army in a lightning assault on France through Belgium, deploying only minimal forces to guard the eastern borders against the Russians until France fell and units could be transferred east. Meanwhile, a Standing Committee on Mobilization Matters set up in December 1912 with representatives from both army and navy concerned itself particularly with the problem of feeding the population in the event of a British naval blockade cutting off imports of grain, and the president of the Reichsbank set about increasing the country's gold reserves by £20 million. He used a variety of measures including purchases of gold from abroad at a loss, to the bewilderment of observers in the City of London.[33]

Several German historians have sought to minimize the significance of Wilhelm's December 1912 War Council on the grounds that neither Bethmann nor any civilian ministers were present, and consequently it was not a decision-making meeting.[34] Yet this was imperial Germany; Wilhelm did not run his government like a British cabinet by compromise and mutual responsibility. He ran it through his separate civil and military *Kabinette*; and as commander-in-chief of the armed services, which lay outside the civil constitution in all respects except a measure of budgetary control, he would not have called a civilian minister into a military meeting. Bethmann was informed by von Müller in writing immediately after the council that a conference on the military-political situation had taken place and he (Bethmann) was required by the Kaiser to alert the people through the press to the great national interests at stake in the Balkans crisis so that if a war should break out they would know what they were fighting for.[35] He was not told of the decisions to prepare army and navy Bills since these were military matters. They would concern him only when they had to be guided through the Reichstag. Such was the disjointed nature of Wilhelm's 'personal rule'; such was the nature of the Prusso-German state in which the military wielded the power and set the tone and Wilhelm played the part expected of him as 'All Highest' warlord.

By 1914 the optimism of *Weltpolitik* had disappeared, replaced at the highest levels of German government by profound pessimism. Instead of opening the way to world influence, the fleet policy had antagonized Britain and swung her into the hostile camp. Meanwhile, to the east, Russia with her vast population appeared to have recovered from humiliation in the Japanese war and the subsequent revolution and was embarked on a massive expansion of her army combined with strategic railway construction, which, when complete, would undermine the whole basis of the Schlieffen Plan by enabling the rapid build-up of troops on Germany's eastern borders. In May 1914 von Moltke told the German Foreign Minister that when Russia completed her armament programme in two or three years the military superiority of the Dual Alliance would be so great he did not know how they might still cope with them, and he saw no alternative to a preventive war while they could still 'more or less pass the test'.[36]

German anxieties were heightened by the condition of their principal ally, Austria-Hungary. The empire was a brittle fusion of nationalities, many with separatist tendencies encouraged by pan-Slav or other subversive or terrorist movements. Of most immediate concern was pan-Serb agitation directed from the independent Balkan state of Serbia to Serbs within the empire. The chief of the Austro-Hungarian General Staff, Conrad von Hoetzendorff, had long advocated a strike against Serbia to root out the poison at source, and in spring 1914, with incipient rebellions in the provinces of Croatia, Bosnia, Herzogovina and Dalmatia, he repeated this view to Wilhelm and von Moltke as well as to his own authorities several times.[37] The problem with such a course was that the Balkan states, recently freed from the rule of Ottoman Turkey, had become a target for Russian expansion and Serbia was a Russian client; consequently any move against her would certainly be opposed by Russia. This had been made plain that year by the Tsar's Foreign Minister: for Russia, Serbian integrity was 'une question de vie et de mort'.[38]

The Serbian issue was equally vital for Austria-Hungary, both for the internal cohesion and prestige of the empire and for its status as a great-power counterweight to Russia in the Balkans. On 28 June 1914 tensions in this cockpit of power rivalries were stretched to breaking point: the Archduke Franz Ferdinand, heir to the throne of Austria-Hungary, and his wife were assassinated while visiting Sarajevo, provincial capital of Bosnia, and the killer was part of a team of young revolutionaries who had crossed over the border from Serbia with this intention. They had been armed by Serb Military Intelligence, whose chief was a zealous campaigner for a 'Greater Serbia' and belonged to a secret terrorist organization called the Black Hand. The necessities of the Austro-Hungarian state and the German Great General Staff fused. In Vienna the Foreign Minister swung round to Conrad's view that Serbia must be brought to heel by force of arms; in Berlin von Moltke knew he had the perfect pretext to strike against the Dual Alliance before the Russian army became too large to handle; for if Austria marched on Serbia, Russia would be drawn into the field and it needed only Germany to support Austria to trigger war between the rival Continental blocs. At the most recent joint staff talks with the Austrians in May he had assured Conrad that Austria would not have to face the Russian army alone for long: 'We hope to be finished with France within six weeks from the commencement of operations, or at least to have got so far that we can transfer our main forces to the east.'[39]

Wilhelm's immediate reaction to the assassinations was outrage. He was racing his yacht at the Kiel regatta when the news was signalled and he cancelled all further events. By this date the conditions agreed at his military council of December 1912 had for the most part been fulfilled: the army had been increased to optimum peacetime strength; it was not possible for internal political reasons to add more divisions.[40] The enlargement of the Kiel Canal had been completed. The people had been alerted to danger from the east and a remarkable thaw had taken place in relations with Britain. As an outward sign officers and men of the 2nd Battle Squadron of the British Home Fleet were participating and enjoying German hospitality at the Kiel regatta. For Wilhelm and his government the big question remained: would Britain's Liberal government with its several committed pacifists enter a Continental war?

Whatever the doubts about Britain, by 5 July the issue of war had been resolved. Wilhelm told an envoy from the government in Vienna that Austria should deal firmly with Serbia and would have Germany's full support. That afternoon he convened a Crown Council attended by Bethmann and the Minister of War, after which Bethmann repeated to the Austrian envoy that if Russia intervened in Austria's dealings with Serbia, Germany would support her. It is known as the 'blank cheque'. It was, of course, a call to arms. No one doubted that Russia would intervene.[41] As John Röhl has put it: 'The decision for war against the three world empires of France, Russia and Britain was taken by a tiny group of men [in Berlin] who seem to have had hardly any idea of the shattering consequences that their decision would have for Germany, for Europe and for the world, right down to the present day.'[42]

Yet it was, perhaps, not so much a decision as release from the intolerable strains that had built up within the Reich during Wilhelm's reign, between the army and the opposing aspirations of the Social Democrats, between the Great General Staff and the Navy Office, between pre-industrial landholders and manufacturers, between the urge to Continental and world power and growing anxiety over Russian armed strength, between contradictory foreign policy goals that had led predictably to isolation. Wilhelm, Bethmann, and von Moltke had come to the end of their political and emotional resources; war was the lightning discharge that released them. For the decision, or flight into fantasy, was taken in the belief that war was inevitable and was noble. It was the mechanism through which in the struggle for existence between nations and empires the fittest imposed their superior culture on the less fit. It was Prussia's destiny.

The plot was hatched in utmost secrecy. Austria would issue Serbia with an ultimatum she could not accept; this would be held back until 23 July, when the French President and premier, due to visit Russia, would be at sea on their return voyage and out of touch. In the meantime outward normality would be maintained. Ministers and senior military and naval commanders of both Germany and Austria retired to their usual summer retreats and spas; Tirpitz's High Seas Fleet was prepared for its annual manoeuvres off Norway; Wilhelm departed on schedule for his annual Baltic cruise in the Royal yacht, *Hohenzollern*.

Behind the show for the outside world German ambassadors in the major capitals were briefed on the posture they should adopt when the ultimatum was delivered. The fleet was mobilized in secret; coal and oil stocks at the major bases were brought up to the 'prescribed war stock'; three new dreadnoughts were hurried towards completion, their ships' companies assembled from training ships. The Asiatic squadron under Vice-Admiral von Spee was instructed to 'keep in certain and constant communication' and in the Mediterranean the battlecruiser *Goeben* was ordered to Pola for boiler repairs and workmen were rushed from Germany to expedite the work.[43]

Tirpitz was left on the sidelines. He had said in April that he needed a further six to eight years before the fleet would be completely ready for war.[44] His protests were futile. His fleet policy had failed and there seemed no prospect of it ever succeeding. Von Moltke and the Great General Staff were calling the tune; Wilhelm and Bethmann had fallen into line.

As the date for the ultimatum approached tension among the conspirators mounted: Wilhelm was advised to continue his cruise lest a sudden return 'alarm the world'.[45] On 23 July Admiral von Müller aboard the *Hohenzollern* with Wilhelm noted in his diary, 'the excitement grows. Fleet has established radio contact with us. Today the ultimatum is going to be handed over'.[46]

In London, Paris and St Petersburg the assassinations in Sarajevo had receded into the past, and Lloyd George spoke in the House of Commons that day of a new feeling on the Continent. 'Take a neighbour of ours' — code for Germany — 'our relations are very much better than they were a few years ago.'[47] He was jolted from this rosy view at Cabinet when a messenger brought in a note detailing the terms of the Austrian ultimatum to

Serbia, and Grey read them aloud. After the meeting Churchill went to the Admiralty and drafted measures to meet the anticipated crisis. Later, at dinner, he sat next to the Hamburg shipowner Albert Ballin, who had been sent by Bethmann to sound out likely British reaction to the outbreak of Continental war. Churchill told him it would be a great mistake to assume that England would do nothing.[48] Bethmann later put much the same proposition to the British ambassador in Berlin: Germany had no desire to 'crush' France in any conflict that might arise, and provided British neutrality were certain, every assurance would be given to the British government that Germany aimed at no territorial acquisition at the expense of France. Asked about the French colonies, he said he was unable to give similar guarantees. Grey read the ambassador's report of the conversation with despair. Clearly Bethmann felt war imminent. But how could he propose a pact that would reflect so badly not only on British honour but on the government's instinct for preservation? Attempting to convene a conference of the great powers to localize the Balkan dispute, he rejected Bethmann's proposal out of hand: 'It would be a disgrace for us to make this bargain with Germany at the expense of France – a disgrace from which the good name of this country would never recover.'[49] He could still not make an unequivocal declaration of support for France, nor give Bethmann an unequivocal warning of British participation because of the strong pacifist wing in the Liberal Cabinet.

Austria pre-empted Grey's proposed conference by declaring war on Serbia. Russia mobilized to support her client state. Germany mobilized in support of Austria, but since the General Staff had discarded the plans for war against Russia alone the majority of German divisions prepared to move west against France. Bethmann dashed off a peremptory note to France and followed it with a declaration of war. When Tirpitz asked him why, he raised both arms despairingly. 'Because the army want to send troops over the frontier.'[50] Tirpitz was reminded of a drowning man. Wilhelm's nerve had already cracked. Perceiving that Britain, France and Russia had plotted to force him to support Austria in order to use the Serbian crisis as pretext for a war of annihilation against Germany, he committed the nightmare to paper: '. . . we are either basely to betray our ally and leave her to the mercy of Russia . . . or as a reward for keeping our pledges get set upon and beaten by the Triple Entente as a body, so that their longing to ruin us completely can finally be satisfied . . .'[51]

There is no need to look farther for the immediate cause of the First World War. Wilhelm ruled the fastest-growing power in Europe. All lines of authority led up to him. In this final cry of despair at the situation he had done so much to create he exposed his pathological incapacity for objective judgement.

Finally, it was the exigencies of the Schlieffen Plan which enabled Grey to overcome Cabinet objections to what he had always regarded as a moral obligation to support France. When on 2 August Germany presented Belgium with an ultimatum to permit the passage of troops through Belgian territory and the King of Belgium appealed to Britain for support, all but the most committed pacifists in the British government dropped their objections to siding with the entente, and Grey was at last able to bring his views to the country through Parliament. He told the Commons he would like the House to approach the crisis 'from the point of view of British interests, British honour, British obligations, free from all passion as to why peace has not been preserved'. After pointing to Britain's 1839 treaty obligation to preserve Belgian integrity, and reading out the appeal from the Belgian King, he came to the crux of his argument:

> I do not believe for a moment that at the end of this war, even if we stood aside and remained aside, we would be in a position, a material position, to use our force decisively to undo what had happened in the course of the war, to prevent the whole of the west of Europe opposite to us – if that had been the result of the war – falling under the domination of a single Power, and I am quite sure that our moral position would be such as to have lost us all respect.[52]

He carried the House, and afterwards composed a simple ultimatum giving Germany forty-eight hours to cease the invasion of Belgium, failing which she would find herself at war with Britain. It was timed to expire at midnight, 4 August. Churchill had already sent the Home (later Grand) Fleet north to its war station at Scapa Flow in the Orkneys, and issued orders for Sir John Jellicoe, the outstanding officer Fisher had groomed for command at the 'Battle of Armageddon', to succeed the ageing commander-in-chief. Against thirteen dreadnoughts at the core of Tirpitz's High Seas Fleet, Jellicoe had twenty-one with class for class more powerful guns. Churchill had maintained decisive British superiority against ferocious opposition in Cabinet, a feat that surely stands comparison with his single-minded leadership in the Second World War.

At 11 p.m. on 4 August – midnight in Berlin – he left the Admiralty building to walk the short distance to 10 Downing Street and report that the fleet was under war orders; he was buoyed by the feeling that his country was 'guiltless of all intended purposes of war'.[53]

For the moguls of the City of London, the feeling was rather of shocked incomprehension. During the crisis at the end of July stocks had fallen precipitately and several firms had failed. On 1 August the Governor of the Bank of England had represented to the government through the Chancellor that the financial and trading interests in the City were 'totally opposed' to Britain intervening in the war.[54] After the German invasion of Belgium and Grey's speech the anti-war stance appears to have been over-taken by a patriotic fervour sweeping the country.[55] Yet real anxiety remained, together with disbelief that the expectation of permanent peace built on the interlocking nature of global trade and finance could be shattered by such apparently inconsequential political causes. One City financier later recalled being 'incredulous that such an incredible thing as a European War should be allowed to break out'.[56]

Prime Ministers who drove British free-trade and anti-slavery policies, (*left*) Lord Palmerston, (*right*) William Gladstone; and (*below*) the power behind diplomacy – the British battle fleet, seen here at the time of the Crimean War

A Royal Naval corvette chasing an Arab dhow crowded with slaves in the Indian Ocean after the Atlantic slave trade had been suppressed. (*below*) Britain's first ironclad warship, HMS *Warrior* (1861). Among the finest ships ever built, she can be seen today restored to her glory at Portsmouth, England

President Abraham Lincoln with General George McClellan (*sixth from left*) and officers on 3 October 1862 after the Union victory at Antietam; next day Lincoln proclaimed the emancipation of slaves in the Southern states. (*below*) The duel between the ironclads USS *Monitor* and the Confederate *Virginia* (ex-USS *Merrimack*) in Hampton Roads, 9 March 1862

The prophet of sea power, Captain A. T. Mahan, USN (*left*), and a most fervent disciple, Theodore Roosevelt (*right*), Assistant Secretary of the US Navy, later US President. (*below*) USS *Oregon* (1896). One of the first three battleships commissioned in the US Navy, she took a decisive role in the battle of Santiago in the Spanish-American War of 1898

An artist's impression of Admiral Haihachiro Togo on the bridge of his flagship at the battle of Tsushima, 1905. Fire control and communication was by speaking trumpet. (*below*) Togo's flagship, *Mikasa*

Arthur Hungerford Pollen (*left*) and Captain Percy Scott, RN (*right*), pioneers of gunnery fire control systems which should have given the Royal Navy a decisive lead in long-range accuracy in the early twentieth century. (*below*) The product of the fire control revolution, HMS *Dreadnought* (1906), which rendered all pre-dreadnought battleships obsolete

Winston Churchill (*left*), First Lord of the Admiralty, and his informal adviser, Admiral Lord Fisher, originator of the *Dreadnought*, leaving a meeting of the Committee of Imperial Defence in August 1913

Kaiser Wilhelm II (*seated front*) with his civil and military advisers: von Bülow (*standing extreme left*), von Moltke (*third from left*), von Tirpitz (*seated extreme right*), Bethmann-Hollweg (*standing second from right*), von Hindenburg (*seated in front of him*). (*below*) The *Friedrich der Grosse*, German flagship at the battle of Jutland

12

War, Coronel and the Falkland Islands, 1914

U NTIL ALMOST THE last Wilhelm had believed the pacifists in the
British Cabinet would prevail. Britain's declaration overwhelmed
him. Close confidants were shocked by his tragic appearance in the early
days of August.[1] Bülow, recalled to the court after years in the wilderness,
found himself 'moved by his pallor, his haggard, almost unnerved look'.[2]
Wilhelm acknowledged no responsibility for the calamitous misjudgement. Nor did Tirpitz, who blamed the Great General Staff for staking all
on a quick victory over France, and Bethmann for trying to secure British
neutrality at the expense of his fleet, unable to see that only a navy as
strong as Britain's would allow Germany to break the British hold on
world power. 'This natural and only goal of the last two decades,' Tirpitz
was to write, 'could never be spoken aloud, but could only be held in
view for when Germany's trade and industry and colonies expanded
further.'[3]

Now Germany's overseas shipping and trade were paralysed, her
colonies defenceless against the Royal Navy's command of the oceans. To
add to his exasperation, he had no say in the employment of the fleet he
had created. This was the province of his rival service department, the
Naval Staff. He deplored their entirely defensive plans, which restricted the
fleet to the defended perimeter of the Heligoland Bight until the blockading British fleet had been reduced by 'numerous and repeated [submarine
and torpedo boat] attacks day and night'; only then was it to emerge
'under favourable circumstances' to give battle.[4]

Wilhelm approved the plans. He wanted *his* fleet preserved for use as a
bargaining counter in peace negotiations after the swift land victory promised by the Great General Staff. So, finally, he set his seal on the divergent
aims and strategies of the two services under his supreme command.

An important element of British oceanic control was her undersea telegraph network. By the final decades of the nineteenth century London was
connected by cable with all twenty-four principal British bases around the

world. Fisher, when called to the Admiralty in 1904, recognized the potential of wireless telegraphy to extend the coverage, and provided each base with its own wireless station able to communicate with ships at sea up to one hundred miles distant; two stations in Britain were given a range of over a thousand miles. This extension of the navy's global communication-information net allowed him to plan for an entirely new strategy of trade protection whereby cruisers and smaller warships on foreign stations were to be withdrawn and scrapped and replaced by fewer, but faster, more powerful armoured cruisers operating in 'flying squadrons' from strategic bases to orders from the Admiralty in London rather than local commanders. This was the true genesis of the battlecruiser.[5]

The new strategy required constant surveillance of merchant shipping and foreign warships and potential commerce raiders worldwide. Fisher had the Naval Intelligence Division (NID) organized for the purpose. Sighting reports from Lloyds signal stations and a host of other sources, amplified by predictions of future movements based on trade analysis and particularly coaling stations, were plotted daily on a large wall chart in what soon became known as the 'War Room' in the Admiralty Old Building. Besides trade protection, the plot provided data for interdicting an enemy's trade; and as conviction of Germany's hostile intent hardened, the Trade Division of the NID occupied itself analysing German shipping movements, overseas suppliers and the economic consequences of cutting off these supplies.[6]

Before long the complexity of information on the War Room chart made it necessary to confine the plot to home waters and furnish a second War Room with a chart for the rest of the world. In addition, attempts were made to decipher intercepted German naval signals. The officer leading the attack, Fleet Paymaster Charles Rotter, spent all his leave in Germany, mixing with German officers, but he failed to break in to the codes.[7]

Similarly the German service monitored British naval signals, and was equally alive to the potential of overseas wireless. The completion in 1914 of a huge transmitter at Nauen, near Berlin, which could reach another powerful station at Kamina in the German West African colony of Togo, allowed communication with other colonial stations in Kamerun (Cameroon), German East Africa (Tanzania) and German South West Africa (Namibia), as well as with ships in a large area of the South Atlantic. Stations in German Pacific islands served cruisers and merchantmen in eastern waters.

The British War Staff concerned with trade protection focused on the need to eliminate all these installations. Detailed planning began in July 1914, and shortly after the outbreak of war British troops from the Gold Coast, neighbouring Togo, moved over the border to destroy transmitters at Lome and Kamina, key to the Africa network, while telegrams to the governments of South Africa, Australia and New Zealand requested them to destroy enemy wireless stations in their areas as a matter of urgency.[8] Meanwhile, on the first night of the war five German undersea cables running down the English Channel from Emden to France, Spain, Africa and the Americas had been dredged up and cut.[9]

On 24 August, as the British Gold Coast force came within sight of Kamina, the Germans blew up the wireless masts and burnt their codes. Over the following weeks New Zealand and Australian forces seized or destroyed German Pacific island stations, and by the end of September the only enemy stations in operation were in German South West Africa. The last was silenced in May 1915.[10]

The Admiralty attack on German codes was now led by Sir Alfred Ewing, Director of Naval Education. His appointment had come about in a rather British way. Known to have an amateur interest in cryptography, he was walking to lunch at his club on the first day of the war with the Director of Naval Intelligence, who asked him whether he would set up a code-breaking section. He agreed. The historian of the section wrote later, 'It was assumed that he would have no difficulty in combining [his] two functions for the few months it was thought the war would last.'[11]

Contrary to traditional accounts, a study by Nicholas Hiley has shown that Ewing was not appointed to continue Charles Rotter's work on tactical naval codes, but to break into the long-wave strategic and diplomatic signals from Nauen.[12] He gathered a team composed mostly of schoolmasters from the naval colleges, Osborne, Dartmouth and Greenwich, who came to the task without previous experience and unsurprisingly, despite cooperating with a cryptographic section established by Military Intelligence, made no progress.

The break in to German codes came about by chance, assisted by German carelessness, when the Admiralty obtained copies of captured signal books. The first, *Signalbuch der kaiserlichen Marine* (SKM), was received in mid-October from the Russians, who had recovered it from a German cruiser in the Baltic after she ran aground in fog. The following month a copy of the *Handelsverkehrsbuch* (HVB), used by the German Naval Staff to communicate with merchantmen, also used in a superenciphered form within the High Seas Fleet, arrived from Australia, where it had been seized from a German merchant vessel. Finally, on

3 December the *Verkehrsbuch* (VB), containing the most secure German naval code, arrived in Ewing's office after being jettisoned by a German destroyer in action and subsequently dredged up accidentally by a Lowestoft trawler. These three prizes fell into Ewing's lap. It is significant that on receipt of the first he did not give it to his cryptographic team working on long-distance signals, but called in Rotter from the German section of the NID.[13] After some days Rotter realized that the code groups derived from the SKM were themselves subjected to a substitution cipher. Assisted by astonishing lapses in German signals procedure, he found the key to one cipher on 25 October – 'the reddest of red-letter days', Ewing called it later[14] – and the following week discovered the key used by the commander-in-chief of the High Seas Fleet. On 5 November he read an order in the C-in-C cipher soon after transmission detailing positions to be taken up by U-boats in the English Channel. The significance was obvious. The following day Ewing's cryptographers were moved into a room numbered 40 close by the War Room on the first floor of the Admiralty Old Building, and began monitoring German naval traffic in watches around the clock.[15]

From the first Room 40 was surrounded by the tightest secrecy. Only two copies were made of each decrypt; one was handed personally to the Chief of Naval War Staff (COS), the other to the Director of Naval Intelligence (DID), who had it entered in a log, then locked in a safe.[16] The new DID, Captain Reginald Hall, had a natural genius for intelligence work and presided over a great expansion of Room 40 and its functions. Direction-finding wireless stations were established along the east coast, enabling the position of any German ship sending a message to be fixed by cross-bearings and marked on the War Room chart; but it was the core work of analysing decrypts of routine signals which proved crucial. As Nicholas Lambert puts it: 'From December 1914 until November 1918, Room 40 provided the Admiralty with twenty-four-hour notice of all except one sortie by the German fleet, thereby giving the British sufficient time to raise steam and proceed to sea before the enemy had even left port.'[17]

Room 40 has been described as Britain's principal war-winning weapon.[18] Certainly decrypts, given the cover name 'Japanese telegrams', brought about every meeting or near-meeting between British and German heavy forces during the war.

The German service established a similar listening and decryption centre, *Entzifferungsdienst*, at Neumünster, south-west of Kiel, late in 1914. The location far from the Naval Staff in Berlin or fleet headquarters at

Wilhelmshaven indicated failure to foresee the significance of code-breaking under the new conditions of warfare, and it was a long time before the potential was realized.

The Admiralty's decision to maintain a distant rather than close blockade of the German coast came as a surprise to the Naval Staff in Berlin, invalidating their plans for reducing British battle-fleet strength by attrition before the 'decisive battle'. At first neither side was aware of its opponent's defensive policy and such was the emotional charge generated by Tirpitz's pre-war challenge that each anticipated immediate action. Everything wooden or inflammable was removed from the great ships – chairs, tables, wardroom sofas and pianos; curtains were sent ashore or dumped overboard; German crews even scraped off thicker encrustations of paint from sides and bulkheads. But with the fleets holding their distance at opposite ends of the North Sea no meeting was possible.

Britain reaped the strategic benefit. Troop transports carrying the British Expeditionary Force to France crossed the Channel unmolested. Meanwhile German overseas trade was cut off by the blockade of the North Sea exits. Only the Baltic remained open to their ships. The few German commerce raiders overseas facing British cruiser squadrons, or in Far Eastern and Pacific waters Japanese and in the Mediterranean French squadrons, did little serious damage to British trade. A War Risks Insurance Scheme instituted by the British government gave shipowners the confidence to operate virtually as normal.

Despite the Royal Navy's overall strategic grip it suffered an early tactical defeat which was to have the most profound consequences. The German Mediterranean Squadron, comprising the battlecruiser *Goeben* and a light cruiser, evaded a more powerful British squadron and escaped through the Dardanelles into neutral Turkish waters. There the ships should have been interned, but a war faction in the Turkish government wanting an alliance with Germany in order to pursue an aggressive policy against Britain in the Middle East colluded with the German ambassador in Constantinople to buy and transfer both ships to the Turkish flag. The German admiral, Wilhelm Souchon, was appointed commander-in-chief of the Turkish fleet and the German ships' companies exchanged their uniform caps for a fez. This failed to provoke the Western Allies into a declaration, so in late October the war faction contrived to send Souchon into the Black Sea with all battle-worthy units of the Turkish fleet to attack Russian ships and bases, and report the action afterwards as retaliation for a Russian attack. The provocation had the desired effect. Russia declared war on Turkey. Britain and France followed suit, and Bulgaria came in on Turkey's side, securing Austria's southern flank. It was a major blow for the entente powers, closing Russia to arms imports via the Mediterranean and dissipating her war effort.

At the same time the Royal Navy suffered a defeat in the Pacific. As with the failure to bring Souchon to action before he reached Turkish waters, the prime cause was poor judgement and confusing orders from the Chief of the Naval War Staff, Vice-Admiral Sir Doveton Sturdee, not the War Room plot or input from Room 40; indeed, a decrypt in early October had alerted the War Staff to the dangerous situation developing: Vice-Admiral Graf von Spee's East Asiatic Squadron headed by two modern 8-inch-gun armoured cruisers, which had been worked up over a two-year commission into crack shooting ships, was steering south-easterly across the Pacific towards South American waters[19] defended by a much weaker British squadron formed around two older 6-inch-gun cruisers manned by reservists hurriedly mobilized on the outbreak of war who had not yet fired their guns in practice. The commander, Rear Admiral Sir Christopher Cradock, was offered a pre-dreadnought battleship, *Canopus*, as reinforcement, but since she would reduce his squadron speed and make it impossible to bring Spee to action, Cradock stationed her at the Falkland Islands as an escort for colliers and ordered a heavy armoured cruiser to join him from the South Atlantic. The War Staff, aware of a German light cruiser operating in the Atlantic, countermanded his order. Consequently, when Cradock met Spee on 1 November some 50 miles off the coast of Chile on the latitude of Coronel, the outcome was hardly in doubt.

Cradock himself had no illusions. He was the beau ideal of a naval officer, a bachelor who lived for the service, and after the service for sport.[20] He knew when he sighted Spee's squadron that his ships were no match, but believed his orders were to seek and destroy the enemy, and instead of retiring as he could have done, he attempted to close to bring his lighter guns into effective range. Spee held off until favoured by the light of the setting sun which silhouetted the British ships while his own merged into the eastern darkness, then began practically undisturbed target practice. Within an hour Cradock's flagship was blown apart by a magazine explosion, and in another hour his second armoured cruiser was sunk. Spee's ships suffered only six hits and two men wounded.

Cradock and his ships' companies had upheld the glorious traditions of the Royal Navy, going down in unequal contest with their battle ensigns flying, yet the defeat was a serious blow to the mystique of Britain's long ascendancy at sea. The news arrived in London as a new Admiralty Board was settling in. Churchill had recalled Fisher as First Sea Lord at the end of October to revitalize the naval war.[21] Fisher's instinct was to send two battlecruisers to annihilate Spee; they had been built for just such a purpose. *Invincible* and *Inflexible* were fitted for foreign service in haste, sailing for the South Atlantic after only three days in dockyard hands with workmen still aboard. In command Fisher sent Sturdee, whom he blamed for the disaster off Coronel;[22] he had already relieved him of his post.

Flying his flag in the *Invincible*, Sturdee attached four armoured cruisers and two light cruisers on station in the South Atlantic, then headed for the Falkland Islands, arriving at the capital, Port Stanley, on 7 December. By extraordinary coincidence Spee arrived off Port Stanley the following morning. The German secret agent, von Rintelen, wrote after the war that Hall as DID had contrived the convergence by having orders sent to Spee in German code to proceed to the Falklands and destroy the wireless station at Port Stanley.[23] The dates do not fit. The *Verkehrsbuch*, which Berlin used to communicate with Spee, did not reach Room 40 until 3 December, only three days before Spee, having rounded Cape Horn, summoned his captains and told them he intended attacking the Falklands and destroying the wireless station, key to British communications in the South Atlantic. Spee was then outside wireless contact and had been for some days. The majority of his captains wished to avoid the Falklands; he nevertheless resolved to attack, believing the islands undefended. Here, perhaps, lies the key to Hall's actual involvement: namely planting false intelligence that the Falklands were not defended. The historian of Room 40 found post-war notes Hall had written for a lecture on intelligence and under the heading 'Propaganda': '1. To deceive the enemy in order to lead him to a certain course for which you are prepared (Falkland Islands) . . .'[24]

In view of the difficulties of finding enemy fleets or squadrons in wide ocean spaces experienced throughout centuries of sea warfare, it seems probable that Hall did influence Spee by disinformation. For Port Stanley was defended. The *Canopus* had berthed at the entrance to the inner harbour and set up an extemporized gunfire observation post in a hut ashore. She would have proved a formidable nut for Spee to crack.

Sturdee's battlecruisers were coaling when two of Spee's scouts were sighted early in the morning of 8 December; consequently it was two hours before his squadron could raise steam. Spee, meanwhile, shocked at the report of tripod masts in Port Stanley, infallible sign of British dreadnoughts, sheered off easterly. Unfortunately for him it was a fine day, the air so crisp and clear that visibility seemed infinite, and although he was hull down by the time Sturdee cleared harbour the dark smudges of his funnel smoke betrayed him. Sturdee hoisted 'General Chase!' conjuring glorious images from the French wars, and followed at full speed, reducing later to allow his slower cruisers to keep up.

By 12.50 he was within 17,000 yards of the rearmost of three light cruisers with Spee and made the general signal to engage. As the giant splashes from the 12-inch salvoes crept closer and straddled the unprotected vessel, Spee made the heroic decision for which he had no doubt prepared himself: ordering the light cruisers to scatter and head for South America, he turned north-easterly to head directly across Sturdee's track and draw his fire. Sturdee had anticipated the move and his own cruisers broke off in chase without a signal as he turned north-easterly to conform to Spee's new course and bring all guns to bear.

In the action now joined between the main battle units Sturdee had overwhelming material superiority: the shells from his 12-inch pieces had over twice the weight and destructive force of Spee's 8.2-inch shells and 3,000 yards advantage in range, 16,400 against 13,500 yards;[25] while he could make at least 3 knots more than the German cruisers and so choose his distance. Yet the vibration transmitted through the structure of the bat-tlecruisers at high speed shook the rangefinders, making it difficult to obtain accurate readings, and the gun-layers and spotting officers up the masts were hampered by thick funnel smoke blown down the range by a light wind from the north-west. The *Inflexible*, following in line astern of the *Invincible*, was especially afflicted as she had both her own and the flagship's funnel and gun smoke blowing across her line of fire. For most of the time her target, *Gneisenau*, following Spee's flagship, *Scharnhorst*, was completely obscured. The smoke made it equally difficult for the range-takers and gun-layers of the *Gneisenau* to see the *Inflexible*, and few hits were made by either rear ship. The *Scharnhorst*, however, gave a superlative exhibition of shooting. As the range came down inside 12,000 yards she straddled the *Invincible* and continued straddling and hitting repeatedly, causing Sturdee to ease away a few degrees to open the distance. At two o'clock, with 16,000 yards separating the forces, fire had ceased on both sides. At this point Sturdee's flagship had scored possibly one hit,[26] certainly no more, a lamentable performance caused by smoke and the Royal Navy's pre-war failure to practise long-range shooting at high speed or provide the necessary fire control apparatus.

Spee turned and ran south. Sturdee chased. By 2.45 he had closed to 15,000 yards and recommenced fire. Spee altered course across his track again to bring his guns into range, and Sturdee again conformed, although not as sharply, so accepting a gradually closing range as the duel continued in an easterly direction. By three only 12,500 yards separated them and Spee's cruisers opened with secondary batteries as well, the *Scharnhorst* especially making superb practice without, however, inflicting serious damage or casualties. Meanwhile, the heavier British shells with their flatter trajectory began to hit, bringing fire and destruction to both German vessels and deciding the action. By 3.30 Spee's flagship was listing and enveloped in smoke from bursting shells and internal fires, whose dull red glow could be seen through holes torn in her side; her upperworks were ravaged, both her masts and one of her funnels were shot away and two other funnels leaned against each other. The *Gneisenau* was also listing from a shell hole below the waterline which had flooded two boiler rooms and reduced her speed. Still both ships continued to fight those guns that had not been disabled, and to score hits.

The end came for the *Scharnhorst* at 4.17. Listing heavily, she rolled over and plunged bows first in an uprush of smoke and steam, taking Spee and his entire ship's company with her. No boats could be sent to the rescue since the *Gneisenau* continued the action. Crippled and facing both British battlecruisers and an armoured cruiser that had caught up with the fight, she refused to strike her colours, but fought on with enormous courage, firing sporadically for more than an hour before her commander gave orders to scuttle her.[27] She heeled over to rest on her side, allowing those of her crew who had escaped the storm of explosions, flames and flying splinters to walk on to her other, upturned, side. Immediately the British ships steered towards her at speed, but she sank before they could reach her, leaving survivors struggling in the icy water. All boats that could still float were lowered and almost two hundred men were rescued.

By contrast with the huge loss of life from Spee's ships, the *Invincible*, which had taken twenty-two hits, had one officer lightly wounded, the *Inflexible* one man killed and three wounded from three hits,[28] corroborating Pakenham's report after Tsushima that when 12-inch guns were firing the effects of lighter pieces passed unnoticed.[29]

Of Spee's light cruisers, two were overhauled and sunk by Sturdee's armoured cruisers; one escaped, but was hunted down and destroyed on the Chilean coast the following March. By then all German cruisers overseas at the outbreak of war had been accounted for and only two armed merchantmen remained to prey on commerce. Both were forced into US ports by lack of coal the following month and interned.

Victory at the Falklands was a timely and terrible retribution for Cradock's defeat off Coronel, and was the most decisive naval battle of the war, restoring British prestige and removing the most dangerous threat to oceanic trade. As the official historian put it, 'in little over four months [from the outbreak of war] the command of the outer seas had been won'.[30] It was not an unblemished triumph. In view of Sturdee's overwhelming superiority and the ideal atmospheric conditions, it had taken a very long time and huge expenditure of ammunition to dispose of Spee's two armoured cruisers. Between them, the British battlecruisers had fired 1,174 shells. In part this was due to Sturdee's insistence on the *Inflexible* following close in the wake of his flagship, whose smoke blinded her fire control team, in part to more fundamental faults in British gunnery and delays in fitting Percy Scott's director firing system. Vickers engineers were aboard Sturdee's flagship for this purpose, and he had controlled the battle from the *Invincible*'s director tower, still lacking sighting apparatus.[31] Afterwards he asked the Vickers engineer overseeing the installation how much the action would have been shortened with his director sights.

'Well, sir, you finished them off in time for dinner. With the director you would have finished them in time for tea.'[32]

This was probably near the mark.

13

The Dogger Bank, 1915

---•---

THE DIFFICULTIES EXPERIENCED by Sturdee's gunners at the Falklands were encountered on the next occasion British battlecruisers saw action. It was January 1915. Room 40 deciphered wireless orders to Rear Admiral Franz von Hipper commanding the battlecruisers attached to the High Seas Fleet to conduct a reconnaissance to the Dogger Bank fishing grounds off Newcastle-upon-Tyne, destroying any enemy light forces he found and examining or seizing fishing boats suspected of acting as scouts for the Royal Navy. The Admiralty planned a warm reception. Vice-Admiral Sir David Beatty commanding the battlecruisers at Rosyth on the Forth was ordered to sea to intercept; destroyer flotillas from Harwich were to rendezvous with him, and Jellicoe at Scapa Flow was directed to bring the Grand Fleet south.

The following morning, the 24th, off the Dogger Bank, the trap was sprung. Hipper, realizing he had run into more than a light scouting group, turned south-easterly for home, working up to 23 knots, the most his rear ship, *Blücher*, could make; she was not a true battlecruiser, but the last of the German armoured cruisers before the dreadnought revolution. Beatty chased, signalling for ever greater speed, finally an impossible 29 knots. With heroic exertions from the stokers below, his three newer battle-cruisers, *Lion* (flag), *Tiger* and *Princess Royal* reached 27 knots or a shade over and began stretching away from two older ships of the 2nd Battle Cruiser Squadron in the rear under Arthur Pollen's former adversary, now Rear Admiral Sir Archibald Moore, flying his flag in the *New Zealand*.

The scene appeared set for a brilliant victory. The morning was clear. Beatty was gaining steadily on Hipper and he had the more powerful and longer-range armament. His three leading ships mounted 13.5-inch guns, whereas Hipper's flagship, *Seydlitz*, and her next astern, *Moltke*, had 11-inch, the third in line, *Derfflinger*, 12-inch, matching Beatty's two older ships under Moore. The *Blücher* in the rear had a main battery of 8.2-inch pieces. With her thinner armour and slower speed she had little defence against her pursuers.

Beatty opened against her with single ranging shots from 20,000 yards shortly before nine. By 9.07 his three leading ships were also in action. Hipper's ships were unable to reply at this great distance. When they did some minutes later they were handicapped by a north-easterly breeze blowing their own funnel and gun smoke down the range. The *Lion* made one hit on the *Blücher* before shifting her sights up the German line as she closed, and when, at 9.35, Moore's flagship, *New Zealand*, was able to come into action against the *Blücher*, Beatty signalled his ships to engage their corresponding vessel in the enemy line. The *Lion* herself soon straddled Hipper's flagship and at 9.43 hit her with an armour-piercing shell that penetrated the 11-inch steel of her after-turret barbette. Red-hot splinters entered the working chamber beneath, igniting cartridges whose flash fire shot upwards and downwards through the ammunition hoist shafts. Men in the munitions handling room sought escape through the handling room of the adjoining turret, but as they unclasped the door fire followed, igniting more cartridges and enveloping that turret complex too. Flames and thick smoke rose from both after turrets high above the masts. Both were wiped out, all the men serving the guns incinerated.[1]

In this first phase Beatty's force had the better of the action, scoring two hits on the *Seydlitz*, reducing her main armament by 50 per cent, two on the *Derfflinger* and one on the *Blücher*, against just two hits on the *Lion*,[2] which caused only superficial damage. Since no peacetime practices had been conducted at such ranges and speeds and the only ship equipped for director firing, *Tiger*, was so newly commissioned her control team had had no realistic practice, it was a remarkable feat. For as at the Falklands the tremendous vibration transmitted through the ships' frames at speed made it hard to take accurate ranges, and conditions inside the turrets were not conducive to good aim. As described by a turret officer in the *New Zealand*, his gun-layers and trainers attempted to lay on the left-hand cloud of smoke on the horizon without being able to see the target ship or indeed any ship; the sighting lenses were dulled by spray and cordite smoke after each round and had to be wiped clean; spray was driving in through the observation slits and water poured through the sighting hoods and washed down into the working chamber below. All hands were soaked and cold.[3]

After the first hour, as the range came down further, the battle began to slip from Beatty. The captain of the *Tiger*, mistakenly believing that both Moore's ships were in action, had joined the *Lion* in firing at Hipper's flagship, leaving the second in line, *Moltke*, unengaged, and both she and the *Seydlitz* with her two forward turrets concentrated on the *Lion* and began

to hit. By 10.01 Beatty's flagship had suffered two heavy blows, the first disabling one gun, the second punching through the side armour and causing
flooding. At 10.18 a further two shells hit the armour belt below the
waterline almost simultaneously, shaking the ship so much it was thought
a torpedo had struck. The flooding increased and damage to a pipe carrying fresh water to the port boiler feed tank allowed salt water to
contaminate the boiler water.[4] The German fire was now so rapid and well
directed the Lion's decks were deluged by green water from close shell
splashes and Beatty began zigzagging to throw out the enemy fire control.

At 10.30 the Blücher was dealt a crippling blow. A shell penetrated her
armoured deck and burst in the central ammunition passage – a feature
unique to her – igniting thirty-five cartridges whose flash flame shot up the
loading shafts of two forward turrets, wiping out their crews and destroying both gun positions.[5] The concussion also damaged her engines and
steering gear; her speed fell away and she sheered off to port.

The Lion, despite zigzagging, was still ploughing through a concentrated
barrage which was raising such close fountains that Beatty's flag captain,
Ernle Chatfield, described it as 'like steaming through a waterfall & our fire
was much affected as gunlayers could not see nor could spotters in the Fore
Top . . . '[6] Ten shells struck the ship in under twenty minutes. Flooding
increased, short-circuiting the last dynamo and leaving her without electricity, even for the wireless, while sea water entering the port boiler feed
tank forced the engineers to shut down the port engine. As speed dropped
to 15 knots and the Tiger surged past, and after her the Princess Royal and
New Zealand, a submarine periscope was reported off the starboard bow.
There was no submarine, but Beatty thought he had seen a periscope too
and ordered an eight-point (90 degree) turn to port, all ships together, followed by 'Course north-east', both made with flag hoists. As the Lion fell
farther astern and he saw all his ships heading towards the Germans' wake,
he tried desperately to direct them back into the fight by signalling 'Attack
the enemy's rear'. The flags for 'Course north-east' were still flying from
the only other halyard not cut by splinters, and both were shortly hauled
down as he wanted to follow with an injunction to 'Keep closer to the
enemy', the nearest his flag lieutenant could find to Nelson's 'Engage
the enemy more closely'.[7]

Now, with the flagship out of the battle, Moore found himself in command; when the Lion's two hoists were hauled down together he deduced
that Beatty meant him to attack the rear enemy ship, Blücher, then bearing
north-easterly, and led the whole force against the already crippled and
blazing cruiser. Hipper had intended a destroyer attack on the British line

to relieve her, but as Beatty's ships had swung to port his destroyers were left out of position and he took the sensible decision to save the rest of his squadron by racing for home, leaving the cruiser to her fate. Like Spee's men at the Falklands, the *Blücher*'s company resisted heroically, and it was not until 12.30 that the ship finally rolled over and sank. By then Hipper was safe.

The result was a strategic victory for the Royal Navy, which had asserted command of the North Sea by driving Hipper home, but those in the know were bitter about Moore's lack of fighting instinct. As Beatty wrote to Jellicoe, 'It is inconceivable that anybody should have thought it necessary for 4 B.C.s 3 of them untouched to have turned on the *Blücher* which was obviously a defeated ship and couldn't steam while 3 others also badly hammered shd have been allowed to escape.'[8] He and his officers overestimated the damage they had inflicted.[9] Disregarding multiple hits on the helpless *Blücher*, Hipper's three battlecruisers had received only six hits, three each on the *Seydlitz* and *Derfflinger*, none on the *Moltke*, while they made six hits on the *Tiger* and sixteen on the *Lion*, knocking her out of the action.[10]

British gunnery officers were not aware of the extent of their failure, but disappointment at missing what had seemed a golden opportunity for eliminating the enemy battlecruiser squadron spurred debate about fire control. It was clear that the system of rate-finding based on observations of range and bearing was inadequate: 'Range-finding was insufficiently accurate, and frequent alterations of course rendered any results so obtained too late to be applicable.'[11] Beatty's flag captain, Chatfield, the most influential gunnery officer in the battlecruiser force, was profoundly impressed by that period when the *Lion*'s gun-layers and control officers aloft had been unable to see their target through the fountains raised by enemy salvoes, and concluded that 'Rapidity of fire and *Short Shots*' – enabling spotting officers to see the splashes – were essential. He wrote to a naval friend: 'Whoever gets the biggest volume of fire that is hitting will gain the ascendancy & keep it as the other fellow can't see to reply . . . The *Lion* fired too slowly hampered by all the orders and restrictions on the subject . . .'[12]

These 'orders and restrictions' were designed to eliminate the danger of a flash fire spreading along the ammunition chain, as had occurred in the *Seydlitz* and *Blücher*, by restricting the number of cartridges exposed during the loading cycle. His drive to speed up the rate of fire in the battlecruiser force contributed to disaster on the next occasion Beatty and Hipper met in battle.[13]

14

The U-boat Offensive, 1915

————•————

THE MARITIME STRATEGIES that had brought Britain victory in earlier wars had been rendered difficult by two unrelated factors: the growth of the United States into a mighty industrial power, and the commitment of the British army to fight alongside the French on the Continent. The first threatened the potency of commercial blockade to cut the enemy from overseas supplies, since the United States was the most powerful neutral supplier and it was imperative not to antagonize her; while the engagement of British troops in Belgium and France effectively ruled out peripheral military campaigns supported by the Royal Navy to draw off enemy troops from the main theatre.[1]

Despite this, in 1915, with the belligerent armies locked in trenches stretching from the Channel coast to Switzerland, just such a diversionary attack was launched on Turkey via the Dardanelles. The campaign had glittering objectives: to relieve Russian troops fighting a Turkish advance to the Caucasus, pre-empt Turkish designs on Egypt and the Suez Canal, recruit more states to the Allied cause in the Balkans, take Constantinople and open a warm-water route between the Black Sea and the Mediterranean for Russian exports of grain and much-needed imports of arms and ammunition from the Western powers; for with the Baltic blocked by the German fleet her only overseas outlet was Archangel in the far north, which was ice-bound for half the year.

For Churchill, the enterprise promised a more belligerent role for the Royal Navy, hence for himself. Denied the troops necessary for a combined operation, since none could be spared from the western front, he initiated a purely naval assault with a fleet of mainly older pre-dreadnought battleships. These were to force their way up the straits after knocking out forts at the southern entrance. It proved beyond them. By the time this became apparent sufficient troops had been found for a landing on the Gallipoli peninsula, but the Turks under the overall command of a Prussian general had been given ample time to prepare defences and the Allied forces, once ashore, were unable to break out from their beachheads.

When a single German U-boat arrived in the Aegean after a voyage around the Atlantic coast of Europe and sank two battleships on successive days the fleet was withdrawn to the safety of harbours in the Greek islands. Deprived of support from the ships' heavy guns, the Allied troops were held in costly trench warfare reminiscent of the western front. Finally, at the end of the year, the peninsula was evacuated.

Churchill and Fisher had both gone long since. Fisher had never agreed with Churchill's exclusively naval assault on the straits, and the consequent friction between the two had caused his resignation in May. In the resulting political crisis Asquith formed a coalition government with the Conservatives and replaced Churchill with Arthur Balfour as First Lord of the Admiralty. The failure weighed heavily on Churchill, and on his reputation; more importantly it was of crucial significance for the war. Had the straits been opened to supplies for the Russian war effort, had Balkan states been encouraged to join the Allies, the strategic stalemate in the west would surely have been turned. Success had been close; it was denied by the British army's commitment to the Continental battleground.

Meanwhile, fear of alienating the neutral United States had blunted Britain's commercial blockade. She had herself colluded in weakening this weapon the previous century after the Crimean War by acquiescing in the Declaration of Paris, denying belligerents the right to seize non-contraband goods from neutral ships;[2] her subsequent foreign policy stance of non-intervention in European affairs with the likelihood of permanent neutral status had led the Foreign Office in the direction of even greater protection for neutral cargoes. The question had come up at Arms Limitation Conferences in 1907 and had led to the Declaration of London (1909), which limited contraband to war materials. Britain had not ratified this, however, and since the United States had never ratified the Declaration of Paris, the legal status of neutral cargoes was left curiously vague.

During the first months of war the British government sought to tighten the rules by declaring foodstuffs, fertilizers, vehicles and forage conditional contraband liable to capture if destined for the armed forces of an enemy; the following month coal was added to the list. The effect was weakened by the simultaneous creation of a Contraband Committee to decide which cargoes should be condemned. Since the committee deliberated in secret and was anxious not to aggravate the United States, many cargoes destined for the enemy which would have been condemned by a properly constituted prize court were allowed through. At the same time, in the neutral ports of Holland, Denmark, Sweden, Norway and Italy, a vast network of dummy import agencies sprang up to channel goods from overseas to Germany and Austria; Rotterdam and Copenhagen became the chief entrepôts for these supplies.[3]

Meanwhile, the German High Command, denied their planned quick victory in the west, and with the fleet locked in port by Wilhelm's preservation order, resolved on a U-boat campaign to knock Britain out of the war by cutting her supply lines. They could not declare a blockade since they had too few U-boats to make it 'effective' under the terms of the Declaration of Paris.[4] Instead, on 4 February 1915 they declared the seas around the British Isles a 'War Zone'; from the 18th any merchant vessel within the zone would be liable to destruction.

The Declaration of Paris also prevented the British government from declaring a blockade, since under modern conditions of mine and torpedo warfare surface patrols could not be maintained off enemy ports. The Royal Navy nonetheless maintained a de facto blockade from a distance, in the English Channel and off the north of Scotland, where armed merchant ships patrolled the stormy waters, stopping merchantmen and sending suspected vessels in to Kirkwall in the Orkneys for examination. The situation for neutrals trading with the belligerents was reminiscent of that during the final phases of the Napoleonic Wars, forbidden by both sides from trading with the other. Then British naval control had ensured that neutrals adhered to the British cause whether they liked it or not.[5] Much the same now occurred. The British system of stopping ships and sending them in for examination was so successful that the majority of neutrals called voluntarily at Kirkwall to avoid delay, or if sailing via the English Channel at the Downs; and by July 1915 no neutral shipowner knowingly accepted goods whose ultimate destination was Germany for fear of the disruption to the voyage and costs consequent on discovery.[6] Baltic trade was an exception. The threat of mines and torpedo craft in the narrow entrances to that sea made it too dangerous for the British fleet; consequently the German navy dominated and ensured that Sweden and Swedish trade were tied to the German war effort.

The real difference between the rival undeclared blockades was that whereas British surface patrols conducted stop-and-search in the time-honoured way without endangering passengers or crew, U-boats could not do so: they lacked boats or sufficient men for boarding parties and if they surfaced risked exposing themselves to gunfire should the merchantman be armed, as more and more were; hence the German threat to 'destroy' ships in the declared War Zone. The United States responded with a strong note pointing out that destroying vessels without first establishing their belligerent nationality or the nature of their cargo constituted an unprecedented and indefensible violation of neutral rights which would be very hard to reconcile with a continuation of friendly relations between their two countries.[7] The German government backed away: US vessels would not be attacked if recognized as such. This opened a wide hole in the German blockade since the obvious stratagem for British ships was to fly a US flag in the danger zone, a recognized ruse of war. It also left US citizens and cargoes on British vessels exposed to the threat of attack without warning. This was soon made tragically explicit.

On 1 May the Cunard liner *Lusitania* sailed from New York for Liverpool with 159 Americans among her passengers, and in her holds boxes of artillery shells, fuses and rifle ammunition. US industry was harnessed to the Allied war effort. On the afternoon of the 7th, off the south coast of Ireland, the liner was struck on the starboard side by a single torpedo fired by an unseen U-boat. The commander who had launched the weapon had no knowledge of the ammunition the liner was carrying, but he had identified her correctly and believed, incorrectly, that she was an armed merchant cruiser, and as such a legitimate target. The explosion of the torpedo was followed by a second, more violent eruption, possibly caused by the ignition of fine coal dust in the bunkers, which had been ripped open by the torpedo.[8]

She quickly took a heavy list which made it difficult to launch lifeboats, then sank so rapidly that hundreds of men and women were plunged into the sea from her decks. As a result, only 764 of her 1,196 passengers and crew were saved in the few lifeboats that floated, or were picked up from the sea later by fishing vessels. Over 1,200 lost their lives, among them 94 children. The news was greeted with outrage around the world, apart from Germany, where the sinking was lauded as a triumphant response to Britain's policy of blockade. For the Western Allies it was confirmation of the barbarity they were fighting. A leader in *The Times* of London expressed the abhorrence felt in a nation insulated so long from great wars and their attendant atrocities: '. . . the sinking of the *Lusitania* . . . makes finally clear, even to the doubters and indifferent, the hideous policy of indiscriminate brutality which has placed the whole German race outside the pale . . . No nation has ever sunk so low in infamy . . .'[9]

The American public was equally affected by what seemed an unprecedented massacre of innocents on the high seas; 128 of those lost were Americans. Many anticipated that the United States would enter the war, but there were strong isolationist sentiments, US industry and finance were profiting hugely from the country's neutral status by supplying the Allies, and the President, Woodrow Wilson, convinced himself that his people had a higher mission to the world. An idealist inspired by religious faith – like Gladstone, who was one of his political models – he revealed more of his own inflexible moralism than the realities of United States history when he told his countrymen in the wake of the disaster that America was a peaceful nation and must set a special example. Behind the scenes he did his utmost in negotiations with the German government to persuade them to return to the established rules of cruiser warfare.

The U-boat campaign Wilhelm had been persuaded to endorse was his most irresponsible wartime folly and was to lead irresistibly to Germany's defeat. There were too few boats to cause serious dislocation to British supply lines and, as Bethmann argued, it antagonized neutrals, especially America, on whose exports they relied. It could be said that the use of U-boats was forced on the Naval Staff by the steel grip of the Grand Fleet, which left them no other option. It was nonetheless reckless beyond belief. It tipped the balance of American opinion against Germany even before the *Lusitania* disaster. In the early months of war Britain had been the target of bitter US protests against the tyranny of her cruiser patrols, but after the declaration of the U-boat offensive, particularly after the loss of lives from the *Lusitania*, Germany replaced Britain as principal maritime villain. The change gave the Foreign Office confidence to draw the undeclared blockade tighter. A statistical department analysing the quantities of different commodities shipped to neutrals around Germany allowed officials to set quotas based on the 'normal' or supposed peacetime requirements of each country; anything considerably above this level was confiscated.[10] And during a serious crisis in US – German relations following the loss of three more American lives from the White Star liner *Arabic*, torpedoed and sunk off southern Ireland in August, the Foreign Office at last felt able to court the wrath of the US South by placing cotton on the absolute contraband list, liable to seizure if destined ultimately for the central powers.

The following month, under intense pressure from President Wilson, the U-boat campaign was abandoned. It was revived again in February 1916. A driving compulsion was fear of a long war. The British 'blockade' had begun to bite. High food prices and shortages were causing dissatisfaction among the people and the prospect of the British exerting ever tighter controls on neutral ships and cargoes was alarming. Moreover, the Chief of the Great General Staff, Erich von Falkenhayn, like Napoleon in the great war of the previous century, had identified Britain as the hub of the enemy alliance, holding it together. Since she could not be reached across waters controlled by the Royal Navy he proposed to knock her out with an 'unrestricted' U-boat campaign against her supply lines – attacking merchant shipping without stopping and searching – while mounting a simultaneous offensive against an objective on the French sector of the western front whose retention was so important they would be compelled to throw in every man they had to defend it. The choice fell on Verdun as the killing ground, and some 1,200 artillery pieces were positioned around the salient.

The bombardment opened on 21 February, followed later by infantry probes. The French defended and countered, and over the following months to the end of the year almost as many German as French soldiers were cut down, pulped, dismembered, buried in shell holes or driven out of their wits in this defining cauldron of industrial war. French army morale survived as narrowly as German; but Verdun was held. Today it is a haunted place. Hellish memory is preserved outside the city in the overgrown outlines of trenches zigzagging through cratered ground shadowed by trees; and in an open space before a great ossuary rank upon rank of crosses mark the unidentified dead, tokens of the warrior ethic.

The simultaneous proposal for reviving U-boat warfare against British supply lines met stiff resistance from Bethmann, and for the same reasons as before. Yet there were now many more U-boats than at the start of the earlier campaign[11] and the Naval Staff had calculated that they could sink 160,000 tons of merchant shipping a month, three times the tonnage that could be replaced in British yards. A new Chief of the Naval Staff, Henning von Holtzendorff, was confident that with all restrictions on their use removed Britain could be brought to her knees within six months before American entry into the war could affect the outcome.[12] Nevertheless, orders to U-boat commanders were heavily influenced by regard for American sensitivities: they were to act in accordance with prize law to ensure the safety of crews, and on no account were passenger ships to be attacked. Only armed merchantmen and troop transports could be sunk without warning.

However carefully framed the orders, commanders had only a limited view through their periscope and little time to interpret what they saw. On 24 March 1916 the lieutenant in command of *UB29* in the English Channel near Dieppe sighted a steamer whose decks were crowded with people. Assuming she was a transport carrying troops to France, he torpedoed her without warning. She was a French cross-Channel packet carrying 325 passengers, including several Americans, four of whom were lost. Over the next weeks President Wilson composed what was in effect an ultimatum to Berlin that unless the Imperial Government abandoned its indiscriminate

U-boat campaign against passenger and cargo vessels the United States would have no choice but to sever diplomatic relations.[13] Falkenhayn advised intensifying the U-boat war, but Wilhelm bowed to Bethmann's caution and orders were issued to all boats to operate against commerce in accordance with the prize regulations of stop-and-search. A new commander-in-chief of the High Seas Fleet, Admiral Reinhard Scheer, considered this too dangerous in view of the numbers of armed merchantmen, and recalled the boats instead. Thus the second attempt to force Britain out of the war by cutting her supplies ended. Scheer now planned to use the U-boats as originally envisaged to whittle down the number of dreadnoughts in the Grand Fleet until he could engage Jellicoe on more equal terms. The scene was set for the climacteric naval engagement of the war and the only meeting between dreadnought battle fleets in history.

15

Jutland, 1916 (Beatty)

SCHEER HAD WORKED under Tirpitz on the fleet expansion pro-grammes and he shared all the great man's pugnacious attitude towards breaking Britain's hold on naval power by any means, including unre-stricted U-boat warfare. Like all German naval officers, his eyes had been fixed on *der Tag* when the two fleets would meet in the critical battle for the future of the world. Despite this, when he took command of the High Seas Fleet in January 1916 its numerical inferiority ruled out direct resort to battle – quite apart from Wilhelm's prohibition. Instead, he resolved on a strategy of raids on the English east coast with his battlecruisers to draw out detachments of the British fleet over U-boat traps, with his battle fleet held in the offing to entrap separated enemy squadrons. This required air-ships for reconnaissance to prevent his ships being cut off by Jellicoe, who took the Grand Fleet out at intervals across the North Sea.

> . . . pictures rise to memory of scenes that will never be repeated . . . the whole horizon covered with warships as the Grand Fleet moves at 17 knots in a SE'ly direction on one of its periodic sweeps . . . in four divisions in line ahead, disposed abeam, the columns being about a mile apart . . . moving as one under one controlling will.[1]

With the assurance of aerial observation, Wilhelm found the courage to give the strategy his consent, and as U-boats from the commerce war returned Scheer drew up plans for a raid on Sunderland, near Newcastle-upon-Tyne, only 100 miles from the Firth of Forth, where Beatty's battlecruiser force was based. Such a provocation could not fail to bring him out in pursuit. He dispatched the U-boats from 17 May to form lines of observation across the North Sea prior to taking up stations on the 23rd off the Firth of Forth, the Moray Firth and the exits to the Grand Fleet base at Scapa Flow in the Orkneys; three were specialized minelayers to lay mines across the expected tracks of the British forces as they emerged. The date for the sortie passed with his airships grounded by wind and bad weather, however, and these conditions persisted. Finally, as the U-boats neared the end of their sea endurance with no possibility of aerial reconnaissance, he cancelled the operation, in its place ordering a sortie northwards up the coast of Denmark to the Skagerrak, so securing himself against the possibility of Jellicoe cutting across his line of retreat. As with the previously planned raid, Hipper was to lead with the battlecruiser squadron and light cruisers; he would follow at a distance with the High Seas Fleet.

The British Naval Staff were already alert. Room 40 had picked up the departure of the U-boats, and as they had not attacked anything since, it was clear that something was afoot. On 28 May Room 40 deciphered a signal ordering the High Seas Fleet to a state of readiness, and on 30 May to assemble in the outer roads of the Jade. At noon that day, Jellicoe and Beatty were each warned by landline telegraph that the High Seas Fleet would probably put to sea early on the 31st.[2] Further decrypts indicated that Scheer would proceed northwards up the Danish coast, and at 5.40 Jellicoe and Beatty were ordered to sea to concentrate their forces 100 miles east of Aberdeen.

They sailed late that evening, untroubled by mines, unseen by U-boats. Early the following morning, 31 May, Hipper left the Jade and steered north for Heligoland; after him Scheer came out with the High Seas Fleet. An hour later, as day was breaking on the other side of the North Sea, *U32*, some seventy miles east of the Firth of Forth, sighted light cruisers of Beatty's advanced screen and fired two torpedoes. Both missed, after which she dived to avoid being rammed. Coming up afterwards she saw two of Beatty's battlecruisers and reported them by wireless, together with two cruisers and destroyers, steering east-south-east. Later she reported picking up British wireless signals indicating that two large warships or squadrons with destroyer flotillas had left Scapa Flow. These reports did not reach Scheer until 7.30 and 8.30 a.m. respectively, by which time he was out of the Heligoland Bight and steering for Horns Reef off the coast of Jutland. Eighteen minutes later he received a third report from a U-boat stationed off the Moray Firth: eight dreadnoughts with light cruisers and destroyers steering north-easterly.[3] He could not have known it, but this was the 2nd Battle Squadron sailing from Cromarty to join the main body of the Grand Fleet from Scapa Flow. Scheer found nothing in the disparate movements to suggest that Jellicoe was out in force; on the contrary, they seemed to offer 'the possibility that our hope of meeting with separate enemy divisions was likely to be fulfilled'.[4] His U-boats had failed in both their tasks of injuring and reporting the enemy, hardly surprising in view of their restricted range of visibility and the zigzag courses the British forces steered from first light.

Through the morning the opposing forces steamed towards their appointment with fate unaware of the movements of the other, Hipper leading up the coast of Jutland with Scheer following some fifty miles astern, Beatty and Jellicoe separated in latitude by about a hundred miles heading easterly on converging courses towards a rendezvous off the Skagerrak. For the British it seemed just another uneventful sweep; and this was confirmed for Jellicoe and Beatty at 12.48 when they received a signal from the Admiralty: 'No definite news of enemy. They made all preparations for sailing early this morning. It was thought Fleet had sailed but directionals place flagship in Jade at 11.10 am. GMT. Apparently they have been unable to carry out air reconnaissance which has delayed them.'[5]

It was crass staff work: the cryptographers of Room 40 knew that the German commander-in-chief transferred his flagship's call sign to a shore station at the mouth of the Jade when he left harbour; but no one in Room 40 had been asked. Jellicoe, with all sense of urgency removed by the message, continued towards his rendezvous with Beatty at an economical speed of 15 knots to conserve fuel. A more serious consequence was that later, when he learned that Scheer *was* at sea, he lost all confidence in further Admiralty intelligence.

The afternoon was glorious. Officers and men not on watch basked in the May sunshine as Beatty's battlecruisers reached the end of their easterly sweep, whereupon they were due to turn north for the rendezvous with Jellicoe. Beatty had an infinitely more powerful force than he had commanded at the Dogger Bank. In addition to the 13.5-inch-gun ships of the 1st Battle Cruiser Squadron, *Lion* (flag), *Princess Royal*, *Queen Mary* and *Tiger*, and the 12-inch-gun 2nd Battle Cruiser Squadron, *New Zealand* and *Indefatigable*, he had four fast 15-inch-gun battleships of the 5th Battle Squadron of the Grand Fleet, *Barham* (flag), *Valiant*, *Warspite* and *Malaya*. They had taken the place of his 3rd Battle Cruiser Squadron, which had been sent to Scapa Flow for gunnery practice and was now with Jellicoe.

Extraordinarily, Beatty appears not to have made any attempt to meet the commander of the 5th Battle Squadron, Rear Admiral Hugh Evan-Thomas, during the week since his ships had joined his flag, nor had Evan-Thomas been given the 'Battle Cruiser Fleet Orders'.[6] Beatty was a devoted disciple of Nelson, but it is impossible to imagine Nelson similarly ignoring an admiral newly joined with a division of ships. The deeper significance of the omission lies in the light it throws on Beatty's overconfident leadership. It affected his whole command. Battlecruiser officers and men thought of themselves as an elite cavalry of the sea, their charismatic leader a hero in the mould of Nelson; indeed, his personal courage and dash had been proved on many occasions, lately at the Dogger Bank, where he had conducted the battle from above the armoured conning tower exposed to shells and flying splinters as the enemy found the range.

Yet his ships' shooting was poor. It had been shown up by Hipper at that encounter, although the extent of the failure had been concealed by the conflagration in the *Seydlitz* and the subsequent signals muddle. More recently it had been revealed in battle practice shoots.[7] As with Chatfield, the lesson Beatty had drawn from the Dogger Bank was the supreme importance of rapid fire. In December he had told Jellicoe that instead of trying to improve accuracy, he wished to use the next firing practice to develop yet greater rapidity of fire so that 'we could pulverise him [the enemy] early'.[8] Naturally this had become the goal for his ships' gunnery teams, and the battlecruisers had broken fleet records for speed of fire. To accomplish this his officers had not only encouraged the dangerous practice of stacking ammunition at several stages in the loading cycle, disregarding the restrictions designed to prevent the spread of cordite flash fires, but had failed to improve their rangefinding and fire control. When in spring 1916 the battlecruisers carried out their next practice shoots the scores were disappointing, the *Tiger*'s so bad her captain was censured.[9]

By 2.15, when Beatty turned his force north towards the rendezvous with Jellicoe, Hipper had reached the same latitude and was only 50 miles to his east off Jutland. The wing vessels of their cruiser screens were a mere 16 miles apart, just below the curve of the horizon from each other. Splitting the distance between was a neutral merchantman. Both sides' cruisers closed to investigate and, sighting each other, wirelessed contact reports and engaged. Beatty and Hipper wheeled towards the gunfire.

Evan-Thomas's 5th Battle Squadron was then some five miles northwest of Beatty and at that distance his yeoman of signals could not read the *Lion*'s flags. Beatty's rear ship, *Tiger*, did not repeat the signal by searchlight, no doubt because the change of course had placed her farther from the 5th Battle Squadron than the *Lion*. Meanwhile, the watch officer in Evan-Thomas's flagship, *Barham*, expecting a turn to the port leg of a zigzag, assumed this was the meaning of the flags and made the turn. Consequently the battleships steered away from the battlecruisers and the 5 miles' separation between the squadrons almost doubled before someone in the *Lion* realized that Evan-Thomas was disappearing to the northwest, and the order was repeated by searchlight.[10]

At about the same time Beatty received reports of smoke 'as though from a fleet';[11] realizing he had come upon at least the German battlecruisers, he turned his force south-east, then east to cut them from their base, finally north-east towards the cruiser action, and increased speed. In the *Barham*, Evan-Thomas managed to make up some of the distance his squadron had lost by cutting across the arc of Beatty's turning courses; while 65 miles to the north Jellicoe cancelled the zigzag the Grand Fleet was following and worked up to 18 knots.

Battlecruiser men enjoying the sunshine on deck or an after-lunch nap below were startled into life by the bugle 'Action Stations!' followed by 'Double!' Ladders shook beneath pounding feet. Hands numbered off at their stations with a sense of shared anticipation mixed with clutches of apprehension, placed gas masks, goggles, lifebelts to hand, checked communications and instruments. In the turret complexes loading machinery was tested, ammunition cages filled and reported to the transmitting station at the base of the foremast through which all orders and corrections from the gunnery control team in the foretop and gun-laying and training angles from the director sight would be relayed to the guns. All the battlecruisers were now fitted with directors. In sickbays and casualty clearing stations surgical instruments, tourniquets, bandages, dressings and drugs were laid out ready for use, and stretchers readied. Fire parties uncoiled hoses and wetted the decks; repair parties assembled splinter mats, leak-stopping gear and timbers for shoring up weakened plates, while in the engine rooms spare parts and tools were distributed in readiness for emergency repairs. The decks pulsed to increasing revolutions and large, white battle ensigns shook in the wind of the ships' progress.

Similar preparations for battle were made in the German squadron as the forces converged. Hipper, in the latest 12-inch-gun *Lützow*, steered west, then north-west, and ordered 25 knots. He was followed by the 12-inch-gun *Derfflinger* and three older 11-inch-gun ships, *Seydlitz*, *Moltke* and *Von der Tann*. Visibility was marginally better for the Germans as the western horizon was brighter, and at 3.22 they sighted the tripod masts of Beatty's 2nd Battle Cruiser Squadron, *New Zealand* and *Indefatigable*, stationed some three miles off the *Lion*'s starboard bow. Two minutes later the smoke from the German squadron was seen from the *New Zealand*, but it was not until almost 3.30 that Beatty made out his opponents.[12] He ordered an alteration of course by flags to east by north to cut astern of them on their north-westerly course, but again this was not read in the *Barham*, and the 5th Battle Squadron continued north-easterly for five minutes before the signal was repeated by searchlight. As the battleships turned they were trailing some eight miles off the *Lion*'s port quarter.

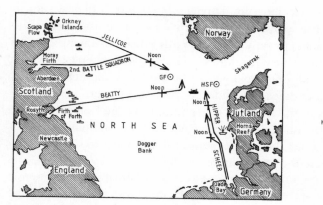

BATTLE LOCATION MAP

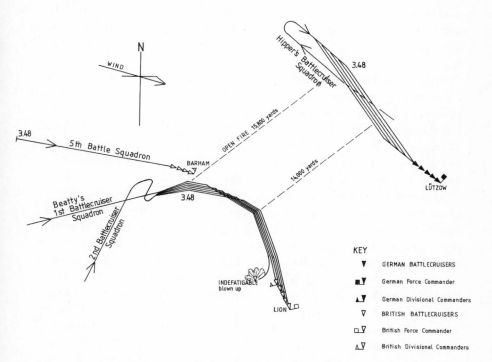

Jutland: Opening of Battlecruiser Action, 31 May 1916

The next few minutes were critical. The distance between the opposing squadrons was some 24,000 yards, closing rapidly towards gun range – over 23,500 yards for Beatty's 1st Battle Cruiser Squadron, 21,000 yards for Hipper's newest 12-inch-gun ships. Hipper reacted with cool professionalism. Reversing course with a starboard turn – away from the enemy – to a south-easterly heading to draw Beatty towards Scheer, following 46 miles to the southward, he formed his ships on a north-westerly line of bearing so that the funnel and gun smoke would be blown by the light westerly breeze down the disengaged side, reduced speed to 18 knots, ordered distribution of fire from the left, that is counting from the head of Beatty's line, and, as the British ships advanced within the maximum range of Beatty's 13.5-inch guns, altered two points towards them to south-south-east in order 'to close the enemy more rapidly'.[13]

By contrast Beatty's deployment was careless. Perhaps he was merely overconfident. Probably he was just being Beatty. From childhood he had been a hard rider to hounds and in his naval career had won rapid promotion by daring leadership. As his flag captain, Ernle Chatfield, wrote: 'He had a love of doing everything at high pressure and high speed. This was not a pose: it was entirely characteristic; whether at sea or in the hunting field . . .'[14]

Now, with Hipper in his sights, he was determined to prevent him escaping a second time. He had ordered the 2nd Battle Cruiser Squadron to form in the wake of his own squadron and reduced to 24 knots to facilitate the manoeuvre at almost the same time as Hipper had begun the turn to reverse his course. To have reduced speed further to allow Evan-Thomas to catch up would have been against all his instincts; in any case, he considered his six battlecruisers more than a match for Hipper's five. Consequently he failed to concentrate the potentially overwhelming power of his force for the crucial opening phase. Instead, he closed the German squadron so precipitately he came within gun range while they were steering across his 'T' on their south-easterly course. He was forced to order a turn to starboard to allow all his guns to bear, and at the same time he signalled a north-westerly line of bearing in an attempt to free his ships from the smoke of their next ahead. A minute later he directed his two leading ships, *Lion* and *Princess Royal*, to prepare to concentrate on the leading enemy. This implied that the third ship, *Queen Mary*, was to take the second German as her target, the fourth the third German, and so on down the line.[15] All three signals were made by flag, and it is not surprising in view of the dense emissions of funnel smoke that the order was not taken in by all ships.

Beatty had informed Jellicoe by wireless of the enemy battlecruisers and their course soon after first sighting them at 3.35, and as his squadron surged towards them, captains endeavouring to spread on a line of bearing before turning to the new east by south course, he was busy on the bridge with another message for Jellicoe. Chatfield was on the compass platform above, fretting. The distance to the enemy had reduced well inside 13.5-inch gun range and he wanted to open fire. He sent a messenger down to the flag lieutenant 'to advise Beatty that the range was closing rapidly and that we ought almost at once to be opening fire'.[16] The answer came back that the vice-admiral was engaged in an important message to the commander-in-chief. Chatfield told the gunnery officer to fire and ordered the '5' flag to 'Engage the enemy' broken out from the yard above. At the same moment Hipper opened fire. Red points of flame rippled down his line. It was thirty seconds after 3.47. The thunderclap of the *Lion*'s first salvo followed. Beatty appeared on the compass platform.

Shells from both sides winged over their targets. Beatty's headlong approach had brought the range down to little over 15,500 yards, but the *Lion*'s rangefinder operators were reporting 18,500 yards, the *Lützow*'s 16,800 yards and the *Derfflinger* and *Seydlitz* next astern 16,400 yards. The *Moltke*, fourth in the German line, had the most accurate range and her first salvo threw up fountains only 300 yards short of her target, *Tiger*. The *Tiger* herself opened a minute later with her forward turrets only – such was her heading as she tried to form line of bearing – and a range of 18,500 yards. Her next ahead, *Queen Mary*, opened after her with a range setting over 17,000 yards, then her next astern, *New Zealand*, at 3.51 with 18,000 yards.[17] By this time, with the *Indefatigable* at the tail of Beatty's line not yet in action, the *Lützow* had found the *Lion*'s range and hit her, and the *Moltke* had scored two hits on the *Tiger*.

British rangefinder operators were still overestimating the range and fire control teams underestimating the closing rate. In addition gunnery officers were hampered by the smoke of destroyers struggling up the engaged side of the battlecruisers to take station with the rest of their flotilla ahead of the *Lion*, as well as by the funnel and gun smoke of the great ships themselves and by huge fountains from enemy near-misses erupting around them. They called down spotting corrections to be applied on the Dreyer Table in the transmitting station below, but Beatty was altering continuously to starboard, first to parallel Hipper's course, then to open the range, which had fallen to 14,000 yards by 3.54. It was far from the steady course for which the Dreyer Table had been adopted, and impossible to obtain reliable rates of change.

Meanwhile, the failure of some ships to take in Beatty's fire distribution signal had resulted in targeting mix-ups: the *Lion* and *Princess Royal* were concentrating on Hipper's flagship, but the third and fourth ships, *Queen Mary* and *Tiger*, had each taken their opposite number in the German line, *Seydlitz* and *Moltke*, leaving the second German battlecruiser, *Derfflinger*, unengaged. Since the *New Zealand* interpreted the fire distribution correctly, both she and the *Tiger* had the *Moltke* as their target; their salvoes were passing over, however, and leaving that ship's fire control team at undisturbed target practice. They made superlative use of the opportunity, repeatedly straddling the *Tiger* and scoring a further seven hits in as many minutes, putting her 'Q' and 'X' turrets out of action and starting numerous fires between decks.

The *Derfflinger,* also enjoying undisturbed practice, was not so effective, and it was not until 3.58, as the range began opening, that she succeeded in hitting the *Princess Royal* with two 12-inch shells. Striking simultaneously, they penetrated 6-inch side armour below 'B' turret and the bridge and shook the whole ship so violently that the main rangefinder and gunnery control position was put out of action. Two minutes later a third 12-inch shell entered and burst on the upper deck forward, spreading death and destruction and starting more fires.

At the same time, at the head of the line, the *Lion* was caught in a succession of accurate salvoes from the *Lützow*.

> . . . all around us huge columns of water, higher than the funnels, were being thrown up as the enemy's shells plunged into the sea. Some of these gigantic splashes curled over and deluged us with water. Occasionally, above the noise of battle, we heard the ominous hum of a shell fragment and caught a glimpse of polished steel as it flashed past us . . .[18]

Shells falling short burst on impact with the sea and threw myriad small fragments of steel high in the air. The *Lion*'s gunnery officer would hear them 'fall on the thin sheet-iron roof of the control top, making a noise like a heavy fall of hail'.[19] When a shell struck the armour belt it felt from inside the control top on the foremast as if the ship was lifted by a giant hand and thrown down again angrily. The *Lion* was hit four times by the *Lützow* in this devastating phase from 4 to 4.03, bringing the total number of hits on her to six and on Beatty's squadron as a whole to at least twenty-three.[20] The Germans had suffered no more than six hits, two on the *Lützow* during this latter period around four o'clock, both probably from the *Lion*, although possibly one came from the *Princess Royal*;[21] two, possibly three hits were made by the *Queen Mary* on the *Seydlitz*, and near the rear the *Tiger* at 4.02 at last succeeded in landing a hit below the water on her tormentor, *Moltke*.

Hipper had won the opening round decisively, not only in number of hits but in their effect. The *Lion*'s 'Q' turret between the after funnels had been knocked out; the *Princess Royal* had been forced into 'B' turret gunnery control and the *Tiger* had been reduced to two working turrets, although one of those disabled was subsequently brought back into action. On the German side only the *Seydlitz*'s main battery had been reduced. The second shell from the *Queen Mary* to hit her had burst while penetrating the 9-inch armour of her after super-firing turret and sent white-hot fragments into the working chamber, wrecking the turret's elevating and training gear and igniting four charges. The flash fire killed all in the chamber and handling rooms below and badly burned most of those in the gunhouse above, but precautions taken after the disastrous ammunition fire at the Dogger Bank prevented the flames spreading beyond the turret.[22]

Hipper ascribed the ascendancy he had achieved in this phase to the British not opening fire until within his effective gun range, 15,000 to 16,000 yards. It was also due to the superiority of the German stereoscopic rangefinders and the steady course Hipper steered during the opening minutes, allowing his gunnery officers to establish the closing rate and find the range rapidly. Moreover, unlike Beatty's officers, they had enjoyed perfect visibility free from smoke down the range.

Of all the hits Beatty's flagship had received, the most dangerous was that on 'Q' turret. The shell from the *Lützow* had struck above the left gun port, blowing off a front portion of the roof plate and killing or grievously wounding all in the gunhouse. The turret officer, Major F. J. W. Harvey of the Royal Marines, was mortally wounded, his legs crushed, but his sergeant with him in the partitioned-off 'silent cabinet' control position, although badly burned, was able to walk, and Harvey sent him to the captain to report the turret out of action. He appeared on the bridge capless, bloodstained and dazed and was directed to the compass platform above, where Beatty and Chatfield, both soaked by spray from near-misses, surveyed the action. On hearing his account, Chatfield ordered the transmitting station to have 'Q' magazine flooded. This undoubtedly saved the ship, for the fire in the gunhouse spread down to the working chamber, igniting the cartridges in the gun-loading cages and sparking a flash fire which jumped down through the trunk. Had the magazine not been closed and flooded the flash would have entered and the flagship would surely have been blown apart, as others were shortly.[23]

First was the rear ship, *Indefatigable*. She was fighting a duel with the rear German, *Von der Tann*, which was firing both main and secondary armament, and at 4.02 landed at least two shells from one salvo on her upper deck aft. Rear Admiral Pakenham on the compass platform of the *New Zealand* immediately ahead saw her draw out of the line to starboard, seemingly settling by the stern. The *New Zealand*'s torpedo officer laid his glasses on her as she swung out some five hundred yards on the starboard quarter, smoke pouring from her after superstructure. She was hit by a further two shells as he watched, one on the fo'c's'le, one on 'A' turret, both exploding on impact. There were no visible effects until perhaps half a minute afterwards when the ship began to erupt, starting from forward.

> The main explosion started with sheets of flame, followed immediately afterwards by a dense, dark smoke, which obscured the ship from view. All sorts of stuff was blown high into the air, a 50-foot steam picket boat, for example, being blown up about 200 feet, apparently intact, though upside down.[24]

Two of her men were picked up later by a German destroyer; 1,117 went down with her.[25]

The range had been opening gradually since Beatty's turns away from Hipper. At 4.10 they were 21,000 yards apart, and Hipper ceased fire. By this time a new element had entered the battle. Evan-Thomas had been steaming at full speed on an easterly course astern of Beatty's battlecruisers and at 4.05 had at last been able to make out Hipper's squadron some ten miles in the east-south-east. He swung round to a southerly course to follow Beatty and at 4.08 his flagship opened fire on the rear German, *Von der Tann*. His was among the best shooting squadrons in the fleet and, although there was little but the high, white stern wave of the enemy to range on, the *Barham* hit the *Von der Tann* within a minute of opening at 19,000 yards. Evan-Thomas then ordered his leading ships, *Barham* and *Valiant*, to concentrate on the fourth in the German line, *Moltke*, leaving the *Von der Tann* to his two rear ships, *Warspite* and *Malaya*. The battleships' 15-inch gun salvoes fell so close about the rear Germans that their hull plates were shaken by the detonations, and both captains began evasive zigzagging. Despite this, the *Moltke* was hit at 4.16 and twice more within the next ten minutes.

Beatty, heartened by the powerful intervention, altered south-easterly towards Hipper and ordered his destroyers to attack the enemy van. While they raced ahead into position to launch the assault, the battlecruiser action resumed, rising to another furious crescendo as the range closed inside 16,000 yards. From each line the salvoes fired by their opponents showed up as red flashes from beneath the layered funnel smoke; afterwards the shells could be seen against the sky. 'They appeared just like big bluebottles flying straight towards you, each time going to hit you in the eye; then they would fall, and the shell would either burst or else ricochet off the water and lollop away above and beyond you, turning over and over in the air.'[26]

The noise was deafening, the concussion from the four-gun salvoes interspersed with 'the shrieking of the enemy's shells falling over or short, and throwing up great sheets of spray',[27] or bouncing high above 'with a whizz sound . . . whilst splinters seemed to creak through the air . . .'[28] From the German line the *Lion* disappeared in a haze of smoke, and the *Derfflinger*'s gunnery officer shifted sights to the *Queen Mary*, which now appeared to be second in the line. At about 4.21 he hit her on 'Q' turret, putting the right gun out of action, and shortly afterwards went into rapid fire, including secondary armament. At 4.25, when the range had fallen to 14,400 yards,[29] a further two shells struck near the *Queen Mary*'s forward turrets. A vivid red flame shot up from her fore part: 'Then came an explosion forward, followed by a much heavier explosion amidships. Black debris flew in to the air and immediately afterwards the whole ship blew up with a terrific explosion. A gigantic cloud of smoke rose, the masts collapsed inwards . . .'[30]

The catastrophe was played out before the eyes of those in the conning tower of the *Tiger*, following some four hundred yards astern of the stricken vessel.

As they [two shells] hit, I saw a dull red glow amidships, and then the ship seemed to open out like a puff ball, or one of those toadstool things when one squeezes it. Then there was another dull red glow somewhere forward, and the whole ship seemed to collapse inwards. The funnels and masts fell into the middle, and the hull was blown outwards. The roofs of the turrets were blown 100 feet high, then everything was smoke, and a bit of the stern was the only part of the ship left above water.[31]

The destroyer *Nicator*, racing up between the lines to take station ahead, had just come up with the *Princess Royal* when the *Queen Mary* blew up. A few minutes earlier she had been abreast of the *Indefatigable* as that ship had exploded. When the smoke cleared from this second eruption and there was nothing to be seen of the great ship they had passed minutes before, those in the destroyer who witnessed it 'seemed quite stunned with horror at the suddenness of the thing, and at the turn that the action seemed to have taken'.[32]

Of the *Queen Mary*'s complement of 1,286, only 20 were picked up later from the sea.[33]

The gunnery officer of the *Derfflinger* pulled his gaze from the monstrous pillar of black smoke marking the battlecruiser's last position and shifted his periscope sight up the line to the *Princess Royal*, straddling her almost immediately and hitting with one shell. The damage was slight, but a signal rating on the compass platform of the *Lion* immediately ahead, seeing the ship disappear completely beneath the smoke of the explosion and fountains raised by the other shells of the salvo, reported her sunk, upon which Beatty made the remark to Chatfield that has since passed into legend, 'There seems to be something wrong with our bloody ships today!'[34]

Few more hits were made by either side as Hipper, beset from astern by the 5th Battle Squadron and from ahead by Beatty's destroyers forming for attack, made successive turns away to the east, opening the range rapidly. At the same time he launched his own destroyers from his disengaged side to attack the British line. Instead the opposing flotillas, approaching each other at a combined speed of over sixty knots, engaged in a furious, twisting gun battle between the lines. Torpedoes were launched but the only hit was on a German destroyer. Another German and two British destroyers were left sinking or dead in the water before the smaller, more lightly armed German vessels retired. Having avoided all torpedoes with his turn away, Hipper altered back to his southerly course, closing the range on Beatty, who was steering south-easterly, and the two lines resumed firing. A few British destroyers that failed to take in a signal for recall flying from the *Lion* made further attacks as Hipper steered south and one torpedo hit the *Seydlitz*, ripping a hole 40 feet long below the armour belt on the starboard side forward and causing substantial flooding, without, however, endangering the ship or even affecting her speed, such was the internal compartmentalization of German dreadnoughts.

Meanwhile the battle had changed suddenly. Beatty's 2nd Light Cruiser Squadron spread some two miles ahead of the *Lion* had sighted Scheer's battlefleet steaming north towards them. It was the first time in the war German battleships had been seen from the British side. They were in line ahead beneath a haze of smoke, their light grey paint reflecting almost white in the westering sun. The cruiser flagship, *Southampton*, flashed the electrifying news by searchlight to the *Lion* at 4.33 – shortly after the start of the destroyer melee – and five minutes later sent an 'urgent priority' wireless message to Jellicoe and Beatty: 'HAVE SIGHTED ENEMY BATTLEFLEET BEARING APPROXIMATELY SE COURSE OF ENEMY N'.[35]

The battleships were soon visible from the *Lion*, and Beatty made a general signal by flags to turn 16 points (180 degrees) to starboard in succession. The cruisers did not comply. They pressed on resolutely to probe the composition of the enemy fleet and the *Southampton* sent another model scouting report by wireless at 4.48 before turning back. The 5th Battle Squadron following 8 miles astern of the battlecruisers also failed to comply with the order to turn, once again because the flags could not be seen and the signal was not repeated by searchlight. Thus Beatty, having reversed course northwards, found Evan-Thomas's four battleships still bearing down towards him. They passed on opposite courses, Evan-Thomas closing the head of the German battle fleet at a combined speed of 40 knots, before turning north. By then he was 2½ miles south of Beatty and well within range of the leading German battleships, some of which shifted their sights from the fleeing light cruisers to his ships.[36] Hipper's battlecruisers also shifted target to his squadron as Beatty moved off northwards; the *Derfflinger* hit his flagship four times, causing extensive internal damage, fires and casualties before Hipper turned his squadron to a northerly course to chase Beatty.

It was twelve minutes past five. The battle had undergone a revolution. Having been lured by Hipper almost under the guns of the High Seas Fleet, Beatty was now leading Hipper and Scheer together into Jellicoe's grasp.

16

Jutland, 1916 (Jellicoe)

J ELLICOE HAD INCREASED speed at 4 p.m. after receiving a message from Beatty that he was engaging the enemy battlecruisers. He was making 20 knots, the best he could reasonably expect from his fleet, steering south-easterly. After receiving the *Southampton*'s 4.30 sighting report of Scheer's battleships he informed the fleet that the enemy's battle fleet was coming north, and at 4.51 sent a message to the Admiralty, 'FLEET ACTION IMMINENT'.

The armoured core of the Grand Fleet comprised twenty-four dreadnought battleships formed in six divisions, each steaming in columns abreast across a 5-mile front. With screening cruisers and destroyer flotillas the formation stretched as far as the eye could see, volcanic grey shapes under layers of smoke with a myriad of white ensigns, 'large and small, silk and bunting, hoisted wherever halyards could be rove'.[1]

Jellicoe in his flagship, *Iron Duke*, led from the centre at the head of the third column from the left. Seconding him astern was the new 15-inch-gun *Royal Oak*. He had one other 15-inch-gun ship, one mounting 14-inch guns, eleven, including the *Iron Duke*, with 13.5-inch guns and ten with 12-inch guns. He also had the 3rd Battle Cruiser Squadron of three 12-inch-gun battlecruisers under Rear Admiral Sir Horace Hood, which had come north for firing practice – in return for which Beatty had acquired Evan-Thomas's fast battleship squadron. Hood had a roving commission on the eastern wing of the fleet, and had advanced some twenty miles ahead of Jellicoe to be in position to intercept any German retreat via the Skagerrak.

Jellicoe's thoughts can only be imagined. This was the supreme moment for which he had been chosen and for which he had worked single-mindedly in the ordnance branch of the Admiralty and at sea for a decade. He was the outstanding gunnery professional. He had devised the top-secret strategem to overwhelm the Germans at their own favoured medium to close range, and had exercised his fleet rigorously in bringing a decisive concentration of fire to bear in the shortest time. Recently he had been forced to rethink. It had become evident on the one hand that the High Seas Fleet would not leave the safety of its defended perimeter, on the other that German long-range gunnery was a good deal better than expected. During 1915 he had ordered experimental firings at ranges from 10,000 to 17,000 yards with target and firing ship moving on courses at speeds involving difficult change of range rate problems.[2] After inspecting the rangefinder plots of the firing ships, Dreyer, now captain of the *Iron Duke* and still his chief gunnery adviser, suggested that 'excellent results can be obtained roughly speaking up to 15,000 yards in clear weather, and good results from 15,000 to 17,000 yards and fair above that'.[3] The argument for opening at long range was strengthened by intelligence reports of a new high-speed German torpedo with a range of 15,000 yards, and in spring 1916 Jellicoe had issued an amendment to the Grand Fleet Battle Orders: 'Until the enemy is beaten by gunfire it is not my intention to risk attack from his torpedoes . . . in the early stages of an action I do not desire to close the range much inside 14,000 yards.'[4]

His tactical adjustment was accompanied by the strategic recognition that while Britain controlled the sea routes – apart from U-boat incursions – and blocked supplies to the central powers, the destruction of the High Seas Fleet was unnecessary and, especially with his medium- to close-range tactics, hazarded the numerical superiority on which British sea control rested. He had conveyed this view to the First Sea Lord only seven weeks earlier, on 12 April, concluding that it was not wise 'to risk unduly the heavy ships of the Grand Fleet in an attempt to hasten the end of the High Seas Fleet, particularly if the risks come, not from the High Seas Fleet itself, but from such attributes as mines and submarines'.[5]

Jellicoe had shifted, therefore, from a thoroughly Nelsonic concept of annihilating the German fleet by weight of close-range gunfire to a defensive compromise based on preserving the status quo. His finely balanced intellect and detailed knowledge of the materiel factors on both sides naturally inclined him to caution. How much this was increased by mental exhaustion is not clear. He was more than halfway through his second year of supreme responsibility for the administration, training and morale of the fleet on which Britain and her empire floated, the only man, as Churchill was to write, who could lose the war in an afternoon. He was conscientious to a degree, and while he made every effort to keep himself physically fit, exercising with a medicine ball aboard his flagship and using every opportunity to go ashore for strenuous walks over the heather or to play golf at the double, the volume of business that he chose to deal with personally wore him down.[6]

There is no question that Jellicoe retained the wholehearted loyalty of the fleet and the respect and affection of his staff. They admired his minute attention to detail and clarity of decision. And however inwardly exhausted or constrained by apprehension of his opponent luring him into torpedo or mine traps, he was keyed up by the prospect of imminent action with the fleet it was his mission to destroy. He instructed Dreyer, with him on the compass platform of the *Iron Duke*, to take bearings all around the horizon to find the best direction for gunnery, while he attempted to gauge from the sound of distant fire just where the enemy would appear, analysing his options for deploying into single line of battle.

Dreyer reported that visibility was clearer to the south, but the advantage to an easterly force would grow as the sun set and threw the western horizon into silhouette. Moreover, the westerly wind would blow the smoke to the disengaged side of the easterly force. Since a position to the east of the Germans would cut off their retreat to base, Jellicoe must already have inclined towards a deployment on his port – easternmost – wing column. First, he had to know precisely where Scheer was. The reports received so far had been confusing and visibility was becoming patchy as the westerly breeze blew boiler soot and gun smoke from the action in the south across the range, and sea mist gathered. In some directions it was possible to see up to 16,000 yards, in others no more than 2,000 to 3,000 yards.[7]

Scheer, meanwhile, unaware of Jellicoe's presence, was bending all efforts to close Evan-Thomas's squadron steering north-westerly after Beatty. This was the object of his sortie: to catch and destroy an isolated unit of the British fleet, and it seemed within his grasp. The 'B' turret officer of the rear British battleship, *Malaya*, assumed from the volume of salvoes splashing close alongside that the ship would be struck at any moment, and 'realised that if any one of those shells should hit us in the right place our speed would be sadly reduced, and then we should fall behind and probably be sunk'.[8]

Scheer's van divisions had altered north-westerly and worked up to maximum revolutions in the effort to close, bringing the leading battleship, *König*, to within 17,000 yards, and between 5.20 and 5.35 the *Malaya* was indeed hit seven times, only narrowly escaping the fate envisaged by her 'B' turret officer. The 5th Battle Squadron was also under fire from Hipper's battlecruisers since Beatty's ships had become lost to view in the haze in the north-west. The *Barham* had already been hit four times in a period of sustained accuracy from the *Derfflinger*, and the *Warspite* at least twice by the *Seydlitz*; and while Evan-Thomas's two rear ships engaged

Scheer's van, the two leading ships took on their opposite numbers in Hipper's line, soon making damaging hits and establishing a clear ascendancy.[9]

Beatty was fast approaching the Grand Fleet on its way south-east-wards. No doubt advised by his navigator that he should adjust his course to starboard for a junction he made the signal to prepare to renew the action, and at 5.33 altered from his north-westerly to a northerly course. Two minutes later his most advanced light cruiser ahead of the *Lion* made out shapes of vessels through the mist. They were armoured cruis-ers at the western end of Jellicoe's advanced screen, although this was not immediately apparent. Hipper, meanwhile, had turned his squadron to port together to try to regain contact with Beatty; consequently the two battlecruiser lines converged, and at 5.41 the *Lion* opened fire again at the *Lützow*, followed shortly by the *Princess Royal*. The range had come down to 14,000 yards, but the *Lion* opened with a gun range of 10,000 yards and corrected upwards after each salvo without making any hits.[10] The *Princess Royal* had better ranges and hit Hipper's flagship after some five minutes. It was Evan-Thomas's two leading ships, however, which continued to cause the most serious damage to Hipper's squadron. The German range-takers and gun-layers, for their part, were blinded by the low sun in the north-west and could see practically nothing of their enemy.

Hipper's leading three battlecruisers had taken heavy punishment by this time: fires were burning between decks, the *Derfflinger*'s fore part was com-pletely filled with smoke, and all had compartments flooded to a greater or lesser extent, while in the rear the *Von der Tann* had all turrets out of action and was keeping station only because her captain saw his duty as remaining a target for guns that would otherwise concentrate on a consort. Hipper resolved to launch his destroyers at Beatty but, diverted by an enemy light cruiser appearing from the east, they were in no position to launch an attack; so Hipper turned away from the British line he could barely see until he was steering east by north.

Beatty, meanwhile, had been altering by degrees to a north-easterly course, and at 5.56 he sighted Jellicoe's starboard – westernmost – column of battleships led by the *Marlborough* some five miles off his port bow. He immediately came round further to east-north-east to head across the Grand Fleet's advancing front; Jellicoe's Grand Fleet Battle Orders required him to take station at the head of the battle line.

From the compass platform of the *Iron Duke* Jellicoe could still see nothing of the action he could hear somewhere off his starboard bow.

He protested to Dreyer, 'I wish someone would tell me who is firing and what they are firing at,'[11] and had the *Marlborough* signalled by light, 'WHAT CAN YOU SEE?' As the *Marlborough* replied Jellicoe saw Beatty's gun flashes himself through the murk and moments later the *Lion* burst out of the mist, followed by the three other surviving battlecruisers heading across his bows in splendid formation, 'lit up by sheets of flame as they fired salvo after salvo at the enemy'.[12] The *Lion* was on fire, smoke pouring from a shell hole in her side forward, 'Q' turret guns cocked up mutely on her disengaged side.

Jellicoe had the query flashed to her, 'WHERE IS THE ENEMY BATTLEFLEET?'

Beatty did not know; even Hipper's battlecruisers had disappeared in the haze.

Jellicoe assumed the enemy to be in the south, the direction of the battlecruisers' fire, and swung the leaders of his divisional columns to a southerly course to meet Scheer head on before deploying into line across his 'T'. He had doubts almost immediately as sounds of battle flared up in the south-east, and returned to his original south-easterly course. At the same time Beatty made out Hipper's ships and signalled by light that the enemy battlecruisers bore south-east.

Jellicoe repeated his question: 'WHERE IS THE ENEMY BATTLE-FLEET?'

The German admirals had even less idea of the situation than Jellicoe. Hipper's cruisers found themselves under fire from heavy ships appearing from the mist in the east and reported four or more battleships engaging them. They were Hood's three battlecruisers steering to Beatty's support. Their intervention from such an unexpected direction caused Hipper to swing his ships to starboard together to fall back on Scheer, oblivious to the approach of the Grand Fleet, now scarcely ten miles away.

Scheer was thus denied any warning of the approaching storm. Like Jellicoe, he was commanding from the centre, but with his ships formed in single column, his flagship, *Friedrich der Grosse*, was eighth from the van, and the leading ships, in pressing after Evan-Thomas, had left him some way astern. He could see little of the action, which he still regarded as a chase after an isolated unit of the British fleet. Like Jellicoe, he had built his career on a technical specialization, in his case torpedoes. He was also a student of naval history and until his recent promotion had been a rigorous commander of the 3rd Squadron of the fleet comprising the most modern dreadnoughts – now ahead of him leading the line. Yet, despite his extreme professionalism, he had on this occasion committed elementary and potentially fatal mistakes.

First, he had given way to pleas from the rear admiral commanding the 2nd Squadron of six pre-dreadnought battleships that they should accompany him; they were following his two dreadnought squadrons. Not only were they too lightly gunned and armoured to fight dreadnoughts, they were slower and reduced his fleet speed by some two knots. The fate of the *Blücher* at the Dogger Bank should have served as a terrible warning against the attachment of such obsolete vessels, known in the service as 'five-minute ships'.

He had also overestimated the reconnaissance value of the comparatively few U-boats he had stationed off the British fleet bases, and had discounted the few but potentially revealing reports they made. It appears that his determination to show the Imperial Navy participating fully in the war alongside the army and his desire to take the fight to the enemy had led him to interpret the reports in the most favourable light for his purpose. It is suggestive that his chief of staff, Captain Adolf von Trotha, characterized him as 'a commander of instinct and instant decisions' and as 'impatient' and needing always to act quickly.[13]

Perhaps his most surprising error was failure to realize that Beatty, in turning and fleeing after sighting his fleet, was not heading for home, which was somewhat south of west, nor even for the fleet base at Scapa Flow, but was steering somewhere into open waters to the east of the Scottish isles. In truth, he was so buoyed up by the chase he gave no thought to where Beatty and Evan-Thomas were heading. If any of his staff did point out the strange courses the enemy were steering they made no mention of it subsequently.

The fleet Scheer was leading blindly into the trap was wholly inadequate to meet the Grand Fleet. Against the twenty-four dreadnought battleships under Jellicoe and Evan-Thomas's four 'Queen Elizabeths', Scheer had sixteen dreadnought battleships and six pre-dreadnoughts. In weight of broadside, including the battlecruiser squadrons on both sides, he had 190,000 pounds against a British total of 396,000 pounds, only marginally reduced by the loss of Beatty's two battlecruisers. Above all, perhaps, Scheer was so restricted in fleet speed by his pre-dreadnoughts that he could not hope to extricate himself if chased in clear weather.

Yet even the report from Hipper's cruiser admiral of four or more battleships to the east seems not to have alerted him to imminent peril. Hipper, after falling back on the van division of battleships led by Rear Admiral Paul Behnke in the *König*, reversed course again and led the fleet in a north-easterly direction, Behnke following. Scheer was content to follow Behnke. Not one of the German admirals had any conception of what they had come up against.

At 6.14 Beatty, now fine on the *Iron Duke*'s starboard bow some two miles ahead of her as he raced eastwards, suddenly saw Behnke's ships emerging from the mist to the south and flashed to Jellicoe, 'HAVE SIGHTED ENEMY'S BATTLEFLEET BEARING SSW'.

As the signalman on the *Iron Duke*'s bridge sang out the bearing, 'sou-sou-west', Jellicoe, a small, alert figure with a white scarf around his neck beneath the collar of a blue raincoat, stepped up on to the platform around the compass. The British historian of the naval war has described the pressure on him:

> Many had been the critical situations which British admirals in the past had been called upon suddenly to solve, but never had there been one which demanded higher qualities of leadership, ripe judgement and quick decision, than that which confronted Admiral Jellicoe in this supreme moment of the naval war. There was not an instant to lose if deployment were to be made in time.[14]

Dreyer never forgot the moment as Jellicoe stared in silence at the magnetic compass card. 'I realized as I watched that he was as cool and unmoved as ever. Then he looked up and broke the silence with the order in his crisp, clear-cut voice to the Fleet Signal Officer: "Hoist equal speed pendant south-east".'[15]

This implied deploying on the port, easternmost, wing column, but since the order as phrased could lead to errors in interpretation, Jellicoe agreed to the signal officer's request to make it a point further to port, to south-east by east. It meant the port wing division continuing on the present south-easterly course with a small adjustment of one point to port, while the leaders of all other columns turned 90 degrees to port, the ships astern turning when they reached their leader's turning point, so forming a line heading towards the port column, and on reaching its wake turning in succession to follow. The evolution would take over twenty minutes to complete, but all ships would be in a dog-leg line with all broadsides open in four minutes.[16] To hasten the movement, Jellicoe told Dreyer to commence the deployment, and the *Iron Duke*'s helm was put over while ships were still acknowledging the signal. The column leaders followed suit. It was 6.15 p.m.

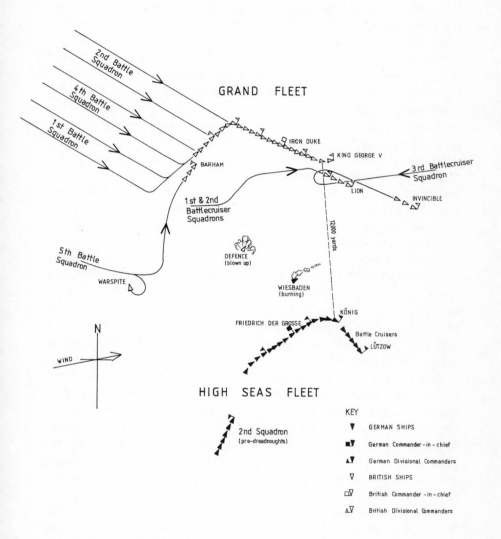

Jutland: Jellicoe's Grand Deployment, 6.30 p.m. 31 May 1916

As he had noted earlier, deployment eastwards conferred all the advantages for gunnery of light and wind direction and blocked any German retreat towards the Skagerrak or Heligoland. He had already ordered two destroyer flotillas to the port, eastern, wing, one to the starboard wing.[17] As it was, the movement placed him at his chosen distance for gun action beyond torpedo range. It must be accounted one of the great moments in British naval history.

Before the effects of the deployment could be realized a series of individual disasters occurred. Two armoured cruisers from Jellicoe's screen, *Defence* and *Warrior*, advanced on one of Hipper's light cruisers, *Wiesbaden*, which had been disabled by Hood's squadron and lay burning between the lines, her smoke obscuring the German heavy ships beyond. As they closed, firing rapidly, they came into view from Hipper's battlecruisers and Behnke's battleships following them, and were subjected to concentrated heavy fire. Both were hit repeatedly and within four minutes the leading cruiser, *Defence*, flagship of Rear Admiral Sir Robert Arbuthnot, was literally blown out of the water; the *Warrior* retired blazing.

Meanwhile, just to the west, Evan-Thomas, properly declining to follow Beatty across the front of the Grand Fleet as it deployed, had made a wide turn to bring his squadron into line astern of the most westerly battleship column led by the *Marlborough*. During the manoeuvre his ships had come under heavy fire from the head of Behnke's line and the *Warspite*'s helm jammed, taking her in a wide circle towards the enemy. She was hit repeatedly by both 12-inch and 5.9-inch shells before her turn took her away again.[18] Extemporized steering was restored, but damage and flooding reduced her speed to 16 knots, and she shortly retired from the action.

Beatty had by this time completed his transit across the front of the Grand Fleet and taken station ahead of the leader of the port column, *King George V*, while Hood had joined from the east and formed his three battlecruisers some distance ahead of the *Lion*; consequently Hood's flagship, *Invincible*, led the fleet on its south-easterly course. The judgement exercised in avoiding collisions as the myriad cruisers and destroyers attached to the different squadrons met and sped past and around each other was of a high, near-miraculous order.

No sooner had Hood turned into line ahead of Beatty – about the time the *Defence* blew up – than he saw Hipper's squadron to the south on an easterly course, and opened fire. His ships were fresh from gunnery practice at Scapa Flow; the range to the *Lützow*, leading and on fire from two recent hits from the *Lion*, was inside 9,000 yards and his squadron was hidden from the Germans by mist. Enjoying uninterrupted practice, his gunnery control quickly found the range and scored repeated, damaging hits. The *Lützow* was struck by eight shells in a six-minute period and so holed forward that some two thousand tons of sea water flooded the compartments, dragging her bows low. The *Derfflinger* was hit three times and the *Seydlitz* once during this period. Hipper turned from the onslaught and reduced speed to relieve the pressure on the still-intact forward bulkheads, when suddenly the mist to the north parted to reveal the *Invincible* outlined against a background of funnel and gun smoke. The *Lützow*'s main armament control was switched to the after position and fire was opened.

Simultaneously, astern of the *Lützow*, the *Derfflinger*'s gunnery officer, who had been aiming and ranging on enemy gun flashes in the mist, also sighted Hood's flagship emerging into silhouette. Training his periscope on her, he opened fire with an observed range of 9,800 yards. The first salvo disappeared over. Ordering 'Down 100!' he went into rapid fire, including secondary armament. The *Lützow*'s after control found the range as rapidly, and both ships recorded hits on their third salvo. Of these, one 12-inch shell penetrated the *Invincible*'s 'Q' turret, bursting inside, blowing off the turret roof and igniting cartridges that projected a flash flame down the ammunition trunk and into the magazine, which blew up, setting off the adjacent 'P' turret magazine and splitting the hull in two.[19] The German control officers again witnessed the awful spectacle of a great ship, rent by successive explosions, disintegrating beneath a gigantic cloud of black smoke, debris and great spurts of coal dust. The two halves of the hull came to rest standing vertically on the shallow seabed some distance apart, both bow and stern projecting above the surface as the following ships raced past. From her complement of 1,032, only six survived, nearly all from the gunnery control team stationed in the foretop.[20]

By this time Scheer's battleships following Hipper's squadron had come under fire from Jellicoe's battle line; Behnke's flagship, *König*, in the lead and lit up for the British by the sun, received seven hits from the *Iron Duke* at a range of 12,000 yards in a period of less than five minutes, and one from the *Monarch*. Of the others, only the fourth in line, *Markgraf*, appears to have been damaged by one hit and a near-miss, but for Scheer it seemed that the entire arc ahead 'from north to east was a sea of fire. The flash from the muzzles of the [British] guns was distinctly seen through the mist and smoke on the horizon, though the ships themselves were not distinguishable'.[21] Behnke was already altering round to starboard after Hipper's battlecruisers, and Scheer signalled, '*Gefechtskehrtwendung nach steuerbord!*' – 'Battle-turn away 180 degrees to starboard!' The evolution started with the rear ship, after which the one ahead of her put her helm over, and so on up the line. It was a frequently practised manoeuvre and was carried out immaculately in the heat of battle. To the British the German fleet seemed to melt away and disappear in the mist. The guns fell silent.

Jellicoe, unsure of just where the enemy had gone, altered southerly by divisions to place himself across their escape route eastwards. Scheer, after a brief respite running south-westerly, decided to reverse course again, and ordered a second battle turn to starboard. His subsequent explanation, adopted by the German official historian, was that he sought to seize the initiative by surprising the British with a combined destroyer and gun attack and create the conditions in which he could escape under cover of darkness.[22] Probably he had still not realized he was up against the entire Grand Fleet and was probing easterly for more certain knowledge of the enemy force. The answer will never be known. So, for the second time that day he advanced straight towards Jellicoe's ships, now heading south across his 'T', and for the second time found himself under fire from a line whose presence was revealed only by gun flashes and shells raining down about his van.

The gun flashes, which had appeared first from the north-east with the rear divisions of the Grand Fleet at some ten thousand yards range, spread southwards, reaching Jellicoe's leading divisions and even Beatty's battle-cruisers ahead of them in the south-east, barring his track ahead. He ordered the preparatory signal for another battle turn away to starboard, and to relieve the pressure on his battle fleet during the turn sent the battlecruisers on a sacrificial charge towards the guns ahead, '*RAN AN DEN FEIND. VOLL EINSETZEN!*' – 'Go at the enemy. Give it everything!' – and followed the flag signal with a wireless order to the same effect, then another flag signal to attack the enemy van.

No sooner had the flags of this second hoist been run up the halyards at 7.14 than the British control officers began to find the range. First to suffer was the *Derfflinger*. The *Lützow* had fallen out of the line and was straggling away south-westwards, her fo'c's'le almost level with the sea; Hipper himself had boarded a destroyer in order to seek another ship from which to control his squadron, and the captain of the *Derfflinger* was leading. He had advanced within 8,000 yards of Jellicoe's rear-division ships without being able to see them when a 15-inch armour-piercing shell penetrated the roof of his aftermost turret, burst over the right ammunition hoist and ignited cartridges in the supply train, creating a flash fire down the trunk which killed all but two of the turret's crew. Shortly afterwards a second 15-inch shell penetrated the other after turret and burst inside, producing a similarly devastating fire and knocking out that turret as well.[23]

Both shells had been fired by the *Revenge* astern of the leader of the rear division, *Marlborough*. In the next few minutes, as the *Derfflinger* led southwards in a desperate charge to comply with the order to attack the enemy van, she was hit by a further three 15-inch shells from the *Revenge* and six 12-inch shells from ships in the next division ahead; the *Seydlitz*, following in her wake, was hit four times, the *Von der Tann* once, and several of Scheer's leading battleships were straddled and hit, the *Grosser Kurfürst* no less than seven times. Even the *Lützow* some way to the south was hit five times by ships of Jellicoe's leading divisions at a range of 18,500 yards. Meanwhile German control officers and gun-layers could see little but 'the great reddish gold flames'[24] from the British guns.

German fire was scarcely more effective in this second encounter with the Grand Fleet than in the first: two shells, probably from the *Seydlitz*, hit the flagship of Jellicoe's 5th Division, but did little damage. Otherwise no British ships were touched. Meanwhile Scheer's leading battleships were turning out of line, slowing, even stopping engines as they attempted to evade the salvoes raining down about them, causing confusion and bunching in the line astern. Scheer made the battle turn away signal executive at 7.17. By then his destroyers were racing ahead to gain position for attack. A few originally ordered to rescue the crew of the cruiser *Wiesbaden* had already launched torpedoes, which were seen and evaded by ships at the rear of Jellicoe's line. The main destroyer attack, authorized by Scheer at 7.21, was met by light cruisers and destroyers from the Grand Fleet and by fire from the battleships' main and secondary armament, which prevented their close approach; but they came in to some 7,500 yards in two waves and fired a total of twenty-one torpedoes. Jellicoe immediately ordered his divisions to turn away two points, and when advised this was not enough, a further two points. As a result, by the time the torpedoes reached the battleships near the head of his line they were approaching the limit of their 10,000-yard endurance and travelling slowly, and were comparatively easily evaded. It was only sharp lookouts, skilful manoeuvring and a measure of good fortune, however, which preserved several ships from damage.[25]

Jellicoe's turn away by divisions to a south-easterly course at the same time as Scheer's battle turn away to a south-westerly course – followed by his battlecruisers, released from their suicidal charge – resulted in the fleets once again losing sight of each other. Jellicoe has been heavily criticized for turning from the enemy at the very moment the head of their line was disintegrating under the guns of his battleships.[26] Yet every other commander in the battle turned away from torpedo attack, including Beatty and Hipper. Jellicoe had said he would do so beforehand and had trained his fleet in just such a tactic to preserve his battleship superiority. Above all, Jellicoe had no inkling of the effect of his fire on the head of the enemy line; nor did he know that Scheer was turning to steer away; all was concealed by smoke and smokescreens laid by the German destroyers and the gathering mists.

Directly the torpedo danger had passed Jellicoe steered southwards, then west-south-west in an attempt to regain contact. By this time Scheer was steering south. He was understandably anxious not to be driven too far west, away from his escape routes, but in view of the length of the northern twilight, the alteration was premature: he should have known he would be pursued and that he needed to retire far enough to avoid being caught again in daylight. He could not guess Jellicoe's precise course, but the two fleets were again converging and would have met had it not been for the intervention of the battlecruisers. For Beatty, taking an independent southwesterly course well ahead of Jellicoe's leading division, came in sight of the four survivors of Hipper's battlecruiser squadron – less the *Lützow*, wallowing far astern – at 8.20, six minutes after sunset. They were stationed to the east of Scheer's battle line and were silhouetted against the bright north-western horizon at ranges of 9,500 yards and under. His own six ships, including the two survivors from Hood's squadron, were scarcely visible against the eastern gloom, and over the next ten minutes he was able to exact some revenge for the drubbing his squadron had received earlier in the day: the *Seydlitz*, which was already severely disabled, took five hits, and the *Derfflinger*, in even worse shape, one hit before all turned away and became lost to sight behind smoke. Of his own ships, only the *Lion* was hit by a 5.9-inch shell which did little damage.

Pre-dreadnoughts leading Scheer's fleet south then came in sight with dreadnoughts following astern. They were engaged briefly and two hits were made against one received before they too turned away and disappeared in the fading light and mist. By driving Scheer's leading ships westward Beatty prevented Jellicoe's van divisions from seeing them. No doubt if they had it would have resulted in a similar withdrawal. Beatty's action was the last encounter between capital ships in the war.

Scheer soon resumed his southerly course and by 9 p.m. Jellicoe's leading division, steering south-westerly after Beatty, was again only 6 miles from the German van, although neither side was aware of it. Night was drawing in with perhaps half an hour before it became completely dark. Jellicoe concluded it was too late to seek further action. The theoretical hazards and the deficiency of British night-fighting preparation and equipment, especially remote searchlight control, had been proved in exercises; above all, torpedo tracks would not be seen. He signalled an alteration of course to south by east to keep between Scheer and his routes home, and at 9.17 ordered the fleet into night cruising formation in three compact columns with the destroyers and cruisers massed astern so that they would not be mistaken for the enemy in the dark.

At practically the same moment Scheer ordered his fleet to a south-easterly course to take him to safety by the shortest route via the Horns Reef swept channel off the coast of Jutland – 105 miles. He had already called urgently for airship reconnaissance off Horns Reef in the morning. Both wireless signals were picked up by the Admiralty monitoring service and went to Room 40 for decoding. By 9.55 the decrypt of the later signal ordering course 'SSE ¾E, speed 16 knots' was in the hands of the operational staff, and fifteen minutes later they were able to read Scheer's urgent request for airship reconnaissance off Horns Reef in the morning.[27] Taken together, the signals left no doubt about Scheer's intention, but for some unaccountable reason only the course and speed order was passed to Jellicoe later. On its own this was a clear indication of how Scheer meant to get home, but during the day the Admiralty had sent several reports of the enemy's position which had not accorded with where they seemed to be, and this latest information was contradicted by the most recent report from Beatty, received in the *Iron Duke* at 9.38, that the enemy fleet was steering west-south-west. This reinforced Jellicoe's own perception of having driven Scheer to the west and his conviction that his opponent would take a more westerly route home in order to avoid a third confrontation. Thus he ignored the Admiralty message and remained on the course he had set to intercept Scheer at first light the following morning, whichever of the westerly routes he chose. Beatty had a similar appreciation of the situation.[28]

It led to one of the more extraordinary nights in the history of naval warfare. For the courses established by the opposing commanders without precise knowledge of their opponent's position converged on a point that Jellicoe would pass through less than twenty minutes before Scheer; this meant that Scheer's van, screened by destroyers and light cruisers, would meet the flotillas massed 5 miles astern of Jellicoe's rear battleship divisions. They did. The night was moonless and the resulting clashes, beginning just before 10 p.m., flared up suddenly between shadowy groups of ships at desperately close range, ceasing as suddenly as the antagonists merged again into darkness, leaving riven and blazing or sinking vessels. German night-firing techniques proved vastly superior: searchlights were remotely controlled by director; secondary as well as main armament of capital ships was in director training, and starshell was employed to illuminate targets. Nonetheless, British destroyers and light cruisers accounted for two German light cruisers and two destroyers, and in a final encounter at first light destroyers torpedoed the pre-dreadnought battleship *Pommern*, igniting a magazine that exploded and broke her in two. The price was five British destroyers and the armoured cruiser *Black Prince*, which strayed inside 1,000 yards of undamaged battleships Scheer had moved from the rear to the head of his line. Subjected to a hail of shell, she was set ablaze and blew apart with the loss of her entire complement of 857. Almost the same number were lost with the *Pommern*.

The separate encounters with Jellicoe's flotillas deflected Scheer briefly and caused much disorder, but failed to weaken his resolve to press on whatever the cost. He knew that if caught the next day before reaching safety he could not escape destruction, and constantly signalled small alterations to keep his capital ships on course for the Horns Reef light vessel.[29] For Jellicoe, who was trying to rest, lying fully clad on a cot just abaft his bridge, the intermittent outbreaks of gunfire and explosions from astern accorded with his view that Scheer would send torpedo craft to attack from this direction; it was one of the reasons he had massed his own flotillas in the wake of the fleet.

Later critics, armed with the tracks of the two fleets that night, could point to the passage of fighting from west to east across his wake as an unambiguous indication of Scheer breaking through in the direction of Horns Reef, but Jellicoe received no reports of heavy ships engaged. The lack of accurate scouting reports, which had been a feature of the day's fighting, persisted through the night.

As the first light of day spread, revealing a calm, grey sea hung with mist, Jellicoe had no inkling that Scheer had broken through astern. He still expected to find him in the west, and soon after 2.30 a.m. reversed the course of the fleet northwards and formed single line of battle. By then Scheer's leading ships were 30 miles to the north-east, scarcely more than an hour's steaming from the Horns Reef channel. German commanders, lookouts, watch officers and guns' crews peered seawards, tense with expectation of British ships emerging from the heavy mist, but as they drew nearer safety with no hint of the enemy, anxiety was replaced by intense relief. The gunnery officer of the *Derfflinger* acknowledged, 'I confess frankly, a load fell from my heart.'[30]

For almost two years officers and men of the Grand Fleet and battle-cruisers had lived in the hope of repeating the deeds of their forebears and winning a second 'Trafalgar' in the North Sea; and the date was auspicious – anniversary of Admiral Howe's triumph over the French at 'The Glorious First of June' in 1794. Disappointment was heightened by the sense that only poor visibility and fading light had robbed them of their chance. No doubt Jellicoe and Beatty felt the failure most keenly and personally. For the wounded and those in damaged ships who had seen the cost in ghastly burns, wounds and blood, and who witnessed that morning the bodies of their shipmates sewn up in hammocks and committed to the deep, dejection was perhaps mixed with relief that action would not be renewed. Their feelings may, perhaps, have been more akin to those described in the diary of a cruiser paymaster after the first major engagement of the war in the Heligoland Bight: 'I have just lived through the horrible experience of an action at sea, and if there is anyone in the world who having once experienced such an event, says he desires to experience another, I should not believe him.'[31]

Scheer and the German press exulted in victory at the Battle of Skagerrak. The tally of ships and lives lost seemed to support the claim. Although by far the inferior fleet, they had sunk three battlecruisers and three armoured cruisers – the crippled *Warrior* having been abandoned under tow in rising seas – and lost only Hipper's flagship, *Lützow*, which had sunk on the way to Horns Reef, and the obsolete battleship *Pommern*. Of the lighter craft, they had lost four light cruisers and five destroyers against eight British destroyers sunk. The casualty figures told a similar story: on the British side 6,094 killed, 674 wounded and 177 taken prisoner, on the German side 2,551 killed and 507 wounded.[32]

Behind the figures lay a single factor: the magazine explosions that annihilated ships and their entire companies in an instant. They accounted for over five thousand British lives. Without them the British would have suffered fewer casualties than the Germans and would not have lost any capital ships. The Germans lost their newest, most powerful battlecruiser, *Lützow*, and the *Seydlitz* and *Derfflinger* were so damaged they barely made it home. Both had suffered ammunition fires that wiped out whole turrets, but their magazines had not blown up.

An immediate Admiralty investigation into the magazine explosions quickly established that in the drive for rapidity of fire ammunition parties in the turrets had deliberately ignored safety regulations.[33] The practice in the battlecruisers and in some at least of the Grand Fleet battleships was to leave the magazine doors open in action for speedy delivery of ammunition, stockpile cartridges in the handing room just outside and open the lids of metal cartridge cases inside the doors even before the cartridges were needed. The full charge for a main armament gun was made up of four parts, each contained in a cylindrical silk case with a gunpowder 'igniter' at each end[34] protected by a tear-off disc. These discs were removed in the handing room before the charges were placed in the hoist leading up to the working chamber below the gunhouse, and in many turrets a small stock-pile of charges, tear-off discs removed, was also kept in the working chamber.[35] The result was an unbroken chain of cordite charges with exposed black powder igniters leading from the working chamber down to an open magazine, inside which cartridge cases often had their lids removed. The Admiralty investigators were left in no doubt of these poten-tially lethal practices, and as early as 5 June a memorandum was sent to all flag officers stipulating that no more than four charges should be allowed outside the magazines at any time.[36]

These initial conclusions, which did not reflect well on the officers of the fleet who had led the drive for rapid fire, from Jellicoe and Beatty down, were obfuscated later for reasons of fleet morale and *amour propre*. The investigation reports were suppressed, papers destroyed and Jellicoe, when appointed First Sea Lord, directed that the loss of the battlecruisers was to be attributed to their insufficient armour protection.[37] There was no evidence for this.[38]

There is another side to the question. At the Dogger Bank in 1915 flash fire had destroyed both the *Seydlitz*'s after turrets. The fire had consumed no fewer than sixty-two complete charges – each made up of a main charge in a brass case and a fore charge in a double silk case – including some charges inside the magazine doors, yet the magazines had not exploded. Despite subsequent modifications to prevent such fires spreading, both the *Derfflinger*'s after turrets had been destroyed by flash fires at Jutland. Yet, again, the magazines had not been ignited, suggesting that German charges were less sensitive than British. A recent authority states categorically that if British charges had been used in German ships the *Seydlitz* would have blown up at the Dogger Bank and at Jutland 'the *Derfflinger* would certainly have blown up as would in all probability the *Seydlitz*, and possibly the *Von der Tann*'.[39] Undoubtedly the German propellant had a different composi-tion and form and a much higher ignition point than the British cordite, and the evidence suggests it was more stable. A German authority has sug-gested the secret lay in a stabilizer invented just before 1914,[40] whereas the distinguished naval historian and former gunnery officer, the late Captain Stephen Roskill, believes the difference lay in purity of manufacture: 'the greater the impurities the greater the rate of deterioration'.[41] Whatever the explanation, eight large British ships were lost to magazine explosion during the war, either from enemy action, accident or spontaneous combustion, whereas the Germans lost only the *Pommern* to this cause after a torpedo explosion, presumably inside a magazine.[42]

In material terms Jutland – Skagerrak – was an undoubted victory for the Germans. In tactics, Hipper won his initial duel with Beatty and proved, perhaps, the most skilful force commander throughout – although latterly deprived of a flagship and unable to direct his squadron. Beatty, while careless at the outset, again proved his qualities of fearlessness and utter commitment to victory despite shocking losses. Jellicoe outmanoeuvred Scheer decisively, although it might be said that Scheer compensated with his bold – or ill-judged and reckless – night dash for Horns Reef through the flotillas astern of the Grand Fleet. Fortunately for him German night-fighting techniques proved decisively superior.

Yet in grand strategic terms none of this mattered. Scheer boasted of victory, but he had run for home by the shortest route, leaving Jellicoe with a practically undamaged Grand Fleet in possession of the sea. No thinking German officer could consider another challenge to British surface mastery.[43] Scheer certainly could not. He sent a confidential memo on the battle to Wilhelm on 4 July in which he ruled out the possibility of 'even the most successful outcome of a [future] Fleet action' forcing Britain to make peace, and concluded: 'A victorious end to the war within a reasonable time can only be achieved through the defeat of British economic life – that is, by using the U-boats against British trade . . .'[44]

17

Unrestricted U-boat War, 1917

IT WAS JANUARY 1917 before Wilhelm accepted that the U-boats would have to be unleashed in an unrestricted campaign against British supply lines. The decision was taken under the influence of the military, Field Marshal Paul von Hindenburg, appointed to supreme command of land forces in August 1916 after the failure of the Verdun offensive, and his intellectual right hand, General Erich Ludendorff. Both were archetypal men of iron descended from the Prussian warrior-landowning nobility. Ludendorff in particular was a repository of the most extreme values of the caste: he regarded war, like Treitschke, as the meaning and ultimate goal of the state.

He was in a position to realize the concept. The war had exposed Wilhelm's temperamental inability to exercise supreme command and the army had seized control, taking the place in the highest council, which Bismarck had devised to concentrate all power in his own hands. In fact, if not in name, Hindenburg and Ludendorff were the military dictators of Germany. They had determined on a ruthless campaign against merchant shipping as the only way to knock out Britain, financier and energizing force of the enemy alliance. It was a desperate gamble, certain to provoke the United States, yet it had to be taken because the central powers could hardly survive another year of blockade. Severe food shortages caused by loss of agricultural labour to the armed services and war industries and lack of fertilizers from abroad had hit the civilian population especially hard – since fighting men were favoured in the distribution of provisions. Rage, presently directed against the British 'Hunger Blockade', could all too easily turn against the government. Unrest was palpable. Meanwhile, the armies were locked in static trench warfare and outnumbered by the Allied armies.

Bethmann argued for a negotiated peace, but since Hindenburg, Ludendorff and the Naval Staff, backed by magnates of heavy industry, insisted on retaining the great swathes of conquered territory occupied by the central powers he was unable to offer anything remotely acceptable to the Allies. He made an approach in December but it was rejected out of hand. Woodrow Wilson then offered to mediate, but neither side wanted an American-imposed solution. Now, like Falkenhayn earlier, Hindenburg and Ludendorff saw U-boats as the only weapon with which to force their annexationist peace.

The Naval Staff had long advocated this course, and on 22 December 1916 the Chief of the Naval Staff, von Holtzendorff, had produced a detailed proposal. From the premise that the Allies were 'only upheld by England's energy and activity', and if England's back were broken the war would immediately be decided in Germany's favour, he proceeded to figures: estimating the total shipping supplying Britain at some 10¾ million tons; assuming from previous results that U-boats unrestricted by the rules of cruiser warfare could sink 600,000 tons a month, and that 'at least two fifths of neutral sea traffic will at once be terrorised into ceasing their voyages to England', he calculated that in five months shipping to and from the British Isles would be reduced by about 39 per cent. 'England would not be able to stand that.'[1] He recognized that such a campaign would probably draw the United States in against them, but discounted the immediate effect: American money could not make up for shortage of supplies and tonnage.

The numerical analysis seemed conclusive. The chief of Wilhelm's naval *Kabinett*, Admiral von Müller, was won round, and at Supreme Headquarters on 8 January 1917 Wilhelm bowed to the logic, telling Hindenburg, Ludendorff and von Holtzendorff that he would support an unrestricted U-boat campaign. He knew Bethmann was opposed, but remarked that it was purely a military matter which did not concern the Chancellor. Bethmann arrived at headquarters to find the decision made. He warned the group of the fatal consequences of American entry and attempted to persuade them of the need to accept Wilson's peace mediation, but made no impression and finally resigned himself to the policy.

Although a mere civilian, Bethmann had the more realistic view. What the professionals had not considered were the possible reactions of their victim. Historically in time of war merchantmen had been protected in escorted convoys. The Allies employed the system for troop transports and vessels with especially valuable freights, but most ships still sailed independently, as in peacetime, chiefly because of the delays and congestion inherent in assembling large numbers of vessels, and a perceived lack of escorts for the increased number of routes served by steam shipping. The possibility that the British might attempt to reduce losses to U-boats by introducing convoy for all ships and the consequences for von Holtzendorff's tonnage forecasts were not probed.

Jellicoe was now First Sea Lord. He had taken up the post at the beginning of December after handing command of the fleet to Beatty. The government had changed at about the same time, Lloyd George succeeding Asquith as Prime Minister. The constitutional succession provides a significant contrast to imperial Germany, where similar lack of confidence in the conduct of the war had led seamlessly to the military taking power – a sure indication of the opposite polarities of the two nations.

Before his appointment as First Sea Lord, Jellicoe had written to the Admiralty expressing anxiety that if merchant shipping losses continued at present rates the effect on imports might by the early summer of 1917 force the government into an undesirable peace.[2] The Admiralty had echoed his concerns in a memorandum to the government and added that no conclusive answer had as yet been found to the problem of submarine attack on merchant vessels; 'perhaps no conclusive answer ever will be found. We must for the present be content with palliation'. It was an astonishing admission from a navy that had controlled the seas of the world for centuries. The only means of detecting a submerged submarine was by listening for its propeller beat with an underwater microphone known as a hydrophone, which was lowered over the side; yet hydrophones did not indicate direction and could be employed only from stationary vessels; otherwise they were jammed by the ship's own engine noise. For destroying submerged boats, two basic methods had been devised: bombs termed 'depth charges' dropped overboard and set to detonate by water pressure at set depths – or fired by howitzer to distances up to 1,200 yards from the ship – and barrages of deep-moored mines across U-boat transit routes, or steel nets studded with mines that detonated if a snared U-boat dragged them alongside.

Through 1916 fewer than two U-boats a month had been destroyed by these methods.[3] Since German shipyards were completing up to seven boats a month, operational numbers had increased, and Allied shipping losses with them. What was not appreciated was that anti-U-boat strategy was as much to blame as inadequate means of detection and destruction. The Royal Navy as an institution and naval officers as individuals were focused on the pursuit and elimination of the enemy in battle; the thrust was for the 'offensive'. Convoys were perceived as 'defensive', hence destroyers and other light surface craft, aeroplanes and airships were deployed on offensive patrols to hunt the undersea enemy. In this sense the policy was based on semantics, not analysis or historical precedent. Mahan had observed that hunting for individual commerce raiders resembled 'looking for a needle in a haystack'.[4] He was writing of the French wars, yet the difficulties of finding submerged U-boats were, if anything, greater than discovering Napoleonic privateers. Recourse to naval history or critical analysis would have shown that the place to find attacking boats was in the immediate vicinity of their merchantmen targets, which, for optimum use of anti-U-boat resources, should be concentrated in convoys. Yet convoys were ruled out, not simply because of the delays they caused, or the practical difficulties of steaming in company, or even because they were seen as 'defensive', but because so many ships gathered together seemed to offer opportunities for mass destruction to the U-boats finding them.[5]

Several officers, including Beatty, had suggested the introduction of convoy, but the Naval Staff and a new Anti Submarine Division created in the wake of Jellicoe's alarm call to coordinate the fight against U-boats rejected the idea, seeking instead to enhance existing systems of patrolled shipping lanes, evasive routing, hunting groups and mine barrages; such was the inertia of official doctrine and the reliance on commonsense or intuitive solutions.

On 31 January 1917 Bethmann rose dutifully in the Reichstag to announce unrestricted U-boat warfare commencing on the following day. There were then 120 operational boats, approximately a third of which could be on patrol at any one time. The majority were based in North Sea ports, twenty-four in the Adriatic for action against Mediterranean traffic. Shipping losses rose with the onset of the campaign, and during February 209 British, Allied and neutral ships of an aggregate 464,599 tons were lost to U-boats; mines and surface raiders brought total losses to 532,856 tons. In addition, many ships were damaged and undergoing repair, others were held in port until it was deemed safe to put out and over six hundred neutrals in British ports refused to put to sea. In March U-boats sank 507,000 tons and shipping losses from all causes amounted to 599,854 tons,[6] for all practical purposes the figure on which von Holtzendorff had staked the success of his plan.

Despite these frightening statistics there was no reassessment of assumptions at the Admiralty. Jellicoe called for the construction of more patrol craft. He was by nature inclined to pessimism, and in the crisis it showed. Rear Admiral A. L. Duff, a torpedo specialist whom he had brought down from the Grand Fleet to head the new Anti Submarine Division, and Duff's assistant, Dreyer, recently Jellicoe's flag captain in the *Iron Duke*, also remained wedded to patrolling and hunting, as did the War Staff, who issued a paper in February maintaining that 'too much stress cannot be laid on the necessity of enemy submarines being constantly harried and hunted and never allowed to rest'.[7]

The United States had not entered the war. Woodrow Wilson had broken off diplomatic relations with Germany after the announcement of the unrestricted campaign, but while he anticipated being forced into a declaration, he knew he had to await a more blatant affront. His political support came from isolationists in the western and southern states, and during a re-election campaign he had won by the narrowest of margins in November, he had emphasized his success in keeping the country out of the European conflict. It was not fortuitous that one of the best-selling songs in sheet music and on records that year had been 'I Didn't Raise My Boy to Be a Soldier'.[8] Yet despite the concerns of his constituents and his personal abhorrence of war, he was committed in principle to the Allied cause. Earlier, he had told his great friend and foreign affairs adviser Colonel Edward House that if Germany won 'it would change the course of civilisation and make the United States a military nation'.[9] This political leaning towards the Allies corresponded to the industrial and financial realities of the nation in this third year of war. US factories were producing vast quantities of arms and ammunition for the Western Alliance; the New York financial market was providing much of the money to pay for them, and Britain had raised so much in loans on Wall Street that the United States had a vital interest in preventing her defeat.[10]

Through March Wilson acquired pretexts for entering the war he wished to avoid. First and most explosive was a message from the German Foreign Minister, Arthur Zimmermann, to his ambassador in Washington for onward transmission to the Mexican embassy, to be placed before the President of Mexico. Room 40 had decrypted it on 17 January, but Hall, the DID, sat on it until he could prove its authenticity without revealing that British Naval Intelligence was routinely reading enciphered German signals. He did this by having a copy of the message as relayed to Mexico City stolen from the Western Union telegraph office there. This showed the German Foreign Minister inciting Mexico to attack the United States if Wilson should join the Allies as a result of the planned unrestricted U-boat campaign. Mexico was offered an alliance and generous financial support to help her reconquer lost territory in Texas, New Mexico and Arizona.[11] It was Zimmermann's way of assisting the military by seeking to prevent full American engagement in Europe.

Wilson was shown the text and after conferring with his Secretary of State, who was in any case convinced of the need to go to war, approved its release to the press. On 1 March the story made headlines throughout America, at a stroke breaking down all but the most extreme isolationist or pro-German sentiment in the country. Some suspicions that it might be a

British forgery were refuted next day when at a press conference in Berlin Zimmermann himself told the correspondent for the anti-British, non-interventionist Hearst newspaper group that he could not deny the story; it was true.[12]

On 18 March three US ships were sunk by U-boats. Wilson's Cabinet, accurately reflecting the changed public mood since the revelation of the 'Zimmermann telegram', at last agreed on war. It remained for Wilson to justify the decision before Congress, summoned to meet in special session on 2 April. He did so on the moral ground of making the world safe for freedom and democracy, which he contrasted with German autocracy.[13] His call touched a chord of patriotic idealism in American society. Congress's vote for war was greeted as fervently across the country as the call to arms had been in European capitals in August 1914;[14] an autobiographical novel written by a US volunteer serving in the British Army on the western front became a runaway best-seller. In the Foreword the author, Arthur Guy Empney, wrote that his experiences had convinced him of 'the nobility, truth and justice of the Allies' cause'; he knew 'their fight to be our fight, because it espouses the principles of the United States of America – democracy, justice and liberty'.[15]

However enthusiastically many Americans responded to the summons, the armed services were unprepared. Hindenburg and Ludendorff had calculated that even if the Americans were drawn in they would be unable to field a major army until 1919; they were largely correct. The US Navy was hardly in better shape. A Naval Appropriations Act of June 1916 designed to create a navy equal to the most powerful in the world was still some way short of that goal; moreover, the Secretary of the Navy was a pacifist who had been more reluctant than Wilson to see the country enter the war, and the Chief of Naval Operations, Admiral William S. Benson, was viscerally anti-British. Consequently very little had been done to move the service from peace routines, a situation the Assistant Secretary of the Navy, Franklin D. Roosevelt, found exasperating. He had been convinced from late 1916 that the United States had to join the Allies.[16]

Yet it was not until after Congress had voted for war that a naval envoy was sent to Britain to sound out the Admiralty on Allied needs and measures for cooperation. This was the Anglophile Admiral William Sims, who had introduced Percy Scott's gunnery methods to the United States Navy at the turn of the century. He arrived in London on 9 April and saw Jellicoe the following day. Jellicoe handed him a memorandum on shipping losses; the projection for April was almost 900,000 tons. Sims was shocked, and said it looked as though the Germans were winning. 'They will win',

Jellicoe replied, 'unless we can stop these losses – and stop them soon.' When Sims asked whether there was no solution, he replied, 'Absolutely none that we can see now.'[17]

Jellicoe's state of mind over the following days as losses continued to rise in line with the predictions and it seemed as if defeat was closing in is difficult to imagine. His responsibility for the fate of the country and empire was greater than when he had commanded the Grand Fleet; then he could have lost the war in a day; now it seemed probable it would be lost in months with a fatal haemorrhage of merchant shipping. On 23 April he drew the crisis to the attention of Lloyd George's War Cabinet in a memorandum detailing recent sinkings: 419,621 tons in the first two weeks in April; 29,705 tons in a single day on the 22nd. 'The only immediate remedy that is possible is the provision of as many destroyers and patrol vessels as can be provided by the United States of America.'[18] He also proposed more intensive mining of U-boat exit routes from the German Bight using a new type of mine. He believed the mines they had been laying were ineffective. His proposals amounted to a continuation of failed strategies with additional or improved material.

Nonetheless, the memorandum was to prove a turning point. For some time Lloyd George had been taking advice from a number of intelligent, historically minded younger officers who advocated convoy. As early as 11 February the secretary of the War Cabinet, Colonel Sir Maurice Hankey, had written a paper probably based on information supplied by one of these officers, Commander Reginald Henderson of the Anti Submarine Division, proposing 'an entire re-organisation of the Admiralty's present scheme of anti-submarine warfare' and 'the substitution of a system of scientifically organised convoys'.[19]

Jellicoe had made no mention of convoy in his memorandum. Lloyd George decided to force the issue, and at a War Cabinet meeting on the 25th gained approval for a personal visit to the Admiralty to investigate anti-submarine measures. Meanwhile, his young naval informant, Commander Henderson, had analysed statistics of arrivals and departures at British ports and by eliminating coastwise and cross-Channel shipping established that some 280 ocean-going ships a week would require convoying,[20] a far smaller number than had been assumed and one that could be managed with existing destroyers and other escort craft – provided, of course, they were taken from patrolling and hunting duties. Whether it was this illumination or the Prime Minister's impending visit that concentrated Admiral Duff's mind, he produced a memorandum for Jellicoe on the 26th, the day after Lloyd George announced his intention to examine

Admiralty methods, detailing the volume of overseas trade, the numbers of escorts necessary to protect it and outlining a system of convoy. He appended a note: 'It seems to me evident that the time has arrived when we must be ready to introduce a comprehensive scheme of convoy at any moment . . .'[21]

After the war Lloyd George claimed that it was his approaching visit which 'galvanised' the Admiralty into looking afresh at Commander Henderson's figures.[22] Jellicoe and Duff denied this strenuously, yet the admirals' conversion to convoy and their subsequent measures to institute a comprehensive system were half-hearted.[23] The coincidence of their volte-face immediately after Lloyd George had announced his intention to investigate anti-submarine organization, and the fact that the civilian First Lord of the Admiralty was a member of the War Cabinet and had known for some time of the Prime Minister's disquiet, leaves no doubt that his visit was at least at the background of their considerations. In any case, it must be accounted a monumental scandal that they mounted sustained opposition to convoy from February to the end of April while merchant shipping losses were rising, chiefly on the grounds of a lack of escorts, without making any attempt to find out how many escorts would be needed.

The experimental convoys proved a success, but the Admiralty also continued with patrolling and hunting, and it was almost the end of June, a month when total shipping losses reached 683,325 tons, their second highest peak,[24] before a Convoy Section was established in the Trade Division of the Admiralty to organize and control convoys,[25] and not until the end of the year that all overseas shipping had been brought into the system. By then it was evident that the corner had been turned. The reason was not simply that U-boats had to confront or at least approach the vicinity of escorting warships in order to attack merchantmen, but that the concentration of ships into widely spaced groups reduced the U-boats' chances of sighting targets, especially as the groups were routed around boats whose wireless signals had enabled their position to be fixed by direction-finding cross-bearings. Thus, U-boat commanders, instead of finding a more or less continuous stream of undefended single ships steering along 'approach routes', were confronted with vistas of empty sea. By December total merchant shipping losses from mines, submarines and surface raiders had dropped below 400,000 tons.[26]

The German High Command had long since realized that the unrestricted campaign would not bring Britain to her knees. In July the leader of the Centre Party in the Reichstag, sensing their doubts, had made a series of powerful speeches refuting the claim that the war could be ended in foreseeable time by even the present rate of merchant shipping destruction. He had contrasted increasing Allied war production with Germany's shortages of food, fuel and raw materials, and with the support of the Social Democrats carried a 'Peace Resolution' renouncing annexations and political, economic or financial oppression. In this crisis for the military Bethmann took responsibility for the loss of confidence in the government and resigned, playing his part loyally to the end. He was replaced by a nominee of Hindenburg and Ludendorff.

Arthur Zimmermann, meanwhile, had attempted another intervention on behalf of the military, this time on the eastern front. In March the Russian imperial capital, Petrograd – formerly St Petersburg – had erupted in mass strikes and troop mutinies brought on by hunger, inflation and shortages. Unable to control the revolutionary ferment, the Tsar's government had resigned and the representative chamber, the Duma, established after the 1905 revolution, and now a centre of opposition to ministers' conduct of the war, had called on the Tsar himself to abdicate. Army chiefs, placing their hopes in representative government to restore order and continue the war, supported the demand; and Nicholas II obliged.

Zimmermann had then taken a hand by having the revolutionary Marxist anti-war intellectual who went by the pseudonym of Lenin smuggled into Russia from exile in Switzerland by way of Germany and neutral Sweden. Lenin had just set out his interpretation of the war as a collision between expansionist empires driven by monopoly finance capitalism, and his simple remedy to prevent future wars: the overthrow of capitalism everywhere.[27] Arriving in Petrograd in April, he had worked to convince his Bolshevik faction of the socialist movement that they must replace the 'bourgeois' provisional government set up by the Duma with a government of the people as represented by the councils of factory workers, soldiers or peasants known as soviets which had sprung up throughout Russia.

In November he realized his aim. A Bolshevik-led coup toppled the provisional government and he was elected chairman of a new Soviet administration. Needing peace to bring about socialism, he called for an immediate armistice, but as talks began at Brest-Litovsk the country split in a ferocious civil war, officers of the former tsarist regime leading 'White' armies against the 'Red' Soviet forces, fatally undermining resistance to German demands. Eventually, in March 1918, Lenin was forced to accept humiliating peace terms in which Russia lost a million square miles of territory, most of its coal and oil deposits and a third of its population. Lenin and his colleagues survived, nonetheless, to drive forward their vision of socialism against the 'Whites' and all 'class enemies' by means of organized terror echoing the bloodiest days of the French Revolution,[28] and as with that great convulsion changing the course of history.

The Russian civil war, the Treaty of Brest-Litovsk and a similar treaty forced on Rumania two months later[29] gave Germany mastery of the continent from the Baltic states and the shores of the Black Sea in the east to Belgium and the most industrially productive north-eastern regions of France in the west, and allowed Hindenburg and Ludendorff to transfer some forty divisions totalling 600,000 troops from the eastern and Italian fronts to face the Allies in the west. They prepared a massive offensive before the Americans arrived in force.

It was too late. US entry into the war had enabled the commercial blockade of the central powers to be tightened. In January 1918 food shortages brought 200,000 workers in Vienna out on strike and towards the end of that month Berlin workers followed suit; they were soon joined by thousands in other major German cities. The demonstrations were suppressed under martial law, but the popular unrest stood in contrast to the relative quiet in Britain, where the diet of workers actually improved after the introduction of a fair system of rationing that year, and mortality rates declined.[30] Von Holtzendorff's U-boat campaign had failed, owing not only to the convoy system, but also to increased merchant ship construction, particularly in the United States, and the enticement of neutral shipowners with high freight rates and war risks insurance. Von Holtzendorff had met his sinking targets at the beginning of the campaign, but the total shipping available to supply Britain far exceeded his estimates.

Hindenburg and Ludendorff launched their final offensive, 'the last desperate *va banque* play of the war',[31] as it has been described, on 21 March 1918, the main thrust aimed at the British sector of the front on the Somme around St Quentin. Achieving tactical surprise and initial success, they squandered it in pursuit of changing tactical objectives. They also lacked transport to bring up supplies. They had 36,000 motor vehicles against 300,000 on the Allied side. It had been an industrial war from the beginning; the advantage had tipped decisively to the Western Allies, both in scale of production and innovation. The tank was one example: the British had over four hundred available for the front, the French over five hundred, the Germans none.[32]

Heavy artillery played an even more significant role in the final phase in the summer of 1918 after the German offensive had been halted and the Allied armies, including substantial numbers of US troops, counter-attacked. The great guns set the pattern of battle. Tanks and infantry advanced behind moving curtains of shellfire directed with previously unattainable accuracy to knock out opposing batteries and isolate enemy positions. The expenditure of ammunition was prodigious. On the British sector a record 943,847 shells were fired in one twenty-four-hour period between 28 and 29 September,[33] an average of over 650 rounds every minute. The Germans termed it the *Materialschlacht* – the materiel battle. It was clear they had lost it. They were also faced with the arrival of ever more fresh American divisions.[34] Morale at the front was already affected by food shortages at home[35] and it was clear to objective staff officers by the end of September that the war was lost irretrievably; they foresaw the disintegration of the army and Bolshevik revolution in the cities unless negotiations were opened with the Allies. Even Hindenburg and Ludendorff were persuaded of the need for an armistice. Wilhelm appointed a new Chancellor, who formed a government representing the majority socialist-liberal coalition in the Reichstag and sent a note to President Wilson seeking peace talks.

Only the Naval Staff planned offensive action. The overriding impulse was concern for the honour of the naval officer corps.[36] The plan was drawn up on 10 October as Operation Order No. 19. Two groups of destroyers would be used as bait to draw the Grand Fleet down over lines of U-boats and new minefields to the southern North Sea, where the High Seas Fleet would be waiting to meet it in the decisive battle off the Dutch coast.

It was not to be. The fleet had been idle for too long; the men had been infected by the collapse in morale of the civilian population and socialist agitation for peace among shipyard workers in the home ports. Grievances over food further embittered relations. The men ate better than shore workers, but their diet lacked variety and they knew the officers enjoyed abundant fare they could only dream of, and wines and tobacco in their messes ashore. It was exposure to the hardships suffered by civilians and radical socialist agitation for peace among workers ashore, however, together with the entry of the United States with its inexhaustible resources, which had the greatest effect on morale.

When, towards the end of October, Hipper ordered the fleet prepared for sea, the men rebelled, suspecting the officers of wishing only to retrieve their honour with a glorious death in battle; their pent-up anger flared. Sailors and stokers refused duty; petty officers were locked in their cabins; officers feared for their lives. Hipper was forced to call off the operation, and in an attempt to split the mutineers dispersed some ships to other bases. This served only to spread the disaffection. Sailors joined industrial work-ers in north German ports and marched behind red flags through the streets. As with the Russian revolution, sailors', workers' and soldiers' councils were formed and the revolt spread inland to the industrial cities. By 9 November it had reached Berlin.

That day Wilhelm's new Chancellor resigned in favour of the leader of the Social Democratic Party in the Reichstag. His representatives had already travelled to Compiègne and in a railway carriage outside the town heard the harsh armistice terms the Allies were imposing on a defeated Germany, including a continuation of the blockade to ensure the conditions were met. Ludendorff, who had suffered a nervous breakdown, had resigned previously; now Scheer reported belatedly to Wilhelm that the fleet could no longer be relied upon. Wilhelm's world had crumbled: his chief ally, Austria-Hungary, had secured an armistice the previous week. Now even his fleet had deserted him. He fled to exile in the Netherlands.

It was fitting that his beloved creation, the fleet, should have been a catalyst for his destruction. Not only had it brought Great Britain and finally the United States into the alliance against him, its personnel policies, designed to defend the privileges of a small corps of executive officers against engineers and other specialists, were, as Holger Herwig has put it, 'a mirror of the Wilhelmine class state with its growing antagonisms that ultimately split and paralysed German society as a whole'.[37]

18

The Baton Passes

SINCE EARLY 1918, when it became apparent that the failure of the unrestricted U-boat campaign and American entry into the war would deny Germany an annexationist victory, Hindenburg and Ludendorff had thought increasingly in terms of a 'second Punic War'. By accepting armistice terms in October while still in possession of enemy territory they had avoided the outward show of military defeat. German soldiers marched home with their rifles, to be garlanded as heroes; no Allied armies staged a triumph in Berlin as had happened in Paris after Napoleon's defeat and again after France's defeat by the Prusso-German armies in 1871. Allied reluctance to press on to the German capital was understandable in view of the number of lives already lost, but in retrospect it was a mistake. It allowed Ludendorff and military propagandists to manufacture a myth that the army had not been beaten in the field, but stabbed in the back by politicians at home.

In reality German troops were surrendering in mass in the final months of the war.[1] The true scale of German defeat was reflected in the armistice terms: German forces were required to retire behind their own borders and surrender major weapons, including all U-boats and most of their warships and merchantmen. To ensure compliance, the Allies continued the blockade.

The greater part of the High Seas Fleet sailed from the Jade for the last time on 21 November and set course for an appointed rendezvous off the Firth of Forth, nine dreadnought battleships, five battlecruisers, seven light cruisers and forty-nine destroyers in single line ahead, guns disarmed and trained fore and aft. They were met by Beatty's Grand Fleet – including US battleships – formed in two great lines 6 miles apart, 370 ships all told, all hands at action stations, guns loaded. The German column, led by a British light cruiser, steered between the British lines, and Beatty reversed course to shepherd them to internment inside the Firth of Forth. During the next few days they were inspected, then escorted in batches to their final anchorage inside the Grand Fleet base at Scapa Flow. At the same time

U-boats arrived in groups at the east coast flotilla base of Harwich, 176 in all; a further eight sank on the way across.

It was an unprecedented end for the fleet of a major power. The British newspapers were scathing about 'so inglorious a surrender' (the *Manchester Guardian*), and reminded their readers of the sinking of the *Lusitania* and other barbarities committed in defiance of all codes of sea warfare. Germans and Austrians felt equal outrage at the Allied naval blockade, which had caused the deaths of untold numbers of civilians through malnutrition and actual starvation, and continued to do so through that winter long after the armistice. The 'Hunger Blockade' was to become as potent a symbol for those seeking vengeance as the myth of the army's 'stab in the back' by civilian ministers.

The other motifs for German militarists and nationalists arose from the peace conference that opened at Versailles in January 1919. As Margaret MacMillan makes clear in her brilliant evocation of the personalities and proceedings, almost everyone gathered there assumed that Germany had started the war:

> Everyone agreed that Germany, and the Germans, deserved punishment. Even [Woodrow] Wilson, who had insisted during the war that his only quarrel was with the German ruling classes, now seemed to blame the whole of the German people. 'They would be shunned and avoided like lepers for generations to come,' he told his intimates . . . Everyone agreed that Germany must somehow be prevented from dragging Europe into war again.[2]

The big three at the conference, Woodrow Wilson, Lloyd George, who led the British Empire delegation, and the French premier, Georges Clemenceau, were agreed upon three broad aims: to punish Germany, to make her pay reparations that reflected the damage caused by the war, and to prevent her starting another war. The scale of the punishment and the size of the reparations caused difficulties, and in the absence of agreement the problem was turned over to a special commission. This did not report until 1921, but Germany's legal liability to pay reparations was set out in the peace treaty signed at Versailles in June, and these so-called 'war guilt' clauses, particularly Article 231 assigning responsibility for all damage caused by the war to Germany and its allies, joined the 'Hunger Blockade' and the 'stab in the back' in the German nationalist propaganda lexicon.

In truth, the whole treaty stuck in the German collective throat. They had trusted Woodrow Wilson to mediate a 'just' settlement. What they received was humiliation. They were stripped of their former overseas colonies, to be divided between Britain, France and Japan, and lost some 13 per cent of the European territory of the Reich with the return of Alsace and Lorraine to France, the reconstruction of an independent Poland in the east and other minor adjustments. They had already been virtually disarmed; they were to be prohibited from manufacturing tanks, armoured cars, warplanes, U–boats or poison gas and limited to an army of 100,000 men; the Great General Staff was to be liquidated and conscription disallowed. To ensure compliance, the Saar valley would be occupied and an Allied Control Commission would have powers to inspect their factories and military and naval installations. The severity of the terms stunned the German delegation; the leader remarked afterwards that the treaty could have been expressed in one clause: 'Germany renounces its existence'.[3]

Over the following weeks the Germans composed a remonstrance against the war guilt clauses and the requirement that Germany alone should disarm and be required to make reparations. The Allies rejected the appeal. The essence of Wilson's vision for an enduring peace was the establishment of a League of Nations which would design and implement a scheme of international disarmament and guarantee the freedom and security of individual nations. The Covenant of the League formed Part 1 of the peace treaty with Germany, and the Allies replied to the German objection to the disarmament clauses by stating that these were 'the first steps toward that general reduction and limitation of armaments which they seek to bring about as one of the most fruitful preventives of war, and which it will be one of the first duties of the League of Nations to promote'.[4] As for reparations, the size of the bill had still to be decided by the special commission, whose conclusions were to be based very largely on German ability to pay.

On 28 June, anniversary of the murders at Sarajevo that had lit the fuse of war, two reluctant delegates from a newly formed German government were ushered into the Hall of Mirrors in the Palace of Versailles, where in 1871 the King of Prussia had been crowned German emperor, and signed what was dubbed by their countrymen 'the peace of shame'. The army High Command had given approval hours before the government secured assent in the National Assembly;[5] nonetheless, nationalists were able to portray the signatures on the treaty as further evidence that the army and country had been sold out by corrupt politicians.

The larger myth of the vindictive and ultimately self-defeating nature of the Versailles settlement with Germany was endorsed from an unlikely quarter. The German delegates who drafted their vain remonstrance against the Allied terms could not have been expected to admit war guilt or remorse for the unimaginable scale of death, dislocation and suffering inflicted on Europe over the past four years, the innumerable broken homes and bereavements, the disablement and disfigurement, famine, malnutrition, disease and material devastation,[6] and there was every reason for them to avoid mentioning the rapacious treaty Germany had forced on Russia at Brest-Litovsk or Germany's annexationist war aims in the west. Wilhelm's government had financed the war largely by borrowing and had always intended to repay the debt by robbing the defeated enemy,[7] much as Napoleon had financed his wars of European conquest by plunder. Now the positions were reversed; it was they who had to plead for mercy. That their arguments should be supported by an influential member of the British team in Paris must have surprised them.

John Maynard Keynes, Chief Treasury Adviser to the British delegation, was an exceedingly clever young economist with advanced views. Contemptuous of his seniors and the leading Allied negotiators, he fell easy prey to German arguments since they suited his own belief that the ruin to which Europe had been reduced could best be repaired by loans to help rebuild the shattered continent rather than by further depressing the economy of the beaten foe with high reparations. Keynes was not alone in criticizing the oppressive terms of the treaty; many in the American and British delegations felt that the opportunity to establish a 'new order' based on Wilson's original principles had been betrayed,[8] but it was Keynes's onslaught on the treaty in *The Economic Consequences of the Peace*, published at the end of 1919 and an immediate best-seller, not least in the German edition, which passed into accepted wisdom, as did his critique of the size of reparations when they were fixed in 1921. Recently historians have come to realize that Germany paid a fraction of the sum imposed and this was, in any case, far less onerous than Keynes and others had asserted. Of the total bill of 132 billion gold marks – some £6.6 billion – fixed by the commission, only 50 billion were for payment in the short term, the remainder becoming payable when the German economy had recovered sufficiently.[9] In the event the majority social democratic government established in Weimar pursued a deliberate policy of currency inflation, deficit financing and regular defaults, which enabled them to avoid paying even the initial 50 billion.[10]

Besides deliberately resisting payment, Weimar's inflationary policy served the vital internal aims of expanding German industry and providing jobs and social welfare to prevent the workers turning to Bolshevism. The deliberate devaluation of the currency also wiped out Germany's internal war debt; instead of robbing the defeated enemy as Wilhelm's ministers had intended, the Weimar government robbed German war bond holders by reducing the real value of their investments ultimately to zero. Niall Ferguson has shown that by 1922 Germany's national debt had been brought down in real terms practically to its pre-war level – $1.3 billion against $1.23 billion. At the same time the victor powers, pursuing sound money policies, continued to service hugely increased internal debts built up during the war – $23.4 billion for the United States, $34.3 billion for Britain, $27.8 billion for France.[11] In addition Britain and France owed the United States $4.7 billion and $4 billion respectively. In financial terms, Germany, defeated in war, won the peace.

For this she paid a terrible social price. By wiping out savings and bank balances, inflation reduced the middle classes to penury and a hand-to-mouth existence, destroyed respect for government and law and promoted speculation, sharp practice and excess over thrift and integrity, unhinging all moral values and the very fabric of society.[12] The peak year was 1923, when the mark rose giddily through millions up to billions to the dollar. The son of a high Prussian official who later fled to England and established himself as a writer under the pseudonym Sebastian Haffner recalled the inward significance:

> In that year an entire generation of Germans had a spiritual organ removed: the organ which gives men steadfastness and balance, but also a certain inertia and stolidity. It may variously appear as conscience, reason, experience, respect for law, morality or the fear of God. A whole generation learned then – or thought it learned – to do without such ballast.[13]

At this date the National Socialist German Workers' ('Nazi') Party was one of several groups and paramilitary organizations espousing extreme nationalist, anti-Marxist socialism and biological anti-Semitism, and working for a revolution to oust the democratic government at Weimar. The government itself prepared the ground. The devaluation of social, intellectual and moral standards under the onset of hyperinflation created the conditions for the revolutionary change that occurred ten years later in the wake of the worldwide financial crisis provoked by the Wall Street 'crash' of 1929. The Nazi Party polled sufficient votes to share in coalition government. Its leader, Adolf Hitler, was appointed Chancellor.

Hitler lost little time in dispensing with representative government, so Germany again came under the supreme direction of a dangerously unbalanced fantasist. Wilhelm II, imbibing the values of the Prussian guards, had imagined himself a feudal warlord. Hitler had come under different influences: addressing public meetings around the country, he had tuned in to the darkest desires and fears of his audiences and, amplifying them, transformed himself into the embodiment of their most primitive emotions.

Hitler also represented the vengefulness and ambition of the Prusso-German elites. His rise to power had depended entirely on support from and compromise with the power groupings behind Germany's initial drive for European, then world, hegemony, the military, landed estate owners and large industrialists. In both armed services a nucleus of officers imbued with traditional warrior values was dedicated to overturning democratic government, unshackling the 'fetters' of Versailles and reversing the decision of the recent war. Both armed services had worked directly to circumvent the disarmament clauses of Versailles. In partnership with industrialists they had set up companies or affiliates in the Netherlands, Sweden and Spain to design and develop U-boats, tanks and warplanes, and under the guise of trade treaties with Soviet Russia conducted secret experiments on Russian soil with tanks, aircraft, poison gas and other weapons in return for providing the Bolsheviks with technical assistance and training.[14] The Weimar government had been complicit. As a result, by the time Hitler seized power everything was in place for rearmament on a grand scale.

Within days of Hitler's appointment as Chancellor on 30 January 1933 he made it clear that he intended to fulfil pledges made to his backers in big business, finance and the military. He told his Cabinet that Germany's future depended 'exclusively and solely on rebuilding the armed forces'. All other expenditure had to be subordinated to rearmament; a few days later he promised to implement a generous road-building scheme and grant tax relief for car manufacture.

Meanwhile, his lieutenants began a campaign of terror against the internal Marxist enemy. This reached a climax after a clandestine team from the paramilitary wing of the party set fire to the Reichstag and left a Dutch communist youth to be caught inside.[15] The outrage served as pretext for rounding up communist, social democrat and trade union leaders according to previously prepared lists. Their absence from a reconvened assembly in the Kroll Opera House and the intimidating effect on representatives of other parties allowed Hitler to change the constitution with an 'Enabling Act' permitting him to govern without parliamentary constraint.

The brief German experiment in democracy was over. The following year the President, Field Marshal von Hindenburg, died. Hitler had arranged that on his death the office of Reich President – including supreme command of the armed forces – would be combined with his own office of Reich Chancellor; and the day after Hindenburg's death he had all members of the armed forces swear an oath of unconditional personal loyalty to himself as Führer and commander-in-chief of the armed forces. He now had total power.[16]

As Germany set course for war, the victor powers sought to perpetuate peace with arms limitation treaties. While in part this was a response to public anti-war sentiment and over-simple demonization of the great armaments barons as 'merchants of death', the real impulse came from the prospect of another naval building race, this time between Britain, the United States and Japan.

Britain had ended the war with a preponderance of naval strength over other powers not seen since the end of the Napoleonic wars; excluding the interned German fleet, the Royal Navy was practically equal to all other navies of the world combined.[17] Equally indisputably the United States had emerged as the greatest industrial and financial power, and New York had supplanted London as the world's banker.[18] Naturally US Navy officers, imbued with the doctrines of Mahan, saw the need to build a fleet able to wield power commensurate with the country's commercial and financial strength. A building programme announced in 1918 to augment the 1916 Naval Appropriations Act provided for a force of fifty-one battleships and battlecruisers, far greater than the Grand Fleet at its zenith and ship for ship more powerful. The evident intention was to supplant the Royal Navy as arbiter of maritime power and usher in the American millennium.[19] It was also inspired by hostility to British imperialism shading to Anglophobia.

The size of the projected fleet raised huge anxiety at the Admiralty in London. For officers raised in the belief that Britain, her empire and dominant position in the world were dependent on the Royal Navy, the prospect of losing supremacy seemed to threaten their very identity. It was not a logical position. The Royal Navy had already shared primacy in the east with Japan, in the Mediterranean with France and in the western hemisphere with the United States. Britain and the United States were both commercial nations with a common heritage and common interests in preserving world peace for trade and financial markets. The logical position would have been to welcome the US Navy as a partner in shouldering the white man's burden. But for British naval officers this would have been to deny their inheritance.

President Wilson's position was hardly more rational. On the one hand the centrepiece of his peace policy was a League of Nations to guarantee 'collective security' and reduction in armaments, on the other he was proposing US naval increases that would have seemed excessive during the Anglo-German naval arms race at the beginning of the century; while American objections to British imperialism were a reflection of US history and culture as well as awakening strength. They were as visceral as British admirals' refusal to contemplate losing sea supremacy.

As a result relations between the US and British delegations to the Paris peace conference were soured by dispute between the naval members. It was particularly unfortunate that the US naval team was headed by Admiral Benson, who impressed Lloyd George as having 'a double dose of Anglo-Phobia'.[20] Neither Benson nor a new British First Sea Lord, Admiral Sir Rosslyn Wemyss, would give an inch in argument about the projected size of the US fleet, and towards the end of March their political chiefs were called to Paris to mediate. The First Lord of the Admiralty reiterated the British position to his US counterpart, Josephus Daniels: the supremacy of the Royal Navy was 'an absolute necessity, not only for the very existence of the British Empire, but even for the peace of the world'[21] – a curious statement so soon after the worldwide bloodletting of the past four years. Benson immediately interjected: the American people demanded that their navy take an equal share in safeguarding civilization; after which he and Wemyss exchanged such bitter comments that Daniels feared they would come to blows.[22]

Diplomats patched up the quarrel in April, and the following month Daniels made it clear to Congress that the 1918 programme would be abandoned. Even before this temporary naval truce members of the British and American delegations were cooperating closely on most other aspects of the peace negotiations, and the relationship continued to flourish during the conference, in marked contrast to British and American relations with other delegations, particularly the French.[23]

The treaty finally agreed at the peace conference opened with a Covenant or Constitution for a League of Nations dedicated to a system of 'collective security' under which national armaments could be reduced. This was the big idea which Wilson had crossed the Atlantic to bestow on the feuding Europeans. Unfortunately the projected League was not provided with the means to enforce its resolutions. US service chiefs doubted the practicability of an international armed force; the British Admiralty was equally sceptical, and argued that the necessity of using force for objects other than the defence of vital national interests could lead to an increase in armaments, so defeating the objects of the League. The saddest irony was that Wilson, after returning home, was unable to convince the US

Senate of the benefits of collective security; consequently the United States did not ratify the treaty – instead signing bilateral peace treaties with the former enemy powers – and never joined the League of Nations established by the Europeans in Geneva.

Wilson himself did not recover from a massive stroke he suffered while taking his arguments for the treaty and the League directly to the American people. In his moral fervour and oratorical power, Wilson bears comparison with Gladstone; and like Gladstone, he refused to compromise with political opponents. This, ultimately, was his undoing and the cause of his failure to bring Congress round to his vision of the United States leading an association of free nations, each secured by mutual guarantees of political independence and territorial integrity.

Japan had been allowed little part in the peace negotiations. She had done well out of the war as Britain's ally. Without mounting major operations she had gained Germany's Pacific island possessions in the Marshall, Mariana and Caroline groups and taken over German concessions on the Shantung peninsula of mainland China opposite Korea. Meanwhile her exports, particularly textiles, had penetrated Eastern markets that the Western powers could no longer supply; her munitions industries had been boosted by Allied orders, her merchant fleet had doubled in response to the increases in trade and her shipbuilding capacity had increased sevenfold.[24] The consequent growth in the economy allowed her to pay off her foreign debts; she had become a creditor nation, and with formidable armed services was indisputably a major power. When the German ships interned in Scapa Flow were scuttled in an act of defiance ordered from Berlin, the Japanese navy became the third largest in the world.

It had been a remarkable transformation in the half-century since the 'Meiji Restoration',[25] but one to which the Western powers had difficulty in adjusting. For one thing, the almost total domination of the world by a few Western nations was interpreted in terms of race rather than weapon systems; consequently Asiatic peoples were viewed in the West as demonstrably inferior. By the same token the British and Americans, the most successful in spreading their civilization around the globe, regarded 'Anglo-Saxons' as the 'master race'. For another thing, Japan, her customs and language remained mysterious and largely inaccessible to Westerners. Added to this was anxiety about the industrious Japanese undercutting the West economically.

For US and British service chiefs it was the evident Japanese ambitions in mainland Asia which caused concern. The US Navy Department had developed a 'Plan Orange' for war against Japan as early as 1907.[26] In 1916 the British Admiralty War Staff had noted the island empire's 'ideas of a greater Japan which will probably comprise parts of China . . . the Dutch East Indies, Singapore and the Malay States'.[27]

Thus the Japanese delegation to the Paris peace conference had been the object of mixed curiosity and suspicion, and largely because of the racial stereotype was accorded less weight than the victorious Western powers. The Japanese kept their own counsel. The head of the delegation, Prince Saionji Kinmochi, was one of the more remarkable statesmen of his time. Descended from an aristocratic line loyal to the imperial dynasty that the Tokugawas sidelined, he had fought in the civil war that restored the young Meiji, and subsequently travelled to Europe with other courtiers on a mission to study and report on Western customs. Settling in Paris, he had taken a French mistress, learned the language and, unlike many of his fellows abroad among the barbarians, enjoyed himself and stayed for nine years, assimilating the liberal and artistic culture of the host nation.

At the Paris peace conference Saionji, then seventy years old, had instructions to ensure that Japan retained control of the former German islands in the Pacific and the Shantung concessions, and to have a clause enshrining racial equality inserted in the Covenant of the League of Nations. He attended no formal sessions, but met and charmed leading members of the other delegations at the many social functions, and when he felt it necessary used the threat of Japanese withdrawal from the conference to strengthen his case. In the end he succeeded in having Japanese rights to her conquests recognized, but failed on the issue of racial equality. The problem was immigration. It was feared that if racial equality were legally adopted large numbers of oriental immigrants would enter the British dominions and the western states of America and subvert the culture. The Japanese press seized on the humiliation; yet it is doubtful that the anger generated by this setback had any real influence on subsequent Japanese policy. The course had already been set in the highest levels of the ruling oligarchy and it was not directed towards peaceful coexistence with the West.

The navy had a vital role in Japanese future planning. The country lacked oil and most natural resources for industry; the navy had not only to guarantee supplies coming in and manufactured goods going out by sea, but in the longer term to ensure the acquisition by conquest of the vital sources of raw materials within a greater Japanese empire. The huge US fleet-building programme was in large part a response to the threat. The Japanese were already building 16-inch-gun battleships equal in power to

American battleships, and in 1920 authorized a programme that would give them sixteen of these super-dreadnoughts within seven years. The British Admiralty had to react: their 1921 naval estimates provided for four 16-inch-gun battlecruisers, to be followed by four 18-inch-gun battleships.[28]

The situation was alarming. German militarism had just been defeated and the League of Nations established, yet the victorious powers were being drawn into another naval armaments race, this time centred on the Pacific. Public opinion in the United States and Britain was outraged, forcing both governments to re-examine the prospects for arms limitation by agreement. It seemed the more urgent since a worldwide trade recession was driving ministers to cut public expenditure. Armaments were a prime target. In the United States Congress undermined the fleet-building programme by halving the 1921 naval budget. In Britain the Treasury demanded equally drastic naval cuts. At the same time the government put out feelers to the incoming US President, Warren Harding, for an Arms Limitation Conference, and made it clear that Britain would accept naval parity with the United States.

It was a historic turning point; but the government had no realistic alternative. The economy was burdened with war debt and reined in by deflationary policies insisted on by the City of London to restore its former primacy. Moreover, the strong tide of public feeling against war and armaments ran alongside demands for better social welfare provision and made spending on a capital shipbuilding programme to match those of the United States and Japan politically impossible. Without it the Royal Navy's pre-Jutland battle fleet would sink into third place.

President Harding faced comparable domestic pressures for cost-cutting and responded to the British approach by convening a naval armaments limitation conference in Washington. Britain, Japan, France and Italy were invited and subsequent invitations were extended to China, the Netherlands, Belgium and Portugal for those sessions relating to the Far East. The American delegation worked with the US Navy General Board in advance to prepare a detailed plan for fleet reduction and the establishment of permanent ratios of naval strength between the major powers based on capital ship tonnage. Delegates were startled when the scheme was outlined by the US Secretary of State at the opening session on 12 November 1921; but having seized the initiative the Americans were able to gain most of their objectives. Ratios of capital ship tonnage between the United States, Britain and Japan were agreed at 5:5:3 respectively, with France and Italy at 1.67 each. The Japanese had held out for 70 per cent of the US allowance but accepted the lower figure in return for a mutual agreement not to fortify bases in the western Pacific. This left their fleet in a commanding position in the area. A prime American objective to break up the Anglo-Japanese Alliance, however, was achieved by replacing it with a Four Power Pact signed between the United States, Britain, Japan and France, which agreed to consult in the event of controversy between any two signatories.

The disappointment, even fury, with which all three major navies reacted to the limitation ratios imposed indicated their success in curbing expenditure, at least on capital shipbuilding. Cruisers, destroyers and submarines, however, were not covered by the agreements and national rivalries transferred to these cheaper vessels, particularly cruisers. In 1927 the United States government attempted to halt the new competition by calling another conference, this time in Geneva under the aegis of the League of Nations, with the aim of applying the Washington ratios to all types of warship. It failed, but the search for a solution was taken up by a new US President, Herbert Hoover, elected in 1928. Determined to end Anglo-American misunderstandings, he found an enthusiastic partner in the British Labour Prime Minister, Ramsay MacDonald, who came to power the following year. When MacDonald made it clear he accepted the US claim to parity in naval strength the way was opened for detailed bilateral discussions prior to another conference of the major naval powers, which MacDonald agreed to host in London.

While British and US naval officers addressed the technical problems of tonnage and gunpower in relation to national needs, Captain Yamamoto Isoroku of the Imperial Japanese Navy General Staff was engaged in similar but informal discussions with a former US navy contact, now President Hoover's naval aide.[29] Yamamoto was recognized in his service as a brilliant officer. After graduating top of his year from the Naval War College he had been sent to America to study English at Harvard, and on return to Japan had served as an instructor at the War College before being appointed to the Air Planning section of the Naval General Staff. He had then been posted to command the navy's top-secret Air Development Station on the shore of the large Lake Kasumigo-Ura north-east of Tokyo. Argument raged in all three major navies at this period between advocates of air power, who foresaw aircraft carriers replacing battleships as the capital units of the future, and traditionalists, who believed great gunned ships would withstand aerial attack and remain the backbone of the fleet. Yamamoto was decidedly an 'air' man. The naval pilots under his command, who took off and landed on flight decks improvised on lakeside wharves and barges, reached levels of skill in bombing and running torpedoes unmatched in either the US or British services at this period.

In 1926 Yamamoto had been posted as naval attaché to the Japanese embassy in Washington. It was there he had made the contacts he used in his discussions prior to the London Naval Conference. He had also monitored a debate on a future Pacific war sparked by a book from a British naval expert and spy named Hector Bywater, earlier 'Jackie' Fisher's most important source on the progress of Tirpitz's building programme.[30] Bywater had subsequently written a fictional 'history' of a US–Japanese conflict set in the 1930s, *The Great Pacific War*,[31] which was the subject of much discussion during Yamamoto's time in Washington prior to the London Naval Conference. Bywater imagined Japan opening hostilities with a surprise attack intended to wipe out the American fleet in the Pacific, just as she had attacked China in 1894 and the Russian Port Arthur fleet in 1904 without declaring war. It did not correspond with current Japanese plans, which had the fleet acting defensively until the superior US fleet had been whittled down by attrition during its passage to the western Pacific, rather as the German Naval Staff had hoped to whittle down the Grand Fleet before the decisive engagement. Nonetheless, Bywater's concept evidently impressed Yamamoto.[32]

Behind a quiet, professional front, Yamamoto hid a combative nature expressed in competitive games, poker and chess in particular. He was small, slight and athletic; at parties he might throw somersaults, perform headstands or dance jigs without inhibition, and he had many party tricks.[33] In his discussions in Washington before the London conference he played a secret game, no doubt relishing it. Unlike the Americans, who genuinely wanted to limit naval building, the Japanese were exploiting the restriction on capital ship construction by pouring funds into the newer arms of the service, particularly submarines and the naval air force. Yamamoto's brief was to convince the Americans that Japan's chief interest was in cruisers to police the empire and essential shipping routes, and steer them away from limits on submarines or naval aircraft.

The tactics succeeded brilliantly at the conference, which opened in January 1930. Japan secured a ratio in practice of 70 per cent of US tonnage in cruisers,[34] 70 per cent in destroyers and parity in submarines; of greater significance, naval aircraft were omitted altogether from the final treaty. Both the USA and Britain had sought, not for the first time, to abolish submarines, but Japanese arguments against abolition had been supported by France and Italy on the grounds that submarines were the weapon of the weaker power. The British and Americans had to be content with a restriction on the size of individual boats to 2,000 tons, and an article stipulating that when attacking merchant ships submarines had to obey international law:

> . . . [they] may not sink or render incapable of navigation a merchant vessel without having first placed passengers, crew and ship's papers in a place of safety. For this purpose the ship's boats are not regarded as a place of safety unless the safety of passengers and crew is assured . . . by the proximity of land, or the presence of another vessel which is in a position to take them on board.[35]

By according the Royal Navy equal first place with the United States Navy, the Washington and London naval treaties veiled Britain's loss of sea supremacy. The outward show remained. Correlli Barnett has captured the 'neo-Victorian' character of the 1930s service as its trim ships showed the flag around the world, the officers hosting 'cocktail parties under broad awnings spread above white decks as the Royal Marine band played the latest popular hits'.[36] That was not the whole story. High standards of war training were maintained and the lessons of the recent conflict were analysed obsessively on tactical boards and in fleet exercises. Materiel deficiencies were corrected; long-base rangefinders were fitted to great gun turrets and the fire control system was redesigned on the lines Pollen had pioneered to provide helm-free gunnery out to 30,000 yards. Night fighting was practised to such an extent that it became accepted there was much to gain from seeking action after dark.

Tradition and pride were kept bright, as the next conflict would prove, but the mastery symbolized by the white ensign had dissolved in the terms imposed by the naval treaties. There were insufficient capital ships for the Admiralty to send a fleet to the Far East while retaining command in home waters, and most were unmodernized. The only two new battleships Britain was allowed to build were by reason of the tonnage limitations foreshortened, all 16-inch guns grouped forward and scarcely able to fire abaft the beam without damaging the bridge structure. The numbers of cruisers and destroyers were wholly inadequate to defend imperial trade routes, or even Atlantic convoys; and there was not one adequately defended base throughout the British Empire. Despite this, as Paul Kennedy has pointed out, the system of imperial defence remained predicated on naval supremacy: 'The gap between theory and actuality was now enormous.'[37]

Much of the decline would have occurred in any case. The triple impositions of war debt, world trade depression after the Wall Street crash and public sentiment against armaments – overlooking the necessity for a world empire acquired in large part by the sword to defend itself by the sword – would have compelled deep cuts in the naval estimates irrespective of limitation agreements.

There were more serious aspects of decline for which public and politicians bore little blame, only naval officers. Whereas Britain and her navy had sailed into the twentieth century as advancing powers and Fisher had set the pace for navies everywhere, since the peace the service had looked backwards. Materiel and tactical failures at Jutland had been analysed endlessly and correctives applied to ensure victory in the great fleet battle of the next war, but strategy based on the surface battle fleet had scarcely been questioned, except by specialists in the newer underwater and air arms. Instead of bringing on submarines and naval aircraft as striking forces in their own right to challenge surface command, the naval staff called them into the service of the great gunned ships for reconnaissance and, when battle was joined, for aircraft to assist fleet fire control by 'spotting' the fall of shot. This failure of imagination was exacerbated by a political decision taken in 1918 to amalgamate the Royal Naval Air Service and the army's Royal Flying Corps to form an independent Royal Air Force. The navy lost control of aircraft development to the new service and fell irreversibly behind the Japanese and Americans in the design and operation of carrier-borne planes. By the 1930s the former mistress of the seas had not only lost the ability to defend the British Empire if beset at opposite sides of the globe, it had dropped to third place in the world's navies in terms of modern fighting strength.

The growth of the US Navy as the Royal Navy's natural successor was hampered by similar factors, financial stringency and public hostility to war extending to President Hoover and his administration. The fleet was not even brought up to the level permitted by the London treaty.

While the US and British services suffered from public indifference or active pacifist disapproval, the Japanese prepared for war. The Japanese merchant class had failed – again – to moderate the warrior ethos imposed by the system. The great merchant cartels disparagingly termed *zaibatsu* had grown immensely rich in the recent commercial expansion and between them controlled the nation's industry, commerce and financial services. Had they conformed to the British–Western model they should have imposed merchant values on government and society. Instead, they had integrated into the ruling oligarchy, adopting the feudal values of the samurai behind the Meiji restoration. Crucially, they had not sought to constrain the emperor set up for veneration as a god to legitimize the regime's hold on power. The constitution established in 1889 was, of course, modelled on Bismarck's constitution, and the situation of the young Emperor Hirohito in the 1930s resembled that of Kaiser Wilhelm II before the war.

In personality they were quite different. Hirohito entirely lacked Wilhelm's flamboyant braggadocio. He was a reticent intellectual with a prodigious memory, well schooled in the focused thought that had eluded Wilhelm. As a youth he had acquired a fascination for the abundant marine life in the waters around Japan; studying it had become an abiding passion and gained him an international reputation in marine biology. His primary dedication was to the advancement of the empire. He saw his mission as following the course set by his great-grandfather, Meiji, to make Japan pre-dominant in Asia and drive out the Westerners. It would be accomplished by military force. Hirohito had been strictly raised in the samurai code; he had also been introduced by his tutor in natural history to Darwin's theories on the survival of the fittest, and the parallels drawn with human affairs suggesting that fit nations must prevail over unfit.[38] He did not doubt Japan's destiny; nor did his close circle of courtiers, who reinforced his vision of Asia under Japanese tutelage.[39]

The essential difference between the Western maritime powers and Japan was that Western heads of state were subject to constitutional law and Hirohito was not. His powers were absolute. He had supreme authority over the general staffs of the armed forces and appointed the civilian prime minister, who was responsible to him alone, not to the Diet, which remained a virtually impotent debating chamber. In 1925 voting rights to its lower house were extended to all males over twenty-five years old, but in return an Act for the Preservation of Public Peace had given the police virtually unlimited powers to suppress dissidents. They were assisted by a number of extreme nationalist societies which employed street thuggery and intimidation to cow the leaders of workers' or socialist or democratic movements. These traditional patriotic societies had close liaison with, on the one hand, the Home Minister, who controlled the special political police, known popularly as the 'Thought Police', and on the other hand with gangsters in the cities who aided them in campaigns of terror.

During the 1920s many Japanese in the cities had taken to Western liberal ideas along with American jazz, Hollywood films, Western social dancing, cocktails, Western fashions for women and, for the wealthier, tennis, golf and skiing. Young people had begun to rebel against traditional social customs such as arranged marriage; aspirations for freedom and real democracy, even pacifism, had seemed to be gaining ground,[40] but the forces of reaction manipulated by Hirohito and his palace cabal proved too strong. When in 1930 the Prime Minister, an ally of the liberal Prince Saionji, refused to agree funding for naval development plans approved by Hirohito, he was assassinated by a gangster commissioned by the extreme nationalist Black Dragon Society.[41]

The following year Hirohito judged the time ripe to move forward in China.[42] Japanese special forces staged a bomb blast on the Japanese-controlled South Manchuria Railroad, providing a pretext for the army to overrun the whole Chinese province of Manchuria. It was renamed Manchukuo and a puppet government was installed to exploit its resources. Hirohito had judged correctly that the Western powers were too preoccupied with their own financial and social problems to intervene militarily. The League of Nations could do nothing but send a Commission of Inquiry to establish the facts.

The most serious repercussions were to occur within Japan. Business leaders favouring economic expansion in cooperation with China rather than military conquest at last combined with liberal 'constitutionalist' politicians to block the war strategy. The revolt came to a head in early 1932 after the military opened a second front in Shanghai, ostensibly to protect Japanese nationals from Chinese harassment. Mitsui and other cartels were asked to contribute to the cost of the operation in defence of their interests. They refused.[43] The cabal around Hirohito responded by unleashing terror against the leaders. Two prominent figures with connections to Mitsui and the leader of the Constitutionalist Party were assassinated. Combined with a surge in popular patriotism induced by the success of Japanese arms, the intimidation cowed the liberal opposition, and all hopes of a Western-style constitutional state died. Only the Communist Party continued underground agitation, and their members were ruthlessly suppressed.[44]

The following year, 1933, the League of Nations Manchurian Commission reported, dismissing Japanese claims that the state of Manchukuo was an expression of a local independence movement, asserting instead that 'a large part of what was indisputably China has been forcibly seized and occupied by the forces of Japan'.[45] The report was approved on 24 February, upon which Japan walked out of the League. Three days later in Berlin the Nazi arson team in the Reichstag staged the pretext for Hitler to dissolve the Weimar constitution. Like Hirohito, Hitler now transcended law. Raised by propaganda to semi-divine status as the leader sent by Providence to deliver the nation from its humiliations, he concentrated expenditure on armaments, like Hirohito using police repression and street intimidation to crush internal opposition. Denied an increase in Germany's permitted force levels at disarmament talks in October, he also left the League.

It has been a feature of maritime power at least from the Dutch ascendancy in the seventeenth century that women in supreme maritime nations are emancipated to a degree unknown to those living under territorial regimes. The difference is exemplified in the opposing world systems of this period. Women in the United States and Britain had since the eighteenth century been able to follow their own rather than their parents' choice in finding a husband and had in general – if with many exceptions – enjoyed companionable marriages; they had taken precedence in domestic matters and leading roles in social functions, charitable foundations and campaigns for moral causes; the fight against slavery had been a notable example. From the 1850s they had fought resolutely for equality with men in education and the workplace and for the right to vote; and while failing to achieve complete equality, they had broken through the wall of male domination in many spheres: middle- and upper-class women were educated to the standard of their brothers and had entered the professions, especially teaching; by 1930 some 14 per cent of British university lecturers were women.[46] Recently they had won the right to vote. Both the United States Congress and the British Parliament had enacted the necessary legislation in 1918, and two years later the US constitution had been amended accordingly after ratification by individual states. It was the inevitable, if somewhat belated, end result of merchant freedoms. It is indicative of the status women enjoyed in both leading maritime powers that at the peace talks in 1919 the Allies demanded that the German and Austrian constitutions enfranchise women.

The contrast with the position of women in Hitler's Germany and Hirohito's Japan is striking. Traditional views of women's roles epitomized in the phrase '*Kinder, Küche, Kirche*' – children, kitchen, Church – persisted in Weimar Germany, reinforced in the periods of hyperinflation and depression when working women were regarded as having contributed to unemployment by taking jobs rightly belonging to men.[47] The voting rights they owed to the former enemy were a source of bewilderment rather than emancipation, and tended to weaken what remained of family stability after the devastation of the lost war.[48]

In the Nazi state women's prime function was to procreate and increase the race. Motherhood was raised to a sacred duty and promoted with a variety of financial incentives, medals and celebrations, all subject, however, to racial vetting,[49] since at the core of Nazi ideology was belief in the superiority of the Aryan-Germanic race; and material rearmament was accompanied by a drive to eliminate physically and racially 'inferior' blood from the national gene pool. Thus the most intimate aspects of women's lives were subject to intrusive investigation. A minority of women sublimated their feelings in hysterical adoration of the leader; most, impressed by the return of national self-respect engendered by Hitler's assertive foreign policy, accepted the accompanying male orientation and regimentation of society.[50]

Male dominance and paternal authority were even more marked in Japanese society. Submission was the prime female virtue. Marriages were not so much a union between two individuals as the recruitment of a wife to the husband's 'house', or extended family, ruled by the head of the family. The wife had no personal freedom; everything she did was subject to her husband's permission and the ethos of the 'house'; if she did not fit in with the other family members she would be divorced and returned to her own family. Western-style individualistic families comprising husband, wife and children could be found in the cities, but the majority of married couples lived with other couples in a 'house' under its patriarchal head.[51]

Imperial Japan and Nazi Germany – like Napoleonic France in the previous century – exhibited striking similarities: each was dominated by a warrior elite whose values, inherited from feudal times, were expressed in male dominance and suppression of the female element. Each was driven by the ruling group under a semi-divine or messianic commander-in-chief identified as the essence and saviour of the nation, who was unconfined by constitutional law and dedicated to the elite vision of territorial expansion by force of arms. Their subjects were conditioned for service to this high purpose, regimented by a central bureaucracy, held in line by a censored, manipulated press and secret political police, and ultimately exploited as expendable.

The systems geared for war inevitably generated war; and the repressed, racially indoctrinated, savagely trained fighting men released their aggression outwards against neighbours. The Pacific war might be said to have begun in 1937 when the Japanese army, after a staged provocation like that preceding the occupation of Manchuria, advanced from Shanghai up the Yangtse valley to Nanking, capital of China. The city fell on 12 December. Two days later its inhabitants and Chinese soldiers within the walls who had donned civilian clothes to avoid capture were subjected to a frenzy of mass murder, torture and rape ordered by the Japanese commander-in-chief,

Hirohito's uncle, Prince Asaka, a prominent member of the palace cabal. Over 200,000 Chinese men were massacred, some 20,000 women raped, and unspeakable acts of sadism committed in this calculated orgy of terror known as 'the Rape of Nanking'.[52] Less than two years later Hitler ignited European war by invading Poland after a more elaborate provocation. Dedicated SS units following the advancing front rounded up and murdered Polish Jews, aristocrats, priests and the intelligentsia in a similar exercise in barbarity, ordered from the top as an act of policy to decapitate the Polish nation and reduce it to a helot state.[53]

19

Hitler's War, 1939

GREAT BRITAIN HAD succeeded the United Provinces (Holland) as supreme maritime power while joined with her in a grand alliance to prevent Louis XIV of France gaining continental hegemony and what was termed 'the universal monarchy'.[1] Similarly, almost a century and a half later, the United States of America took over from Great Britain while in partnership with her to stop Hitler realizing his ambitions for European and world mastery. The course of events was different, but the fundamentals were the same: the two leading merchant trading powers united against the dominant territorial power threatening to overrun the continent. It is a curious coincidence that the US President leading the maritime alliance, the former Assistant Secretary of the Navy, Franklin D. Roosevelt, was descended from Dutch settler stock.

He had taken office in 1933 in the great depression following the Wall Street crash when the imperative had been to restore the US economy and provide work for millions unemployed. His commitment to American sea power remained firm, and in his first measure to stimulate industry with government funds, the National Industrial Recovery Act, over $200 million was allocated to naval construction. It was not until 1937, however, after reports that Japan was applying 24 per cent of her entire annual budget to her navy and had laid down 'monster' battleships in secret, that his administration began a major naval rearmament programme with $1.1 billion authorized by Congress.

It was at the end of this year, 1937, that the Japanese army had advanced up the Yangtse and committed hideous atrocities in Nanking. A US spy gunboat, *Panay*, observing operations from the river, was sunk by Japanese aircraft. Afterwards Roosevelt had approached the British ambassador in Washington with a proposal that their two countries cooperate in intelligence as they had in the world war. Little of immediate significance had come from the initiative,[2] but it is indicative of Roosevelt's recognition of the congruence of US and British interests at a time when Congress and the American people were deeply isolationist and even suspected that

Britain intended dragging them into another war with Germany or Japan in defence of her empire.

Roosevelt's vision of Britain and particularly her fleet as vital to American security was demonstrated again in early summer 1939 when secret talks were held in Washington with an officer from the Admiralty Planning Division and agreement was reached that if Britain were forced into war with Germany the United States Navy would assure command of the Pacific and of the western and southern Atlantic.[3] Notwithstanding his strategy of defending America and American interests worldwide by supporting the Western democracies, Roosevelt was not prepared to run ahead of public opinion. When Hitler invaded Poland at the beginning of September 1939, provoking Britain and France to honour treaty commitments to Poland by declaring war on Germany, he broadcast to the American people to reassure them that the United States would remain neutral: 'I hope the United States will keep out of this war . . . And I will give you assurances that every effort of your government will be directed toward that end.'[4]

Eight days later, on 11 September, he sent a personal note to Chamberlain expressing the hope that the Prime Minister would feel free to write to him 'personally and outside diplomatic procedure about any problems as they arise'.[5] Lacking confidence in Chamberlain, on the same day he sent a similar note to Winston Churchill, who had been appointed to his former post as First Lord of the Admiralty and seemed from his pre-war stand against 'appeasement' to be Chamberlain's most likely successor. It was the beginning of a correspondence that was to form a significant personal hinge throughout the Anglo-American alliance.

Originally Hitler had intended avoiding Wilhelm II's mistake of challenging the British fleet, and had made it clear to the commander-in-chief of the Kriegsmarine, Admiral Erich Raeder, that construction must be held to a level that could not possibly alarm Britain. In early March 1935 he had proposed to formalize this with an agreement to limit the German service to 35 per cent of the strength of the Royal Navy.[6] His aim was to split the Western Allies and ensure that Britain kept out of the conflict when he struck east against Russia for 'living space' and raw materials in eastern Europe – in accordance with the concepts of Halford Mackinder transmitted through his own geopolitical mentor, Professor Karl Haushofer.[7] When he had gained the continent it would be time for the reckoning with Britain and the United States for world mastery. This was also Raeder's view, as his discussion with Hitler over the 35 per cent ratio makes clear: 'Commander in Chief stated his opinion that the fleet would have to be developed later against England.'[8]

The British Naval Staff had taken the bait.[9] Lacking resources to defend the empire against a Japanese attack in the east while engaged against a German–Italian combination in the west, they had jumped at the chance to limit the scale of the European threat and accepted the proffered 35 per cent ratio, together with a German demand to build U-boats in contravention of the Versailles Treaty. The Anglo-German Naval Agreement was signed on 18 June 1935. Hitler had been delighted. The British government should not have been. Shamelessly deserting France and acquiescing in the final abandonment of the Versailles aspirations to preserve peace through collective security, it had gained only an empty pledge. In part stampeded by the Naval Staff, who had been utterly bamboozled by the German negotiators, they had also been influenced by the idea, propagated by Hitler, that Nazi Germany formed a bulwark against the spread of international communism. In extreme form, as expressed by the Governor of the Bank of England, Hitler and the president of the Reichsbank were the 'bulwarks of civilisation . . . fighting the war of our system of society against Communism.'[10]

Hitler's joy at his triumph was short lived as he came to realize he had deceived himself as much as the British. In 1937, when Britain had at last woken to the need to rearm, he told his service chiefs that Germany had to reckon with 'two hate enemies, England and France', who would not welcome a German colossus in the middle of Europe.[11] This received confirmation from the British Foreign Secretary in spring 1938 after Hitler had annexed Austria and was poised to march on Czechoslovakia. He was advised, as Wilhelm and Bethmann had been before the first war, that he should not count on Britain standing aside. He sent Raeder proposals for greatly accelerated naval construction, particularly in U-boats and large battleships. Raeder, who already thought war with Britain inevitable, ordered his 1st Staff Officer Operations to study the implications. The resulting report concluded that Britain's weakness was dependence on overseas shipping, hence it followed that 'The sea war is the battle over economic and military sea communications',[12] a judgement diametrically opposed to Mahan's battle-fleet doctrine on which Tirpitz had based his fleet policy.

The study led to a grandiose building programme termed the 'Z Plan' for huge battleships, aircraft carriers, armoured and light cruisers and no fewer than 249 U-boats to be completed by various dates up to 1947. It was a fantasy: the resources needed could only have been found at the expense of the requirements of the other armed services and essential civil projects;

and the fuel required to drive such a fleet exceeded Germany's total annual oil consumption. It serves to reveal the colossal ambition of Raeder and his staff and the chaos to which German planning had been reduced by Hitler's personal style of leadership.[13]

Raeder anticipated war with Britain, but he had been assured repeatedly by Hitler that he need not expect it before about 1944; when it erupted in September 1939 he was unprepared. His fleet comprised two modern battlecruisers mounting 11-inch guns, three armoured cruisers with 11-inch guns, termed by the British 'pocket battleships', a number of cruisers and flotilla craft and fewer than fifty operational U-boats, patently insufficient to sever Britain's supply lines and bring about what he termed 'the final solution to the English question'. German strategic thought was harnessed to concepts of the 'decisive' battle or the 'final' solution. When news came of Britain's declaration of war he poured out his frustration in a memorandum: his navy 'could only show that it knew how to die with honour in order to create the foundations for later reconstruction'.[14]

Certainly the British fleet was far superior in numbers, yet adherence to the naval limitation treaties had seriously affected its capabilities. It was headed by twelve battleships, three battlecruisers and six aircraft carriers, but the great gunned ships were of first war vintage, apart from two that were too slow even to catch the German 'pocket battleships'. Of the three battlecruisers swift enough to do so, only one, the *Hood*, matched the speed of the German battlecruisers; yet she, too, was of pre-Jutland design and had not been thoroughly modernized.

Of more concern in the light of Raeder's conversion to the *guerre de course* was a lack of escort craft for merchant shipping. With the Naval Staff focus on the lessons of Jutland for the next fleet battle, perhaps against the Japanese in the Pacific, lessons from the unrestricted U-boat campaign had received scant attention. Trade protection entirely lacked the glamour of fleet action; in any case the Germans had no U-boats before the 1935 naval agreement – although the Japanese had. Above all, perhaps, the development of a system for detecting submerged submarines had induced complacency. Termed 'Asdic', acronym for the Allied Submarine Detection Investigation Committee, where the concept had originated in 1917, the apparatus – known now as sonar – beamed out ultrasonic pulses that could be trained in any direction underwater; these bounced back from dense objects and the time elapsed was converted into range. So much confidence was placed in the system that in 1937 the First Lord of the Admiralty had stated in the Commons, 'the submarine is no longer a danger to the security of the British empire'.[15] Yet the maximum range of

Asdic in good conditions was some 2,500 yards, less than that of a modern torpedo, and it was little use against surfaced submarines. A study of the first war U-boat campaign would have revealed that in 1918 half of all U-boat attacks on merchant shipping had been delivered on the surface at night.[16]

Such statistics were not available. In the drive for economy, work on Naval Staff histories of the war had been abandoned before reaching the final years. It seems scarcely credible in the light of the terrifyingly narrow margin by which Britain had avoided defeat, but the lessons learned then had to be relearned in the second war at great cost.[17] H. P. Willmott has pointed out that with the new German U-boat arm in its infancy there had never been the cash for trade defence: 'Any attempt to have built up British anti-submarine forces before the last couple of years prior to the outbreak of war would have been for both the nation and the navy financially irresponsible and strategically irrelevant.'[18]

Yet the contrast between the Naval Staff obsession with the lessons of Jutland – a strategic victory – and their failure to evaluate near defeat by the U-boats in 1917/18 suggests more profound reasons for the comparative neglect of trade protection. Chief among these surely were the glorious traditions of the service. From their earliest days at naval college officers had held before them the example of famous admirals and victorious fleet engagements, and had been imbued with that cult of the 'offensive' which had played such a central role in retarding the introduction of convoy in the first war.

There was something else. The contrast between Britain and the Royal Navy as advancing powers at the start of the century yet by the 1920s and 1930s looking backwards has been mentioned. Britain's traditional industries were in decline; the City of London struggled to compete with Wall Street; the Royal Navy had fallen irretrievably behind the US and Japanese navies in the new air and underwater fighting arms. It seems that historical forces were at work favouring younger nations and navies at the expense of the old.

The opening moves in September 1939 were reminiscent of those in August 1914: the Home Fleet, considerably smaller than Jellicoe's Grand Fleet, had taken station in Scapa Flow in the Orkneys to block the northern exits to the Atlantic and support a Northern Patrol of cruisers examining merchantmen for contraband. A similar contraband control was exercised in the Dover Strait and for Mediterranean traffic from Gibraltar, Malta, Haifa and Aden. Maritime blockade of Germany, declared on the first day of war, remained a principal tool of strategy and, as in August 1914, convoys of troopships carried a British Expeditionary Force to France to fight alongside the French army.

On the German side two pocket battleships and their supply ships, which had sailed before the outbreak, were waiting in the Atlantic, and eighteen ocean-going U-boats, which had also been dispatched in secret, lay to the west of the British Isles and as far south as the Strait of Gibraltar; smaller coastal U-boats were on station in the North Sea and the Baltic. Although Hitler had promised to avoid war with Britain, Raeder had made these precautionary moves before the attack on Poland.

The U-boats were controlled by Kapitän zur See Karl Dönitz, Führer der U-boote (FdU), from an extemporized headquarters in a timber barrack hut on the outskirts of Wilhelmshaven. During the first war Dönitz had been transferred to U-boats and in 1918 had commanded his own boat in the Mediterranean until, on diving for a submerged attack on a convoy, his chief engineer had lost control of stability. Dönitz had been taken prisoner. The British interrogating officer found it extremely difficult to get him to talk or even to write his name, and reported on him as 'very moody and almost violent at times'.[19] As a prisoner of war he had feigned madness convincingly enough to have gained early repatriation.

While Germany developed U-boats in secret during the late 1920s he had been appointed to command a half-flotilla of torpedo boats. It was a significant posting, for the basic tactics in which he trained his half-flotilla were applicable to surfaced U-boats: forming reconnaissance lines by day to seek the enemy, holding touch at extreme range below the horizon and moving in to attack by night. It is significant that his excellent service report in 1930 was endorsed by one of the officers leading clandestine U-boat development, who signed himself 'BdU – Befehlshaber der U-boote' or Commander-in-Chief U-boats[20] – a post that did not officially exist.

In 1935, the year the U-boat arm emerged officially, Dönitz was appointed to lead it. He had set about the task with customary verve and diligence and to such effect that his station chief at Kiel reported that his few boats were by spring 1936 'ready for employment on war tasks', and added, 'Military and comradely spirit in the flotilla is above all praise.'[21] He was referring to a spirit of confidence in their weapon and a sense of belonging to an elite that Dönitz consciously inspired in his officers and men. It is also apparent from the record that he had been developing a new type of group tactics for surfaced U-boats and that these were modelled on the tactics in which he had trained his torpedo boats. At this stage they were designed for action against warships or troop transports in the Baltic and Mediterranean. By the end of 1937, however, as the view took hold that war with Britain might not be avoided after all, his mind had turned to commerce war,[22] and in early 1939 he had played a war game pitting U–boats and an armoured cruiser against five heavily escorted convoys bound for Britain through the north and south Atlantic. The boats, dispersed in groups to the west and south-west of the British Isles, found only one convoy. The boat that sighted it called up the others in its group, but all were later adjudged to have been destroyed by the convoy escorts as they approached.[23]

Somehow Dönitz had conjured positive conclusions from almost complete failure. There had been great advances in radio technology since the first war which enabled boats to transmit and receive messages over huge distances, even when submerged to periscope depth, and in his report on the war game he pointed out that this allowed a concentration of U-boats to be brought against the concentration of merchant ships in a convoy.

For the war against trade he recommended Type VII and Type IX boats, the former of some 750 tons with a speed of 17 knots on the surface, 8 knots underwater and a range of 6,500 miles at a cruising speed of 12 knots; the latter rather larger, just over 1,000 tons, marginally faster on the surface, with a range of some 8,000 miles. Both classes were far smaller than submarines developed in the US and Japanese navies for the great distances of the Pacific, and were half the size of the 'cruiser U-boats' favoured for the trade war by the Naval Staff in Berlin. Dönitz wanted them because they could be built in greater numbers; he needed numbers for his group or *Rudel* – wolf pack – tactics. Specifically he wanted 'Ninety continuously operational boats in total, thus [to allow for voyage and repair time at base] at least some 300 of these types are necessary for successful operations'.[24] He continued to cite this number of 300 after the war; with 300 boats at the start he could have brought England to her knees. Yet the number could not have been calculated from the results of his war game – nor of course could he have known the number of escorts the British Admiralty might have built if faced with the construction of such a monstrous U-boat fleet. He probably chose 300 because he felt it came within the limits of the possible; it was not a great deal larger than the total provided for in the Z Plan.

Raeder had wanted to declare a blockade zone around the British Isles on the outbreak of war and conduct unrestricted U-boat warfare within it, but Hitler still hoped to avoid an irreparable breach with Britain and forbade it. Consequently Dönitz's orders to his commanders in waiting positions were to conduct operations strictly according to the Prize Law as formulated in the London Naval Treaty.[25] The Naval Staff anticipated being able to lift restrictions in due course by arguing that armed merchantmen should be treated as warships.[26]

A serious breach of orders occurred on the first evening of the war. The commander of *U-30* patrolling some 250 miles north-west of Ireland found himself right ahead of the passenger liner *Athenia*, and submerged for torpedo attack. What he was thinking of will never be known since he did not survive the war and the relevant page of his log was torn out on his return to base. Dönitz claimed later that he mistook the liner for an auxiliary cruiser, but this was a standard excuse and there was no justification for it since she was obviously a passenger liner far out in the Atlantic and steering a steady westerly course. He sank her with a single torpedo; 118 lives were lost, among them 22 American citizens. Shock waves radiated around the world: it recalled the sinking of the *Lusitania* and seemed to presage similar frightfulness.

When he heard the news, Dönitz had all boats signalled to emphasize the orders to operate according to the Prize Rules. Hitler, alarmed about reaction in the United States, prohibited action against any passenger ships even if sailing in convoy, while his propaganda chief, Josef Goebbels, accused Churchill of having the *Athenia* sunk to bring the United States into the war against Germany, and confused the issue so successfully that many Americans were in doubt about the true cause of the liner's loss until the evidence was produced at the Nuremberg trials after the war.[27]

The British Admiralty introduced convoy on some routes from the first, but sufficient escorts were lacking and numbers of ships sailed independently. It was among these that Dönitz's commanders found most of their targets. They also claimed two major warships. With the acute shortage of escorts precluding a complete convoy system, the Naval Staff resorted to the failed first war strategy of patrolling focal areas of shipping and establishing 'hunting groups'; two of these, each comprising an aircraft carrier and destroyers, were attacked by patrolling U-boats and one carrier was sunk; the other escaped only because the torpedoes detonated prematurely. Both U-boats were then located with Asdic by the accompanying destroyers and depth-charged; one was destroyed. The Admiralty deployed no more carrier hunting groups.

The exploit was followed by a more spectacular feat: *U-47* succeeded in penetrating the Home Fleet base at Scapa Flow and sinking a battleship. Dönitz had planned the operation in detail and entrusted it to one of his favourite commanders, Günther Prien, who on return found himself lionized as a national hero. An American correspondent who attended a press conference to show him off assessed him as 'clean-cut, cocky, a fanatical Nazi and obviously capable'.[28] Prien's political convictions matched those of his chief. Dönitz had been an ardent supporter of the Nazi Party from at least the early 1930s. His allegiance to Hitler and the party was as intense as his commitment to his U-boats and the young men who hazarded their lives in them.[29]

After Prien's achievement Dönitz was stepped up from FdU to BdU – Commander-in-Chief U-boats. He had already convinced Raeder of the need to build up his force as quickly as possible to the magic number of 300, and Raeder used every audience he had with Hitler to press for a priority allocation of materials for U-boat construction. He also pressed him repeatedly to permit unrestricted U-boat warfare. Hitler refused him priority in materials on account of the needs of the army, and would not agree to lift restrictions on the U-boat campaign for fear of the effect this would have on President Roosevelt and opinion in the United States. Nonetheless, restrictions were being removed progressively as the Naval Staff had intended without public announcement. It had started on 24 September when Dönitz ordered all boats to use force against vessels using their wireless when ordered to stop on the grounds that they were a part of the enemy anti-submarine network. On 2 October he had extended permission to use force against all vessels sailing without lights.[30] By November Dönitz had committed his commanders to a completely unrestricted campaign in the waters around the British Isles and extending to 20 degrees west in the Atlantic, still without any formal announcement.[31] It was made explicit in Order 154 to his commanders:

> Rescue no one and take no one with you. Have no care for the ships' boats. Weather conditions and the proximity of land are of no account. Care only for your own boat and strive to achieve the next success as soon as possible! We must be hard in this war. The enemy started this war in order to destroy us, therefore nothing else matters.[32]

Abandonment of the Prize Rules was most clearly demonstrated in the new year by increased use of night attack on the surface when in most cases commanders could not identify their victims. In February 1940 the Admiralty Anti-Submarine Warfare Division reported that sinkings in night surface attacks had risen from 33 per cent of all sinkings the previous October to 53 per cent, and commented 'the great advantage of such a method is that the U-boat can escape at speed on the surface'.[33] The division took comfort, however, in the apparent success of the convoy system:

'Out of 164 ships sunk during the first six months [to the end of February 1940] only seven were in convoys escorted by anti-submarine vessels',[34] from which it was deduced that U-boats had 'a marked antipathy against attacking convoys, preferring lone neutrals and stragglers'. This was the opposite of the truth so far as Dönitz was concerned. The relative immunity of convoys was a result of the difficulty of finding them with the very few boats at his disposal. New construction had not kept pace with losses and he now had fewer boats than at the outbreak of war.

His other serious problem was torpedo failure. Non-contact magnetic pistols designed to detonate the charge under ships' hulls to break their backs were firing prematurely and contact pistols sometimes not at all. From his commanders' reports he estimated 'At least 30 per cent of torpedoes are duds',[35] and calculated that 'at least 300,000 tons [of merchant shipping] which might have been sunk can be reckoned to have been lost due to torpedo failure'.[36] Despite this his boats had done very much better than the surface raiders: in six months Raeder's two powerful battlecruisers and three pocket battleships had sunk only sixteen ships of some 63,000 tons at the cost of one pocket battleship, the *Admiral Graf Spee*. She had been engaged by three British cruisers in the doughtiest traditions of the Royal Navy and driven in to the River Plate, where her commander had chosen to scuttle her rather than condemn his ship's company to a hopeless fight against heavy ships he was led to believe were gathering outside; in reality there were none. In the same period the U-boats had sunk 199 ships of an aggregate 702,000 tons,[37] insufficient to threaten Britain's war economy.

In March Dönitz had to withdraw most of his boats from the Atlantic on orders to screen an amphibious invasion of Norway and Denmark. Designed originally to protect vital iron ore shipments from the northern port of Narvik down through Norwegian territorial waters, the landings pre-empted British plans to stop the traffic by occupying Narvik and other key ports. Fierce naval battles erupted, providing the U-boats with ample targets, but they were robbed of success by their torpedoes. In the most contested area off Narvik, Prien and another 'ace', Herbert Schultze, the first commander to have sunk over 100,000 tons of merchant shipping, reported torpedo failures against two cruisers, the battleship *Warspite*, two destroyers and, inside one inlet, a 'solid wall' of anchored troop transports, cruisers and destroyers. Dönitz received so many similar reports of torpedo malfunction that he unilaterally withdrew his boats southwards.

The landings succeeded nonetheless; and Hitler became master of Denmark and Norway. In Britain the shock of the campaign brought

dissatisfaction with Chamberlain's war leadership to a head and he was succeeded as Prime Minister by Winston Churchill, who formed a National
Government from all three main political parties. As First Lord of the
Admiralty Churchill had played a large role in the bungled response to
the German strike; had the Royal Navy lost the battleship *Warspite* and the
cruisers, destroyers and transports Prien and Schultze had attacked at short
range his reputation would probably have suffered such damage he would
not have come to power. On such random chance history turns.

In Churchill Britain found an instinctive leader guided by emotion, imagination and intuition – resembling Hitler in these respects. Yet he was a
student of war and his mind was stocked with the great sweep of British
history defined by defiance of Continental tyrants. Above all, perhaps, he
had a strong heart schooled in adversity. Aspects of his childhood had, like
Hitler's, been shaped by trauma, in his case parental and especially mater-
nal neglect. He had known despair and continued to experience that
bottomless pit which he called his 'black dog'. Possibly no other British
leader would have been capable of his perverse refusal to admit defeat over
the coming weeks. For on the day he took office, 10 May, Hitler launched
an attack on France through Holland and Belgium and a surprise thrust
through the Ardennes which severed the French divisions from the British
Expeditionary Force to their north, and drove the British towards the
coast. They were saved by a miracle comparable to that of the dud torpedoes in the Norwegian campaign; Hitler halted his armoured columns 15
miles from Dunkirk, allowing time for British and Allied destroyers assisted
by privately owned small craft to evacuate some 350,000 troops from the
beaches. Guns, transport and supplies were abandoned, but repatriation of
the men who would form the nucleus of a re-equipped army gave
Churchill heart to remain defiant as the French armies crumbled and
Benito Mussolini brought Italy into the war on Hitler's side. 'We shall go
on to the end,' Churchill declared in the House of Commons. 'We shall
never surrender.'[38]

Paris fell on 14 June. The French government had fled, re-establishing
itself in Bordeaux. It is scarcely remembered now, but on the 16th
Churchill made a desperate attempt to keep French forces in the war and
prevent the French navy from falling into Hitler's hands by proposing an
'indissoluble union' between Britain and France with a single war cabinet
and joint organs of government.[39] French ministers were too convinced of
defeat and too prejudiced against English duplicity to give this extraordinary proposal proper consideration; instead the Prime Minister resigned

(*right*) August Bebel, German Socialist leader who opened a clandestine correspondence with the British Foreign Office to warn that Tirpitz's fleet was 'directed against England & England alone'; (*below left*) Admiral Reinhard Scheer, Commander-in-Chief of the High Seas Fleet at the battle of Jutland; (*right*) Vice Admiral Franz von Hipper, his battlecruiser force commander

Admiral Sir John Jellicoe (*left*), Commander-in-Chief of the British Grand Fleet at the battle of Jutland, and (*right*) Vice Admiral Sir David Beatty, his battlecruiser force commander. (*below*) Jellicoe's flagship, HMS *Iron Duke*

Beatty's flagship, HMS *Lion*, is hit on 'Q' turret between the after funnels during the battle of Jutland; note the flash rising above mast height; (*centre*) a magazine explosion in HMS *Invincible* blows her apart; (*below*) the German battlecruiser, *Seydlitz*, engulfed in flames during Hipper's suicidal charge at the British line

US Presidents whose support for Britain was tempered by national interests: (*left*) Woodrow Wilson on his way to the Paris Peace Conference, 1919; (*below*) Franklin Roosevelt with Churchill aboard HMS *Prince of Wales* at the 'Atlantic Charter' meeting, August 1941. Standing behind them Admiral King and US and British Chiefs of Staff. (*above*) The shape of things to come: the US carrier, *Yorktown*, with aircraft, 1941

Grossadmiral Karl Dönitz (*centre*), Commander-in-Chief *Kriegsmarine*, with Adolf Hitler (*left*) and the *Luftwaffe* chief, Hermann Göring. (*below*) Two U-boat 'aces' of the first 'fortunate time': (*left*) Joachim Schepke, (*right*) Otto Kretschmer, whose tonnage sinking record was never surpassed

Japan's god-Emperor Hirohito, who bore ultimate responsibility for attacking the United States, and (*above right*) Japanese planes prepared for take-off for the attack on Pearl Harbor; (*below left*) Admiral Isoroku Yamamoto, Commander-in-Chief of the Japanese Combined Fleet, (*right*) Vice Admiral Chuichi Nagumo, commander of the carrier fleet

(*from left*) Admiral Chester Nimitz, US Commander Pacific Ocean Area; Admiral Ernest King, Commander-in-Chief US Fleet (COMINCH); and Admiral Raymond Spruance, commander of US carrier Task Force 16 at the battle of Midway, and later of the US Fifth Fleet. (*below*) USS *Yorktown* hit by a Japanese air-launched torpedo at the battle of Midway, 4 June 1942

The monster Japanese battleship *Yamato* is hit by a bomb from US aircraft near her forward 18.1-inch gun turret during the Leyte Gulf campaign, 24 October 1944. (*below*) The Japanese delegation aboard USS *Missouri* for the surrender ceremony in Tokyo Bay, 2 September 1945, The Japanese Foreign Minister in front

and Marshal Pétain, linked indissolubly in the French psyche with the defence of Verdun in the first war, formed a new administration and sought an armistice. Hitler craved vengeance, but the terms he dictated were comparatively mild, for he needed peace with Britain afterwards so that he could pursue his real war in the east without hindrance. A core of central and southern France was left to Pétain to govern as a puppet from Vichy; the northern and western departments bordering the Channel and Atlantic coasts were to be occupied by German forces. The French navy was to be assembled in French ports to be 'demobilised under German or Italian control'.[40]

Not only had Britain lost her partner in arms, her strategic position was now compromised by enemy control of the entire European coast from the North Cape of Norway down to Biscay; moreover, no reliance could be placed on assurances that the French fleet would be disarmed under German or Italian control. The Admiralty gathered a special force of heavy ships for the Mediterranean and instructed the admiral commanding to offer French naval units the choice of coming over to the British or scuttling their ships; failing either he was to destroy them. The commander-in-chief of the most powerful French squadron at Mers-el-Kebir, near Oran, rejected the ultimatum and the British force opened fire, destroying one battleship, seriously damaging two other heavy ships and a number of smaller vessels and inflicting great loss of life. A tragic envoi to Churchill's offer of indissoluble Franco-British union, it was similarly rooted in misunderstanding. Other French units abroad were immobilized by negotiation or by force; those warships that had already sailed to British ports of their own volition were boarded and seized. With these rough actions Churchill sent a clear message that Britain would fight on alone.

German control of the coasts flanking the British Isles could not be addressed so directly. Air attacks on shipping using southern British ports became so heavy that the Trade Division of the Admiralty, which controlled merchant shipping worldwide, diverted oceanic convoys and independents from the English Channel, re-routing them to north-western ports, Liverpool and the Clyde. The resulting internal disruption caused a significant fall in imports on its own.[41] Of wider concern was the prospect of bases on the French Atlantic seaboard coming into use for U-boats and surface raiders.

Dönitz lost no time in making a personal survey of harbours in Brittany suitable for his boats. His first choice fell on Lorient, and just outside, at Kerneval on the north bank of the river serving the port, he found a small chateau which he determined to convert into a command post.

20

The Warlords

———•———

THE SHAPE OF the looming world war was established in summer 1940 after the collapse of France. Hitler bludgeoned Britain with bombers and the threat of invasion to force her to terms. Through secret channels he offered a peace which would leave her with navy and empire intact; all he wanted in return was a free hand in Europe. Had the outcome been dictated by reason the offer must have been accepted. Germany's position on the Continent was unassailable. Many in British governing circles, including the Foreign Secretary, Lord Halifax, believed a compromise peace was the best hope,[1] as on paper it was.

Yet in the wider historical perspective the present threat was only the latest chapter in a story begun with the repulse of the armadas of Philip II of Spain, continuing through the invasion attempts of the Bourbon kings of France and Napoleon to the defeat of Kaiser Wilhelm II. Churchill's mind was furnished with this magnificent tapestry and the warriors, statesmen and thinkers who had wrought it in defence of British freedoms, not least his famous ancestor, John Churchill, first Duke of Marlborough. Conscious always of the weight of the past, he expressed the theme constantly. In a speech to Parliament reporting on the fall of France and anticipating the battle to defend Britain against invasion, he warned that British life and the long continuity of her institutions and empire depended on the outcome: 'Let us therefore brace ourselves to our duty and so bear ourselves that if the British Empire and its Commonwealth lasts for a thousand years men will still say, "This was their finest hour".'[2]

He saw Hitler as the antithesis of all that Britain stood for, the 'dark curse to be lifted from our age',[3] and had dedicated himself to this cause.[4] At the same time he revelled in the war he was running.[5] It is also true that his simple patriotism reflected a national mood of defiance. His was the authentic voice of a proud imperial people.

The strategy with which he intended defeating Hitler rested at this early stage on two assumptions: that he could draw the Americans into the fight and could amass a sufficient bomber force to destroy Germany from the air. Before the fall of France, Roosevelt had promised material support, and Churchill believed, as he told the House of Commons on 20 June, that if only Britain could hold out until after the US presidential elections in November, he did not doubt that 'the whole English-speaking world will be in line together'.[6]

Nonetheless, he put his faith primarily in bomber aircraft. He could see 'only one sure path' to win the war, he minuted the Minister of Aircraft Production in July, 'and that is an absolutely devastating, exterminating attack by very heavy bombers from this country upon the Nazi homeland'.[7] This was a huge overestimation of the potential of strategic bombing given the navigational techniques, bombs, bombsights and training of the time,[8] and was to have unfortunate consequences in the war against the U-boats.

His faith in Roosevelt was also misplaced. Roosevelt won in November but, like Woodrow Wilson in the first war, on a platform of avoiding participation in foreign wars: 'we will not send our army, naval or air forces to fight in foreign lands outside of the Americas, except in case of attack',[9] and in response to his opponent's charge that he *would* do so, he told parents, 'Your boys are not going to be sent into foreign wars. They are going into training to form a force so strong that, by its very existence, it will keep the threat of war away from our shores.'[10] Undoubtedly he regarded Britain's fight as vital to the defence of America and of democracy itself, and constantly tried to convey this in broadcasts to his people, but while Britain was prepared to pay for large shipments of arms and munitions from US factories and do the fighting, Roosevelt had no incentive to persuade his deeply isolationist Congress and people to go beyond material support and take part in the war; nor could he have done so.[11]

He was, moreover, an opponent of imperialism, as were most Americans whose own history of fighting for independence from the British Crown seemed a sufficient reason. Roosevelt also regarded Britain as a major trade rival of the United States; his own ancestors, the Delanos, had experienced this at first hand in China.[12] Meanwhile America's vital interests were not injured by the conflict in Europe; quite the reverse. In geopolitical terms the United States was growing stronger as her world power rivals, particularly Britain, expended their strength.

Nor had Roosevelt any personal affinity with Churchill despite the correspondence he had initiated earlier. He had met him first in 1918 when, as Assistant Secretary of the US Navy, he had spoken at a dinner in London which Churchill attended. He had come away appalled by the former First Lord of the Admiralty 'lording it all over us', and referred to him later as 'a stinker'.[13]

Both men were patricians, though raised in very different societies. Of the two, it has been remarked that Roosevelt conformed more to the image of the reserved Englishman concealing his thoughts and emotions, Churchill to the outgoing and transparently direct American. All those who worked for Churchill knew just what he felt at any moment, and what he required. This could not be said of Roosevelt, whose closest colleagues were frequently left guessing about his true feelings and intentions.[14] Both men energized their administrations by the power of personality, but while Roosevelt operated in the sphere of the feasible, Churchill was, in the words of Isaiah Berlin, 'preoccupied by his own vivid world, and it is doubtful how far he has ever been aware of what actually goes on in the heads or hearts of others'.[15]

Churchill also courted Stalin. Here, too, he had a record. In 1919, during the Russian civil war when Stalin had been a member of Lenin's Politburo, Churchill had been one of the most violent critics of Bolshevism and supporter of intervention against the Reds. Since then Nazism had eclipsed communism as a threat to the British Empire, so he had told the Soviet ambassador in London in 1938;[16] and in June 1940 he sent a carefully worded letter to the Soviet dictator suggesting they both had an interest in deciding how to react to the prospect of Germany establishing hegemony over the European continent.[17] He was snubbed. Nonetheless, Churchill was convinced that if Britain could hold out against invasion, Hitler would recoil eastwards. As it became apparent in autumn 1940 that the Royal Air Force had won the battle in the skies over Britain, precluding invasion, he directed a grand deception campaign to influence Hitler in that direction. The gambit was to prove embarrassingly successful when Hitler's deputy, Rudolf Hess, flew to Scotland in May 1941 expecting to contact a British 'Peace Party'.[18]

Churchill's deception worked because it contained elements of truth and played to Hitler's most fundamental desire to concentrate his forces in the east without concern for a hostile Britain at his back. Hitler gave his first intimations of a move east in July; as noted by the Chief of the German General Staff in his diary at the end of that month:

> *England's hope is Russia and America. If hope of Russia falls away, so too falls America* because falling away of Russia means huge increase of value of Japan in Far East . . .
> . . . *If however Russia is smashed, then England's last hope is eradicated.* The master of Europe and the Balkans is then Germany.[19]

Stalin knew that Hitler would turn on him eventually. Shocked by the speed of France's collapse, he had rushed troops into the Baltic states, Lithuania, Latvia and Estonia, to create a northern buffer zone, and in the south had taken over Bessarabia, easternmost province of Rumania bordering the Ukraine and the Black Sea.

Like Hitler, Stalin was a legatee of revolution. Lenin and the civil war following the Bolshevik coup had destroyed the social, legal and economic structures of tsarist Russia more surely even than the Weimar government's inflationary policy had untied traditional social and moral values in Germany. As in Germany, the party led by the most amoral, ruthless and power-hungry political gangster had won the resulting battle for ascendancy. As Donald Rayfield has put it, Stalin was 'no more a Communist than a Borgia Pope was a Catholic'; he merely 'made revolutionary socialism a hollow container for his own fascism'.[20] In terms of numbers forced from their homes, wiped out by hunger resulting from farm 'collectivization', sent to gulags in Siberia, worked to death as slave labourers, purged as 'enemies of the state', tortured and murdered by the sadists of the NKVD – the People's Commissariat of Internal Affairs – Stalin's crimes were on a scale Hitler had not begun to match; already in 1940 Stalin's victims were counted in millions. Churchill must have known Stalin was a monster, the creed he professed more inimical to the capitalist system of the Western democracies than Nazism. Yet he was prepared to make common cause with him against Germany because he regarded Hitler as the greater immediate threat.

In addition to danger on his western front Stalin was anxious about his Far Eastern flank. In 1936 Japan had signed an Anti Comintern Pact with Germany, pledging both nations to prevent the spread of communism. Stalin had received assurances from his master spy, Richard Sorge, in Tokyo that there were no secret military clauses; both signatories had merely agreed to support each other diplomatically in the event of either becoming involved in war with Russia. Since then, however, there had been border incidents and in May 1939 Japanese forces had invaded the Soviet protectorate of Outer Mongolia. Sorge reported this as a limited probe only, and no prelude to war, but Stalin sent an able tank specialist, Lieutenant General Georgi Zhukov, to retrieve the position. Zhukov had done so in August with an irresistible armoured thrust supported by aircraft.

Zhukov's victory was not unwelcome to Hirohito and his palace cabal. They remained determined to strike south for the oil and raw materials of the Western colonial powers; Zhukov's demonstration of the superiority of

Russian tanks helped to win over strong factions in both armed services advocating a strike north against Russia.[21] Yet striking south carried great risks. The war in China had not been won; the principal cities and seaports had been brought under Japanese control, but a Nationalist Chinese government continued the struggle from the interior, aided materially by the Western powers, and the United States had threatened Japan with sanctions. A strike south would probably trigger war with her.

This should have been difficult to contemplate. Despite a great expansion of Japanese exports, especially textiles, and a threefold increase in the output of heavy industry and armaments over the past decade,[22] Japan remained a pygmy beside the United States, whose national income was seventeen times greater.[23] The really alarming comparison for the regime was that whereas Japan devoted 70 per cent of government expenditure to the armed forces, the United States spent under 12 per cent, representing a minute 1.6 per cent of her gross national product. As Paul Kennedy has pointed out, 'An increase in the defence-spending share of the American GNP to bring it close to the proportions devoted to armaments by the fascist states would automatically make the United States the most powerful military state in the world.'[24]

The fall of France in June 1940 had triggered the start of just such a process. Congress voted huge additional funds for aircraft production and a 'two-ocean navy'. The Japanese naval staff calculated that this would propel the US Navy from its present 10:7 advantage over their own navy to 10:5 in 1943 and a crushing 10:3 in 1944.[25] Against such odds they had no hope. If they were to strike south it had to be soon. Yamamoto, now an admiral and Commander-in-Chief of the Combined Fleet, believed that if so the US Pacific fleet had to be knocked out at the start by a surprise attack. Yet his knowledge of America's vastly greater economy and advanced technology and production methods made him profoundly pessimistic about the eventual outcome even if the first strike were successful.

The enormity of the decision was not lost on Hirohito, but the choice had already been made. The outbreak of war in Europe had offered the opportunity to strike at the Western colonies while their forces were engaged, and France's unexpected collapse increased pressure to act. Japanese troops were ordered in to French Indochina. At the same time alliance negotiations were reopened with the victorious fascist powers. Hitler had proposed alliance with Japan the previous year in the hope that this would tie down Stalin's troops in the Far East. Talks were now brought to a successful conclusion with a Tripartite Pact, signed on 27 September

1940: Japan recognized German and Italian leadership in establishing a 'new order in Europe', while they in their turn recognized Japan's leading role in a 'new order in Asia'; and all parties pledged each other political, economic and military assistance should any of them be attacked by the United States.

Notwithstanding the opportunities opened for Japan by the European war, it is hard to account for Hirohito's determination to pursue a course that would in all probability lead to war with a power so much stronger than Japan. Was he influenced by his own regime's constant nationalist propaganda, portraying the Japanese people as a master race predestined to dominion in the east? Had the veneration he was accorded as a god and the flattery of self-serving counsellors corrupted his perceptions? Was he more conscious of his duty to fulfil the sacred mission imposed on him by his ancestors, or of peer pressure from his palace cabal? Was it the sheer momentum of the war economy sustaining the fighting in China driving the need to acquire the oil and raw materials of the British, Dutch, French and Portuguese colonies to the south? Without these Japan would continue to be dependent on America and the West and vulnerable to economic pressure; with them she would dispose of vast resources within a perimeter whose extent would provide defence in depth. To forgo the opportunity would not only deny the policy pursued over the past decade, but admit defeat in the face of US and Western opposition to the war in China. Perhaps there was no rational solution to the problem, which boiled down to a simple choice between going va banque or retreating in humiliation.[26]

Whatever induced Hirohito to maintain the drive towards conflict with the United States it was rationalized in moral terms echoing current propaganda: the superior military spirit of the Japanese contrasted with Western degeneracy. The Americans in particular were perceived as enfeebled by luxury and lacking in stamina for a protracted struggle. Japanese misconceptions of the West fully equalled Western misjudgements of the Japanese.

Meanwhile American economic pressure grew. At the end of July 1940 Roosevelt announced that US exports of aviation fuel would be limited to the western hemisphere and British Commonwealth countries, and in September, as Japanese troops entered French Indochina, he laid a similar embargo on scrap iron and steel vital for the Japanese armaments industry, and loaned $25 million to the Chinese Nationalists.

Roosevelt's most immediate concern, however, was to keep Britain afloat. American aid in the supply of arms, ships, ship repair, aircraft and pilot training facilities already strained the limits of neutrality. After the fall of France Roosevelt dropped any pretence of standing outside the struggle and agreed to exchange fifty first-war, previously mothballed US Navy destroyers for eight bases on British territory in the western Atlantic and Caribbean. The destroyers required extensive refitting, but they were a morale-boosting token of American commitment at a time when merchant shipping losses to U-boats were rising ominously.

21

The Battle of the Atlantic, 1940–1

A FTER THE SHOCKING torpedo failures during the Norwegian campaign the U-boat staff had debated whether to resume the war against merchant shipping or wait until all faults had been eliminated and new detonating pistols proved. Dönitz himself believed that to hold the boats at base would damage morale and fighting efficiency, and determined on a renewed offensive in the Atlantic.

He still had few boats. Despite Raeder's efforts, new construction had not kept pace with losses, and several boats were engaged on supply missions to Norway or refitting after being used for supply. He began by sending out four boats in early May. One of these, commanded by Viktor Oehrn, sank one neutral early in his patrol but then experienced five successive failures firing with magnetic pistols. He reported it by radio. Dönitz responded by banning the use of magnetic detonators and ordered all boats to use only contact pistols, after which Oehrn enjoyed perfect results. He returned to an enthusiastic reception at Wilhelmshaven on 9 June, played in by a band on the quay and flying ten victory pennants on lines rigged from his raised periscope, as was the practice in the U-boat arm. Each pennant represented a ship sunk and was marked with the estimated tonnage of the victim. For this cruise they totalled 43,000 tons.[1]

Oehrn's remarkable tally showed what could be done, and Dönitz committed the rest of his force of only twenty-four ocean-going boats to an all-out campaign in the Atlantic. Eleven sailed in early June; six more followed before the end of the month. Burning to prove his *Rudel* tactic, Dönitz formed the first wave into two groups stationed across the estimated tracks of two homeward-bound convoys reported by the radio monitoring and decrypting service, B-Dienst, and assigned one commander in each group to take tactical control 'if necessary',[2] until which time all boats were to keep radio silence. Neither convoy was seen, but over the following weeks the commanders, acting independently, took a toll of lone vessels and ships from weakly protected convoys in the Western Approaches. Prien alone claimed ten ships totalling over 68,000 tons – reduced by post-war research to eight ships of 51,483 tons.[3] Losses from surface raiders, aircraft and mines brought the month's total to 140 ships of 585,500 tons,[4] a staggering figure reminiscent of the first war U-boat campaign, which sounded alarm bells at the Admiralty, in Churchill's War Cabinet and among US naval observers in London.

Sinkings fell in July as most boats returned to their home ports in Germany, but Dönitz ordered four to Lorient, where an advanced party of technicians was establishing the first U-boat base on the Biscay coast. By cutting out the long homeward passage around the north of Scotland, these boats would gain almost an extra fortnight in the operational area. By 2 August Lorient was a fully operational U-boat base with the engineering facilities of the former French naval dockyard brought into service for major overhauls and refits; and on 15 August Hitler formalized the unrestricted campaign Dönitz had been waging for the past nine months by announcing the 'Blockade of Britain'. It was felt to be less provocative than 'unrestricted warfare', although it was strictly illegal since there were insufficient U-boats to make it effective. At the same time he warned neutrals that they risked destruction if they entered the 'war zone' around the British Isles. It was scarcely news: neutral shipowners had lost over 100,000 tons of shipping in the last two months alone[5] – not US shipowners, though, since Roosevelt had established 'European Danger Zones' around the British Isles, Scandinavia and since June throughout the Mediterranean in which US ships were prohibited.

By this time the German media had adopted a new U-boat 'ace', Otto Kretschmer. Known to his comrades as 'Silent Otto', Kretschmer was described in his service report as 'an unusually quiet, well-formed character, yet with inner strength. Very likeable, unassuming, well-mannered in behaviour and demeanour'.[6] In command of a coastal U-boat at the outbreak of war, he had been stepped up in spring 1940 to commission the ocean-going Type VII, *U-99*. He had worked her up in the Baltic and sailed towards the end of June for the Atlantic, where he claimed seven merchantmen totalling almost 23,000 tons[7] before putting in to Lorient to replenish. Turning round in only four days, he steered up for the southwestern approaches to Ireland and on the fourth day out sank a 13,200-ton liner. Two days later he sank two medium-sized cargo liners and the following day, 31 July, sighted an escorted outward-bound convoy, which he shadowed from over the edge of the horizon by day, closing at dusk for three days until the escorts turned back for home; he then attacked, torpedoing and, as he thought, sinking three tankers. Two days later he claimed a final victim from a homeward-bound convoy, bringing his tally by his own calculation to seven ships totalling 46,118 tons. He reported this to U-boat headquarters and headed back for Lorient.

Raeder and Dönitz were both waiting for him on the quay as he brought U-99 in flying seven victory pennants. Dönitz knew from B-Dienst intercepts that the three tankers claimed had not sunk; this was not unusual since the internal compartmentalization of tanker hulls made them hard to put down, especially when sailing in ballast. He evidently wanted a new U-boat ace to boost morale, however, or was persuaded by the navy propaganda department that he should have one, and had increased the tonnage claimed for the patrol to 65,137 tons in order to bring Kretschmer's aggregate sinkings in both commands to over 100,000 tons.[8] This was the qualifying figure for the *Ritterkreuz*, the Knight's Cross of the Iron Cross with which aces were distinguished. After U-99 had made fast alongside, Raeder went aboard and bestowed the order on Kretschmer personally while news cameras clicked. Those members of the crew interviewed talked of a reserved but popular commander of unflappable temperament, whose sangfroid gave all hands 'a feeling of absolute security'.[9] This was perhaps the most important attribute of a good submarine captain.

Kretschmer was the fifth U-boat commander to achieve the Ritterkreuz; two more followed before the end of August, others in the autumn as the U-boat arm enjoyed what came to be known as the *glückliche Zeit* – the 'fortunate' or 'happy' time – and monthly sinking figures rose to almost 300,000 tons in September, 352,400 tons in October. Mines, aircraft and surface raiders claimed fewer victims, however, and total sinkings never reached the June figure.

It was during September and October that Dönitz's aim of attacking convoys with groups of U-boats was finally realized. B-Dienst provided the information for the first occasion by intercepting and deciphering a signal giving the position at which escorts were to meet a slow convoy from Canada. Dönitz, established in temporary headquarters in Paris pending conversion of the chateau he had marked out at Kerneval outside Lorient, sent four boats to form an interception line at the rendezvous. He had by now discarded the idea of a group commander; once in contact each boat was to attack without attempting to coordinate her movements with any other.

The convoy was picked up by U-65 after the escort of two destroyers, two corvettes and three armed trawlers had joined, and she was forced to submerge. Surfacing later and regaining touch, she shadowed in rising wind and seas, her reports enabling Prien in U-47 to home in that evening,

6 September. Prien attacked in darkness on the surface in wild conditions, sinking three ships before the arrival of Coastal Command flying boats at dawn forced him down. He and *U-65* surfaced later, made their best speed in the direction in which the convoy had been heading, found it again and shadowed, reporting position and course. The signals brought up two new boats, and after dark all moved in for another surface attack. Because of the wild sea conditions only two more ships were sunk, but Dönitz was encouraged that the group principles of shadowing and directing other boats on to a convoy had been proved. This seemed to be confirmed by further successful group attacks on the surface at night in the following weeks.

Although let down in the opening phase by their torpedo detonators, U-boat commanders enjoyed superb optical and fire control instruments, superior to those in any other navy at this period. For surface attack they had sophisticated rangefinder binoculars – *Überwasserzieloptik*, or *ÜZO* for short – which were carried up from below and fixed on a special *ÜZO* post on the bridge. As the attack officer trained the instrument on the target the bearing was automatically transmitted to the fire control computer – *Vorhaltrechner* – in the conning tower below. Set with target data, this electromechanical instrument provided the torpedo firing angle as a continuous solution and transmitted it to the gyro compasses of the torpedoes in their tubes, which could thus be fired whatever course the U-boat itself was steering, provided it was within 90 degrees of the course set on the torpedoes. Later models could actually be fed with data from up to five separate targets and would set five different solutions in individual torpedoes. German periscopes for submerged attack were also more sophisticated than those in other services, and as with the *ÜZO*, the target bearing was transmitted automatically to the *Vorhaltrechner* from the periscope bearing ring.

Weather had a great influence on the outcome of the night surface tactics U-boats were employing. Calm seas, clear skies and moonlight provided the setting for the most devastating group attacks in October. Dönitz had spread a line of boats far to the west of Ireland. At first storms and fog denied the group success, but on the night of 16 October, as the seas subsided and the moon came out, lookouts on the bridge of *U-48* sighted shadows on the rim of the horizon; they were ships of another slow convoy from Canada. *U-48* shadowed, plotting the convoy's course and speed, reported to U-boat headquarters, and shortly before midnight closed on the surface and torpedoed a tanker and two freighters – one of which remained afloat. The convoy made an emergency turn; the three escorts, which had never worked together, wheeled outwards firing starshell but failed to locate the U-boat, which continued shadowing on the surface, trimmed low. With daylight a Coastal Command flying boat arrived, forcing her under. She lost the convoy, but U-38 homed in and took over as shadower, sending reports that enabled the rest of the group to position themselves ahead of the convoy's track, five boats under experienced commanders, including Kretschmer in U-99 and the latest aces, Joachim Schepke in U-100 and Engelbert Endrass, formerly Prien's First Watch Officer, who had since made a reputation in his own right, in U-46.

The attack began soon after 10.15 on the evening of the 18th. The night was clear with a bright moon shining between scattered clouds. The sea heaved gently, rippled by a light wind from the south-east. The low silhouettes of the U-boats, decks almost awash, were not sighted as the commanders closed. Apart from Kretschmer and the commander of U-101, who had seen each other and exchanged signals by light some hours before, none knew where the others were; each manoeuvred on his own. The first indication of the attack was a torpedo detonating within the convoy. The escorts, now augmented by others for the final leg home, made routine turns outward, firing starshell. The U-boat commanders probed the gaps left, each First Watch Officer lining up the shape of a merchantman across the illuminated hairline of his night sight, and when satisfied pulling the torpedo firing lever. Detonation followed detonation; fountains of water lit by flame rose above the victims, which slowed and settled lower, crews scrambling to launch lifeboats.

The commanders who took part in this wholesale massacre signalled claims to U-boat headquarters totalling thirty ships of an aggregate 197,000 tons; Kretschmer himself claimed seven ships of 45,000 tons. Several claimed the same vessel, however, and British reports suggest the true totals were twenty ships of 79,600 tons, Kretschmer's share being six and one shared vessel totalling 29,000 tons.[10] Even this reduced total represented 57 per cent of the convoy of thirty-five ships which had sailed from Canada.

Prien in U-47 arrived too late to take part, but ran into another homeward-bound convoy the same day. He reported and Dönitz ordered four commanders to the scene who had not expended all torpedoes in the previous nights' battles. They arrived in the evening, finding conditions little changed, a bright moon shining on light clouds, a calm sea and columns of ships silhouetted against a luminous sky. Despite a more powerful escort including two destroyers capable of outrunning surfaced U-boats, the scenes of destruction were repeated. From 9.15 until three the following

morning, the 20th, the darkness was rent by the flash and blast of detonations and brightened by starshells and white-hot explosions of tanker
cargoes shooting blazing oil. After it was over the five commanders
reported a total of seventeen ships sunk aggregating 113,000 tons – of
which Prien himself claimed eight of over 50,000 tons. Again this was
exaggeration born of the chaotic conditions of a night battle; the true figures were twelve ships of 75,000 tons.[11] Fortunately for British and neutral
sailors the commanders had now expended all their torpedoes and were
heading home. Not a boat had been lost.

Dönitz was jubilant, entering in his war diary: 'by joint attack in the last
three days 7 U-boats with 300 men in the crews have sunk 47 ships
totalling about 310,000 tons. A colossal success'.[12] He drew the conclusion:

> The operations prove that the development of U-boat tactics since 1935, and
> the training based on the principle of countering the concentration of ships
> in a convoy by a concentration of U-boats attacking, was correct . . .
>
> Further, if there were more U-boats the English supply routes would not
> be left free after such attacks because, as today, nearly all boats have to return
> after using all their torpedoes . . .[13]

Bad weather also contributed to a marked decrease in sinkings as winter
gripped the north Atlantic. Gales raised furious seas. Winds of force seven
or above were recorded on fifty-two out of the ninety-two days from
November through January 1941.[14] From the low bridges of the four to
eight U-boats on patrol at any one time visibility was practically limited
to the driven crests of wild, spume-veined slopes on every hand. For the
watch on deck, one officer and four lookouts, one for each quadrant of
the compass, there was no respite from the buffeting of breaking seas. 'We
do not look down on to the sea,' one wrote, 'but up out of it, enveloped
in water like swimmers . . . we see with the eyes of the sea.'[15] They wore
steel harnesses clipped to the bridge structure to secure them against
being washed overboard, but needed all their strength to resist the surge of
the water as it beat over them and swirled waist deep. Straightening afterwards and lifting binoculars to their eyes with numb fingers, brows and
beards stiff with salt, boots filled, bodies achingly wet beneath sou'west-
ers, oilskins and sweaters, they tried to steady themselves against the
motions of the boat.

There was little more comfort for the watch below. Braced in their
bunks against the rising, descending, corkscrewing movements, they could
scarcely sleep, but only dozed, feeling the slam and judder of the seas,

hearing the wash and gurgle of water across the deck casing through their twilight consciousness. Condensation streamed in rivulets down the inside of the hull plates and fell in drops from the massed pipes and cables overhead. Everything was wet. Clothes never dried. Bread grew soggy; fresh food rotted. Nothing could be cooked. To gain relief from unending, wearying movement, to cook and eat it was necessary to take the boat down over 160 feet.

On the few calmer days individual boats attacked ships sailing independently or stragglers from convoys, but from early December until the end of January 1941 there were no group convoy battles, and the monthly sinking figures fell to an average of 162,000 tons, scarcely over half that of the preceding three months.[16] The figures might have been boosted by a flotilla of Italian submarines sent from the Mediterranean to a base prepared for them at Bordeaux and placed under Dönitz's operational control, but their crews lacked the intensive training the U-boat men underwent and they proved more of an encumbrance. Dönitz deployed them in areas where 'the way they let themselves be sighted, their radio traffic, their clumsy attacks'[17] would not compromise his own boats.

For his own men, Dönitz spared no effort. He had moved into his new headquarters in Kerneval in November, from where he could see the Lorient boats departing or returning upriver from their solitary patrols, and had established additional bases on the Atlantic coast at Brest, St Nazaire and La Pallice, near La Rochelle. He tried to greet each returning boat personally and impress each member of the crew with a sense of individual value. Bands played the boats in, and as the men came ashore after his brief inspection, finding the solid ground unsteady beneath their feet, nurses bestowed flowers and smiles. Afterwards they enjoyed a homecoming celebration with champagne, the fresh Brittany food they had missed for weeks and as much German beer as they could drink. For those going on leave there was a special express known as the BdU-train to Bremen and Hamburg via Nantes and Paris; for the others rest hostels in coastal resorts away from the bases, with chateaux or hotels requisitioned for officers. The uninhibited scenes in the Bar Royal of the Hotel Majestic in La Baule, near St Nazaire, in the opening of Lothar-Günther Buchheim's classic *Das Boot*, have been condemned as gross exaggeration by U-boat veterans; yet they contain a core of truth: these were very young officers, on the one hand glorified in press, radio and newsreels as Hitler's knights, on the other responsible at sea for the safety of their boat and crew, and for setting an example of imperturbability under attack, and scoring. There was intense rivalry. Newer commanders looked up to the aces who were already legends, Prien, 'the Bull of Scapa', Kretschmer, 'the Tonnage King', Schepke of film-star good looks, and determined to emulate them.

For the British Admiralty the U-boats' concentrated attacks by night on the surface where Asdic was of little use had come as the shocking surprise Dönitz always intended. Defeat had focused minds, though; and much was, in any case, under way to remedy the defects exposed. Over 120 new corvettes from emergency building programmes had been launched by the end of the year; most were in commission, and hundreds more were on the stocks in British and Canadian yards; the Royal Canadian Navy was training thousands of new recruits to man them. Of a simple whale-catcher design with a basic reciprocating engine, they lacked the speed to catch U-boats on the surface and their violent motion in any seaway was exhausting, even dangerous for ships' companies, yet they were sturdy, quick to build and had the range to cross the Atlantic; they were to provide the backbone of the convoy escort force for the rest of the war.

Of equal consequence, Coastal Command was being supplied with more and better aircraft. The crucial role of the air in anti-submarine work had been relearned. It was not necessary for aircraft to destroy U-boats, only to force a shadowing boat to submerge, when its low underwater speed and endurance usually ensured that it lost the convoy.[18] Although the Air Ministry and Churchill gave priority to bombing German cities, American Lockheed Hudson bombers with greater range than Coastal Command's obsolete models were now being supplied for shipping protection, and they and even longer-range Sunderland flying boats were being fitted with a primitive search radar. This lacked the range or definition to be more than an occasional aid in locating surfaced U-boats, but work on a vastly improved set employing a cavity magnetron to produce a very short, centimetric wavelength beam was nearing completion.

In the meantime the Admiralty Trade Division attempted to route convoys around U-boat patrol lines as plotted by the Submarine Tracking section of the Operational Intelligence Centre.[19] But perhaps the most important lesson the Anti-Submarine Warfare Division of the Admiralty had absorbed from the autumn battles was that escorts assigned to convoys on an ad hoc basis as they became available could not be expected to work together effectively. Escorts were now being formed into permanent groups, 'each under its own leader, each working as a team and sharing a common training',[20] as it was put in the division's November report. In

addition both surface escorts and aircraft were being fitted with radio telephones for intercommunication during operations, and Coastal Command
aircraft were at last being supplied with depth charges instead of bombs.

The cumulative effect transformed the terms of battle. A U-boat 'spring
offensive' launched towards the end of February 1941 met fierce resistance
and Dönitz's three top-scoring aces failed to return. First to be lost was
Prien in *U-47*. The exact circumstances of his end have not been defini-
tively established. All that is certain is that in early March he, Kretschmer
and others attacked an outward convoy escorted by a well-trained group
under Captain James Rowland, which beat them off and destroyed two
boats, including *U-47*, and forced another to retire for the loss of only two
merchantmen.[21] Scarcely over a week later both Schepke and Kretschmer
fell victim to an exceptionally powerful escort group under Captain
Donald Macintyre while attacking a homeward convoy.

Schepke was located first, forced under and depth-charged. This fearful
experience has been described by many: the sound of propellers above
increasing in volume; the metallic chirp of the Asdic beam striking the hull
at ever shorter intervals; the crew silent in stockinged feet bracing themselves against solid fixtures, suspense building until, as Buchheim has
described it, the hull of the boat became like the skin of the men inside, the
smallest noise like a nerve touched. The click of the first *Wasserbomb*, or
Wabo, reaching its depth setting was followed by thunderous explosions as
the charges detonated near by, hurling the boat about. Electrics shorted,
lights flickered out, instrument glasses smashed, hand-held flashlights
probed the dark, lighting up falling flakes of paint and cork.

After more than an hour, during which several charges exploded very
close, Schepke was forced to the surface. He tried to evade a destroyer closing fast to ram and was calling down to his crew to abandon ship when the
destroyer's bows hit and crushed him between the side of the bridge and
the periscope standard, killing him instantly. Kretschmer, who had claimed
six victims from the convoy, was then located near by and was also forced
to the surface by depth charges. Coming up between two destroyers, he
ordered Abandon Ship and survived, together with all but three of his
men.[22]

The loss of the three aces defined the end of the U-boat 'Happy Time'.
Dönitz, whose feelings for his missing favourites were betrayed only by
deeper reserve, continued to believe that with numbers the Atlantic battle
could still be won, for U-boat production was at last increasing. The
remaining aces and the 'Young Turks' at the Biscay bases continued to vie
for reputation and the *Ritterkreuz*. Yet the balance had already tipped

against them. No subsequent commander would reach Kretschmer's confirmed sinkings of forty-three ships totalling 247,000 tons.[23]

March 1941 was also the month in which the British Admiralty obtained a breakthrough into the code used by all German naval units, including U-boats. The code was generated by an Enigma machine. It had a keyboard like a typewriter. When a letter was pressed its enciphered equivalent was illuminated on a display panel and at the same time an alphabet rotor turned, changing subsequent encipherment paths. There were three such rotors in the machine and after the first rotor had completed a full revolution of twenty-six steps – one for each letter – the second rotor began to turn, and after that the third. Consequently it was not until 26 to the power of 3 (17,576) keys had been pressed that the same encipherment pattern recurred. Further variations were introduced by inserting pairs of plugs into lettered sockets in a switchboard below the keyboard, and to add to the complications naval machines were supplied with eight different rotors from which the three in use were chosen according to a table of settings. It was theoretically impossible to break such a machine code, and the Government Code and Cipher School – GC and CS – at Bletchley Park, successor to the Admiralty's Room 40 and the cryptanalytical section of the War Office, had not done so. The Admiralty therefore laid plans to capture a naval Enigma machine and tables of settings. The first success was achieved in early March during a raid on the Lofoten Islands off northern Norway, when a haul of material was seized from an armed trawler.[24] The real prize in the signals war was obtained two days later from *U-110*, a Type IX boat commanded by the officer who had torpedoed the *Athenia* on the first day of the war, Fritz-Julius Lemp. He had since become an experienced commander and holder of the *Ritterkreuz*, but remained capable of egregious error. He attacked a convoy south of Iceland protected by two powerful escort groups, one of which would shortly have parted, and disastrously for U-boat Command and his own reputation, when his boat was brought to the surface by depth-charge attack and he ordered his crew to abandon her he failed to ensure that the Enigma machine and coding materials were jettisoned.

The boat did not sink, and the Enigma, all its rotors, tables of settings for April and June, charts of the Atlantic showing mine-free approaches to the Biscay bases and a wealth of priceless secret material were retrieved by a boarding party from the destroyer of the senior escort officer, Commander A. J. Baker-Cresswell. He had engineered the capture by calling off a consort about to ram the surfaced boat, and had had the German survivors in the water taken to another ship and hurried below decks to prevent them seeing their vessel boarded;[25] consequently no hint of the possible seizure of coding materials ever reached Dönitz. Lemp himself did not survive.[26]

The coup was the single most valuable contribution to the intelligence war, and has been compared to a major victory at sea. The experience gained by the cryptographers at Bletchley Park from reading signals through June on a daily basis, together with the provision of more of the analytical machines known as *bombes*, enabled the naval section to provide the Admiralty with decrypts of U-boat signals with usually no more than a thirty-six-hour delay from August 1941 virtually to the end of the war, with a small gap in early 1942.[27]

The immediate result was the location and destruction of German tankers and supply ships stationed overseas to replenish surface raiders and long-distance U-boats. The long-term effect was to give the Admiralty Submarine Tracking Room sufficient information to plot all U-boat patrol lines accurately in real time, allowing the Trade Division to route convoys around them. The German authority on the U-boat war, Jürgen Rohwer, has estimated that evasive routing saved some three hundred merchantmen of a total of 1½–2 million tons from destruction in the second half of 1941,[28] and suggests this was the decisive period when Dönitz lost the tonnage battle. Such a purely mathematical analysis overestimates the effects, since it takes no account of the growing capability of British counter-measures, in both material and training, or of the increasing involvement of the Royal Canadian and US navies in the western Atlantic.[29] Nonetheless, the tonnage sunk by U-boats from July to December fell to half that sunk in the first six months of the year, and the vital figure for Dönitz, the tonnage sunk per U-boat per day at sea, went down from a high of 486 tons in May to a mere 126 tons in November; it had been almost 1,000 tons in October 1940.[30]

German surface warships and converted merchant raiders had broken out from time to time in the high northern latitudes and ranged over the oceans, avoiding confrontations with British heavy ships, but their depredations were a pinprick in comparison to the losses wrought by U-boats. Raeder's hopes were now pinned on two new battleships, *Bismarck* and *Tirpitz*, which were considerably larger, faster and more powerfully armed than the latest Royal Navy battleships. Together, he believed, they could deliver a mortal blow to British supply lines. First to complete her work-up was the *Bismarck*. He intended dispatching her with the battlecruisers against Atlantic convoys, but one battlecruiser was refitting and just before the intended sortie the other was damaged in a torpedo attack delivered from heroically close range by a Coastal Command aircraft. Anxious to keep the pressure on the British in the Atlantic, he nonetheless sent the *Bismarck* out in May 1941 with only the heavy cruiser *Prinz Eugen* in company.

The story of the pursuit and destruction of the *Bismarck* has been told many times. Shadowed by cruisers in the Denmark Strait between Iceland and Greenland, she was intercepted as she emerged into the Atlantic by the elderly battlecruiser *Hood* and the battleship *Prince of Wales*, which was so new she still had dockyard fitters and technicians aboard. In the ensuing action the combination of accurate German long-range fire and inadequate protection over the *Hood*'s magazines resulted in the veteran British battle-cruiser blowing apart like her predecessors at Jutland. Of her ship's company, only three survived. German fire was then concentrated on the *Prince of Wales*, which was forced to turn away, her after turret jammed, although not before she had made two hits on the *Bismarck* with her forward guns. Together, these caused an oil leak and fuel contamination which restricted *Bismarck*'s range, and the force commander, Vice-Admiral Günther Lütjens, ordering the *Prinz Eugen* to proceed with the mission, headed back for St Nazaire for repairs.

The Admiralty directed all available units towards him, and finally it was Swordfish aircraft from the carrier *Ark Royal* summoned from the Mediterranean which delivered the fatal blow. Attacking from low cloud in stormy weather, they scored two hits, one of which jammed the *Bismarck*'s rudders, leaving her crippled and unable to escape her pursuers. The following morning, 27 May, two battleships of the Home Fleet closed and overwhelmed her with concentrated salvoes. Reduced to a blazing shambles, she fought to the end, going down, flag flying, only after her sea cocks had been opened, carrying Lütjens and all but 110 of her company of over two thousand with her.

From the start of the war Dönitz had been pressing for the immense resources devoted to the surface fleet to be diverted to U-boats; they could be built far more quickly at far less cost than major warships, and only they, he argued, could get through the British blockade to cut her supply lines.[31] The loss of the *Bismarck* seemed a convincing demonstration, and almost overnight the U-boat arm became the focus of German naval effort. The lesson was driven home over the following weeks when, as a result of the cipher settings seized from *U-110*, German tankers and supply ships stationed overseas to support surface raiders were destroyed. The few commerce raiders still at large were also hunted down or, like the *Prinz Eugen*, returned home. By the end of the summer U-boats were fighting the trade war virtually on their own.

The Royal Navy was equally successful in containing Italian surface warships in the Mediterranean. The previous November two waves of Swordfish aircraft from the carrier HMS *Illustrious* had surprised the Italian battle fleet in the harbour of Taranto; coming in under balloon defences in the face of fierce anti-aircraft fire, they had launched torpedoes that sank three battleships at their moorings for the loss of only two planes. The Swordfish, a biplane with a top speed scarcely over 150 m.p.h., obsolete by the standards of US and Japanese naval aircraft, had given the clearest demonstration yet of the new dimension of power at sea. The Japanese Assistant Naval Attaché in Berlin flew to Taranto to investigate. The moral ascendancy of the British Mediterranean fleet was reinforced with a notable victory off Cape Matapan in March 1941.

Hitler's attention, meanwhile, was focused eastward. Notwithstanding the weakness of his Axis partner in the Mediterranean theatre, or Britain's refusal to come to terms, he had made the decision to attack Russia. He had given the campaign the code name 'Barbarossa' after the twelfth-century German emperor and crusader Frederick Barbarossa. It was his crusade. The purpose was to destroy Bolshevism and under cover of the confusion of war destroy the Jewish race in Europe. At the deepest psychological level this was a race war to cleanse the German bloodstock and win space to colonize eastern Europe and dominate the continent. In this sense his vision was no different from Hirohito's ambition to establish a new Japanese order in east Asia.

The German public had been prepared by three recent anti-Semitic films, *Die Rothschilds*, *Jud Süss* and, at the turn of the year, *Der ewige Jude*, which achieved notoriety by juxtaposing scenes of Jews and sewer rats.[32] Himmler, chief of the SS, was the chosen instrument. He was instructed to prepare for the '*Endlösung*', or 'final solution' to the Jewish problem.[33] Special formations of SS and police units were designated to follow each of the army groups spearheading the assault into Russia to round up and liquidate Bolshevik functionaries and Jews behind the lines. The generals had private doubts about initiating a two-front war, but made no significant remonstrance. Hitler's conquests had established him, not least in his own eyes, as the greatest warlord of all time – shortened by sceptics to the acronym 'GröFAZ'. Of the service chiefs, only Raeder proposed an alternative strategy for advancing in the Middle East and taking the Suez Canal in order to knock Britain out before the United States entered the war on her side. Hitler disregarded him and there was no collective organ of government or chiefs of staff committee to make informed judgements. National governance had dissolved. There were only competing and overlapping authorities taking their own decisions in the light of 'the leader's' will.[34]

Barbarossa was launched in the early hours of 22 June, a peculiarly inauspicious date 129 years to the day since a former warlord and would-be master of the continent, Napoleon Bonaparte, had crossed the River Niemen into Russia. The German assault was on an incomparably larger scale: more than three million men deployed with tanks, personnel carriers, artillery and aircraft over the length of the Soviet border from the Baltic to the Black Sea. Astonishingly, complete tactical surprise was achieved. Stalin had been gulled into believing that the show of military might on his frontier was a bluff to force concessions.[35] The Red Army paid the price. Over a thousand Russian aircraft were destroyed within hours of the beginning of the assault; without air cover Russian forward positions were overrun or encircled and cut off. Within a week the army groups in the north and centre had penetrated some 300 miles, by the beginning of September 500 miles, into Soviet territory. History had never seen such powerful forces engaged, nor murder on such a monstrous scale, as the special SS and police formations following the front line exploited the hatreds engendered by Stalin's policies in the Baltic provinces and the Ukraine to recruit local auxiliaries for the mass liquidation of communist officials and Jews.

The shift of the German war effort eastwards provided respite for Britain as Hitler diverted U-boats to the Baltic and Arctic and in the autumn insisted on the dispatch of twenty U-boats to the Mediterranean to help Italy keep open sea lines of communication with Axis forces in North Africa. These boats achieved spectacular triumphs against the British Mediterranean fleet, sinking a battleship and the carrier *Ark Royal*, but the tonnage war in the Atlantic waned. In this respect Hitler's turn east against Russia and Churchill's peripheral strategy against Italy in the Mediterranean together ended any small chance Dönitz might have had of winning the Atlantic supply war before British anti-submarine defences became too strong for conventional U-boats to combat.

Roosevelt had by this time brought the United States to what seemed the brink of war in support of Britain. His first step after winning a third term in November 1940 had been to ensure the continuance of American arms supplies. Britain was fast running out of gold and foreign exchange to pay for her huge orders. He had proposed that when that time arrived the United States should continue to supply war materials on lease or loan, to be returned in kind after the war, justifying it on the grounds 'that it may still prove true that the best defense of Great Britain is the best defense of the United States';[36] The 'Lend-Lease' Act in March 1941 gave Roosevelt authority to aid any country whose defence he believed to be necessary to the security of the United States. Soviet Russia now fell into that category. Lend-Lease was to be vital in maintaining both Britain's and Russia's ability to fight; it was also used as a subtle instrument to keep Britain financially subservient while US exporters broke into pre-war British markets.[37]

As Lend-Lease was being debated representatives of the British chiefs of staff and US officers meeting in Washington agreed that in the event of the United States entering the war, the fight against Hitler in Europe would take precedence over operations against Japan in the Far East.[38] In April Roosevelt further compromised US neutrality by pushing the boundary of a so-called 'Pan-American Security Zone' patrolled by the US Navy into mid-Atlantic. Preparations were then made to take control of convoys within the western half of the north Atlantic: bases were developed in Greenland and at Argentia, Newfoundland – acquired the previous year from Britain in the destroyers-for-bases deal – and US Marines took over defence of a base at Reykjavik, Iceland, from British and Canadian troops.

In August Churchill sailed with senior naval and military officers for a secret meeting with Roosevelt and his service chiefs in Placentia Bay off Argentia. They agreed a joint statement of post-war aims called 'The Atlantic Charter', reminiscent of Wilson's 'Fourteen Points' in the first war: disarmament, peoples' rights to choose their own form of government, equal access to trade for all states, the freedom of the seas.[39] Behind the public accord, the service chiefs confirmed the strategy of dealing with Germany first should the United States enter the war.

With the US Navy now taking an active part in convoy duties in the western Atlantic, encounters with U-boats were unavoidable. In October two US destroyer escorts were torpedoed, and one sank with the loss of 115 of her company. Had Roosevelt wished to bring the country into open war with Germany, he had the perfect pretexts, but this was not his intention, possibly because his armed forces were not ready. The decision was about to be made for him. In Japan a carrier task force under Vice-Admiral Chuichi Nagumo was making final preparations for the most audacious venture in the nation's imperial history.

Stalin had learned from Richard Sorge in Tokyo as early as September that Japan was preparing to strike against Britain and America, not Russia. Confirmed by army intelligence, it had allowed him to order the transfer of half his Far Eastern Army with tanks and aircraft west for the defence of

Moscow. On 5 December he unleashed these fresh divisions against the enemy threatening the capital. The temperature was minus 15 degrees Fahrenheit. The Russian troops in capacious white snowsuits were equipped with heaters, skis and sledges; the Germans were not; their planning had been predicated on rapid victory before winter set in. Surprised by the new divisions and ill prepared for the arctic conditions, they were forced to give ground. Moscow was saved.

In the open spaces of the north Pacific Nagumo's task force, observing strict radio silence, neared the Hawaiian islands. US Navy intelligence had been bamboozled by Japanese wireless disinformation signals and had no inkling of its approach. By the early hours of 7 December Nagumo was just over two hundred miles north of the island of Oahu; still the Americans had no suspicion. He signalled his six carriers to alter easterly into the wind to fly their aircraft off. The ships pitched heavily into the swell but the first wave of planes lifted off with scarcely a hitch and at about 6.20 a.m. headed for Pearl Harbor, forty-three fighters, forty-nine high-altitude bombers, fifty-one dive-bombers and forty torpedo planes,[40] a force incomparably more advanced and powerful than the few Royal Navy Swordfish that had attacked Taranto the previous year. Little over an hour later they were followed by a second wave almost as strong.

Shortly before eight o'clock Admiral Husband E. Kimmel, commander-in-chief of the US Pacific Fleet, was called to the telephone in his residence overlooking the harbour and told the base was under attack. Not yet fully dressed, he dashed outside to find the sky filled with turning and diving planes, their wings emblazoned with the red rising sun of Japan. He stared 'in utter disbelief and completely stunned'.[41]

For the Japanese the success of their surprise strike was a source of immense pride: the US Pacific battle fleet had been eliminated – although not the carriers – for the loss of only twenty-nine Japanese aircraft. For the Americans and Roosevelt it was an act of perfidy which would be avenged. It is instructive, however, that when Roosevelt delivered a considered speech the next day asking Congress to declare a state of war with Japan, he did not include Germany. It was left to Hitler to include himself. With his Russian campaign stalled until at least the end of winter, angered by American aid to Britain and the US Navy's undeclared war in the western Atlantic, he was delighted by Japan's explosive entry into the conflict. Much of the US war effort must now be diverted to the Pacific, and Britain's too, since her eastern empire had been struck by Japanese forces at the time of the assault on Pearl Harbor.[42] He was not technically committed to joining Japan as the Tripartite Treaty was a defensive alliance, and it was Japan which had attacked America. Nonetheless he had assured the Japanese Foreign Minister that he could count on Germany in any conflict with the United States;[4] and believing in any case that Roosevelt was seeking a pretext to enter the European conflict, this was one promise he kept. He declared war formally on the United States on 11 December. Since Churchill had already committed Britain to war with Japan, the conflict had become global in scale and ferocity.

22

The Pacific, 1942

———•———

THE SCALE OF Japan's maritime assault on the Western empires was unprecedented. Numerous other Japanese expeditionary forces had been under way during Nagumo's silent passage across the north Pacific; it was their more obvious moves towards jumping-off points for the invasion of the Philippines, north and south, the Malay peninsula and the Dutch East Indies which had occupied US Naval Intelligence and successfully diverted attention from the Pearl Harbor strike force.

Even before Nagumo's first wave struck the US fleet base Japanese troops had come ashore in British Malaya to fight their way towards the airbase at Kota Bharu; and as the day advanced Japanese aircraft raided Guam, Wake Island, Hong Kong and US airbases on Luzon in the Philippines, ravaging bombers and fighters on the ground and establishing air supremacy prior to invasion. For the Admiralty in London it was the dread situation for which no answer had been found.[1] Singapore at the southern tip of the Malay peninsula had been conceived after the first war as the main fleet base for the defence of the eastern empire, yet Treasury demands for economy and the politics of disarmament had left the Royal Navy without sufficient ships to provide a Far Eastern fleet if engaged against Germany and Italy; and Singapore had not been provided with adequate defences against overland attack. Air power had been recognized as crucial in this respect but the airfields in Malaya had been built on widely dispersed sites too close to the shore to be defensible against determined assault from the sea.

In the period of tension prior to the Japanese strikes Churchill had insisted on the dispatch of capital ships to Singapore as a deterrent, also to signal to the governments of Australia and New Zealand that Britain was committed to their defence. The Naval Staff needed all modern units to meet the threat posed by the new German battleship, *Tirpitz*, in the Atlantic, but had reluctantly agreed to send the modern battleship *Prince of Wales*, the old battlecruiser *Repulse* and an aircraft carrier.[2] Accidental grounding damage to the carrier prevented her sailing; consequently the squadron that arrived in Singapore on 2 December comprised only the *Prince of Wales*, *Repulse* and four destroyers.

In command was (acting) Admiral Sir T. S. V. Phillips, recently Vice-Chief of Naval Staff, who had been arguing forcefully against the dispatch of this token deterrent. By then it was plain he had been right. Two signals from the First Sea Lord suggested he should consider taking the capital ships to sea to confuse the Japanese as to their whereabouts, but before he had time to respond, a report of escorted Japanese transports off southern Indochina heading westwards, followed by reports of the attack on Pearl Harbor and landings at Kota Bharu and Singora (Songkhla) on the Malay peninsula, left him little choice. The fate of Singapore depended ultimately on the threatened airfields to the north; the navy could not abandon their defenders. Calling on the Royal Air Force for fighter cover over Singora on Wednesday the 10th, he took his small squadron to sea under cover of darkness on the 8th and stood north-easterly, away from the land, to avoid discovery, later altering northerly, intending to make a surprise raid on the Japanese transports, then head off rapidly seawards.

Early the next morning he received ominous news from his chief of staff, whom he had left in Singapore as a liaison: fighter protection would not, 'repeat not, be possible' on the 10th. Kota Bharu airfield had already been evacuated and the other airfields put out of action by Japanese air strikes. Further, 'Japanese have large bomber forces based southern Indo-China and possibly also in Thailand'.[3] Phillips decided, nonetheless, to press on. He was a small man, nicknamed 'Tom Thumb', with a pugnacious temperament. Given his character and the weight of British naval tradition, it is difficult to imagine him doing other. In theory his flagship had formidable anti-aircraft defences, including the secondary battery of sixteen dual-purpose 5.25-inch guns in high-angle director control. It is possible that Phillips, although a gunnery specialist, was not aware of the ineffectiveness of this system, which used estimates rather than measurements of an aircraft's speed of approach to apply aim-off, giving results no better than guesswork.[4] And the level of skill Japanese navy pilots had attained in dive-bombing and torpedo attack was, as yet, unknown.

In the early afternoon the squadron crossed a Japanese submarine patrol line established south of the landings and was sighted and reported. Phillips was unaware of this, but later that afternoon Japanese scouting aircraft were sighted. With surprise now lost and the prospect of coming under mass air attack as he neared the landings, Phillips knew it was futile to continue. He altered course north-westerly towards Singora for the benefit of the shadowing aircraft, and after dark turned and retired southwards.

Scarcely over four hours later, in the early hours of the 10th, a message came in from his chief of staff in Singapore reporting new Japanese landings at Kuantan, some 170 miles south of Kota Bharu. Phillips decided he could surprise and disrupt this latest force and altered towards the land, increasing speed to 25 knots. He did not call for air cover in case the Japanese should locate him from intercepts. Soon reaching the Japanese submarine patrol line again, he almost ran over one boat, which fired a salvo of five torpedoes. All missed. On the strength of her report, however, a Japanese naval air flotilla at Saigon, which had been alerted by the earlier reports, was launched, thirty-four aircraft armed with bombs, fifty-one with torpedoes. They did not expect the British squadron so close to the land, and found only a destroyer Phillips had detached earlier. She evaded their attacks.

Phillips, meanwhile, had found Kuantan entirely peaceful. The report had been false. Then his luck ran out: a reconnaissance plane on the last leg of its patrol sighted his squadron and called in the strike aircraft, now turning for home. The first flight of nine high-level bombers was sighted from the flagship soon after eleven, small silver specks high up in the sky in line abreast. Thus far Phillips had conducted the sortie with exemplary skill and boldness; now, no doubt weary after the continuous tension of the past two days, he made serious mistakes, attempting to control the movements of the two capital ships by flag signal and failing to order a smokescreen. He had also neglected, after realizing he had been sighted, to call for fighter aircraft from Singapore.

The first wave of bombers flew unscathed through the barrage of anti-aircraft fire thrown up by the ships and straddled the *Repulse*, hitting her aft with one bomb without causing serious damage. Phillips realized his initial mistake and signalled to her to manoeuvre independently. Next, sixteen torpedo planes closed; nine targeted the *Prince of Wales*, descending to 100 feet as they came in in waves of three and launched their weapons. The flagship brought one plane down, but was hit by two, probably three, torpedoes on the port side, which caused extensive damage and flooding. The *Repulse* was not hit, and evaded further waves of torpedo planes and a second high-level bombing attack, before her captain, seeing the flagship in extreme difficulties, steered towards her to offer assistance. The two ships were some eight hundred yards apart when more torpedo planes came in, attacking from both sides. Unable to comb the tracks from different directions, the *Repulse* was hit once, the *Prince of Wales* four times. Nine fresh torpedo planes then concentrated on the *Repulse*, flying in from all angles. She brought down two with her guns, but four torpedoes went home, the explosions sending terrific shock waves throughout her structure, shaking the masts and rigging, and she began listing to port. Her captain, sensing it was the end for his veteran command, called all hands on deck. They scrambled up, forming orderly lines on the starboard side, and as she went over farther, climbed the deck rails and walked on to the side plates and down towards the sea.[5]

Phillips ordered two of his accompanying destroyers to rescue survivors, and requested tugs from Singapore, but it was fighter aircraft standing by for a call he never made which arrived to witness the last moments of his flagship. It was 1320 hours when she rolled over and sank. Of 2,921 officers and men from the two British capital ships, 2,408 were rescued by the destroyers; neither Phillips nor his flag captain was among them.

The interwar debate in all navies between advocates of carrier air power and those who regarded battleships as the arbiters of naval war was finally settled. It had taken the Japanese 22nd Naval Air Flotilla less than an hour and a half to demolish Britain's newest battleship and a modernized battlecruiser manoeuvring freely in open water. Nor was there any doubt that Britain's reign as mistress of the seas was over, and with it her hold over her empire in the east. The wide separation of her colonies, formerly her strength when she had controlled the seas between, was now her weakness. Hong Kong had been taken; Malaya, Burma, India, Australia and New Zealand lay open to invasion. In the two white dominions there was anxiety, verging on panic, and a natural leaning towards the United States for protection.

The absence of US carriers from Pearl Harbor during the Japanese attack had not been fortuitous. Washington had issued a war warning to all US Pacific commands on 27 November after diplomatic negotiations with the Japanese government had evidently broken down; and Kimmel had been instructed to send his carriers away from the base. It was a precautionary measure; no one in the Navy Department imagined a Japanese strike on Oahu. Despite a report from the US ambassador in Tokyo in January that year that 'in the event of trouble with the United States' Japan planned a 'surprise mass attack on Pearl Harbor',[6] Kimmel had been sent a paraphrase, with a qualification: 'The Division of Naval Intelligence places no credence in these rumors.'[7] The 'rumors' had not been followed up. The report had lain forgotten beneath many later intelligence assessments. No one doubted that the Japanese would open hostilities before a declaration, but all recent intelligence pointed to moves southwards aimed probably at the Philippines or Malaya. It seems that the dispersal of the carriers was ordered simply because they were the fastest units of the fleet with the greatest range.

Whatever the motive, the directive to Kimmel had historic significance: the carriers alone stood between Japan and her ambition to dominate the Pacific, for although the Americans had powerful submarines on station in theory capable of making things difficult for Japanese invasion forces, in practice in the opening phases of the war these failed utterly.

Individual US 'fleet' submarines were formidable fighting machines, by far superior to those in any other service. Of some 1,500 tons, twice the size of a Type VII U-boat, they could make 20 knots on the surface, 10 knots submerged, and they carried twenty-four torpedoes in total in bow and stern tubes. A Torpedo Data Computer – TDC – provided continuous firing solutions, and like the U-boats' *Vorhaltrechner* set the gyro compasses of individual torpedoes in the tubes so that a commander could fire at any time whatever his course. The size of the boats also allowed superb accommodation: a separate messroom, a washroom with showers, and air conditioning, which was not so much a luxury as a practical measure to improve the health and alertness of the men in the tropics and prevent deterioration of electrical and other equipment through condensation. The potential of these boats was not realized, however, because the torpedoes' depth-keeping mechanism and detonators constantly failed. The war also showed up deficiencies in training, which had encouraged caution, and in the appointment of commanding officers. Inevitably those qualities of aggression and determination tempered by precise calculation under stress were not necessarily touchstones for selection in peacetime.[8]

As a result of the unreliability of the torpedoes and the often excessive caution shown by commanders on their first war patrols – with notable exceptions – a magnificent force of twenty-three fleet submarines and six smaller 'S' class boats based at Manila in the Philippines failed to impede the invasion of Luzon or the southern island of Mindanao. Between them they sank just one 5,500-ton transport and a small freighter. Twelve of the latest fleet submarines and nine older boats from Pearl Harbor did no better against invasion of Wake Island or on patrol off Japanese bases. By the end of December the fifty submarines of the Pacific and Asiatic commands had between them sunk ten Japanese ships totalling 43,600 tons.[9]

Nor in the opening phase could the American carriers pose a threat to Japanese invasion forces. They were required to defend Pearl Harbor from another strike. Admiral Kimmel and the senior Army Air Force commanders had been recalled to answer for their conduct before a Commission of Inquiry, and when Kimmel's successor, Admiral Chester Nimitz, assumed command in January 1942, his priority was to maintain the line of communication with Australia, which had to be held at all cost.

He used practically his entire remaining fleet, including carriers, to escort Marine reinforcements to Samoa to prevent the island falling to the enemy and to secure it for use as a staging post for a future assault into the Japanese island perimeter. Japanese forces, meanwhile, advanced like wildfire down Malaya towards Singapore and northwards into Burma, through the Philippines and into Borneo and Celebes in the Dutch East Indies. By 9 February 1942 Japanese troops had gained Singapore Island itself, and on the 15th the base was surrendered. A major disaster for British arms, it was a mortal blow for British and European prestige in the east.

Five days later a powerful Japanese carrier force and an air flotilla based on Celebes Island launched a surprise strike on Darwin in northern Australia, crippling the port and sinking much of the shipping there. Meanwhile Japanese amphibious forces had penetrated farther in the Dutch East Indies, and on the 26th an Allied squadron cobbled together from Dutch, British, Australian and American cruisers and destroyers in the area sailed under Rear Admiral K. W. F. M. Doorman of the Royal Netherlands Navy to intercept an invasion force heading for the principal Dutch island, Java. Doorman's squadron was approximately equal in gunpower to the Japanese covering force, but not in speed, and the ships had not worked together and lacked common signals. Moreover, the Japanese had air support, which they lacked. This proved crucial during a night engagement on the 27th when flares dropped by aircraft over the Allied ships enabled the Japanese to torpedo and sink the Dutch flagship and another cruiser. In subsequent actions the three remaining Allied cruisers, fighting stubbornly to their last shells, were overwhelmed.

The Battle of the Java Sea was the last flicker of naval resistance on the part of the European colonial powers in the Far East. In the next two months the Japanese consolidated their position in the Dutch East Indies and the Philippines and advanced through Burma to the border of India, while their carriers ranged the Indian Ocean, attacked Colombo and the Royal Naval base at Trincomalee in Ceylon (Sri Lanka), catching and sinking one light carrier and two cruisers, and ravaging merchant ships in the Bay of Bengal; a total of 112,300 tons of shipping was sunk in five days.[10] A recently formed British Eastern Fleet with two carriers and five veteran battleships from the first war wisely avoided engagement and finally retired to East Africa.

The historian of the British war at sea, Captain Stephen Roskill, wrote of this period: 'If ever students, in the years to come, seek an example of the consequences of loss of maritime control over waters adjacent to countries in which world powers held great interests, they will surely need to look no further than the events in the Pacific and Indian Ocean during the early months of 1942.'[11]

Like the German advance into Russia, the Japanese rampage through East Asia was distinguished by atrocity. Both armed services used humiliation and cruelty as deliberate training tools and means of so charging the men with suppressed anger that they would unleash it in action against the enemy; and they treated those who fell into their hands as they themselves had been used. Ethnic Chinese continued to be particular victims. Thousands of Chinese made prisoner at the fall of Singapore were tortured and executed by the secret police or used by the army as living targets for bayonet or sword practice.[12] Women were routinely abused. The assumption of male dominance that marked Japanese society found expression in the enslavement by the end of the conflict of some 250,000 Korean, Chinese, Filipina, Indonesian and even Dutch girls and women in brothels to 'service' troops, administrators and businessmen in the conquered territories.[13] One Dutch woman who survived work in a brothel serving the occupying elite of Samarang, Java, has described dreading Sundays when lower-rank soldiers were admitted.[14] Allied prisoners of war and Asian civilians were used as slave labourers in mines, construction works and industry, and succumbed in thousands to malnutrition, disease, savage punishments and unremitting toil. A Japanese scholar who lived through the period has described the greater Japanese empire as 'a Kafkaesque state dedicated to the abuse of human rights'.[15]

More horrifying even than the merciless exploitation of prisoners of war and 'comfort women' were the activities of the secret medical Unit 731 and associated groups known collectively for camouflage as Epidemic Prevention and Water Purification units. Established by General Shiri Ishii as early as 1932 in Manchuria, Unit 731's primary function was research into ways of transmitting deadly diseases to the enemy. Unsuspecting Chinese, Korean or Manchurian civilians were infected with bubonic plague, anthrax, typhus, cholera or other diseases, and afterwards, while still alive, their organs were removed for study without anaesthetic. The unit also tested the efficacy of grenades and flame throwers on human victims staked out at various distances, and studied the effects on other 'test subjects' of freezing, limb amputation and disembowelling; indeed, it is clear that sadistic voyeurism played as large a part as scientific enquiry in the unit's activities.[16]

As the Japanese began their conquests in early 1942 preparations were under way in Berlin for systematizing the drive to exterminate Jews, Bolshevik functionaries and other 'contaminants' of the Germanic race in eastern Europe. Experiments to find a more efficient method of killing, less stressful to those taking part than mass shootings, had already been tried in Poland. The choice had fallen on a prussic acid gas called Zyklon B, used commercially for eliminating vermin; and after the infamous Berlin-Wannsee conference at which all ministries and departments concerned with the occupied territories in the east or the 'Jewish problem' were briefed on their role in the extermination programme,[17] the first planned death camp with a fixed gas chamber was constructed at Belzec, south of Lublin in Poland. It began operations in mid-March. Other specialized extermination camps followed through the early summer, including Sobibor, Treblinka and Auschwitz-Birkenau, which was to become a byword for industrial murder.

Himmler, who presided over this 'final solution' to the Jewish problem on behalf of Hitler, also patronized doctors and scientists prepared, like those employed by Unit 731 of the Imperial Japanese Army, to conduct experiments on human victims. Dr Josef Mengele is perhaps best known, but long before his genetic studies at Auschwitz, Himmler was supplying women from his concentration camp at Ravensbrück as subjects for sterilization experiments devised by a Professor Carl Clauberg using a caustic solution to block their fallopian tubes. Male concentration camp inmates were used to study the possibilities of mass sterilization by X-rays of the testes. At Dachau concentration camp Himmler had an air-tight chamber constructed for high altitude research on behalf of the Luftwaffe. In simulated descents without oxygen, test subjects suffered intense pain, convulsions, temporary blindness and paralysis. Dr Sigmund Rascher, who conducted these experiments, also subjected prisoners to prolonged immersion in freezing water to test methods of resuscitation, again on behalf of the Luftwaffe, concerned about aircrew shot down over the sea.[18]

The humiliation and enslavement of beaten enemies, torture, rape and mass killing are as old as human history, but never before 1942 had they been practised on this monstrous scale. It was as if the German and Japanese peoples, claiming racial superiority in their spheres as reprisal for the lack of respect shown them by the Western colonial powers, projected their savage sense of rejection on to all outside the ethnic circle.

The foundation stone of the Allied partnership that would run the Second World War was laid on 31 December 1941 during a conference in Washington between Roosevelt, Churchill and their advisers. Roosevelt agreed to a British proposal for unifying strategic command by linking both nations' military leaders in a Combined Chiefs of Staff (CCS) organization.

By the end of the conference in January 1942 it had been agreed that CCS headquarters would be in Washington with the British chiefs represented by a permanent Joint Staff Mission. The existing 'Germany first' strategy was reaffirmed and the world divided into operational theatres, India and the Middle East falling naturally to the British, the Pacific and south Atlantic to the Americans. Subsequently the American chiefs of staff split the Pacific into four operational areas, the South-West under General Douglas MacArthur, who established his headquarters in Australia as the Japanese overran his command in the Philippines, and the North, Central and Southern areas, together constituting the Pacific Ocean Area under Admiral Nimitz at Pearl Harbor. Nimitz answered to the Commander-in-Chief, US Fleet (COMINCH), Admiral Ernest King, in Washington.

Both Nimitz and King were examples of the openness of American society. Both came from immigrant stock, German in Nimitz's case, while King had a Scottish father and an English mother; both had seized the opportunity provided by the US Naval Academy for those who passed the competitive entrance examination to benefit from higher education at state expense. Nimitz had specialized in the new submarine arm; King familiarized himself with both new arms, submarine and aviation, entering the Submarine School course as a captain aged forty-one, although not taking the final exams; and learning to fly and obtaining his wings on the approach of his fiftieth birthday. Intensely ambitious, he aimed to fit himself for the higher posts in the service.

In character the two men were very different. Nimitz was calm and courteous. On taking over at Pearl Harbor he made a point of retaining Kimmel's staff officers and assuring them of his confidence in their abilities, so steadying morale. King, by contrast, was a driven character. Throughout a career marked in earlier days by wild drinking and womanizing, he had spared neither himself nor his subordinates, nor on occasions the feelings of his superiors, in pursuit of perfection. Described by the US naval historian Samuel Eliot Morison as 'tall and spare and taut with piercing brown eyes, a powerful Roman nose and deeply cleft chin',[19] he inspired awe and fear rather than affection. Although in theory committed to the overall 'Germany first' strategy, he was emotionally committed to the Pacific theatre and his allocation of resources frequently infuriated the British. To Colonel Sir Ian Jacob, the percipient secretary of the British chiefs of staff, he appeared 'to wear a protective covering of horn',[20] although he perceived inner depths to his character. Roosevelt had utter confidence in King, and in March 1942 agreed to him becoming Chief of Naval Operations as well as COMINCH, and gave him authority over the offices

of the Navy Department as well, making him the most powerful naval officer in history with complete control of every aspect of his service.

King's Pacific strategy was offensive from the start. While holding the
line of communications from Hawaii to Australia by building up operating
and refuelling bases at Samoa, Fiji, New Caledonia, Tonga and other island
groups in the south Pacific, his aim, once these were 'reasonably secure',
was to 'drive north-west from the New Hebrides into the Solomons',
drawing Japanese forces there and 'thus relieving pressure elsewhere'.[21] In
the meantime, he urged Nimitz to strike the enemy wherever he could. In
practice this meant using single-carrier task forces for hit-and-run raids on
Japanese island bases. It breached the principle of concentration of force
which had served the Japanese well in all their carrier operations, and had
no discernible effect on the Japanese drive south-eastwards towards the
island groups King needed to secure communications with Australia. Yet,
exploited for propaganda, the strikes boosted morale in the fleet and at
home, which was undoubtedly King's primary objective.[22]

The military weakness of the strategy was exposed at the time of its most
spectacular propaganda triumph: on 18 April a flight of sixteen US Army
Air Force long-range B-25 bombers under Lieutenant Colonel James
Doolittle took off from the carrier *Hornet* in the north Pacific and flew over
six hundred miles to Tokyo, Yokohama and other Japanese cities, achieving complete surprise as they dropped their bombs. Flying on afterwards,
they landed or in many cases crash-landed in China or Chinese waters as
their fuel ran out. It was a heroic venture, and the psychological impact was
immense on both sides of the Pacific. Yet the operation had taken the
Hornet and an accompanying carrier, *Enterprise*, thousands of miles from the
south Pacific islands whose protection was King's top priority, and just
at a time when signals intelligence was pointing to a Japanese thrust into
this area.

US cryptographers had broken the Japanese diplomatic machine code in
September 1940, but Japanese naval codes remained inviolable until early
1942 when the first incursions were made at the Code and Signals Section
at the US base at Corregidor, Manila Bay. After the evacuation of the
Philippines the attack on naval codes had continued in Washington and at
Pearl Harbor, where Lieutenant Commander Joseph Rochefort and a team
of cryptographers worked around the clock on the stream of intercepted
Japanese signals, seldom leaving their basement offices below the navy's
waterfront headquarters. The target was not a machine cipher, but a code
of five-digit groups encrypted by subtracting other five-digit groups on
a list in the possession of both sender and recipient. By early April

Rochefort's team was reading a significant proportion of the groups, and although the Japanese geographical grid had not been broken, a combination of cryptanalysis, radio direction finding and traffic analysis – deducing the identity of call signs and monitoring the patterns of activity – was producing a remarkably accurate picture of Japanese movements and intentions. At the time of the Doolittle raid these pointed to an amphibious assault on Port Moresby on the southern coast of the Australian portion of New Guinea, barely over seventy miles across the Torres Strait from the northernmost cape of Australia itself.

Nimitz had one carrier, *Yorktown*, in the south Pacific. Of his four others, one was under repair after torpedo damage from a Japanese submarine earlier in the year. He directed the other three to join the *Yorktown*. The *Lexington* reached her in the Coral Sea south of the Solomon Islands on 1 May as the Japanese forces approached, but the two carriers involved in the Doolittle raid were still on passage back to Pearl Harbor and could not join for another fortnight. Such was the cost of King's dispersion of force. Nimitz had acceded only reluctantly to the plan.

The Japanese High Command had more serious differences of opinion. The Naval General Staff, supposedly the strategic planning authority, aimed at extending Japanese conquests eastwards to Fiji and Samoa across the US lines of communication with Australia and had reached agreement with the Army General Staff for the necessary troops – which was not easy since the army and navy staffs had very different strategic goals. Yet Yamamoto, as Commander-in-Chief of the Combined Fleet, would not accept the plan. He insisted, as he had in the months before the war, that the enemy fleet had to be the target. His first thoughts had been for a second strike on Pearl Harbor, but it was evident the Hawaiian base was now too heavily patrolled and defended and could not be surprised again. He settled on an invasion of the US Midway Island base as a means of luring out the US fleet, including carriers, for the 'decisive battle' to settle the outcome of the war. His concern was that operations in the south Pacific would allow time for American industry to gear up and overwhelm Japan. Her naval power had to be smashed and her will broken before this could happen.

Yamamoto's prestige as author of the triumph at Pearl Harbor and his reputation with the Japanese people, who associated him with the naval successes that had marked the war, gave him formidable authority, especially as it appeared he was ready to resign over this issue. In early April the Naval General Staff gave way and approved his project. Shortly afterwards the shock of Doolittle's raid on the capital reinforced the decision and converted the Army General Staff to the strategy. Yamamoto's victory was not as complete as he would have wished, however. In their recent study of these operations from the Japanese perspective, Jonathan Parshall and Anthony Tully have demonstrated that Yamamoto was forced to include in his plans for Midway a General Staff requirement to seize strategic points in the western Aleutians in order to expand Japan's defensive perimeter into the northern Pacific;[23] second, to agree to support a limited operation beforehand to take Port Moresby in southern New Guinea, together with the small island of Tulagi in the Solomon group for use as a seaplane base; this was the operation US Intelligence had discerned. Yamamoto agreed to assign the two newest of his six fleet carriers for the project.

Thus, instead of a single operation, Yamamoto found himself saddled with three more or less simultaneous projects, invasion of the western Aleutians – Operation AL – the seizure of Midway Island – Operation MI – and when the Americans came out to defend Midway the 'decisive fleet battle'. And first he had to part with two of his six heavy carriers to support the invasions of Port Moresby and Tulagi – Operation MO. This was to have a major impact on his Midway plan. For the US carriers *Yorktown* and *Lexington*, which Nimitz had directed to the Coral Sea on the strength of his cryptanalysts' assessment, ambushed the Japanese forces, sank one light carrier, wrecked the flight deck of one of Yamamoto's heavy carriers, *Shokaku*, and decimated the aircrews of the other, *Zuikaku*. In the course of these actions over 7/8 May, the first carrier battle in history, during which the opposing ships never saw each other, the Americans lost the *Lexington*, yet they halted the invasion of Port Moresby and accounted for ninety-two Japanese aircraft, against sixty-six US planes. This was to prove crucial for in the Japanese service air groups were integral to their carrier and losses were not simply made good with other trained crews, as they were in the US service; the whole group had to be reconstituted and retrained.[24] Since Operation MI was scheduled for early June there was no time for this.

Parshall and Tully argue that Yamamoto had sufficient operational aircraft and trained crews to have slotted them in to what was left of *Zuikaku*'s group, and would have done so if he had considered it necessary.[25] Evidently he felt no urgency. It was believed that both US carriers had been eliminated in the recent battle; consequently the Americans had only two, or at most three, carriers in the Pacific, and Yamamoto could assume that his four carriers with their experienced air groups would be more than a match for these. Yet there was no confirmation of the US carrier losses in the Coral Sea, and Midway itself was an airbase that should have been brought into the reckoning.

23

Midway, 1942

———•———

YAMAMOTO'S RELAXED VIEW of the force required to defeat the Americans in the decisive fleet battle stemmed from underestimating them. The series of easy Japanese victories had induced overconfidence; the opinion in the Japanese service, which he evidently shared, was that the Americans lacked the fighting spirit of the Japanese, had inferior weapons and had been so beaten their morale was shaken. The view survived the battle of the Coral Sea since it was believed both American carriers had been sunk. The question of how they had been in position to interdict the Port Moresby forces did not raise suspicions that Japanese operational codes might have been penetrated. Yamamoto did not consider the possibility. Confident that he would be able to surprise the Americans at Midway – although long-range Catalina aircraft were known to be patrolling from the island base – his plan allowed three days from initial air strikes on the base defences before the US fleet could reach the area from Pearl Harbor.

The assumption that he could achieve surprise was matched by other misconceptions: that the Americans would bring out their surviving battleships with the carriers, and the corollary that if confronted with the full might of the Japanese Combined Fleet battle group headed by his flagship, *Yamato*, the largest battleship in the world with a main armament of 18-inch guns, the American fleet would not accept battle. Despite promoting fleet air power during his professional career, despite the sinking of the *Prince of Wales* and *Repulse*, Yamamoto still believed in the battle fleet. Therefore in planning the Midway operation as a lure to bring out the American fleet, he aimed to keep his main battle group well out of reconnaissance range to the west. The fleet carriers under Nagumo would launch air strikes to reduce the base, then move some five hundred miles north–north-easterly, leaving the Invasion Force Main Body as the target for the American fleet steaming up from Hawaii. When they appeared Nagumo would move southwards to close the trap; and Yamamoto, some three hundred miles west of Nagumo, would move south-eastwards to complete the destruction. Thus, in his care to entice the Americans out without frightening them off, and while simultaneously carrying out Operation AL against the Aleutians to the north, Yamamoto and his Combined Fleet planners dispersed their separate forces too widely for mutual support. As an operational design employing the greater part of the Japanese navy, no less than eleven battleships, four fleet carriers, four light carriers, over thirty cruisers and sixty destroyers, together with twenty-one submarines,[1] the plan was absurdly over-elaborate and depended for success on the Americans doing exactly what was expected of them.

Instead Nimitz set a trap for the Japanese. He was able to do so because Rochefort's code-breakers, who suspected the coming operation was directed at Midway, confirmed it with a brilliant ruse: transmitting a bogus report in clear that the desalination plant at Midway had broken down, they provoked a Japanese order, which they intercepted and decoded the next day, for a water ship to be added to Operation MI invasion forces. That clinched it.

Nimitz packed Midway with as many aircraft as the tiny atoll could accommodate, and reinforced the garrison with Marines who beavered night and day to extend and strengthen the defences against landings. When the *Yorktown* arrived back in Pearl Harbor from the Coral Sea on 27 May needing an extensive refit, Nimitz had 1,400 workmen swarm aboard to make emergency repairs sufficient to get her to sea again in the shortest possible time. She and the two Doolittle raid carriers, *Enterprise* and *Hornet*, were his first and last line of defence against the coming Japanese assault. Of only two other operational carriers in the US service, one was completing repairs on the west coast, the other was in the Mediterranean ferrying aircraft for the defence of Malta.

Nimitz dispatched the *Enterprise* and *Hornet*, designated Task Force 16 under the command of Rear Admiral Raymond Spruance, on 28 May. The repair gangs, working around the clock on the *Yorktown*, had her ready for operations on the 30th, and he sent her out as Task Force 17 under Vice-Admiral Frank Fletcher to join Spruance at a position wishfully named 'Point Luck' some three hundred miles north-east of Midway. From there they could ambush Nagumo's carriers as they approached the island from the north-west. Fletcher, who had directed the US task force at the Coral Sea, was in overall command. Both he and Spruance had verbal instructions from Nimitz to hold Midway, but to yield the island rather than risk losing the carriers; their written orders were to the same effect: '. . . you will be governed by the principles of calculated risk, which you shall interpret to mean avoidance of exposure of your forces to attack by superior enemy forces without good prospect of inflicting, as a result of such exposure, greater damage to the enemy'.[2]

It was a fine line indeed. If numbers of aircraft had been the sole consideration the Americans would have had the edge over Nagumo. Altogether the three US carriers mustered 231 aircraft against 223 on Nagumo's four carriers, although another two dozen were carried aboard the Japanese carriers for use from the Midway base after its capture.[3] The Americans also had ninety-five aircraft based on Midway and thirty-nine Catalina patrol seaplanes, which could be used to launch torpedo attacks. American aircraft were generally outclassed by their Japanese counterparts in offensive capability, however, and their pilots were less experienced. Most of the fighter aircraft on Midway were obsolete Brewster Buffaloes lacking the speed, manoeuvrability and firepower of the outstanding Japanese Type O carrier fighter, the 'Zero'; and many of the bombers were also too slow or otherwise unsuitable for attacking warships; while the American torpedoes, whether launched from Midway- or carrier-based planes, were unreliable and too slow to endanger fast ships. Against this, the American carriers had radar to alert them to attack, and in this operation, again, the precious advantage of surprise.

Yamamoto had hoped to establish the position of the American fleet prior to the Midway attack by aerial reconnaissance of Pearl Harbor. Lacking aircraft with the necessary range, he had planned to establish a temporary flying boat refuelling base at an islet called French Frigate Shoal between Midway and Pearl Harbor. This 'Operation K' had been penetrated by Rochefort's code-breakers, however, and Nimitz had pre-empted him. When the Japanese submarines converted to aviation fuel tankers arrived off the islet on 26 May they found a US seaplane tender and destroyer escort in occupation and had to abort. No reconnaissance was flown. Yamamoto also dispatched eleven submarines to form a patrol line to the north of French Frigate Shoal across the route he expected the US fleet to take on its course towards Midway. These did not struggle into place until 3 June, by which time both of Nimitz's carrier task forces had passed west of them to make their rendezvous at Point Luck. Consequently Yamamoto did not know where the American carriers were.

Nimitz had all Pearl Harbor submarines not out on distant patrol deployed for the coming battle, eleven disposed in an arc extending from west to north of Midway from 50 to 200 miles out, three 420 miles to the east of the island in case the carriers were forced to retire, and four north of Pearl Harbor to guard against a feint in that direction. The disposition of the main group has been criticized as too close to Midway, inside the distance at which Nagumo's carriers would launch their strikes, hence unable to report or attack the main enemy target.[4]

Fletcher, in the patched-up *Yorktown*, joined Spruance at Point Luck on 2 June. Nagumo with his carrier task force, or *kido butai*, was ploughing eastwards towards him in thick weather, preserving radio silence. His four carriers, *Akagi* (flag), *Kaga, Soryu* and *Hiryu*, were supported by two battleships and two new heavy cruisers and screened by eleven destroyers. Over 500 miles to his south the different elements of the Midway invasion forces were heading directly towards their target and 300 miles to his west Yamamoto was following with the battleships of the Main Body. To the north the separate components of the Aleutians operation steered towards Dutch Harbor, Kiska and Adak. Simply to list these forces spreading out across the Pacific suggests the overweening confidence of the Imperial Japanese Navy at this juncture six months into the war.

Two invasion groups were sighted by patrolling Catalinas from Midway early in the morning of 3 June 700 miles west of the island; high-level bombers were sent out from the base, but failed to score any hits. The report of their attack was received by both Yamamoto and Nagumo, the latter now on a south-easterly course towards his launch position for the Midway strike. For Fletcher, the sighting report confirmed his concept of the Japanese plan, and that evening he set a south-westerly course to position himself close to the track he supposed their carriers would take. So the opposing forces converged through the night. The outcome would depend on which side could locate and strike the enemy first; and here Fletcher had the advantage since he knew the sector in which he expected to find the Japanese. Nagumo did not expect American carriers anywhere.

The searches flown by each side early the following morning, 4 June, reflected the difference. Nagumo was not an aviation specialist; he had been appointed by virtue of seniority. For the technicalities of carrier operations he relied on his Air Staff Officer, Commander Minoru Genda, who had served him in this position throughout the war. He could have had no better counsel. Genda was the outstanding aviation professional in the Japanese service and largely responsible for the creation of the combined carrier force for mass air operations. It was he who had worked up Yamamoto's original outline for an attack on Pearl Harbor into an operational plan. And after that strike he had immediately appreciated the significance of the missing American carriers and urged Nagumo to remain in the area until he had found and destroyed them. This was not provided for in the orders and Nagumo had rejected his advice. Now, in the early hours of 4 June, as Nagumo's carrier aircraft were armed for the strike on Midway, Genda directed a search pattern which he was later to admit was 'slipshod',[5] seven planes fanning out like the spokes of a wheel from north-north-east through

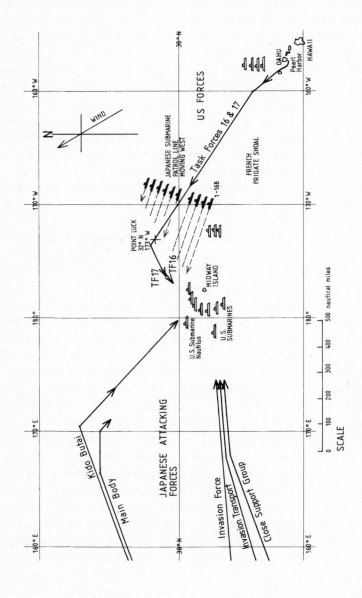

Midway: The Position at 4.30 a.m. 4 June 1942

east to south for 300 miles, altering 90 degrees to port for a 60-mile leg, then returning. Seven planes were insufficient to cover the area, particularly as clouds limited visibility; but neither Genda nor Nagumo expected to find American heavy forces; they were simply going through the routine.

Fletcher's staff also miscalculated, sending search planes out 100 miles westward when Nagumo was over 200 miles distant. It was left to Catalinas from Midway to report the Japanese. The first sighting came in at 5.34, but without details of the enemy position, course or composition; the pilot was dodging in and out of cloud to escape Zeros. Ten minutes later a second Catalina reported 'Many planes heading Midway bearing 320 distance 150'.[6] It was intensely frustrating for Fletcher: Nagumo was evidently unaware of his presence since he had committed his strike force against the base, but where was he? He had to contain himself until 6.03 when the second Catalina reported 'Two carriers and battleships bearing 320 distance 180 course 135 speed 25'.[7] The four Japanese carriers were disposed in a box formation with some four miles between each, but only one side of the box had been seen. Fletcher had to make a critical decision: whether to launch his whole strike force against the two carriers reported or with-hold aircraft for use against the other two carriers believed to be with Nagumo but, it now seemed, separated from him. He took little time. At 6.07 he ordered Spruance with Task Force 16, *Enterprise* and *Hornet*, to 'Proceed southwesterly and attack enemy carriers as soon as definitely located'.[8] Meanwhile he headed into the easterly wind to recover return-ing patrol planes, holding *Yorktown*'s strike aircraft ready to attack the second detachment of enemy carriers should they be reported.

Spruance's professional situation was akin to Nagumo's. He was not an aviation specialist. He had been plucked from command of the cruisers of Task Force 16 when the force commander, Vice-Admiral William Halsey, had gone down with a crippling attack of shingles on return from the Doolittle raid. Halsey had recommended Spruance with such conviction that Nimitz had appointed him to succeed to the command despite his complete lack of carrier experience. A quiet man noted for 'attention to detail, poise and power of intelligent decision',[9] Spruance was said to be the only flag officer who Admiral King recognized as smarter than himself.[10] Intellect and calculation occur in most descriptions of the man. Never were these attributes more necessary. The distance to the enemy force was such that he would not be ideally placed to launch his strike until nine o'clock, but as reports came in from Midway of the Japanese attack on the base he decided to bring the launch time forward by two hours to seven; the enemy would be barely within the 175-mile operational range of his

Wildcat fighters and Devastator torpedo bombers, and some might not make it back, but they would catch Nagumo at his most vulnerable, recovering and refuelling his returning aircraft.

Nagumo's strike planes were already heading back. They had found the American base fully prepared for their arrival with fighters aloft and no aircraft on the ground or in the lagoon. All had been dispatched on search or strike missions. The American fighters fell on the leading formation of bombers and shot four down before the Zeros covering the flight set on them, picking off the more sluggish American planes almost at will. With the way cleared, the Japanese high-level bombers came in from the east along the axis of the two larger islets forming the base. They ran into a barrage of accurate anti-aircraft fire, but lost only one more plane as they dropped their bombs. They were followed by dive-bombers, and after them the Zeros with strafing runs. Fuel storage tanks were set alight, the command post and numerous maintenance buildings and pipelines destroyed, and the runways on Eastern Island cratered, although not so badly as to be unusable. Nor were the islands' defences subdued. The strike leader reported ten minutes into his return flight that a second attack was necessary.

The message was handed to Nagumo on the bridge of *Akagi* at seven, just as, some 175 miles to the east, Spruance's two carriers began launching aircraft. Nagumo had anticipated the need for a second strike, but it posed a dilemma. Before sailing, Yamamoto had told the Air Staff that during the attack on Midway a reserve force should be held back in an anti-shipping role. The larger part of this reserve, forty-three planes, fuelled and armed with torpedoes, stood in the hangar decks of his two 1st Division carriers, *Akagi* and *Kaga*; the remainder in his 2nd Division carriers, *Hiryu* and *Soryu*, altogether thirty-seven dive-bombers, fuelled but unarmed. They would receive their bombs after being brought up to the flight deck; this had not been done since it would have impeded the constant launch and recovery of fighters for the Combat Air Patrol – CAP – covering the group. In present circumstances, with no report of enemy surface forces, it seemed hardly sensible to retain the anti-shipping reserve while recovering, refuelling, rearming and no doubt repairing the returning Midway strike planes for the second attack on the island base. It would be a better use of time and resources to arm, or in the case of the torpedo aircraft rearm, the reserve force with bombs for land targets and send them off for the second strike. Yet this was contrary to Yamamoto's instructions.

Nagumo was considering the problem when aircraft from Midway were sighted, altogether ten torpedo bombers approaching in two groups from the south-east. They had no fighter cover and the CAP Zeros, rounding to intercept, fell on their tails long before they came within torpedo range of the leading carriers. The result could not be in doubt. Resolutely though the American pilots held on towards the Japanese formation and their rear gunners fired back, shooting down two Zeros, the bombers were holed repeatedly and one after another plunged into the sea. A few dropped torpedoes outside effective range; only three survived to make it back to base.

The attack was scarcely over, the racket of anti-aircraft fire and whining engines stilled, before Nagumo came to a decision to disregard Yamamoto's instructions to hold back the reserve. Perhaps inspired by the evidence of Midway's offensive capacity, however inexpertly wielded, he issued orders for the reserve force to be armed with bombs and stand by to attack.[11]

Rearming the torpedo planes was neither simple nor quick. Each 17-foot-long weapon had to be detached from its brackets under the fuselage and winched down on to a cart which was then pushed manually and guided through the other parked planes on the hangar deck to the lift from the magazine. Since bombs for land attack were coming up on the lift, the torpedo had to be hauled up by block and tackle for temporary storage on nearby bulkhead brackets designed for the purpose. The cart could then be loaded with a bomb and pushed back to the plane, whose armourers would be replacing the torpedo holding brackets with bomb brackets. There were fewer ordnance carts than aircraft in a ratio of about one to three, hence to rearm all torpedo aircraft took three times longer than the procedure described; Parshall and Tully have estimated one and a half hours as necessary to complete the process in the two 1st Division carriers.[12] Afterwards each plane would be manhandled to the elevator to the flight deck, and up on deck manhandled to its position – termed 'spotting' – after which it would need to stand while the engines were warmed up – altogether another forty-five minutes at least. Nagumo had given his order to rearm at 7.15. He could not expect to launch before about 9.30 at the earliest. The dive-bombers of the 2nd Division carriers could fly off earlier, but alone would not have constituted the balanced force required by Japanese doctrine.

In any case, the process was soon interrupted. First, one of the search aircraft sent out that morning sighted a group of ten US warships, and at 7.28 reported their position, course and speed, but not their type. It was Spruance's Task Force 16. Nagumo had the message by about 7.40 and after rapid consultation with Genda and his staff gave instructions to cease rearming, and ordered the search plane to retain contact[13] and 'Ascertain ship types'.[14]

He now had to decide whether to prepare a strike against this American group by having the anti-shipping reserve brought up from the hangar decks before the return of the Midway strike force, due back in about half an hour, or to wait and recover those planes first, then send up the reserve strike. The second option would cost him time – almost two hours against some forty-five minutes for an immediate strike – but the first option would cost him strength, as about a third of the torpedo planes had been rearmed with bombs and could not be re-equipped in time.

The nub of the matter was whether the American group contained a carrier. His deliberations were interrupted by the arrival of a second wave of sixteen dive-bombers from Midway. The pilots lacked experience, so their commander, Major Lofton Henderson, led them down in a shallow 'glide-bombing' descent, heading for the leading carrier on the port side of the box formation, *Hiryu*. Again the Americans had no fighter escort and the CAP Zeros were soon on their tails. Henderson's plane and five others were brought down long before they reached their target. The remainder pressed on through bursting anti-aircraft shells from the ships before dropping their bombs so close to the *Hiryu* she was temporarily hidden behind towering water columns; but they failed to hit her. Eight of the original sixteen made it back to Midway, six so badly holed they were written off.[15]

Even before Henderson's planes launched their attack Japanese lookouts spotted a third wave of aircraft from Midway. These were B-17 'Flying Fortresses' at 20,000 feet. They divided into three groups, each targeting a carrier, but the time the bombs took to fall from such an altitude allowed the carrier captains to swing their ships clear, and again no hits were made. Nagumo's returning Midway strike planes appeared during this attack, but held their distance as the carriers manoeuvred under extreme helm.

At 8.20, as the B-17s turned for home, Nagumo received a report from his search plane watching the American surface force that the enemy was accompanied by 'what appears to be a carrier'.[16] He scarcely had time to digest the unwelcome news before another wave of dive-bombers from Midway approached, again unescorted by fighters, and a submarine periscope was sighted close outside his now irregular formation. Both threats were beaten off, but the constant attacks had closed the option of launching the reserve strike against the American ships: his Midway planes had been waiting to land for almost an hour. Several were damaged and all would soon run out of fuel. At 8.27 he had the signal indicating decks clear for landing broken out from *Akagi*'s halyards.[17]

Spruance's strike forces from *Enterprise* and *Hornet* had now been in the air for some time. Fletcher, who had been waiting vainly for news of a second Japanese carrier group, was on the point of launching *Yorktown*'s strike at the same target. The American operations, however, bore no comparison to the smooth coordination of the air groups from different carriers routinely achieved by the *kido butai*. It was understandable: Japan had been at war with China since the early 1930s and preparing for the conquest of the Pacific island groups for almost as long. All American aviators had known until six months before had been peacetime exercises.

Spruance had decided to strike Nagumo with all his force. Neither of his carriers, however, had space on the flight deck to launch its whole air group in one operation and they had to 'spot' and fly off a part of the total before bringing up the remainder from the hangar deck and sending them off. In Spruance's flagship, *Enterprise*, thirty-three Dauntless dive-bombers were sent up first to circle and await the second contingent of fourteen Devastator torpedo bombers and ten Wildcat fighters, which had shorter endurance. The operation dragged out; Spruance felt time pressing. He was aware of the Japanese search plane keeping his group under observation, keenly conscious of the need to catch Nagumo while recovering his Midway strike planes, and at 7.52, before the second-stage aircraft had left the deck, he sent the dive-bombers off on their own. They headed off south-west, led by the carrier's air group chief, Lieutenant Commander Clarence Wade McClusky.

The *Hornet* completed launching her strike force shortly afterwards, thirty-five Dauntless dive-bombers, fifteen Devastator torpedo bombers and ten Wildcat fighters, and these departed on a more westerly course at 7.55. Ten minutes later the *Enterprise*'s second wave, including fighter escort, was airborne and flying off on yet another course. The fragmentation was increased twenty minutes later when the leader of the *Hornet*'s torpedo bombers, Lieutenant Commander John Waldron, who had not agreed with the course set by his air group commander, took it upon himself to break away to port and steer his squadron in a more southerly direction. There were now four waves of aircraft from Spruance's two carriers heading on separate tracks for different positions at which their flight leaders estimated they would find the Japanese. Finally, at 8.38, as their target, Nagumo, flew the signal for his waiting planes to land, Fletcher began *Yorktown*'s launch operation. Holding back a squadron of dive-bombers in case a second Japanese carrier group should be reported, he sent up seventeen Dauntless dive-bombers, followed in a second wave by twelve Devastator torpedo bombers and six Wildcat fighters. There were now five American groups comprising 126 strike aircraft and 26 fighters heading in various directions from westerly to south-westerly to intercept the enemy.[18]

By this time the Japanese Midway strike aircraft had landed on their carriers and Nagumo had altered north-easterly to close the American group.

His search plane had reported *Yorktown*'s first wave of torpedo bombers heading towards him. He was not alarmed. He believed the American force to consist of one carrier, five cruisers and five destroyers, and had reported this to Yamamoto at 8.55, adding that he was heading towards them – the implication being that he would destroy them. His reserve strike aircraft were still below in the hangars, however, and could not be sent up until the Midway strike planes had been cleared from the elevators and the flight decks had been freed from operations to maintain the CAP with fresh fighters.

The first wave of American carrier aircraft was sighted at 9.18 in the north-east. They were the torpedo bombers from the *Hornet*. Their leader, John Waldron, who had broken away from his air group, had somehow steered a direct course for Nagumo, but as a result, like the earlier torpedo plane strikes from Midway, he was without fighter cover. The results were similarly shocking. Beset by Zeros, the lumbering Devastators were riven and sent blazing into the sea. Only one survived to launch a torpedo at the northernmost carrier, *Soryu*, which evaded easily. The lone aircraft was brought down before it could clear the formation, although the pilot, Ensign George Gay, managed to scramble from his cockpit as the plane sank beneath him. He was the sole survivor of Waldron's gallant band.

The Japanese ships had turned to run from the attack and were still heading west when another flight was seen coming in from the south. This was the torpedo squadron from the *Enterprise*, which had started off with its ten-Wildcat escort almost a quarter of an hour after Spruance had sent the dive-bombers off under McClusky. The fighters had since become separated. Flying high to gain advantage over the CAP Zeros, they had lost sight of their charges and latched on to Waldron's flight instead before losing him, too, prior to his heroic sortie.

The new arrivals were led by Lieutenant Commander Eugene Lindsey, who directed his attack at the southernmost carrier, *Kaga*, arranging his planes in two divisions to take her between them in a pincer. The Japanese ships turned away northwards. Straining to overtake, Lindsey called on his radio for the fighters to come down in support, but his calls were not heard, and as the Zeros homed in from their engagement on the farther perimeter, joined presently by fresh flights launched from both 1st Division carriers, the earlier scenes of destruction were repeated. Seven planes did come through the hail of fire, chiefly perhaps because those Zeros that had repulsed Waldron were low on ammunition, but their torpedoes launched at long range were all evaded. Only four planes made it back to the *Enterprise*; Lindsey's was not among them.

The firing had scarcely died away when two other American flights approached from opposite directions: the *Yorktown's* complete air strike of dive- and torpedo bombers escorted by six Wildcat fighters from the east, the *Enterprise's* unescorted dive-bombers under Wade McClusky from the south-west.

McClusky had been in the air for the best part of three hours. During this time Nagumo's alterations to close the American task force, fly on aircraft and evade attacks had left him considerably north of the intercept position McClusky had worked out. On reaching this position at about 9.30 and finding the ocean empty, McClusky had turned north-west along the reciprocal of the original Japanese course towards Midway, and shortly before ten sighted what he took to be a lone enemy cruiser moving fast in a north-north-easterly direction. Assuming she might be joining Nagumo, he turned to follow. He was correct. She was one of the *kido butai's* screen destroyers and had been hunting the American submarine that had appeared earlier. Judging she had held the boat down sufficiently far from the force, she was hastening to rejoin; and by one of those fateful turns of history, she led McClusky straight to his target. At 10.02 he reported to Spruance, 'Have sighted the enemy.'[19]

Spruance's strike force could scarcely have arrived in a less coordinated pattern over the past forty-five minutes. The torpedo aircrew from both carriers had paid a terrible price for going in piecemeal without fighter cover; the *Hornet's* dive-bombers and escorting Wildcats had failed to find the target and were on their way back; the *Enterprise's* Wildcats had been too high to see either of the torpedo bomber attacks; and the radio system that should have brought them in had failed. Individualism could not have been carried farther, nor individual resolution in face of the fearsome Zeros and cordons of exploding shells put up by Nagumo's force. Any objective analysis must conclude that it was magnificent but it was not war, not at any rate professional war. Yet those heroic American airmen had not given their lives in vain. They had in a magnificently haphazard way and quite fortuitously set up the perfect situation for the final killer blow. The constant series of raids had prevented Nagumo from getting his reserve strike force up to attack the American task forces, and although none of his ships had suffered so much as a strained plate, several Zeros had been destroyed and many of the pilots were weary and running low on fuel or ammunition when the final attack waves homed in practically simultaneously a few minutes after ten o'clock.

The *Yorktown's* torpedo bombers were sighted from Nagumo's flagship some thirty miles off at 10.06 coming in from the east-south-east. Other

Japanese lookouts and the pilots of the Combat Air Patrol were soon absorbed by this latest threat, to the exclusion, it seems, of the seventeen *Yorktown* dive-bombers way above. These were flying at 10,000 feet over scattered cloud, which may partly have accounted for the lapse. They were led by Lieutenant Commander Maxwell Leslie, who eased to starboard to head around the enemy formation, now running north-westerly from the lower-level torpedo threat; his intention was to come in from a northerly direction as the slower torpedo bombers launched their attack from the east.

The *Yorktown*'s six Wildcat fighters led by Lieutenant Commander John 'Jimmy' Thach were far below, flying on two levels just behind the torpedo planes. The Zeros concentrated on them first. Failing to notice the dive-bombers high above, at least half the thirty-five-strong CAP swarmed around Thach, as he wrote later, 'coming in on us like a stream from astern'.[20] His few planes were overwhelmed by the numbers lining up to attack. He had devised a weaving, scissor-like defensive tactic which he and his wingmen now applied for the first time with such success that they accounted for six Zeros and lost only one Wildcat – a spectacular reversal of results in former contests – but engulfed in continuous life-and-death engagements he was unable to protect the torpedo planes when a second cohort of Zeros, reinforced by fresh planes sent up by the 2nd Division carriers, set on them. 'I saw a second large group [of Zeros] streaming right past us onto the torpedo planes,' Thach wrote. 'The air was like a beehive.'[21]

The *Yorktown*'s torpedo planes were led by Lieutenant Commander Lance Massey. The attack on Thach had allowed him to fly in closer to the Japanese ships than previous American attacks, but once the second wave of Zeros tore into his sluggish formation the former scenes of destruction were repeated; Massey was one of the first to go down. The survivors, splitting into two groups to head for the nearest carrier, *Hiryu*, as she ran from them, were thinned drastically.

Yet, by holding the attention of the Japanese fighter pilots and, it seems, all lookouts and all carrier Air Officers responsible for directing the Combat Air Patrol, Massey's flight performed a crucial role: no one noticed either Leslie's or McClusky's dive-bombers high above. How this was possible is hard to understand. Thach, defending himself against the Zeros, saw 'this glint in the sun and it just looked like a beautiful silver waterfall'[22] as the bombers tilted into their dives. But by then, of course, it was too late for the Zeros on a lower level around him and the surviving torpedo planes. So far as the Japanese lookouts and Air Officers were concerned, battle fatigue was no doubt a factor. The *kido butai* had been absorbing raids for the past three hours. The air officers had been launching and recovering aircraft since before dawn.

The real fault lay with the Japanese system, or lack of system, which in turn resulted from their overweening confidence and focus on the 'decisive battle': everything was geared to offence rather than defence. The speed and manoeuvrability of the Zero fighter were in part due to light construction and lack of protective armour for the pilot; the carriers' flight decks were unarmoured, their magazines had minimal protection and their damage control systems entirely lacked the reserve capability or specialized equipment fitted in American carriers. Above all, there was no overall system for directing the CAP fighters. While air groups from every carrier were routinely coordinated into a mass strike, fighter cover over the *kido butai* was left to individual Air Control Officers whose main task was to direct their own flight deck operations. In any case, once the Zeros were aloft the Air Officers lost control as the radio system was so unreliable pilots seldom used it. In practice, therefore, it was up to the fighter pilots themselves to spot threats and react accordingly, a simple enough task in face of single raids spaced at intervals, far more complex when several raids came in simultaneously, as they did in the twenty minutes after ten o'clock. The lack of any control organization was all the more surprising since, unlike the Americans, the Japanese had no radar to warn them of approaching flights in good time.

McClusky was first to strike. He was leading two squadrons, each of which in US practice should have taken a separate target. Owing to a misunderstanding, both followed him down as he dived on the south-westernmost and nearest carrier, *Kaga*. Her 1st Division consort, Nagumo's flagship, *Akagi*, would not have received any attention if the leader of the rear squadron, Lieutenant Richard Best, had not sized up the situation rapidly and broken away towards her. His planes on either wing followed, but the remainder stayed with McClusky. Consequently, while three bombers headed for Nagumo's flagship, thirty dived on the *Kaga*. She hurled up a barrage of shell and put on extreme starboard helm, but there were no fighters up to divert the American pilots in their headlong trajectory. Their bombs raised gigantic water columns close by the carrier as she wheeled, others struck at intervals along her flight deck, passing through and detonating among the torpedo bombers of the reserve strike, fuelled, armed and ready to go, and the recovered first-strike planes, dismembering them and the plane handlers, armourers and mechanics in the hangar and crew spaces astern, and igniting high-octane fuel fires. One bomb hit the forward end of the island structure, killing the captain and senior officers on the bridge.

Some distance away officers on the bridge of the *Soryu* had turned from satisfied observation of the Zeros destroying Massey's torpedo planes heading for their nearer consort, *Hiryu*, and were watching aghast as flames and black smoke welled from the stricken carrier. They had little time to take it in. A lookout yelled, 'Enemy dive bombers !'[23] Gazing up, they saw through a gap in the clouds American planes making for them, lit by the sun. These were the *Yorktown* squadron led by Leslie. Again, complete surprise was achieved. The results were shockingly similar. Amid fountains from near-misses three bombs hit the flight deck, ploughing through and shaking the ship bodily as they exploded below with the same devastating effects on the reserve strike bombers and human flesh as in the *Kaga*'s hangar deck. On the flight deck itself Zeros were blown overboard or shattered and set ablaze, their pilots and the plane-handling teams reduced to lifeless heaps where the blast had flung them. Way below, the force of the explosions transmitted through the ship's structure severed steam pipes serving the main propulsion turbines, which stopped turning.

Before she had lost way, Best and the two pilots with him who had peeled off McClusky's dive were homing in on *Akagi*. The attention of the flagship's officers and lookouts must have been fixed on the smoking ruin of the *Kaga*, or perhaps the *Soryu*, for again surprise was complete. Two bombs shaved *Akagi*'s port side forward and under the stern, one aimed by Best himself struck plumb at mid-length on the edge of the elevator, forcing it down and detonating below among the torpedo bombers of the reserve strike and the plane-handling crews with the same fearful effects as before, igniting fires there and in the lower hangar deck.

The bombers levelled out and headed away, pursued by Zeros and anti-aircraft fire, while not far to port five torpedo bombers, the last survivors from Massey's squadron, still beset by Zeros, made their final run in to launching positions against the only carrier to have escaped the bombers, *Hiryu*. She evaded their torpedoes and as the planes turned to head for home the Zeros went with them. Only two made it back to the *Yorktown*.

Yet in the space of those few volcanic minutes between 10.22 and 10.30 the complexion of the Pacific war had undergone a sea-change. The *kido butai*, which had swept all before it, had proved mortal. The deficiencies of its fighter cover in face of multiple threats, and the vulnerability of the thin-skinned fleet carriers themselves to precision strikes by expert dive-bomber pilots, had been exposed. Three of its carriers had been eliminated, for the fuel fires raging below their decks were to prove impossible to control. Small wonder that a shocked Nagumo refused to leave the bridge to transfer his flag until reminded very directly by the ship's captain that he had a duty to direct the fleet and he could no longer do so from *Akagi*.

In *Yorktown* news of the loss of so many aircrews produced a grim mood. Then Leslie's dive-bombers began arriving in small groups or singly, many badly holed or out of fuel, flopping in the water, some with landing or arrester gear shot off, crashing on deck; but the atmosphere changed immediately. As described by one ordnanceman aboard: 'The bomber pilots could hardly contain themselves. They were shouting and laughing as they jumped out of the cockpit, and the ship which had been so sombre a moment before when the torpedo planes returned became now hysterically excited.'[24]

The contrast with conditions in the blazing Japanese carriers could not have been starker. The scenes below were horrific beyond words. Those not killed instantly by the blast in the hangar decks were stunned, burned or choking on smoke and fumes. As Parshall and Tully put it: 'The few men who survived there were undoubtedly shocked into near insensibility.'[25]

The battle had passed its climax, but it was not over. The *Hiryu* had survived. She flew the flag of the rear admiral commanding the 2nd Division carriers, and shortly before eleven he launched a dive-bomber strike on the American force reported by search planes. It was led by Lieutenant Michio Kobayashi. The *Yorktown*'s radar operator picked up Kobayashi's incoming flight 40 miles away a few minutes before noon and the air patrol fighters were vectored on to it. The Wildcats broke up the Japanese formation and escorting Zeros, shooting down or disabling so many that only seven bombers emerged from the melee to make their dives. These punched through the exploding barrage put up by the carrier and screening cruisers and destroyers and scored three hits which penetrated the flight deck, starting numerous fires below and fracturing the boiler uptakes to the funnels, causing the engines to lose power. The carrier's aviation fuel lines had been drained as a precaution before the attack, however, – which had not been the case in the Japanese carriers – and damage control teams were able to suppress the fires. They also succeeded in extemporizing repairs to the uptakes, enabling the engineers to raise steam in four boilers, sufficient for a speed of almost twenty knots.

Nagumo, meanwhile, had transferred his flag to a light cruiser and recovered his battle spirit. He was leading his heavy units east towards the Americans, intending to engage them in a gun action. He now knew they had three carriers; the information had been extracted from downed US aircrew. The *Hiryu*'s dive-bombers had crippled one carrier – so it was believed – and a second strike of torpedo bombers had been launched to take out another. Instead, the flight, led by Lieutenant Joichi Tomenaga, found the *Yorktown* again, making a good speed and showing no signs of fire – evidently not the carrier their dive-bombers had left blazing. Tomenaga went in. Only five of his planes survived the fighter and anti-air-craft cordon, but they scored two torpedo hits which caused extensive flooding and knocked out power throughout the vessel. With the pumps out of action, she took an alarming list and at three o'clock, less than half an hour after the attack, her captain, fearing she would turn right over, ordered all hands to abandon ship.

By this time search planes Fletcher had sent out earlier had located the *Hiryu* 110 miles to the west, and Spruance's two carriers were 'spotting' strike planes on their flight decks; they were dispatched before 4 p.m., twenty-five dive-bombers from *Enterprise*, led by Lieutenant Wilmer Gallaher, sixteen following from *Hornet*. They had no fighter escort; all sur-viving Wildcats were retained to chase off Japanese search planes and provide cover in case of another enemy raid.

At 4.45 Gallaher sighted Nagumo's force and altered to skirt round it to the south in order to make his attack from the west out of the sun. The tactic succeeded. Again, despite patrolling Zeros, surprise was achieved and it was not until shortly after five, when Gallaher was about to nose into his dive, that the flight was seen from the *Hiryu* in the centre of the enemy formation. It was too late, and the incoming bombers were too numerous to be denied. High water spouts erupted around the carrier as she turned at speed, then four bombs crashed through her flight deck forward, the explosions rending and incinerating the light wooden aircraft parked in the hangar below. The forward elevator was ripped up and a section blown back against the island structure with such force that all on the bridge were knocked off their feet. The carrier continued turning at speed and with the wind of her progress fanning the flames aft it was not long before she was ablaze from end to end.

Between them, Fletcher and Spruance and the US dive-bomber pilots, aided by the self-sacrificing forlorn attempts of the torpedo aircrews, had achieved what would have seemed before the battle an impossibly decisive victory. For the loss of the *Yorktown* – and this was not yet certain – Nagumo's carriers had been eliminated. All four were blazing uncontrol-lably, and through that evening and the following early morning all were sent to the bottom, as it appears from Parshall and Tully's researches, by their own hands to Nagumo's orders, *Akagi* last of all.[26] By this time Nagumo had finally admitted to himself that the battle was lost, and Yamamoto had called off the operation.

On the American side Fletcher, without a flagship, had conceded tactical command to Spruance, who retired east until midnight, then after a brief alteration north, headed west at slow speed to be in position to defend Midway should it come under attack during the day. By then the Japanese were in retreat. He followed, launching searches that failed to find any further enemy carriers or the Japanese main forces, which had now joined together under Yamamoto.

So far only one submarine had taken an active role: USS *Nautilus* under Lieutenant Commander William Brockman had closed and attacked the enemy force without success, but in so doing served as the unwitting instrument of McClusky's perfectly timed arrival over the Japanese carriers. Now a Japanese boat took a part. *I-168* under Lieutenant Commander Yahachi Tanabe was ordered to seek the crippled carrier – *Yorktown* – north-east of Midway. He made his way submerged towards her reported position throughout the 5th, surfacing after dark to recharge batteries and refresh his crew; and soon after 4 a.m. on the 6th sighted the mastheads of a group of ships over the horizon. He steered towards them until he judged he might be seen, then dived for a submerged approach.

The *Yorktown* was at the centre of the group. She had remained afloat and damage control teams had reboarded; a destroyer had been made fast alongside to provide power for her pumps and she was under way towards Pearl Harbor at 3 knots. Five other destroyers were screening her. Tanabe resolved to move inside them to be certain of hitting. It was an agonizingly drawn-out approach. Without air conditioning, the heat built up unbearably, and tension mounted as regular pulses from the destroyers' sonar (Asdic) were magnified in the hydrophones. As the screen was closed about midday the pulses ceased, no doubt deflected by a thermal layer in the water, for despite the destroyers' slow speed the operators picked up no echo as Tanabe passed beneath; nor were his propeller noises heard. At 1.31 he raised his scope for a final observation and fired four torpedoes with a narrow spread, set to strike the carrier at mid-length. One hit the destroyer alongside, ripping her apart; two struck as intended, exploding opposite gaping holes torn by the *Hiryu*'s torpedo planes and destroying what remained of the mid-length compartments. It was the final blow. The sea rose inside the hull and shortly before four the order was given to abandon ship. She sank early the following morning.

Tanabe and his crew barely survived their triumph. The boat was rocked by depth charges and driven deep, and was fortunate to escape finally under cover of night.

24

Allied Victory, 1943–5

LIKE NAPOLEON AFTER the battle of Trafalgar, Hirohito was not pre-pared to tell his people of the disaster off Midway; instead, like Napoleon, he fed them a brazen lie. On 10 June Tokyo Radio announced a great naval victory in which two American aircraft carriers and 120 air-craft had been destroyed for the loss of one Japanese carrier and thirty-five aircraft. The true figures were closer to 100 American against 228 Japanese aircraft destroyed.[1] Casualties were even more disproportionate, 307 Americans against over three thousand Japanese killed. Nearly seven hun-dred of these had been from the engine and boiler rooms of the four carriers. Although not directly affected by bombs, these men had been unable to escape through the fires raging and blistering the decks above and had been carried down with their ships. To keep the shocking facts of the defeat secret, even from the army staff, home leave was withheld when the forces returned to base and the wounded were transferred under the strictest security to naval hospitals at Yokosuka, Kure or Sasebo, placed under carefully vetted doctors and nurses and not allowed to communicate with anyone outside, or even to write home.

It is a moot question as to whether Midway was 'decisive'. Certainly it did not decide the Pacific war as Tsushima had decided the Russo-Japanese war. It might loosely be compared with Trafalgar, which had not decided the Napoleonic War either. In both cases victory went to the numerically inferior side and much grim fighting was to follow. There any resemblances end.

The prime reason for the American victory was the brilliant work of Rochefort's team at Pearl Harbor; in most other respects the Japanese were architects of their own defeat, which was caused not so much by hubris, although this had run high throughout the fleet, as by Yamamoto's refusal to accept the authority of the Naval General Staff and the compromises he was forced to accept in return for having his own way. The Japanese Combined Fleet was so much stronger than the US Pacific Fleet at this time, its air component so much more proficient, that had either the General Staff plan for operations in the south Pacific or Yamamoto's plan for Midway and the decisive fleet battle been adopted undiluted it is difficult to see how the Americans could have won. The absence of two of the *kido butai*'s six fleet carriers from the Midway action as a result of the engagement in the Coral Sea and the diversion of resources for the Aleutians combined with the over-subtlety of his own plans to 'bait' the trap for the Americans turned what had been an overwhelming superiority into something like equality between the opposing main strike forces at the point of contact. In consequence the American advantage of surprise was decisive and the widely dispersed Japanese forces were unable to recover.

The main reason why Midway was not, in the German term, 'war-decisive', however, was that, win or lose this battle, the Americans were bound in the longer term to win the war. The products of Roosevelt's 'two-ocean navy' programme of 1940 and expanded US aircraft production would over the next two years tip the military balance overwhelmingly in America's favour; and nothing Japan could do would alter the odds. She lacked the shipyard or industrial capacity to compete and had no ally in the east. All her oil and strategic raw materials had to be imported by sea and were therefore vulnerable to naval blockade. Equally critical, she was technologically far behind the Americans, particularly in radar and radio communications. Centimetric radar was the trump. This invention by British scientists had been handed to the Americans along with other secret patents in the summer of 1940 in order to harness the superior productive power of the US electrical industry to the British war effort.[2] It was to prove crucial in aerial warfare and in the defeat of Dönitz's U-boats in the Atlantic; equally it was to give US submarines in the Pacific a decisive advantage over Japanese anti-submarine forces. It was, of course, the disparity in material and technological potential between Japan and the United States which had driven Yamamoto to attempt his knockout blows on the US Pacific Fleet at Pearl Harbor, then at Midway. Now he had failed it was apparent to those at the top of the navy and in Hirohito's inner council that Japan had lost her gamble and must go down to defeat.

This could not be admitted. The expansion of the empire had been too dazzling; the people were too well indoctrinated in their role as the masters of East Asia, too geared for war and sacrifice, too committed to the Emperor and the 'holy' cause to be given a hint that all the national triumphs might have been for nothing and they would have to bow to the enemy they had been conditioned to despise. It was difficult for the Emperor's inner circle to take it in themselves. On a practical level it was foolish to admit weakness by extending peace feelers in the aftermath of a major defeat. Inevitably

Hirohito and his counsellors decided to enhance their bargaining position for future negotiations by further territorial conquest. The chosen directions were overland through New Guinea towards Port Moresby and north-eastern Australia and overseas via the Solomon group east of Australia to disrupt communications between that country and the United States.

Midway had given King and Nimitz confidence to take the offensive in the same direction. On 7 August 11,000 men of the US 1st Marine Division were landed on both the islands in the Solomons occupied by the Japanese, Tulagi and Guadalcanal. On the former the garrison resisted fanatically to the last man; on Guadalcanal a half-finished airfield was abandoned to the Marines, who completed it and named it after the Marine officer Major Lofton Henderson, killed while leading his raw dive-bomber pilots in their forlorn attack on the *Hiryu*. Hirohito reacted by assembling troops from the former Midway invasion forces and island garrisons to wrest back Henderson Field. So began the protracted struggle for Guadalcanal, fought in dense jungle ashore and in the air, at sea and beneath the sea, which etched itself in US history and legend.

Possession of Henderson Field eventually allowed US forces to prevail in the struggle to supply Guadalcanal, and the Japanese withdrew from the Solomons in February 1943. Not only had the Americans taken the first step in puncturing the enemy perimeter, they were the power best able to replace losses; consequently the tremendous rate of attrition of men and materiel during the campaign worked in their favour. This applied particularly in the air. The US aircraft industry not only outproduced the Japanese, but King and Nimitz had established a system of rotating operational squadrons back home which preserved experienced aircrew.[3] Japanese pilots were not rotated; they remained with their air groups; consequently the huge aircraft losses in the Solomons led to the extinction of most experienced pilots.

By this time the tide of war had turned in favour of the Allies in every theatre. In the Mediterranean the British and Commonwealth army under a new general, Bernard Montgomery, reinforced with men and materiel including American Sherman tanks and self-propelled assault guns via the long sea route around the Cape of Good Hope, had broken through the Axis lines at El Alamein and driven the enemy into precipitate retreat westwards. At the other end of North Africa a large Anglo-American expeditionary force had come ashore in Morocco and Algeria under the US general Dwight Eisenhower, and was advancing eastwards to catch them between the pincers.

In southern Russia the German 6th Army had been trapped in Stalingrad by a giant Soviet encircling movement, and after weeks of desperate fighting, street by devastated street, the survivors had reached the limit of endurance and, incapable of further compliance with Hitler's order to resist 'to the last man and last bullet',[4] laid down their arms. Stalingrad was the Continental equivalent of Midway, a turning point in the world struggle.[5]

The significance of the defeat was not lost on Hitler. The realization that victory in the two-front war against Russia and the Anglo-Americans was beyond his grasp afflicted him physically.[6] His back bowed, his left hand developed an uncontrollable tremor and he suffered blinding headaches and occasional giddiness.[7] This was apparent only in his closest circle. To most Germans guided by Dr Goebbels' Propaganda Ministry, he remained the leader bestowed on them by Providence. He could no more be seen to admit the possibility of failure than Hirohito. He adopted a strategy of holding every metre of ground won in the east and persuaded himself that the enemy alliance must crack.

The Soviet triumph at Stalingrad was a result of the extraordinary resilience of the Russian soldiery – aided by terror – an equally astonishing revival of tank, aircraft and artillery production in plants relocated and extemporized in the Urals, Kazakhstan and Siberia.[8] It did not of itself guarantee Russia's survival, let alone her rise to world power, for which she needed Western aid. So far this had not amounted to much, but in the months following Lend-Lease goods poured in through the Pacific port of Vladivostok and the far northern ports, Murmansk and Archangel, and overland from the head of the Persian Gulf. In addition to metals and other raw materials, guns, tanks, aircraft, aviation fuel, chemicals, machine tools and vast quantities of canned meat, butter and other foodstuffs, the crucial deliveries were steel rails for the worn-out railway system and jeeps and army trucks to give the Red Army logistic mobility, and in particular radio stations, radio sets, field telephones and telephone cable, which allowed Soviet commanders tighter control over their units in the field and in the air, enabling them, in Richard Overy's words, 'to confront German forces during the summer campaigning season [of 1943] in the sort of pitched battles of manoeuvre at which German commanders had hitherto excelled'.[9] This transfer of Western technology was critical. In private both Stalin and his Deputy Supreme Commander, Marshal Zhukov, acknowledged that without Western aid the Soviet Union 'could not have continued the war'.[10]

Aid to Continental allies had always been a vital strand in the strategy of dominant maritime power. Now British and huge American supplies to the Soviet Union enabled a resurgent Red Army to bleed Germany of men and material and force Hitler to concentrate resources in the east. He had already lost confidence in his navy: the brilliant defence of an Arctic convoy by British cruisers and destroyers against a pocket battleship and heavy cruiser in the dying hours of 1942 proved the final straw. He lectured Raeder for an hour and a half on the uselessness of the surface fleet, virtually forcing his resignation. Dönitz had taken over from him at the end of January 1943, resolved to subordinate everything to the U-boat campaign against enemy merchant shipping.

By this date he had the astonishing total of 409 U-boats, 222 of which were operational – the others on training or trials; 178 were assigned to the Atlantic, allowing seventy or more on patrol at any one time.[11] Commanders had enjoyed a second *'glückliche'*, or 'fortunate', time off the American coast in the early months of 1942 when they had caught the US Navy completely off guard. Since then they had been forced out into mid-Atlantic again, where conditions were tougher than ever before. Air patrols over convoys, escorts trained as a team and fitted with centimetric radar and high-frequency radio detection sets, HF/DF or 'Huff Duff', which located transmitting U-boats, had rendered pack attacks on convoys perilous. Dönitz sent long-range Type IX boats to the south Atlantic and into the Indian Ocean, where sinkings were easier, but maintained his campaign against the vital north Atlantic convoy routes with groups of boats stationed in a comparatively narrow central area south-east of Greenland beyond the range of Allied air patrols, known as the 'air gap'. These groups achieved such success in February and March,[12] that Dönitz was bolstered in his belief that with even more boats he could raise monthly sinking figures to a level the Western Allies could not bear; and in April he persuaded Hitler to increase U-boat building to twenty-seven boats a month.

It was not rational. Not only had the convoy battles resulted in record losses of U-boats, nineteen in February alone, but a massive American merchant shipbuilding programme had raised the target sinking figure from von Holtzendorff's 600,000 tons a month in 1917 to 1.3 million tons. The size of the US programme owed much to the American industrialist Henry Kaiser, who had initiated and organized a wholly novel method of prefabricating simple cargo vessels in sections to be assembled and welded together on the launching ways. These standardized freighters of 10,500 tons, christened 'Liberty ships', were being completed at a rate of over sixty a month. Simple arithmetic should have shown that, even with U-boat production raised to twenty-seven a month, if losses of boats continued at the current rate it would take over a year to reach the required number, during which time some two hundred more boats and their increasingly scarce trained crews would have been lost. The 'tonnage war' was in practice unwinnable with existing types of boats. By refusing to acknowledge this Dönitz squandered time he might have used to drive forward the development of more advanced types with a high underwater speed – designs for which had already been proposed – meanwhile condemning his young crews to a lethal struggle in craft whose technology had been rendered obsolescent by the new enemy measures.

The convoy losses in March which had encouraged Dönitz shocked the Allies into overdue action. The 'air gap' existed only because long-range Lancaster bombers and American Liberators were being used by Bomber Command, with Churchill's enthusiastic support, for a campaign designed to bomb German industrial workers from their homes; and more recently because Admiral King was assigning Liberators to non-urgent reconnaissance duties in the Pacific instead of making them available to close the north Atlantic 'air gap'. News of the convoy losses in mid–March prompted Roosevelt to ask King where the Liberators had been when these ships were sunk. King was stung into action, and specially adapted ultra-long-range Liberators were sent to Newfoundland and Iceland. Results were immediate. With radar-fitted aircraft covering the north Atlantic shipping routes from end to end U-boats approaching convoys were either forced under or picked off.[13]

The turning point came in May. U-boats in potentially annihilating numbers were concentrated successfully against north Atlantic convoys but were located by aircraft or surface escorts fitted with HF/DF and forced down or destroyed before they could get among the ships, suffering more losses than they inflicted. By the 22nd, when thirty–one U-boats had reported themselves sinking or had failed to answer when called, Dönitz at last bowed to arithmetic and withdrew the survivors southwards into safer waters. The conclusion was drawn in the U-boat Command War Diary next day: 'it is at present not possible with available weapons to fight a convoy with a strong air escort'.[14]

Although the defeat of Dönitz's U-boats had been one of the most pressing problems for the Allied Combined Chiefs, King made no lateral jump from the Atlantic to his Pacific domain. Japan and her island empire were as dependent on seaborne supplies as Britain; her anti-submarine forces were less numerous, less organized and technologically far inferior, her merchant shipbuilding capacity was smaller and she had no allies to provide extra tonnage. She was the perfect target for the kind of commerce war Dönitz had been waging. Moreover, US fleet submarines were larger and potentially more powerful than German U-boats; yet neither King nor Nimitz nor MacArthur in the Pacific even considered using the magnificent submarine forces based on Pearl Harbor and Brisbane to paralyse Japan by cutting her supply lines. Instead they adhered to the pre-war plan of advancing from island to island group towards the enemy homeland, and employed submarines on reconnaissance missions for the fleet, patrolling off enemy fleet bases, intercepting enemy forces whose movements had been learned from signal decrypts and innumerable special tasks connected with the island-hopping strategy; attacks on merchant shipping occurred almost by default.

Despite torpedo failures and the low priority given to commerce destruction, US submarines and carrier aircraft were, by the end of 1943, sinking more supply shipping than the Japanese could replace, and the total Japanese merchant fleet had been reduced to under five million tons, a million tons below her needs. The Japanese reacted by consolidating local escort commands into a single Combined Escort Fleet controlled from Tokyo, and attempted to boost the number of escort vessels. It was too late, and the 'decisive battle' still occupied the high ground of service thought and ambition, leaving too little in human or material resources for such 'defensive' measures as commerce protection; above all, Japanese technology lagged too far behind American.

A few US fleet submarines were by this time operating a version of pack tactics with a group commander in one boat directing two 'flankers', but results were patchy and the rate of sinkings fell in early 1944 as both Pearl Harbor and Brisbane submarines were directed to support amphibious operations to seize the Gilbert and Marshal Island groups; and enemy capital units remained the priority. It was not until the second half of the year, when the rate of sinkings by submarine pack attacks in the East China Sea and Luzon Strait increased, that the Naval Staff in Washington became wise to the fact that Japan was vulnerable to blockade. King proposed the capture of Formosa (Taiwan) to establish bases there and on the Chinese coast from which to mount patrols to cut Japan from her southern sources of oil and raw materials. The concept was turned down by MacArthur, who had promised to return to the Philippines and wished to do so in martial style, and also by Nimitz and Spruance, now commander-in-chief of the Central Pacific Fifth Fleet, who were doubtful about the logistics.

Spruance's fleet was by this time far stronger than the Japanese Combined Fleet at the height of its power. His fast carrier task force, which sailed from the Marshals on 6 June for the invasion of the Marianas, comprised the veteran *Enterprise*, six new large fleet carriers and eight new light fleet carriers with altogether over nine hundred aircraft embarked, and was accompanied by seven fast new battleships. Seven older battleships and troop transports would follow, the whole supported by a logistical fleet train comprising oil tankers, ammunition and supply ships, hospital ships, repair ships, floating dry docks, tugs and cranes.

There was a synchronism to the campaigns in all three major theatres in this penultimate summer of the war. On the day that Spruance's fast carriers set out for the invasion of the Marianas, on the opposite side of the world an armada of landing ships and craft, battleships for shore bombardment, cruisers, gunboats and innumerable destroyers, frigates, corvettes and other escort vessels, covered overhead by nearly two thousand fighters and 350 specialized anti-submarine aircraft, crossed the English Channel to land British Commonwealth and American invasion forces on the beaches of German-occupied Normandy from the mouth of the Seine to the Cherbourg peninsula.

At the same time, in the east, Soviet forces were moving to jumping-off points for a massive armoured offensive against a German salient around Minsk on the central front. Operations were opened on 9 June in the far north to lure German reinforcements to the Baltic states. The major offensive against Army Group Centre began a fortnight later on the third anniversary of the German invasion of Russia with similarly massive force – 2,715 tanks, 1,355 self-propelled guns, 166 infantry divisions, 24,000 guns and heavy mortars supplied by up to 100 trains a day with 12,000 lorries for distribution at the front, and supported overhead by 6,000 aircraft.[15] It was industrial war on a vaster scale than 1914–18, and the linking factor in all theatres was American production. British and Russian factories were between them turning out more tanks, aircraft and armaments than Germany, but American industry, now producing more than Britain and Russia combined, gave the Allies both crushing materiel superiority and a decisive technological edge.[16]

The other crucial factor in both European theatres was successful deception. This was not so critical in the Pacific since Spruance enjoyed overwhelming superiority, and naval forces are, in any case, able to strike in any direction. The Japanese could not be sure where the blow would fall. Yamamoto was dead, the victim of a planned strike on his aircraft after the Americans had decoded a signal detailing his itinerary for an inspection tour of the Solomons the previous April. It is clear from a poem he left that he knew of the danger and embraced a warrior's death in battle.[17] His successor, Admiral Soemu Toyoda, expected Spruance to support MacArthur in New Guinea, and had concentrated practically all that remained of Japan's battle strength, designated the First Mobile Fleet, in the Celebes Sea. Commanded by Admiral Jisiburo Ozawa, the force comprised the two large fleet carriers that had missed Midway and a brand-new fleet carrier, *Taiho*, serving as his flagship, together with six medium carriers converted from fast liners or fleet auxiliaries, and seven battleships. Only 430 planes were embarked, less than half the number in Spruance's fleet, and there were few, if any, experienced pilots; nearly all had been lost over the Solomons and other island bases. The intention was to compensate by luring Spruance within reach of shore-based aircraft on Ulithi, the Palaus and western Carolines. Directly it was realized that Spruance's attacks in the Marianas were not feints, however, Ozawa was ordered northwards for the critical engagement, 'A-Go' – 'Operation-A'.

His movements were reported to Spruance from US submarines deployed for the purpose. This was to be the first time submarines would play a significant role in a fleet engagement, initially by reporting Ozawa's movements, then by sinking two of his fleet carriers. First to go down in the early afternoon of 19 June was the veteran *Shokaku*, hit by Lieutenant Commander Herman Kossler of the *Cavalla* with three, possibly four, torpedoes. She was the first large carrier to fall victim to submarine attack. Earlier that morning Ozawa's flagship, *Taiho*, had been hit by a single torpedo fired by Lieutenant Commander James Blanchard of the *Albacore*. This had torn open aviation fuel tanks and jammed the forward aircraft elevator. The ship herself had not seemed in danger, but in attempting to disperse the fumes from the ruptured tanks the damage control team spread them throughout the ship and created an explosive mixture in some compartments, which erupted that afternoon, raising the flight deck, blowing out the sides and destroying the vessel.

By that time the battle in the air had been decided. Ozawa had located Spruance's fast carriers and launched his strike aircraft that morning in four waves. These had been picked up on radar while still 100 miles from the American carriers; fighters had been vectored on to them by Fighter Director Teams tracking enemy and own flights by radar and providing fighter leaders with intercept courses and altitudes by radio, a system beyond Japanese capabilities. All incoming raids were jumped 50 miles or more from their targets. The Americans now had a superior fighter, the Grumman Hellcat, developed with aircrew input, and their seasoned pilots decimated the enemy formations. The handful of planes that did reach attacking positions over the carriers caused no serious damage. Of 373 Japanese aircraft taking part some three hundred were lost, against only twenty-nine US planes.[18] The jubilant Americans christened it 'the Great Marianas Turkey Shoot'. The following afternoon Spruance's search planes located Ozawa for the first time and he dispatched 131 torpedo and dive-bombers, covered by eighty-five Hellcats, which reached the Japanese force that evening and sank one medium carrier, seriously damaged four others, including the fleet carrier, *Zuikaku*, to which Ozawa had transferred his flag, a battleship, a cruiser and two tankers. Ozawa ordered preparations for a night attack on the American force with sixty-one aircraft remaining to him, but Toyoda instructed him to withdraw.

The Battle of the Philippine Sea was decisive, but not in the sense the Japanese had planned. It was now evident that the Americans could not be halted by conventional means. They were dominant in the air, and given the comparative rates of aircraft production must become more so. If the Japanese homeland was to be preserved, radical measures were needed. The concept of suicide tactics by pilots steering their aircraft into enemy ships as guided bombs had already been studied as a more effective use of resources; and a submarine-launched human torpedo named *kaiten* had been developed by two young submarine officers. It was essentially a standard 24-inch-diameter torpedo with an enclosed compartment for the pilot at mid-length equipped with steering and depth controls, compass and periscope. The Naval General Staff ordered production of *kaiten* to begin.

Reverence for death in battle is common to warrior societies, and sacrificial death now became the motif of the Japanese war. As Spruance's Marines overran the garrison on Saipan in the Marianas, the navy chief on the island, Admiral Nagumo, former commander of the *kido butai*, committed ceremonial suicide; afterwards the remnants of his men made a suicidal charge at the US lines, and over the following days thousands of Japanese civilians accepted an invitation from Hirohito to achieve similar heroic status in the spirit world by ending their lives rather than falling into the hands of the American invaders. Thousands did so by hurling themselves, their wives and children from the island cliffs in desperate scenes, some recorded on film.[19]

In October, as the Americans launched an invasion of the Philippines, Admiral Toyoda staged a grand suicide ride with what was left of his fleet. Expecting his ships to 'bloom as flowers of death',[20] he concealed his purpose with a typically convoluted plan to use Ozawa's depleted carrier force with barely a hundred aircraft remaining as bait to lure the American carriers away from the landing beaches and allow his battle groups to close and destroy the invasion forces. The operation was designated '*Sho*(victory)-1', the ultimate euphemism.

It resulted in the effective extinction of the Japanese navy. Although Admiral William Halsey, alternating with Spruance as Pacific Fleet commander, fell for the ploy and chased the decoy carriers, the US landings on the island of Leyte were not impeded and Toyoda lost three battleships, one large and three small fleet carriers and numerous smaller ships against American losses of one light carrier, two escort carriers, three destroyers and a submarine.

It is no coincidence that as the battle ended the first six Japanese suicide, or kamikaze, pilots – so named after a providential wind that in Japanese tradition had dispersed a Mongol invasion fleet in 1281 – took off from the island of Mindanao to attack a more southerly group of US escort carriers. Two were shot down before reaching their targets, two succeeded in crash-diving on separate carriers, breaking through the flight decks and igniting fires in the hangars below, without, however, sinking the ships, and two returned to base to report the results. These were judged a success and over the following months units of the Pacific Fleet covering the invasion of the Philippines and the next push up to the island of Okinawa were subjected to kamikaze attacks of increasing scale and ferocity, which inflicted serious damage, sank over fifty smaller vessels and put ships' companies under enormous stress. Initially commanders alerted to coming mass raids by signals intelligence warned their men, but the practice was discontinued once it was found that 'the strain of waiting, the anticipated terror, made vivid from past experience sent some men into hysteria, insanity, break-down'.[21] Fanatically though the young kamikazes pursued their violent deaths in battle, they could not turn aside the American juggernaut. The result was only, as Ronald Spector has put it, 'to add still another level of fatalism and bloodshed to what was already a grim and merciless war'.[22]

In Europe Germany was gripped in a similar frenzy of self-destruction. Hitler had lost his ally, Mussolini, the previous year after the Western Allies had invaded Italy. British Commonwealth and American armies were pressing in from west and south, the Red Army from the east. Aware that the war was irretrievably lost, a group of army officers had attempted to assassinate Hitler with a bomb in his East Prussian headquarters in July, but had failed, and over the following months they suffered a fearful retribution.

Dönitz, who had proclaimed himself consumed by 'Holy wrath and boundless fury'[23] over the conspiracy, was already sending young men out on what were effectively suicide missions in midget submersible craft. The smallest, *Neger*, was a modified torpedo like a Japanese *kaiten* with a compartment for a pilot with breathing apparatus; it was not a suicide weapon since a standard torpedo was slung beneath; but as with other 'Small Battle Units' being turned out in quantity the chances of returning from a mission were negligible. Yet new types of ocean-going U-boat with huge battery arrays for high underwater speed were already in production. With these *Elektro*-boats, designated Types XXI and XXIII, Dönitz expected to seize back the initiative in the 'tonnage war', and could have done so had he switched construction from existing types sooner. Yet even after defeat in the battle of the Atlantic he had continued building and sending out conventional boats; 344 had been lost between the end of May 1943 and November 1944 with little effect on Allied shipping tonnage; of greater significance than the loss of the boats, over thirty thousand trained officers and men had failed to return.[24]

He continued sending boats out on patrol as the Allied armies advanced inside the borders of Germany. His exhortations to fanatic defiance grew ever more strident, his naval police more savage in the arbitrary execution of deserters and defeatists as the end approached. Like Hitler and Himmler, like Hirohito and his cabal, he was better able to call for resistance to the death since the Allies were demanding unconditional surrender. The Americans and British were determined that this time German militarism would be crushed and seen to be crushed so that it could never rise again to initiate a third world war;[25] the Soviets were resolved to defeat fascism and exact revenge for their millionfold losses in the war Hitler had unleashed. As for Japan, the Americans were intent on vengeance for Pearl Harbor, and the British chiefs accepted that the Pacific war was their affair.[26]

The British were not yet fully aware of the extent of US ambitions in Asia, nor how far Roosevelt had moved towards the concept of a Soviet–American settlement to the exclusion of Britain and the other European colonial powers, whose greed he blamed for creating the conditions from which war had sprung.[27] The Americans were looking on China and East Asia as a vast field for commercial and cultural penetration,[28] sensing no irony in simultaneously anathematizing the former colonial powers, since while they were projecting American values and the American way of commerce in the region, the indigenous peoples, including the Japanese, would be free and independent. The British chiefs of staff recognized the need for a Royal Naval presence in the Pacific as a political counterweight to American domination but had almost as much difficulty convincing Churchill[29] as in persuading Admiral King. Eventually a British Pacific Fleet was formed, and in March 1945 joined Nimitz's command; but it was little more than an appendage to the vast array of American naval might.

The diminutive size of the British Pacific fleet in relation to the American was an accurate index of the changed power relationship between the two allies. The USA was now driving the war in Europe as much as in the Pacific. With four armies in the field to Britain's one, it was natural that the supreme commander should be an American, General Eisenhower. His strategy, backed by Roosevelt and the US Joint Chiefs, took no account of Churchill's anxieties about the Soviets dominating eastern Europe after the war. No attempt was made to reach Berlin before the Red Army, nor to prevent Soviet penetration of the Balkans. The reason was that Stalin had replaced Churchill as Roosevelt's principal partner in the Grand Alliance.[30]

The unlikely partnership between a democratic American President and a bloodstained Soviet tyrant seems to have resulted from a genuine meeting of minds. Stalin's recent biographer, Simon Sebag Montefiore, concludes that 'Stalin's fondness for Roosevelt was as genuine a diplomatic friendship as he ever managed with any imperialist',[31] not that Roosevelt would have accepted the epithet. Roosevelt himself looked forward to working with the Soviet leader for the post-war reconstruction of the world order under the aegis of a United Nations institution representing free and independent peoples – for the eastern Europeans a historic misjudgement.

Britain's influence was further diminished since expenditure on the war had bankrupted her. From being the wealthiest creditor nation before the first German war, she now had overseas debts almost fifteen times greater than her reserves of gold and foreign currency; and in concentrating on war production her export trade had fallen to a third of its pre-war level.[32] Her ability to maintain the war had become entirely dependent on American Lend-Lease. This instrument, with which Roosevelt had supported and encouraged Churchill to stay in the fight against Hitler, had ruined her, as indeed it had promoted the ruin of Germany, America's other great trading rival. It is difficult to believe that either consequence was entirely unforeseen or unintended.[33]

Roosevelt died of a cerebral haemorrhage on 12 March 1945, little more than a month before the Red Army reached Berlin and precipitated the macabre series of suicides in the Führer's bunker below the ruins of the Reich Chancellery. Hitler was convinced he had been let down by his generals and the German people. He excepted Dönitz, and before placing a pistol to his temple, appointed him as his successor. The enemy was in control of most of the country, and after vain attempts to negotiate a separate peace with the Western Allies, Dönitz had no choice but to accept unconditional surrender. It came into force at midnight on 8 May. He had already sent instructions to his U-boat commanders at sea to surrender their boats, the first two Type XXI *Elektro*-boats among them. They had been too late to affect the outcome.

In all during the war 790 U-boats had been destroyed – excluding those surrendered or scuttled at the end – and of 40,600 officers and men who had passed through U-boat training 30,246 had been killed or died of wounds and a further 5,338 had been taken prisoner,[34] a loss ratio possibly unique in the annals of war.

By this date in the Pacific US submarines and aircraft had obtained a stranglehold over Japan's supply lines. By the end of 1944 her merchant shipping tonnage had been reduced to little over 2½ million tons,[35] entirely inadequate to sustain her economy. The few convoys running skirted close inshore, aiming for sheltered anchorages by night, their terrified sailors attempting to jump ship when they made port. The Luzon Strait, a particular haunt of American submarine wolf packs, had become 'the devil's sea'.[36] Since then submarine packs in the Inland Sea and aircraft-laid mine barriers across Japan's ports had cut the home islands even from mainland Asia. Oil and aviation fuel tanks were dry; industry extemporized where possible; the people subsisted on less than 1,700 calories a day and from 9 March the inhabitants of Tokyo and other major cities experienced mass air attacks with incendiary bombs creating firestorms similar to those that German civilians had suffered in the final months of the war in Europe. The last heavy unit of the Japanese fleet, the monster 18-inch-gun battleship *Yamato*, had sailed on a suicide mission on 6 April with fuel for a one-way passage only to 'charge' a US invasion fleet at Okinawa; she duly met her end under a rain of bombs and torpedoes from carrier aircraft. *Kaitens* and other midget suicide craft were now gathered at points around the coasts of the home islands to repel the anticipated invasion, and obsolescent aircraft were hidden in forest airstrips for the use of thousands of young men under training as kamikaze pilots.

Hirohito and his cabal had long known their gamble was doomed, but were still not prepared to admit defeat before obtaining guarantees for the continuance of the emperor system. These were not forthcoming. The Allied leaders, meeting at Potsdam in July, only reiterated their demand for 'the unconditional surrender of all Japanese armed forces . . . The alternative for Japan is prompt and utter destruction'.[37]

The novel and catastrophic nature of the promised destruction was not specified. It was to be the consummation of a United States project to create a nuclear fission weapon before Hitler's scientists. The first test 'atomic' bomb had been detonated in New Mexico with awesome results ten days before the Potsdam warning. Roosevelt's successor, Harry Truman, was advised that using this latest weapon to force Japanese surrender would save a million and a half, perhaps many more, Allied casualties during an invasion of the home islands, and tens of thousands of Allied prisoners of war who might be executed or simply allowed to starve to death in the event of invasion. The decision was not difficult. None of the key policy-makers, civilian or military, raised objections to the use of the bomb against Japan. It was not a matter for moral or ethical debate; civilians were already being firebombed in conventional raids over Japanese cities.

The first uranium-235 bomb, 'Thin Boy', was dropped over Hiroshima, southern Honshu, on 6 August; bursting 1,500 feet above ground level it annihilated 60,000 people instantly in a fireball and reduced the city centre to rubble and ash. Many more people outside the radius of destruction suffered fearful burns and irradiation. Three days later a second, plutonium, bomb, 'Fat Boy', was released over Nagasaki, Kyushu, with equally horrifying results. These two demonstrations, and the prospect of Tokyo and the imperial cabal being liquidated next in a blinding sheet of flame, at last released the scales of myth, hope, fear, double-think and double-talk that had prevented a decision on peace. Hirohito himself insisted on surrender for the sake of national survival.[38]

The formal ceremony took place in the morning of 2 September on the quarterdeck of the battleship *Missouri*, in Tokyo Bay. Together with Nimitz's flag as Commander-in-Chief US Pacific Fleet, she flew the personal flag of General Douglas MacArthur, appointed by the Allies Supreme Commander for the occupation of Japan. Proceedings after the Japanese delegation came up the side were as carefully choreographed as those in the *Queen Elizabeth* at the end of the previous war. First, the Japanese Foreign Minister signed the instrument of surrender; he was followed by the Japanese Chief of the Army General Staff, after which MacArthur, as commanding a presence as Beatty, signed for the Allies; next came Nimitz, followed by a representative of Nationalist China, America's chosen partner for the reconstruction of East Asia, after him the commander of the British Pacific Fleet, followed by Soviet and other Allied representatives.

The baton had passed. A new and mightier power had risen as mistress of the seas to give the law to the world.

25

The 'Cold War' – and After

THE NAVAL AIRBASE on Midway remained a link in the chain of US global command until the introduction of reconnaissance satellites and nuclear-powered submarines in the 1970s. Thereafter its strategic role diminished. In 1992 the naval air facilities were closed down, and four years later the atoll was transferred to the Department of the Interior and placed under the US Fish and Wildlife Service to be managed as a National Wildlife Refuge in the chain of Hawaiian refuges.

As such Midway is vital for the survival of many species, especially perhaps the Laysan albatross. Its islands and islets support the world's largest breeding colony of this albatross, which rears some half a million chicks annually. Of these an unnatural proportion perish from starvation or dehydration, principally because they have been fed by their parents with plastic flotsam brought to the atoll on currents from all the lands bordering the Pacific.[1]

The albatross was chosen in 1798 by Samuel Taylor Coleridge for his epic *The Rime of the Ancient Mariner*. The story of the great seabird that followed the ship of the ancient mariner until one day he shot it dead was an allegory of the evils consequent on mankind breaking the unity of nature: 'The man hath penance done, And penance more will do'.[2]

Now, 200 years later, as the results of mankind's reckless abuse of nature have become everywhere apparent, the dread portents of the Romantic movement have become a commonplace of political, scientific, even economic discourse. The first book to alert a worldwide reading public was Rachel Carson's *Silent Spring* in 1962. Carson married poetic insight with scientific training as a marine biologist and long experience working for the US Bureau of Fisheries, later the US Fish and Wildlife Service. Her target was industrial farming, specifically the production and use of synthetic pesticides, a by-product of chemical warfare research during the Second World War. Her argument that the indiscriminate barrage of chemicals laid down against insects poisoned the whole chain of life, including man, raised a storm of alarm and was generally heeded. The pesticides that concerned her were banned or strictly regulated. It did not stop intensive farming. In England, more than thirty years after *Silent Spring*, Graham Harvey was moved to write *The Killing of the Countryside*, describing with similar passion the ditches poisoned with chemicals and the fields bereft of wild flowers, butterflies and birds.

Beyond the dangers of chemical pollution, Rachel Carson's bigger theme was the complex interrelationship between all living things, the reactive, ever-changing nature of the balance achieved and the incalculable consequences of human intervention. She ascribed the idea of controlling nature to 'the Neanderthal age of biology and philosophy',[3] when nature was viewed as a convenience for mankind.

In the early 1970s Dr James Lovelock took the concept of man as part and prisoner of nature to the ultimate level by proposing that Planet Earth was itself a living organism, its animate and inanimate constituents interacting mechanistically to stabilize the physical and chemical environment. He named this entity after the ancient Greek earth goddess and brought the theory to popular attention in 1979 with the publication of *Gaia: A New Look at Life on Earth*. In his most recent exposition, *The Revenge of Gaia*, he points out that Rachel Carson's 'silent spring' was not simply the product of pesticides: 'the birds died because there was no longer space for them in our intensively farmed world'.[4] By treating the land and the oceans as if they existed for man's benefit alone rather than for the community of ecosystems that serve all life, 'humans . . . have usurped Gaia's authority and thwarted her obligation to keep the planet fit for life'.[5]

For the biologist Professor E. O. Wilson, the increasing rate of extinction of species and the resultant loss of biodiversity is the wake-up call. He lists the causes as, again, habitat loss, pollution, over-harvesting – hunting, fishing, gathering – and at the root of them all human overpopulation. Humanity, he asserts, has itself become a geophysical force: 'We have spread thousands of toxic chemicals worldwide, appropriated 40 per cent of the solar energy available for photosynthesis, converted almost all the easily arable land, dammed most of the rivers . . . and now . . . we are close to running out of fresh water.'[6]

The realization that we have by our own actions reached a point of possibly irreversible damage to the life systems that support us on earth places the United States in an unenviable position. As inheritor of the capitalist trading system, known now as the global economy, hence champion of the free market and the individual freedoms that spring from it, she must confront the dread consequences of the system. There is no simple palliative. The World Bank, the great facilitator of capital projects for infrastructure, energy and agriculture in the developing world, has created a Vice Presidency of Environmentally Sustainable Development;[7] but with world population rising, and developing countries seeking for their own often huge populations the wealth and way of life enjoyed in the West, 'sustainable development' is at best escapism, at worst the road to hell on earth.

Many trust that by feeding environmental costs such as carbon emissions into project accounting, investing in new, 'clean' technology and discouraging pollution by imposing 'green' taxes, free market forces can still preserve the conditions necessary for human life on earth, so preventing our extinction as a species. This is to underestimate both the pressure of human expectations and the multiplicity of dangers facing the environment.

If the United States does not rise to this greatest of all moral and intellectual challenges by inspiring a radically new way of thinking and leading free peoples in a new direction the probability is that our descendants will not survive; certainly our civilizations built up over millennia will join that of Ozymandias, King of Kings.

> . . . Round the decay
> Of that colossal wreck, boundless and bare,
> The lone and level sands stretch far away.[8]

The United States ended the Second World War as dominant world power. Her industrial production had surged by almost 50 per cent since 1939 and was more than equal to that of all other nations combined. Not all production had been for armaments. Her people enjoyed the highest standard of living in the world with an income per head almost twice that of the next-richest group of nations, the British Commonwealth and Switzerland. She was also the greatest exporter, the greatest creditor nation and owned three-quarters of the world's gold.[9] The dollar ruled.[10] As she was the sole possessor of the atomic bomb her armed might was unchallengeable; and her navy was greater than the navies of the rest of the world combined.

Her cultural influence was as wide. Ragtime, jazz, blues and swing derived from dances and songs of southern American Negro slaves had swept the post-first-war world and influenced music everywhere; at the height of the Second World War British 'black' propaganda stations transmitted 'American jazz' to attract German military personnel to their broadcasts, with great success; U-boat crews were especially responsive.[11] The foxtrot, also derived from southern Negro dances, was popular around the world, as were songs from Broadway 'musicals', a distinct new form of musical theatre inaugurated in 1927 by *Show Boat*, in which a believable storyline initiated songs and dance; the genre blossomed in the 1940s with such classics as *Oklahoma* and towards the end of the decade *South Pacific*, conjuring romance from the recent conflict. Hollywood films were even more potent as showcases for the American way of affluence, American individualism and optimism.

In historical terms, America after the war occupied the place in the world and in men's imagination that Britain had in the period after Napoleon's defeat in 1815. European visitors to the United States were stunned by the sheer scale of American wealth and modernity,[12] just as nineteenth-century visitors to Britain had been overwhelmed by the prosperity and luxury they found everywhere. That most perceptive of French economic philosophers, Alexis de Tocqueville, visiting Britain in the 1830s, described it as 'the Eden of modern civilisation' with 'more dazzling riches than anywhere else in the world'. On completion of his tour he felt he had visited 'the most powerful, the most active, the most successful social entity on earth'.[13]

Going back two centuries, the Dutch republic, the United Provinces, had drawn similar expressions of wonderment from foreign visitors during her golden age from the 1650s after her merchant trading companies had engrossed the commerce of much of the world and her fighting admirals had driven the Spanish from the seas; Amsterdam was then fulcrum and motor of the Western financial system; one gazetteer of the time observed, 'The whole world stands amazed at its riches,'[14] and an English visitor in 1660 wrote, ''Tis commonly said that this city is very like Venice. For my part I believe Amsterdam to be much superior in riches.'[15] He noted that the signs of prosperity and ease extended throughout the population. A well-travelled Dutchman ascribed the 'present grandeur' of his countrymen to 'their political wisdom in postponing everything to merchandise and navigation [and] the unlimited liberty of conscience that is enjoyed among them . . .'[16] Here he referred not simply to freedom of worship, but freedom of speech, which was a source of as much astonishment to visitors as the prosperity of the country.

Freedom of expression is the golden thread running from the Dutch republic and Great Britain at the height of their power to the United States. It is the symptom of merchant ascendancy spun from trading wealth, its essential complements devolved, consultative systems of government and an independent judiciary. These distinguished the great maritime trading powers from their land-based contemporaries ruled by autocrats or centralizing bureaucracies employing regulations, extreme censorship and executive justice. Each state in the United Provinces was, at least in theory, sovereign; in Britain in the eighteenth and nineteenth centuries, apart from centralized tax collection, each county, each town and parish, looked after its own interests virtually unaffected by the government at Westminster, just as individual states in the United States have powers of taxation and considerable autonomy from Washington. Supreme maritime nations have always been politically exceptional and have viewed themselves as uniquely 'moral' compared with the 'old world' of top-down government and acquiescent or subservient peoples.

There could have been no more extreme version of the latter than the Soviet Union, which emerged from the world war as the second major power after the United States. Every area of life was subject to central control imposed by terror. In pursuit of Marxist-Leninist orthodoxy, Stalin had liquidated untold millions of his own people, over twice as many as the Jews and others exterminated by the Nazis, many more than the number of Soviet soldiers who had died fighting Hitler.[17] More recently the Soviet system had been imposed on eastern European countries overrun by the Red Army on the way to Berlin. Sir Owen O'Malley, British ambassador to the Polish government-in-exile, had raised the moral issue as early as April 1943, asking how the British government could contemplate the surrender of central and south-eastern Europe 'to the cruel and heathenish tyranny of the Soviets'.[18] Field Marshal Sir Alan Brooke, Chief of the Imperial General Staff, had expressed similar views that year,[19] and by July 1944, convinced that Russia must become 'the main threat in 15 years from now', he was proposing a post-war policy of gradually rebuilding Germany instead of dismembering her, and bringing her into a federation of western Europe to meet the Soviet threat.[20]

The Americans became equally alarmed about Soviet policy in East Asia. In April 1945, before the end of the war in Europe, the US Office of Strategic Services warned of the emergence after the war of an immensely powerful Soviet Union with which the United States might come into conflict, and advised, against the trend of Roosevelt's policies, that the United States 'should realize its interests in the maintenance of the British, French and Dutch colonial empires' in order to check 'Soviet influence in the stimulation of colonial revolt'. Apart from disorder in the region, any policy aimed at weakening the colonial empires 'may at the same time alienate from us the European states whose help we need to balance the Soviet power'.[21] This pragmatic view replaced ingrained American anti-colonialism.

Such were the origins of the 'cold war' between the West and Soviet

Russia in the decades after the Second World War. It was the age-old conflict between the mutually antagonistic systems of maritime and territorial power, between commerce and conquest, but given an ideological instead of a dynastic or religious rationale. In this way 1945 was different from 1815. After Napoleon's defeat Britain had stood supreme without a rival, and had been able to set about reshaping the world in her own image with minimal expenditure on arms. When after victory in the Second World War the United States embarked on her own mission to create a new world, she faced a powerful enemy intent on exporting her own opposing values; the result was an arms race of unprecedented magnitude and danger, combined with worldwide competition for spheres of influence.

American aims were little different from Britain's in her heyday; like Britain's ruling class then, US statesmen felt they had saved the world for freedom and it was their duty as much as it was in their commercial self-interest to spread freedom and all blessings of the American way of life to the less fortunate, especially in Asia.[22] Like the British, they placed the emphasis on free trade; unlike the British, they were resolved, in accordance with the principle enunciated by Abraham Lincoln at Gettysburg of 'government of the people, for the people, by the people',[23] to promote democracy and self-determination.

In Japan their proconsul, General Douglas MacArthur, generally succeeded: disbanding the armed services and working with the existing Japanese bureaucracy to reform the pre-war political system, encouraging liberals and trade unionists, even releasing Marxists from jail, cutting down police powers, restoring free speech and civil liberties, creating local democracy, breaking up the great *zaibatsu*, redistributing agricultural land to tenant farmers, he brought into being what appeared to be a modern democratic state with universal suffrage in the Western image. There were two major anomalies. To manage this wholesale redirection MacArthur had decided to utilize the people's veneration for their god-emperor, Hirohito, which had survived all the sacrifices and devastation of the failed war. Instead of being put on trial as a war criminal, the Emperor was retained as 'the symbol of the State and of the unity of the people, deriving his position from the will of the people with whom resides sovereign power'[24] – a very American interpretation of constitutional monarchy. He was deprived of powers relating to government. The more remarkable aspect of the new constitution was contained in Article IX: '. . . the Japanese people forever renounce war as a sovereign right of the nation'; consequently 'land, sea and air forces, as well as other war potential, will never be maintained'.[25] Deprived of the essential instruments of sovereignty, Japan became, in effect, a protectorate of the United States, bound to her by treaties of mutual security, with American forces based on her soil.

Article IX did not long survive the exigencies of the cold war. When in June 1950 communist North Korea, prompted by Moscow, launched an attack on the southern, pro-Western half of that country, American troops stationed in Japan were rushed across to support the South Koreans, and MacArthur, still in command of the forces occupying Japan, ordered the Japanese to establish a 75,000-strong paramilitary police force to take the place of the US troops. Subsequently expanded with naval and air arms, this nucleus grew into the Self-Defence Forces, which were increased in line with the country's growing industrial strength under the American umbrella. They were military forces in all but name, although nuclear weapons were, for emotional/historical reasons, ruled out.

Japan is an enigma: an island nation ideally placed off the coast of East Asia to dominate the trade of the region, protected by sea from continental invasion, the question of why the martial ethos of her landholding aristocracy was never challenged, as in Holland and England, by the values of her successful merchant-trading class remains unanswered. Merchants had failed to impose themselves in the fifteenth and early sixteenth centuries, and failed again during the long period of national seclusion under the Tokegawas.[26] Merchant families gained control of the economic life of the country and acquired great wealth, yet when Japan was forcibly opened to trade in the mid-nineteenth century it was samurai who forged the revolution to catch up technologically with the West and set the course for military conquest.

Whether American ideals of freedom and democracy have taken deep root since defeat seems questionable. In many ways traditional values have simply been redirected: in politics, government and business decisions are made by traditional Japanese consensual means; the Ministry of Finance, the Okurasho, directs the economy nationalistically in defiance of free market principles;[27] big business takes paternalistic responsibility for employees in return for absolute loyalty; the cultural inequality of women is reflected in their less permanent role in the workplace, hence lower incomes;[28] the fiercely competitive education system is as single-mindedly devoted to the needs of industrial society as it was once to the warrior nation. In short, individualism has not generally triumphed over nationalism, conformity, deference and the corporate spirit. Moreover, reliance on America for defence and foreign policy has prevented the country from growing up or, as Ian Buruma puts it: 'If people cannot be trusted . . . to exert democratic control over matters of war they are unlikely to have enough confidence to maintain their freedoms in times of danger.'[29]

The most worrying symptom of Japanese failure to assimilate American freedoms has been refusal to face up to responsibility for the Pacific war or the sub-bestial manner in which Japanese forces conducted it. By contrast with German acceptance of responsibility for genocide, or the exaggerated guilt expressed by British liberal intellectuals for the British Empire, Japanese politicians have quibbled endlessly over ways to apologize to their Asian neighbours without appearing to do so, and have failed to compensate either their wartime 'comfort women' or the former Allied prisoners of war whom they used so cruelly.[30] Barbarities such as Unit 731 and the Nanking Massacre have been expunged from Japanese history books. A former West German Chancellor, Helmut Schmidt, who met Hirohito and all the leading Japanese politicians during his long period in office, wrote in his memoirs that 'the Japanese seem to lack any sense of guilt'.[31] What can people understand of freedom who deny themselves any expression of shame?

Helmut Schmidt also noted during his visits to Japan 'a widespread and for the most part carefully concealed arrogance, a feeling of superiority in comparison to almost all the neighbouring nations'.[32] He observed, too, that women remained 'second class citizens'.[33] Historically, this has been a sign of societies that have not developed individual freedoms. Can it be simply that East is East and West is West, that the factors preventing the symptoms of supreme maritime power from applying in the East were cultural or genetic?

Laurens van der Post, who survived a Japanese prisoner-of-war camp where he had been made to watch Japanese soldiers conducting bayonet practice on live prisoners tied between bamboo posts, and executions performed by beheading, strangling, burial alive, 'but, most significantly, never by just shooting', came to realize that 'the Japanese were themselves the puppets of immense impersonal forces to such an extent they truly did not know what they were doing'.[34]

To ascribe Japanese behaviour to dark impersonal forces was no doubt a form of survival strategy; in a sense it was also true, and applied equally to the Germans practising genocide – and, perhaps, to the directors and viewers of 'torture pornography' films today – but it is of little help in solving the historical conundrum of why Japan took such a diametrically opposite tack to that of the Western maritime powers. Van der Post describes the 'profound disregard of the importance of life' in the Japanese military, and the belief that they were instruments of a historical revenge on the Europeans for their invasion of the east.[35] This hardly accounts for their hideous barbarity towards the Chinese and other East Asians during the war, and simply returns the argument to the beginning and the predominant Anglo-Saxon view of history as random, lacking plot, pattern or purpose. H. A. L. Fisher, who was decidedly of this view, ascribed differences to culture:

> We Europeans are the children of Hellas. Our civilisation, which has its roots in the brilliant city life of the eastern Aegean, has never lost traces of its origin, and stamps us with a character by which we are distinguished from the other great civilisations of the human family, from the Chinese, the Hindus, the Persians and the Semites.[36]

We, then, are the anomaly, in which case the overarching thesis of these volumes falls. It can be argued, however, that the Japanese had a cultural and artistic life as brilliant as that of ancient Greece.

In Europe in 1945 the victorious Allies carved Germany into four occupation zones, the Russian in the east, the American, British and French in the west; in addition the Western powers each took an enclave in Berlin, which was enclosed in the Soviet eastern zone. The original aims of the Western Allies were to de-Nazify, demilitarize and decentralize Germany to prevent her rising again to threaten the peace of Europe, but they found themselves with urgent economic and humanitarian problems. Communications had been shattered and vast areas of the cities reduced to rubble by Allied bombing. Acute housing and food shortages were exacerbated by millions of refugees from the east, and that winter people starved and froze to death in the ruins. Helmut Schmidt recalled subsisting on 896 calories a day.[37] Allied priorities had to be adjusted to rebuild the economy and, in the light of Russian behaviour, to bring the three western zones together to form a bulwark against Soviet expansion.

American policy was based on a report from a diplomat in the US embassy in Moscow named George Kennan. Before the war Kennan had been sent to study Russian thought, language and culture at Berlin University. Posted to Moscow in 1944, he had become highly critical of Roosevelt's close relationship with Stalin, and when in February 1946 he was required to reply to a message from the US Treasury asking why the Russians were making difficulties at the World Bank, then being set up in Washington, he fired off an essay-long analysis broken up into five telegrams to make it more digestible. The basic message was that Stalin believed peaceful coexistence with the West impossible and was determined to do everything to advance Soviet power wherever he could; Kennan likened world communism to a 'malignant parasite, which feeds only on diseased tissue', and suggested the most effective response was to build up the health of American society.[38] The 'long telegram' created a sensation in Washington and Kennan was called home and appointed director of policy planning at the State Department. Here he found another analogy for Soviet policy: as a fluid stream that sought to fill every cranny of world power, but would, if confronted with unassailable barriers, accommodate itself to them and temporize or retreat. The United States, he argued, should pursue a strategy of 'long-term, patient but firm and vigilant containment of Russian expansive tendencies'.[39]

Truman first applied the policy of containment to the Soviet drive towards the Mediterranean. Greece and Turkey were in danger of falling to communist insurrection; Britain could no longer afford her traditional support for their governments and Truman stepped in with US economic and military aid. In explaining his action he formulated what came to be known as 'the Truman doctrine' of helping 'free peoples to maintain their institutions and their integrity against aggressive movements that seek to impose upon them totalitarian regimes'.[40] He next sought to apply the doctrine to Europe as a whole by offering dollar aid to restore the shattered Continental economies. This was conceived in the spirit of Kennan's belief that communism could best be defeated by building up strong, healthy societies. Stalin rejected what he perceived, no doubt correctly, as the tentacles of American capitalism penetrating his tightly controlled imperium; consequently American finance, known loosely after the US Secretary of State as 'Marshall Aid', was only taken up in the west European countries, including the Western-occupied zones of Germany.

Stalin's rejection of aid reinforced the existing division of Europe between a Western free market and an eastern communist bloc, so formally institutionalizing the cold war. It can be compared to Kaiser Wilhelm II's decision in 1914 to support Austria against Russia. As the First World War had shattered British expectations that international trade and interlocking economies would ensure universal peace, so in 1947 American hopes for building a new world of free democratic trading nations were dashed by Stalin's hostility. In both cases reasonable assumptions of progress came up against the irrationality of the world expressed through a single, all-powerful but unstable individual. For Stalin's prestige had been so enhanced by victory over Nazi Germany that his word was absolute among his ruling coterie, which he dominated with a mixture of secrecy and mystery, bullying, humiliation and whim.[41]

Marshall Aid, together with reform of the German currency, the removal of surviving Nazi wage and price controls and food rationing, and the consolidation of the three western zones of occupation and West Berlin into a West German republic with a decentralized constitution unleashed a seemingly miraculous rebirth of the economy, or *Wirtschaftswunder*, which turned the new state into an industrial powerhouse. Marshall Aid was equally crucial in the revival of the other western European economies,[42] and with the help of covert payments from the US Central Intelligence Agency — CIA, formed in 1947 — prevented France and Italy from falling to the communists within.

Alongside economic containment Truman created a military alliance to counter the vast standing army Stalin maintained in eastern Europe. The North Atlantic Treaty Organization — NATO — bound the United States to most countries of western Europe, Canada and Iceland in a mutual defence pact, underwritten militarily and financially by the United States. It was complemented by similar alliances and bilateral treaties which Truman and his successors formed with countries of the Far East, South-East Asia and the Middle East, encircling the Soviet Union and China — where communists under Mao Zedong had triumphed in 1949 — with regional coalitions backed by US naval and military power. There would be eruptions around the periphery, in Korea, British Malaya and French Indochina, but the main focus of the cold war remained the central front in Europe.

By 1949 the Soviets had developed an atomic bomb; and such was their supremacy in ground troops, it seemed they could sweep through the NATO forces and reach the Channel coast within days. West Germany was co-opted to help redress the balance, and in May 1955 the Western occupation was lifted and the German Federal Republic proclaimed as a sovereign state. The following day she joined NATO. Like Japan on the eastern flank, Germany had flourished as an American protégé and, as Helmut Schmidt expressed it, had become 'linked with the Americans by shared values concerning freedom and the role of the individual, the open society and the democratic form of government'.[43]

Stalin had died the previous year. His successor, Nikita Khrushchev, reacted to German membership of NATO by forming the Warsaw Pact, a military alliance between the Soviet Union and its east European satellites with a unified command, although designed as much to cement Soviet control over eastern Europe as to confront the West. An arms race already under way between the two superpowers now escalated in every dimension, particularly in nuclear weapons and delivery systems.

The United States followed a traditional maritime strategy, like Britain before her, deploying naval forces from a network of bases in every ocean: the First, later renamed the Third, Fleet in the Pacific; the Second Fleet in the Atlantic, working closely with navies of the other NATO nations; the Sixth Fleet commanding the Mediterranean on the southern flank of NATO and providing squadrons for the Indian Ocean; the Seventh Fleet operating from Subic Bay in the Philippines to cover East Asian waters. The Soviet Union, like all great continental powers in history, built a fleet to challenge American encirclement, concentrating particularly on submarines to disrupt Western supply lines; the Soviet navy as a strategic force was constrained by geography, however, lacked carrier-borne strike power and logistic support for long-distance operations, and like the grand fleets built by Bourbon France or imperial Germany suffered, and in war would have suffered more, from the priority accorded land forces in a continental power. The US naval historian Clark Reynolds was probably not wide of the mark in commenting, 'the Russians kept up appearances and have fumbled accordingly in many spheres of maritime activity'.[44]

In addition to encircling the Soviet Union and China with naval power, the United States ringed the communist empires with nuclear bomber forces and later with nuclear ballistic and cruise missiles based in South Korea, Okinawa, Taiwan, Guam and other Pacific island bases, Turkey, Greece, Morocco, western European countries, Iceland and Greenland; nuclear bomb components without warheads were even stored in Japan, whose government and people were opposed to nuclear armaments.

Containment was accompanied by global surveillance. In both Britain and America signals and electronic intelligence – the monitoring of non-communication signals from radar and missiles – was accorded the major share of secret service funding. The British Government Communications Headquarters – GCHQ, successor to the wartime GC & CS at Bletchley Park – and the US National Security Agency – NSA, formed by Truman in 1952 – grew into the premier Western intelligence agencies, employing more staff than all conventional intelligence services combined.[45] The wartime intelligence cooperation between the Western Allies continued under a revised agreement, known as the UKUSA treaty, and special Liaison Offices were established for the NSA in London and for GCHQ in Virginia. Among other things the UKUSA treaty allowed the Americans to take advantage of cryptographic agencies and intercept stations in the British Commonwealth and imperial bases such as Hong Kong, Singapore, Colombo and elsewhere in the Indian Ocean and Persian Gulf. Besides land-based stations, NSA installed monitoring equipment in 'spy planes', ships, submarines and orbiting satellites, creating a multidimensional eaves-dropping system which could pick up and record any transmission anywhere.

The CIA, meanwhile, was employing the oldest intelligence-gathering expedient, strictly illegal in the United States, of opening letters. Between 1954 and 1973 all mail to and from the Soviet Union passing through the port of New York was read and some two per cent judged to be of inter-est was photographed.[46]

Equal effort was devoted to penetrating the closed communist empire with the message of freedom. American Lend-Lease equipment acquired by the Soviets during the war had enabled them to become proficient at jamming enemy radio; they used this expertise in the post-war years to jam Radio Free Europe, Voice of America, the BBC and other Western stations. To counter this, the US National Security Council oversaw an operation termed 'the Ring Plan' to surround the Eastern Bloc with powerful transmitters, the strength of whose signal was such that, as one ebullient radio warrior quipped, 'anybody with a metal filling in his mouth is going to be able to pick up the Voice of America'.[47]

In parallel with the enormous propaganda effort the CIA and special operations and psychological warfare divisions of the US military engaged in covert schemes to support dissident groups within the Eastern Bloc in a manner reminiscent of SOE's subversive activities in Nazi-occupied Europe during the war. There was little coordination behind the projects: some aimed at bringing about the collapse of the Soviet empire from within, others at establishing partisan groups behind enemy lines for the hot war deemed inescapable. The belief that war was inevitable, meanwhile, led American strategists to consider a pre-emptive nuclear strike before the Soviets developed delivery systems capable of reaching the United States. The British military and intelligence communities viewed an American first strike as all too frighteningly probable.[48]

The balance soon shifted. In 1953 Russia followed only nine months behind America in the development of a hydrogen bomb immensely more destructive than the atomic bomb, and thereafter progressed so rapidly in missile technology that US cities became vulnerable to nuclear attack. With both major powers facing total annihilation if war broke out between them, aptly defined by the acronym MAD for Mutually Assured Destruction, both turned to managing coexistence.[49]

Finally the Soviet empire collapsed from within. It had been pre-dicted by many, but when it happened it came as a shock to both sides.

The problem was colossal inefficiency in the closed and centrally controlled Soviet economy, exacerbated by mounting defence expenditure.[50] Coexistence with the West had not ended the arms race, merely channelled it in different directions, into space and especially into competition for spheres of influence around the world. For this an oceanic navy was essential. Soviet naval expansion was reminiscent of French fleet-building to rival British naval power in the years before 1789, leading to government bankruptcy, food riots and revolution. Similarly, Soviet concentration on naval and military production crowded out the domestic economy and retarded living standards by comparison with those of the flourishing free-trading world outside.

The contrast had always been most evident in Berlin, where the regimented inhabitants of the tenements of the eastern zone were confronted with the glittering shops of the western sector, and received radio and television portrayals of a materially richer, more diverse and attractive way of life. So great was the lure of the West that in order to stem an exodus of skilled workers and professionals the East German government had erected a barbed-wire barricade across the city and around the western zone, later replaced by a 10-foot-high concrete wall guarded by armed sentries. The border between East and West Germany had already been sealed; over the following years the defences were strengthened with razor wire, automatic guns, mines, anti-vehicle ditches, guards and guard dogs to prevent the citizens of what was brazenly named the German Democratic Republic from voting with their feet to escape.

It did not solve the basic problems caused by Marxist-Leninist orthodoxy and the disproportionate resources directed towards the military by ministers and officials whose power was vested in the sector. By 1985, when a comparatively young leader, Mikhail Gorbachev, took power, the economy had stalled; targets laid down for industry and improvements in the standard of living had not been met; agricultural productivity was so low food was imported, and hard currency earnings had been hit by falls in the world price of oil and natural gas, which together made up 60 per cent of Soviet foreign receipts. The country was in crisis. Gorbachev responded with radical departures from Leninist policy: in foreign affairs he sought rapprochement with the United States, proposing mutual reductions in nuclear missiles, even their elimination, in order to release resources for domestic and export production, and talked of joining the International Monetary Fund and the Western trading club, the General Agreement on Tariffs and Trade. He sounded, and with his personable wife, Raisa, looked, like a different kind of Soviet leader. He convinced Helmut

Schmidt that 'even the Communist leaders of Russia are finally discovering their membership in the "common European home"'.[51]

Internally he attempted to regenerate economic growth by permitting some discussion within the system and encouraging small-scale private enterprise, particularly in farming. When it became evident that these tentative reforms had failed to lift the dead hand of central control he plunged further in imitation of the West, influenced by his new friends, the United States President, Ronald Reagan, the British Prime Minister, Margaret Thatcher, and the German Chancellor, Helmut Kohl, by allowing unprecedented freedom of expression in the media (glasnost) while attempting to democratize the Communist Party and introduce free market mechanisms in industry (perestroika). His mission was to fire up the Marxist-Leninist economy. Instead, the injection of antithetical Western values destroyed it. Finally, in 1988, with cracks opening in the party and the Union, he made the ultimate break with orthodoxy by proclaiming he would no longer intervene in the internal affairs of the east European satellites. Nationalist disaffection had long been rife within these states, and once deprived of Russian military support their governments lost confidence and gave way before popular uprisings. The collapse of the Warsaw Pact was symbolized by the opening of the border between East and West Germany late in 1989, the unification of the two Germanies the following year and the subsequent destruction of the Berlin Wall. A year later the Soviet Union itself broke apart. Gorbachev was awarded the Nobel Peace Prize for bringing about the end of the cold war; in reality he had contributed with much courage and eloquence to a historic demonstration of the law of unintended consequences.

The other victor of the world war, the former mistress of the seas, fared little better. The conflict itself had borne out Churchill's prediction that if the British Empire and Commonwealth lasted a thousand years, 'This was their finest hour';[52] for after the fall of France in 1940 Britain could have retired with her navy and empire intact had she allowed Hitler a free hand on the Continent to smash the Soviet Union. The offer had been made many times and finally brought to Britain in person by Hitler's deputy, Rudolf Hess;[53] instead she had fought on under Churchill's leadership for honour and freedom against tyranny. Seldom has moral principle so overridden material aims and accountancy in any great war. Seldom has good triumphed so unambiguously over evil.

It was magnificent, but a swansong. By the end of the conflict in which she alone of the victor nations had fought since the first day, she was ruined financially. During the course of the war she had run down her gold and dollar reserves and become the world's largest debtor nation, owing £3,355 million abroad. Her exports had fallen by almost a half and her imports had risen, producing a visible trade gap of over £1,000 million,[54] yet she had naval and military establishments on an imperial scale. When US Lend-Lease was cut off at the end of the Pacific war she faced bankruptcy unless further American aid was forthcoming. Keynes was dispatched to Washington to plead the case. The Americans made generous recognition of Britain's crucial contribution to victory against the dictatorships by cancelling $20 billions owed on the Lend-Lease account.[55] The rescue loan they finally agreed was $3.75 billion at 2 per cent interest, rather less than the interest-free sum Keynes had hoped for, but topped up by a loan from Canada, it kept the country afloat.

The British people had celebrated victory by voting in a socialist – Labour – government led by Clement Attlee, Deputy Prime Minister in Churchill's wartime coalition. Labour was expected to promote a fairer society sheltered by welfare provisions outlined by the economist Sir William Beveridge, at government request, in 1942. The war had accustomed people to government controls and austerity and they got more of the same as Labour attempted to juggle the state takeover of major industries – iron and steel, coal, railways, road transport, docks and harbours, electricity generation – and the creation of a welfare state with a hugely ambitious National Health Service at its core, while still preserving the appearance of great-power status by acquiring a nuclear bomb and maintaining a powerful navy, occupation forces in Germany and costly overseas establishments. Had the United States not come to the rescue again with Marshall Aid it could not have been managed.

As it was, sterling had to be drastically devalued and the great pillar of the eastern empire relinquished. Attlee, like the Americans, had long favoured self-government for India, but after the war there was no alternative. A national movement for Indian independence, institutionalized in the Hindu Congress Party and the All-India Muslim League, had been gaining momentum since the early years of the century and would not be denied; Britain lacked the military or economic strength to attempt to hold on, and her moral authority had been shattered by the loss of Singapore and her Far Eastern possessions to Japan during the war. Lord Louis Mountbatten, who as Supreme Commander South-East Asia had led the campaign driving the Japanese from Burma, was appointed last Viceroy of India to conduct the handover. It was hoped the subcontinent could be kept as a single entity, but the Muslim League demanded a separate homeland. Lines of partition were hastily drawn on the map and when Mountbatten formally ceded power in August 1947 two states came into being, India and Pakistan, the latter divided into East and West, which later separated. It was a precipitate withdrawal and the occasion of much bloodshed as refugees from different faith communities, cut off from their own kind by arbitrary lines of partition, were massacred. Nonetheless, both India and Pakistan emerged as democracies committed to the rule of law and other British values; both joined the Commonwealth, formerly the British Commonwealth of Nations; and their men continued to worship at the shrine of cricket. The United States subsequently subsidized both governments in order to preserve the subcontinent from Soviet or Chinese penetration, and as showcases for democracy in Asia. As William Roger Louis and Ronald Robinson have observed, under cold war pressure 'a once British empire modulated strategically into an Anglo-American field of influence'[56] backed by US economic and military might.

Ceylon (Sri Lanka) and Burma also gained independence – only Ceylon joined the Commonwealth – and Britain relinquished her mandates in the Middle East, withdrawing from Transjordan and Palestine as the state of Israel was formed, evacuating Egypt except for the Suez Canal zone, and abandoning traditional guarantees to Greece and Turkey, which were taken up by Truman. Britain's pretensions to world power were exposed in 1956 when the United States and the Soviet Union forced her to withdraw from an invasion of Egypt concerted with France and Israel after Egypt nationalized the Suez Canal. Subsequently she retreated from one after another of her remaining colonies in Africa and elsewhere, often after struggles with nationalist forces, a regression aptly described by Paul Kennedy as 'the death spasms of a sinking empire'.[57] Nonetheless, the former colonies generally joined the Commonwealth and, like India and Pakistan, received American development aid under the aegis of the World Bank to prevent them falling to communism; thus, again, Britain's formal empire gave way to an informal Anglo-American imperium. As Louis and Robinson put it, the United States had learned, like Palmerston and even Gladstone, 'that the international economy required imperial protection'.[58]

It was at home that Britain's decline was most precipitous. She had come out of the war with much of her industry and transport system worn out, and while state subsidies would have been necessary to restore the railways and no doubt other sectors, the wholesale nationalization and welfare programmes on which Labour embarked with insufficient funds, however well meaning, were hardly conducive to manufacturing innovation or productivity; nor was her resumption of traditional trades within the Commonwealth. For victors in the war there was little incentive to change, and management and worker relations remained hierarchical. Above all, neither Labour nor Conservative governments were able to control the increased sense of power of organized labour. For whatever causes, Britain failed to match the economic growth of West Germany, and during the 1960s fell behind France and Japan too.[59]

By this time Conservatives were in power. The Prime Minister, Harold Macmillan, suddenly perceived the likely explanation for Britain's relative economic failure; perhaps it was not so much government control of major industries or lack of investment or appalling industrial relations – which Margaret Thatcher would combat so effectively later – or even high spending on defence and overseas commitments to maintain a seat at the top table of international diplomacy, or the strain of supporting sterling as a world currency, but simply because Britain had refused to join the European Economic Community – EEC – formed in 1957 and led by France and Germany. He set about rectifying the 'mistake'. The situation was analogous, although not directly comparable, with that of the Dutch republic after she lost maritime supremacy in the eighteenth century; having supported her successor, Great Britain, against Bourbon France, in January 1795 she threw open her gates to welcome in the armies of revolutionary France, thereby losing the 'true freedom' which had been her pride, and paying a terrible economic price.[60]

The concept of the EEC had sprung from anti-war idealism in the wake of the mass slaughter of the First World War. Convinced that the war had been caused by the egotism of individual nations, minds had turned to 'intergovernmental' or 'supranational' organizations that could maintain international peace and security. The League of Nations had been established for this purpose, and it was two officials of the League who instigated the EEC after the Second World War: an Englishman, Arthur Salter, and a French political economist, Jean Monnet. Salter had published a collection of papers in 1931 entitled *The United States of Europe*; the fundamental idea, borrowed from the customs union formed by the individual states of Germany in the nineteenth century, was that the European nations should join to form a 'common market' surrounded by a tariff wall for imports from outside; he drew the conclusion:

the commercial and tariff policy of European states is so central and crucial a part of their general policy, the receipts from Customs are so central and substantial a part of their revenue, that a common political authority, deciding for all Europe what tariffs should be imposed and how they should be distributed, would be for every country almost as important, or even more important than, the national governments, and would in effect reduce the latter to the status of municipal authorities.[61]

Salter saw this 'common political authority' as a body composed of officials who had transcended nationality and owed allegiance only to the supranational authority they served. This was the seed Monnet planted in the torn soil of western Europe after the Second World War, deliberately obscuring his supranational goal, first in the so-called Schuman Plan of 1950 integrating the coal and steel industries of France, Germany, Belgium, Holland and Luxembourg, next in the 1957 Treaty of Rome bringing into being the EEC – or 'Common Market' – comprising the above-mentioned five countries and Italy, and formally dedicated to 'ever closer union'.[62]

If Monnet was the visionary schemer, the impetus and funding came from the United States; indeed, Marshall Aid was designed to encourage a federal – not supranational – United States of Europe on the lines of a United States of America; the CIA's largest operation in western Europe was directed towards that goal.[63] This was chiefly for the purposes of containing communism and safeguarding the large western European market for US business, but it was also driven by the American urge to export US values and political culture; many of those working for the CIA towards a united Europe were liberals or idealists with a strong belief in the United Nations.[64]

Instead of a democratic, free-trading polity in the image of the United States they helped Monnet create the nucleus of its polar opposite, an inward-looking protectionist bloc directed by a supranational body named the 'European Commission' sitting in Brussels. The Commission was complemented by a 'Council of Ministers' representing the member countries of the EEC, a 'European Court of Justice' to interpret Community law, which overrode the laws of member countries, and an 'Assembly' of delegates from national parliaments, later turned into a 'European Parliament' with members elected in member countries. Like Bismarck's Reichstag and the Japanese Diet of the Meiji era, the European Parliament was a democratic fig leaf with no power to originate legislation; all new laws and regulations were and are proposed by the Commission in Brussels, negotiated in secret by a committee of bureaucrats from the member countries and approved or not, again in secret, by the Council of Ministers with a system of qualified majority voting. Member countries can veto new laws only in especially sensitive areas of policy, and these have been constantly eroded. Since the Commissioners are appointed, not elected, and cannot be voted out of office, the system is profoundly anti-democratic and designed to be so to cut out national 'egotism'. It has closer affinities to the Bolshevik apparatus of Party Secretariat and Politburo than to any Anglo-Saxon system of representative government; and since the public has no access to the work of the Commission or Council of Ministers, corruption, jobbery and all forms of political skulduggery are built in.

This was the Frenchified system of top-down government by professional bureaucrats Macmillan proposed to join in order to cure Britain's disappointing economic performance. The Labour leader, Hugh Gaitskell, warned of the consequences in a remarkable speech to his party conference in 1962: with 'ever-closer union' as laid down in the Treaty of Rome, Britain would become no more than a province of Europe. 'We must be clear about this: it does mean . . . the end of Britain as an independent state . . . it means the end of a thousand years of history.'[65]

He exaggerated. It meant the end of 273 years of British history since the 'Glorious Revolution' had imposed parliamentary checks on the executive power of the monarch. Neither Macmillan's Cabinet nor the media seemed to care. It was left to France in the person of General de Gaulle to veto British entry – a fine irony except that, as Christopher Booker and Richard North have argued, de Gaulle feared that Britain as a member of the Community would block a proposed Common Agricultural Policy – CAP – designed to rescue the French rural economy from collapse.[66] It was only after France had tied Germany, the major European industrial power, in to the CAP that Britain was permitted to join.

By this time Macmillan's Minister for Europe, Edward Heath, was Prime Minister, and it had become clear that the Community was moving on to the next stage of 'ever-closer union', towards economic and monetary integration. A Foreign Office report for Heath spelled out the consequences for British entry, in effect echoing Gaitskell's predictions of loss of sovereignty to a European superstate. Somehow the report's authors saw 'no real reason why UK interests should significantly suffer'.[67] Heath was, in any case, personally committed to the European project. He plunged into negotiations, swallowing the grotesque Common Agricultural Policy, which was to do so much to poison the English countryside, alienate Commonwealth countries and produce obscene mountains of surplus foodstuffs, and surrendering the rich fishing grounds around Britain to a Common Fisheries Policy which allowed all member countries equal access. At the same time he led a campaign to convince the people they were doing no more than joining a 'common market' which would lead to an increase in trade and prosperity.

This was the great betrayal. It was not the rush to join — Heath's motives were idealistic — it was the deliberate deception played on the British people about what a government White Paper of the time called the loss of 'essential national sovereignty'.[68] With national sovereignty gone, freedom would inevitably wither, since the historical record is clear that individual freedoms can be preserved only by checking the power of the executive. The EEC was built on the opposing principle of absolute power: the European Commission, in effect its combined legislature and executive, is deliberately designed to transcend the concerns of the member countries and peoples in pursuit of a theoretical common good.

Heath was aided in his campaign of concealment by the liberal intelligentsia in the Foreign Office, the BBC and press — with honourable exceptions — and ultimately by the British people, who again demonstrated impermeability to ideas. Once this had been a healthy trait — they had not fallen for French theories or Bolshevik utopias — but over recent years their lack of curiosity on matters not practical and present has allowed them to vote in two Labour prime ministers dedicated to surrendering the country, bound and constitutionally tied to the Community, now called the European Union, or EU. No doubt the British are aware of practical dangers from the EU, but unless they awake to the more abstract lessons of European history they will soon lose those individual liberties which Edmund Burke described as 'an entailed inheritance derived to us from our forefathers, and to be transmitted to our posterity'.[69] The signs are only too apparent.

The burden falling on the United States cannot be overstated. The old ways that brought her to world power can no longer serve. Hitherto the costs of growth were ignored since the price was paid by other species and ecosystems and the earth itself in depletion of resources. Now that countries with enormous populations have dedicated themselves to economic growth in the image of the West it will no longer be possible: cost is rising exponentially as space and resources diminish. Economic growth cannot be indefinitely sustainable, and we are approaching the limits in a number of areas;[70] on the other hand economic decline is a recipe for strife and anarchy. It is probably only a free people which can think itself out of this perilous paradox, not the demos, but the few geniuses nourished in freedom and empowered by free institutions. Britain, whose record in ideas and inventions is second to none, will inevitably lose her freedoms as she submits to the European embrace. The European Union itself will stagnate and, like the former Soviet Union, implode before the economic advance of China and the Pacific Rim. China, the looming world power, has never been free, and may also disintegrate as market necessities grind against Communist Party control.

Over the past 400 years, as these volumes have sought to demonstrate, a few great maritime powers have consistently triumphed over their continental rivals, and their societies have enjoyed greater levels of personal freedom and material prosperity. Now that their economic system has brought the world to the edge of the abyss, some humility is due, some acceptance of responsibility for crowding out other species, some recognition of the often hideous cruelty involved in the use of other species as commodities in the mass production of food and as subjects for scientific experimentation – and some acknowledgement that material acquisition, like conquest, leads to ever more unsatisfied desires and broken societies. The free market and science and technology have brought us to the precipice. What else can lead us away? Historians cannot foresee the future, but any historian attempting to base predictions on the bloody record of the 400 years covered by these volumes can hardly be optimistic.

Notes

Introduction

1. J. S. Mill, Introduction to Tocqueville, ii, p. xlvii.
2. E. L. Jones, p. 1; and see Padfield, *Maritime Power*, p. 13.
3. Ferguson, *Empire*, p. xxv.

Chapter 1: The British Empire

1. In full *An Inquiry into the Nature and Causes of the Wealth of Nations, published in 2 vols 1776–78, with additions and corrections 1784.*
2. Pierre Verger, cited Thomas, p. 575.
3. See Sir James Watt, 'The Health of Seamen in Anti-slavery Squadrons', Mar.M, vol. 88, no. 1 (Feb. 2002), pp. 70ff; and see Padfield, *Rule Britannia*, pp. 113–14.
4. Hansard, *Parliamentary Debates*, 10 March 1830, cited Guedalla, p. 129.
5. Cited Thomas, p. 734.
6. Ibid., p. 746.
7. Cain and Hopkins, p. 35.
8. Rothschild's view recorded in Francis Bamford and the Duke of Wellington (eds), *The Journal of Mrs Arbuthnot*, London, 1950, I, pp. 390–91; cited Kynaston, II, p. 42; see also ibid., p. 124.
9. See Thornton, pp.47–8
10. Kynaston, I, p. 167.
11. Select Committee on the Bank Acts, P.P. 1857–58, 99. 1700–02; cited Kynaston, I, p. 167.
12. Ferguson, *Banker*, p. 132; and see Ferguson, *Cash Nexus*, p. 290.
13. See Cain and Hopkins, pp. 299, 307 (re. Chile), 315 (re. Argentina).
14. M. L. Magill, 'John H. Dunn and the Bankers', in Johnson, *Historical Essays on Upper Canada*, p. 214; cited Cain and Hopkins, p. 271.
15. See Ferguson, *Banker*, p. 272; and Ferguson, *Cash Nexus*, p. 290, quoting Heinrich Heine.
16. H. Heine, 'Ludwig Börne' (1840), in *Sämtliche Schriften*, Munich, 1971, IV, p. 28; cited Ferguson, *Banker*, p. 228.
17. See Cain and Hopkins, pp. 119–20.
18. See Kynaston, I, p. 166.
19. See Cain and Hopkins, pp. 31f; A. N. Wilson, *Victorians*, pp. 279ff.
20. Hughes, p. 401.

319

21. Macaulay, p. 293.
22. Mr Roebuck, cited Arnold, pp. 18–19.
23. Captain Cooper Key, cited Colomb, p. 178.
24. Ibid., p. 164.
25. Arnold, 'Heinrich Heine', p. 132.
26. Ibid., p. 133.
27. Arnold, 'The Function of Criticism at the Present Time', p. 12.
28. Burke, pp. 183–4.
29. Arnold, 'The Function of Criticism at the Present Time', p. 14.
30. Ferguson, *Empire*, p. xxii.
31. Montaigne, 'Apology for Raymond de Sebonde', in *Essays*, Bordeaux, 1588; cited Singer, p. 199.

Chapter 2: The Russian (Crimean) War, 1854

1. Magnus, p. 35.
2. Ibid., p. 110; also pp. 105–8; and see A. N. Wilson, *Victorians*, p. 356.
3. Cited A. N. Wilson, *Victorians*, p. 174.
4. 28 March 1854; Magnus, p. 115.
5. Graham to Dundas, 24 Jan. 1854; cited A. Lambert, p. 84.
6. Kennedy, *Great Powers*, p. 226.
7. Ibid., p. 393.
8. Dundas to Admiralty, 4 June 1855; Bonner-Smith, p. 60.
9. Dundas to Admiralty, 13 Aug. 1855; ibid., p. 185.
10. Rear Admiral Pénaud to Minister of Marine, 11 Aug. 1855; cited *The Times*, London, 20 Aug. 1855.
11. *The Times*, London, 9 Oct. 1855; cited Bonner-Smith, p. 11.
12. See Padfield, *Battleship*, p. 16.
13. Cited Baxter, p. 301.
14. Exports were down four-fifths on 1853 figures, imports down only by one third; ibid., pp. 298–9.
15. Kynaston, II, p. 191.
16. See A. Lambert, p. 332.

Chapter 3: The Indian Mutiny, 1857

1. See David, p. 9: 45,000 European to 232,000 Indian soldiers.
2. James, p. 121.
3. 'Minute on Education', cited David, p. 73.
4. David, p. 146.
5. Ferguson, *Empire*, p. 174, provides figures showing that the Indian army constituted 62 per cent of all British garrisons in the empire in 1881, and quotes Lord Salisbury's description of India as 'an English barracks in the Oriental Seas from which we may draw any number of troops without paying for them'; and see Cain and Hopkins, p. 330.
6. See Padfield, *Maritime Power*, pp. 371–4.
7. See Lubbock, p. 4.

8. See Padfield, *Maritime Power*, pp. 19–21.
9. See Reischauer, pp. 110–11.

Chapter 4: The American Civil War, 1861

1. Cited Derek Tangye, *The Confusion Room*, Michael Joseph, 1996, p. 111.
2. J. S. Gordon, p. 86.
3. See Batty and Parish, p. 20.
4. John L. O'Sullivan in *United States Magazine and Democratic Review*, July/Aug. 1845; cited *Encycl. Britannica*, VII, p. 777.
5. Cited *Encycl. Britannica*, XXIII, p. 44.
6. Cited Batty and Parish, p. 49.
7. To Layard, Foreign Office, 20 Oct. 1861; BM Add Mss 38987; cited Guedalla, p. 376.
8. Cited *Encycl. Britannica*, XXIII, p. 45.
9. Secretary of Confederate Navy; cited H. W. Wilson, I, p. 3.
10. See Padfield, *Battleship*, pp. 25–6.
11. Cited. Kemp, p. 555.
12. See Reynolds, pp. 384–5.
13. Hill, p. 119.
14. Cited Batty and Parish, p. 93.
15. The fifth of five ms. copies which must have reflected afterthoughts inserted in the address; *Encycl. Britannica*, V, p. 229.
16. Cited Burrows and Wallace, p. 877.
17. See pp. 38–9.
18. Cited Hill, p. 135.
19. J. S. Gordon, p. 94.
20. Foreign Office memo, 5 Oct. 1861; FO 84/1150; cited ibid., p. 775.
21. Antonio Maria Fabié, *Diario del congreso*, 1864–65, 6 May 1865; cited ibid., p. 781.
22. Ibid., pp. 784–5.
23. See Cain and Hopkins, pp. 300–301.
24. See p. 42.

Chapter 5: Pax Britannica

1. See Magnus, pp. 149, 150.
2. P. H. Colomb, *Slave Catching in the Indian Ocean*, Longman Green, 1873, p. 269; cited Padfield, *Rule Britannia*, p. 124.
3. C. Darwin, *On the Origin of Species by Natural Selection, or the Preservation of Favoured Races in the Struggle for Life*, John Murray, 1859; cited *Encycl. Britannica*, vol. XVIII, p. 857.
4. Warner, p. 259.
5. Fox, p. 28.
6. Burrows and Wallace, p. 733.
7. Cain and Hopkins, p. 364.
8. Padfield, *Rule Britannia*, p. 171.
9. Cain and Hopkins, p. 365.

10. Kynaston, I, p. 338.
11. Cited Padfield, *Battleship*, p. 100.
12. Hill, p. 185; Padfield, *Battleship*, p. 100.
13. 13 Sept. 1882.
14. Selborne to Salisbury, 26 March 1896; cited Pakenham, p. 47.
15. See Pakenham, p. 20.
16. See ibid., pp. 31–2.
17. Ibid., p. 259.
18. Kynaston, II, p. 196; and see p. 54 above.
19. Salisbury to Lansdowne, 30 Aug. 1899; cited Pakenham, p. 94.
20. Kynaston, II, p. 197.
21. Pakenham, p. 249.
22. Ferguson, *Empire*, p. 277, states that 27,927 Boers died in the camps, the majority children; for conditions in the camps, see Pakenham, pp. 505 ff; and p. 572 states that deaths in the camps were estimated at between 18,000 and 28,000, against *c.* 7,000 Boers serving in commandos killed. For the Anglophobic propaganda uses of British concentration camps, see Kennedy, *Anglo-German Antagonism*, p. 247.
23. See Pakenham, pp. 486–7, 511–12.
24. See, for instance, Hobsbawm, *Age of Empire*, pp. 66–7, 72–3.
25. Cain and Hopkins, p. 393.
26. See Ferguson, *Empire*, pp. 240, 242–3; Kennedy, *Great Powers*, pp. 285, 296; *Times Atlas of World History*, pp. 252–3.
27. Cain and Hopkins, p. 170.
28. Ibid., p. 395.
29. Hobsbawm, *Age of Empire*, p. 350.
30. Cited Padfield, *Battleship*, p. 114.

Chapter 6: Aspirant Navies: the United States

1. See Kennedy, *Naval Mastery*, pp. 188–90.
2. This phrase from John Seeley, *The Expansion of England*, London, 1883; cited ibid., pp. 190–91.
3. Mackinder, *Britain and the British Seas*, p. 343.
4. Mackinder, *Geographical Pivot*, pp. 30, 41.
5. Ibid., p. 41.
6. Ibid.
7. Ibid., p. 43.
8. Mahan, *Sea Power upon History*, p. 88.
9. Kennedy, *Great Powers*, pp. 209, 261.
10. See Thiesen, pp. 428ff.
11. Scott, pp. 149–52.
12. Speech before the Hamilton Club, Chicago, April 1899, in Roosevelt, pp. 19–20.
13. See Hill, p. 198.
14. R. D. Evans, captain of USS *Iowa*, *A Sailor's Log*, Appleton, 1938, p. 445.
15. Ibid.

16. Treaty of Paris, Dec. 1898.
17. Speech before the Hamilton Club, Chicago, April 1899; Roosevelt, p. 31.
18. In *The Independent*, 21 Dec. 1899; ibid., p. 45.

Chapter 7: Aspirant Navies: Imperial Japan

1. See Lord Selborne memorandum, 'Balance of Naval Power in the Far East', 4 Sept. 1901; PRO Cabinet Papers 37/58/87; cited Kennedy, *Naval Mastery*, p. 213.
2. See p. 31 above.
3. See Jones, p. 151.
4. Ibid., p. 155.
5. Captain Vasilii Galownin, *Memoirs of Captivity in Japan in the Years 1811, 1812 and 1813*, London, 1824, pp. 82–94; cited Livingston et al., p. 10.
6. Ibid., p. 11.
7. See W. G. Beasley, 'Town Life and Tokugawa Culture', in Livingston et al., p. 63.
8. 'Imperial Rescripts: The Great Principles of Education, 1879', in Livingston et al., p. 152.
9. See Herbert Passin, 'Mori Arinori', in Livingston et al., pp. 148–51.
10. See E. H. Norman, 'Early Industrialisation', in Livingston et al., pp. 117–21.
11. See Nobutaka Ike, 'Ito and the Constitution', in Livingston et al., pp. 187–9.
12. See Walter McLaren, 'A Political History of Japan during the Meiji Era', in Livingston et al., p. 207; Bix, pp. 8–10, 28–9; Bergamini, pp. 277–8.
13. See Marlene Mayo, 'Attitudes towards Asia and the Beginnings of Japanese Empire', in Livingston et al., p. 214.
14. See Padfield, *Battleship*, pp. 134–6.
15. Ibid., p. 134.
16. See p. 66 above.
17. See James Crowley, 'Creation of an Empire, 1896–1910', in Livingston et al., pp. 225–6.

Chapter 8: Aspirant Navies: Imperial Germany

1. Ousby, p. 155; Kennedy, *Great Powers*, p. 255.
2. Kennedy, *Great Powers*, p. 257.
3. Ibid., p. 190.
4. Ousby, p. 156.
5. Ernest Renan, *La Guerre entre la France et l'Allemagne*, 1870, in *Oeuvres complètes*, I, p. 433; cited Ousby, p. 159.
6. To Charles Norton, 1897; cited Birkenhead, pp. 183–4.
7. Cited Padfield, *Naval Race*, p. 104.
8. H. O. Arnold-Foster, 'Notes on a visit to Kiel and Wilhelmshaven', Aug. 1902; PRO ADM 116/940B.
9. Remarks on ibid. by Admiral R. Custance.
10. See Röhl, *Kaiser and Court*, p.119 : 'the conclusion seems inescapable that Kaiser Wilhelm II was the originator and co-author of the 'Tirpitz Plan', this is even more the case in relation to the second Navy Bill of 1900'.
11. See ibid., p. 25.

12. Vicky to Queen Victoria, 28 Apr. 1863 and 10 Dec. 1866, in R. Fulford, *Dearest Mama*, Evans, 1968.
13. See Padfield, *Naval Race*, p. 32.
14. See Röhl, *Kaiser and Court*, pp. 3–4.
15. To Karl Marx, 13 Apr. 1866; cited Crankshaw, p. 233.
16. Röhl, *Kaiser and Court*, p. 4.
17. See ibid., p. 5; Kennedy, 'The Kaiser and German *Weltpolitik*', in Röhl and Sombart, pp. 146ff.
18. See p. 75.
19. Marschall von Bieberstein diary entry, 5 Feb. 1895; cited Röhl, *Kaiser and Court*, p. 119.
20. Cited Dorpalen, p. 232.
21. See Kennedy, *Anglo-German Antagonism*, p. 226.
22. Ibid., p. 227.
23. Cited in Appendix, Steinberg.
24. A. v. Tirpitz, *Politische Dokumente der Aufbau der deutschen Weltmacht,* Berlin, 1924, I, p. 136; cited Kennedy, '*Maritime Strategieprobleme der deutsch-englischen Flotten rivalität*', in Schottelius and Deist, p. 179.
25. Szögyeny to Goluchowski, 5 Feb. 1900, HHSt.A Vienna, PA III/153; cited Kennedy, *Anglo-German Antagonism*, p. 241.
26. See V. Berghahn, '*Der Tirpitz Plan und die Krisis des presussisch-deutschen Herrschaftssystems*', in Schottelius and Deist, pp. 93–4.
27. Cited Steinberg, p. 195.
28. Röhl, *Kaiser and Court*, p. 119.
29. See Padfield, *Naval Race*, p. 93.
30. See Tirpitz's *Stichpunkte für seinem Immediatvortrag in Rominten*, 28 Sept. 1899; cited V. Berghahn, '*Der Tirpitz Plan und die Krisis des preussisch-deutschen Herrschaftssystems*', in Schottelius and Deist, p. 95.
31. See pp. 62, 65.
32. See p. 73.
33. See Sumida, *Naval Supremacy*, esp. p. 38; and N. A. Lambert, *Fisher's Naval Revolution*, esp. p. 294.
34. Fisher had a similar blind spot for the mathematics of gunnery; see Anthony Pollen, p. 51.
35. For analysis of the technical, strategic, economic and political context in which the *Dreadnought* was designed, see Grove, pp. 415ff.
36. See Sumida, *Naval Supremacy*, pp. 50–71; and Bacon, *From 1900*, p. 101.
37. See Padfield, *Battleship*, p. 195.
38. See V. Berghahn, '*Der Tirpitz Plan*', in Schottelius and Deist, pp. 97–9.
39. Grey to Spring-Rice, 19 Feb. 1906; cited Monger, p. 281.

Chapter: 9 Tsushima, 1905

1. See p. 61.
2. Capt. D. Daragan, formerly Russian Imperial Navy, to author, 18 Oct. 1968.
3. Cdr Okuda, Imperial Japanese Navy, cited Padfield, *Rule Britannia*, p. vi.

4. Capt. D. Daragan, to author, 18 Oct. 1968; Novikoff-Priboy, esp. p. 72.
5. Cited T. Ropp, *The Development of a Modern Navy*, unpublished dissertation; cited Marder, *British Naval Policy*, p. 436.
6. Capt. D. Daragan, to author, 24 Sept. 1968.
7. *Russo-Japanese War*, vol. 1, p. 166.
8. Ibid., p. 161.
9. Ibid., p. 163.
10. Description from Capt. D. Daragan, to author, 24 Sept. 1968.
11. Novikoff-Priboy, p. 40.
12. See ibid, pp. 47–50.
13. Ibid., p. 61.
14. Ibid., p. 75.
15. Grant and Temperley, p. 346.
16. Novikoff-Priboy, p. 141.
17. Ibid., p. 103.
18. Ibid., p. 135.
19. See *Russo-Japanese War*, vol. 3, p. 50; for 'Dotter', see Padfield, *Aim Straight*, pp. 80–81.
20. *Russo-Japanese War*, vol. 3, p. 47.
21. See ibid., p. 64.
22. See Padfield, *Battleship*, p. 176.
23. See Novikoff-Priboy, p. 163.
24. *Russo-Japanese War*, vol. 3, p. 64.
25. Ibid.
26. Ibid., p. 65.
27. Ibid.
28. See Novikoff-Priboy, pp. 165–70.
29. Semenov, *Rasplata*; cited Padfield, *Battleship*, p. 178.
30. *Russo-Japanese War*, vol. 3, pp. 67–8.
31. Ibid., p. 70.
32. Ibid.
33. See Novikoff-Priboy, pp. 247–8.
34. *Russo-Japanese War*, vol. 3, p. 75.
35. See David Cannadine (ed.), *Admiral Lord Nelson: Context and Legacy*, Palgrave Macmillan, 2005, pp. 159–60.
36. Association of Old Worcesters, *Newsletter*, July 2005, pp. 13–15; *Daily Telegraph*, 6 Jan. 2005.
37. See James Crowley, 'Creation of an Empire, 1896–1910', in Livingston et al., p. 228; Reischauer, p. 140.

Chapter: 10 Long-range Gunnery

1. See Sumida, *Naval Supremacy*, pp. 75–7; Anthony Pollen, pp. 17–19.
2. *Russo-Japanese War*, vol. 3, p.163.
3. See Padfield, *Aim Straight*, pp. 146–50.
4. See Pollen's letter from HMS *Jupiter*, May 1906; Sumida, *Pollen Papers*, pp.93–4, 99.

5. A. H. Pollen testimony to Royal Commission on Awards to Inventors, 1 Aug. 1925, vol. 9, p. 84; and see Pollen to Dreyer, 18 Dec. 1907; both cited Sumida, *Naval Supremacy*, p. 123; and Sir Henry Jackson, 3rd Sea Lord, to Pollen before the trials, 'If your gear can be broken down Wilson can break it – so look out'; cited ibid., p. 126.

6. See Sumida, *Naval Supremacy*, p. 121, citing undated printed history, probably prepared for Royal Commission on Awards to Inventors hearings; also log of HMS *Ariadne*, the ship in which Pollen's gear was fitted; PRO ADM 53 17318.

7. Pollen to Hughes-Onslow, 1 Nov. 1909; cited from typescript made by Anthony Pollen from draft ms. Letter in Pollen Papers; Sumida, *Naval Supremacy*, pp. 172–3.

8. 25 Aug. 1910; Sumida, *Naval Supremacy*, p. 203; Moore had ordered the adoption of Dreyer's scheme on 13 Aug. 1910; see note 9 below.

9. Moore memo and minute, 13 Aug. 1910, in 'Invention of Range-finding System', PRO ADM 1/8131; cited Sumida, *Naval Supremacy*, p. 218.

10. See Padfield, *Guns at Sea*, pp. 226–31.

11. The Royal Commission on Awards to Inventors, 1925, judged that the Argo Clock 'directly contributed to the evolution of the clock mechanism of the earlier types of Dreyer Table into a form which served the same function and was based on the same principle as the Argo Clock and while we acquit all concerned of any intention or desire to copy or take unacknowledged the benefit of the claimant's [Pollen's] work . . . we think it impossible to question the influence of that work upon the ultimate result.' Cited Anthony Pollen, p. 255.

12. A. H. Pollen's notes of a telephone conversation with Prince Louis of Battenberg, First Sea Lord, 18 Dec. 1912; cited Sumida, *Naval Supremacy*, p. 232.

13. See Padfield, *Guns at Sea*, p. 259.

14. Peirse to Battenberg, 7 Sept. 1912; Battenberg Papers, IWM DS/MISC/20; cited Sumida, *Naval Supremacy*, p. 226.

15. Rear Admiral R. Peirse, 'Some Remarks on Mr Pollen's Plotting System', Aug. 1912; cited ibid., p. 227.

16. See especially J. T. Sumida, 'The Quest for Reach . . .'; 'A Matter of Timing . . .'; and 'Information Dominance . . .'

17. Sumida, 'Matter of Timing', pp. 95–6.

18. Ibid., Tables 1, 3, pp. 97–8.

19. Lt Cdr R. G. Studd, 'Changes in Naval Construction and Tactics', NR, Aug. 1921, p. 424.

20. John Brooks, in *Dreadnought Gunnery*, has attempted to refute Sumida's main theses. Brooks maintains that Pollen was the author of his own misfortune in his dealings with the Admiralty, and that the poor gunnery of the battlecruisers at Jutland was due to Beatty's tactical mismanagement rather than failure in fire control by the Dreyer Table. There is no doubt much truth in both points, but the book as a whole is badly organized: there is no sequential narrative of the decisive trials; and excerpts from trial reports suggest selective quotation – whether or not this is the case. The book does not carry conviction. Until Brooks or another historian technically competent in gunnery and fire control is able to organize a narrative for the enlightenment rather than the mystification of readers, Sumida will hold the field, and deservedly so.

21. For details of German fire control instrumentation see Schmallenbach, pp. 90–2.

22. See Padfield, *Guns at Sea*, pp. 258–60; Arthur Pollen, p. 199 states, 'there has been no feature of gunnery action more regularly reproduced than the rapidity with which the Germans find the range at the beginning of an action'.

Chapter 11: Towards Armageddon

1. Ferguson, *Pity of War*, esp. pp. 68ff. Ferguson's bibliography, however, lacks key works on Kaiser Wilhelm II, Tirpitz and the German fleet, notably: Berghahn's *Der Tirpitz Plan*, Steinberg's *Yesterday's Deterrent*, Röhl's *The Kaiser and his Court*; and while he lists Schottelius and Deist (eds), *Marine und Marinepolitik im kaiserlichen Deutschland*, he does not mention either Paul Kennedy's or Volker Berghahn's contributions in this volume – respectively '*Maritime Strategieprobleme der deutsche-englischen Flottenrivalität*' and '*Der Tirpitz Plan und die Krisis des preussisch-deutschen Herrschaftsystems*'. Nor does he list Paul Kennedy's 'The Kaiser and German *Weltpolitik*: Reflexions on Wilhelm II's place in the making of German foreign policy' in Röhl and Sombart (eds), *Kaiser Wilhelm II: New Interpretations*. There are other monographs he has missed, particularly by Paul Kennedy, Berghahn, Deist and Röhl, which analyse pre-1914 German governance and strategy, understandable, no doubt, in view of his wide range of sources and particular focus on economics, but symptomatic of neglect both of the reality of Wilhelm II's 'personal rule' and of Wilhelm's inspiration and support for Tirpitz's fleet. While he employs formidable intellect to demolish 'myths' surrounding the First World War his demolition of the Prussian will to war is based on false premises and insufficient research on naval affairs. It is noteworthy that Paul Kennedy's classic *The Rise and Fall of British Naval Mastery* is not included in his bibliography. These remarks apply equally to Hew Strachan's masterly recent *The First World War*.

2. See Marder, *Dreadnought to Scapa Flow*, I, p. 116.

3. See Fisher's testimony to Committee of Imperial Defence, 1909, cited T-124, p. 37; and Marder, *Dreadnought to Scapa Flow*, I, p. 119.

4. Field Marshal Sir W. Nicholson, cited Marder, *Dreadnought to Scapa Flow*, I, p. 391.

5. Wilson–Dubail agreement, July 1911; see ibid., p. 388; and see T-124, pp. 41–2.

6. Cited V. Bonham-Carter, *Winston Churchill as I Knew Him*, Eyre & Spottiswoode, 1965; cited Padfield, *Naval Race*, p. 259.

7. Churchill, I, p. 272.

8. Fisher to Spender, 31 Oct. 1911; and to G. Fiennes, 8 Feb. 1912; cited Marder, *Fear God*, II, pp. 409, 429.

9. Padfield, *Naval Race*, p. 211.

10. See ibid., p. 179: it was not until 1906 that a sum for submarine development was included in the German naval budget, and then only 5 million marks, a fraction of the cost of a single dreadnought.

11. See ibid., p. 159.

12. 7 March 1908; cited Brett, II, p. 294.

13. Padfield, *Naval Race*, p. 186.

14. To Bülow, 8 March 1906; Lepsius et al., XXIV, pp. 44–6.

15. 16 July 1908; ibid., p. 103.

16. Bülow, pp. 312–13.

17. See Padfield, *Naval Race*, p. 234n. Between 1901 and 1909 some 2,444 million marks (*c.* £122 million) had been spent on the navy, a figure that matched almost exactly the loans raised in the same period to cover deficits in Reich budgets.

18. See Ferguson, *Pity of War*, pp. 129–30, and for graphs of bond prices, pp. 133–4; and see Sumida, *Naval Supremacy*, p. 336.

19. See Berghahn, '*Der Tirpitz Plan*,' in Schottelius and Deist, pp. 105–6.

20. See Ferguson, *Pity of War*, pp. 137–40; Berghahn, '*Der Tirpitz Plan*,' in Schottelius and Deist, p. 110.

21. In Great Britain *c.* 60 per cent of defence budget went to the navy, *c.* 40 per cent to the army; in Germany 19–26 per cent went to the navy, the rest to the army; see Kennedy, 'Tirpitz, England and the second Navy Law'.

22. For instance, Lord Selborne: '[Britain's] Credit and its Navy seem to me to be the two main pillars on which the strength of this country rests, and each is essential to the other'; cited Kennedy, *Anglo-German Antagonism*, p. 325.

23. To Harden, July 1909; cited Cecil, p. 160.

24. Bülow, pp. 417–18.

25. Sir Henry Angst to Tyrrell (FO), 4 Oct. 1910; PRO FO 800 104 (Grey Papers), pp. 113–17; and see R. J. Crampton, 'August Bebel and the British Foreign Office', *History*, June 1973, pp. 218ff.

26. Marder, *Dreadnought to Scapa Flow*, I, pp. 283–4.

27. 26 March 1912; cited R. S. Churchill, *Winston Churchill 1901–1914*, Heinemann, 1967, p. 556.

28. Admiralty memo on the general naval situation, 26 Aug. 1912; Asquith Papers, Box 24, Oxford. This must have been worked up from an earlier paper as Churchill used similar phrases in a CID meeting on 11 July; see Marder, *Dreadnought to Scapa Flow*, I, p. 296.

29. See Marder, *Dreadnought to Scapa Flow*, I, p. 112.

30. Cited Röhl, 'Admiral von Müller', p. 664; and see Röhl, *Kaiser and Court*, p. 173.

31. Röhl, *Kaiser and Court*, pp. 162–5.

32. General von Wenninger to Bavarian Minister of War, cited ibid., p. 164.

33. For these preparations, see Röhl, *Kaiser and Court*, pp. 185–7.

34. Wolfgang Mommsen and others, cited ibid., pp. 177–8.

35. Ibid., pp. 178–9.

36. F. Fischer, *War of Illusions: German Policies from 1911 to 1914*, London/NY, 1975, pp. 164–7; cited Ferguson, *Pity of War*, p. 100.

37. Grant and Temperley, p. 387.

38. Röhl, *Delusion or Design?*, pp. 82–3; and see Grant and Temperley, p. 388.

39. Fischer, *Germany's Aims*, p. 37.

40. Dieter Groh, '*Je eher, desto besser! Innenpolitische Faktoren für die Präventivkriegsbereitschaft des deutschen Reiches, 1913/14*', *Politische Vierteljahresschrift*, 13 (1972), p. 506; cited Röhl, *Kaiser and Court*, p. 188.

41. See Prince Lichnowsky memo, Jan. 1915; cited Röhl, *Delusion or Design?*, pp. 82–3.

42. Röhl, *Kaiser and Court*, p. 8.
43. For all these preparations, see Berghahn and Deist, esp. p. 47. It is extraordinary that this vital monograph has been ignored by general historians studying the outbreak of the First World War.
44. Tirpitz to Capt. Hopman, 'beginning July' 1914; cited ibid., p. 46.
45. J. E. Sutton, *The Imperial Navy, 1910–1914*, unpublished doctoral dissertation, Indiana University, 1953, pp. 559–60.
46. Röhl, 'Admiral von Müller', p. 669.
47. Hansard, 5th Series, IXV, pp. 726–9.
48. Churchill, I, p. 193.
49. Grey, p. 325.
50. Tirpitz, I, p. 277.
51. 31 July 1914; cited Balfour, pp. 350–51.
52. Grey, pp. 14–15.
53. Churchill, I, p. 228.
54. Kynaston, II, p. 609.
55. See ibid., p. 610; and see Ferguson, *Pity of War*, pp. 201ff.
56. Baron E. B. d'Erlanger, *My English Souvenirs*, 1979, p. 238; cited Kynaston, II, p. 610.

Chapter 12: War, Coronel and the Falkland Islands, 1914

1. See Tirpitz, I, p. 280.
2. Bülow, p. 143.
3. Cited Padfield, *Naval Race*, citing Kennedy, *Strategieprobleme*.
4. Cited Kennedy, 'German naval operations plans', p. 69.
5. See N. A. Lambert, 'Strategic Command . . . ', pp. 377–8.
6. Admiralty Trade Division, '1909 German Trade and Shipping', undated, but 1908/09; cited ibid., p. 381.
7. See Hiley, p. 246.
8. Ibid., p. 258.
9. Beesly, p. 2.
10. Hiley, p. 259.
11. Beesly, p. 9; see also Admiral Sir W. James, p. 50.
12. See Hiley, pp. 246–8, 252–5, 266.
13. Ibid., pp. 262–3.
14. A. W. Ewing, 'Some Special War Work', Lecture, 13 Dec. 1927, p. 72; cited ibid., p. 263.
15. Beesly, p. 15; Hiley, pp. 263–4.
16. See Beesly, pp. 16–17; and Marder, *Dreadnought to Scapa Flow*, II, p. 132.
17. N. A. Lambert, 'Strategic Command . . . ', p. 403; see also Hiley, pp. 265–6.
18. Admiral Sir W. James, cited Marder, *Dreadnought to Scapa Flow*, II, p. 133.
19. Corbett, I, p. 305.
20. For an insight into Cradock's character and the ethos of the early twentieth-century Royal Navy, see Christopher Cradock, *Whispers from the Fleet*, J. Griffin, London and Portsmouth, 2nd edn, 1908.
21. Fisher's predecessor as First Sea Lord, Prince Louis of Battenberg, was not

hounded from office because of his German name and ancestry, as popular legend has it; see Marder, *Dreadnought to Scapa Flow*, II, p. 88: 'The initiative for Battenberg's resignation definitely came from the Cabinet, which wanted him removed . . .'

22. See Fisher to Beatty, 19 Nov. 1914: 'Never such utter rot as perpetrated by Sturdee in his world-wide dispersal of weak units! Strong nowhere, weak everywhere!'; Marder, *Fear God*, III, p. 77. Sturdee, however, had urged the dispatch of a battle-cruiser force to the South Atlantic after learning that von Spee was crossing the Pacific, but he had been blocked; see Marder, *Dreadnought to Scapa Flow*, II, p. 128.

23. Rintelen, pp. 218–20.

24. Beesly, p. 77.

25. See Marder, *Dreadnought to Scapa Flow*, II, p. 122.

26. Schmallenbach, p. 93, states no hits in the first half-hour.

27. For a description of the damage to the ship, see Hans Pockhammer, *Before Jutland; Admiral Spee's Last Voyage*, Jarrolds, 1931, pp. 210, 217–22, summarized in Massie, pp. 271–4; see also *Gneisenau's* gunnery officer paraphrased in Padfield, *Salt and Steel*, pp. 494–5.

28. Corbett, I, p. 426 has no casualties in either ship.

29. See *Russo-Japanese War*, vol. 3, p. 75.

30. Corbett, I, p. 436.

31. From where the enemy was always in sight: Admiral H. E. Dannreuther (gunnery officer, HMS *Invincible* at the Falklands battle) to author, 1965.

32. Interview with the engineer, Lancelot Leveson, 28 June 1965.

Chapter 13: The Dogger Bank, 1915

1. See Schmallenbach, pp. 79–80; and see anti-flash discussion at the Admiralty, PRO ADM 116/2348; and Campbell, pp. 373–4.

2. Campbell, p. 7.

3. Padfield, *Aim Straight*, p. 233; paraphrase of report in the library of HMS *Excellent*, Whale Island, now dispersed.

4. See Marder, *Dreadnought to Scapa Flow*, II, p. 160.

5. Schmallenbach, p. 78.

6. Letter to a friend, cited Thompson, p. 95.

7. Corbett, II, pp. 95–7; Marder, *Dreadnought to Scapa Flow*, II, p. 163.

8. Beatty to Jellicoe, 8 Feb. 1915; cited Marder, *Dreadnought to Scapa Flow*, II, pp. 167–8.

9. See Chatfield's letter to a friend, cited Thompson, p. 95.

10. Campbell, p. 8.

11. Naval Staff, *Technical History and Index: Fire Control in H.M. Ships*, Admiralty (TH 23), 1919, p. 21.

12. Letter to a friend, cited Thompson, pp. 100–101.

13. See ibid., pp. 101–102.

Chapter 14: The U-boat Offensive, 1915

1. See pp. 114–16.
2. See pp. 25–6.
3. See Richmond, p. 137; Chatterton, p. 62.
4. Germany had only twenty long-range U-boats and ten obsolescent coastal boats.
5. See Padfield, *Maritime Power*, pp. 266ff.
6. See Chatterton, pp. 112, 120.
7. See Corbett, II, pp. 266–7.
8. See the War Diary of Kapitänleutnant Walter Schwieger of *U20*, in *Der Krieg zur See, 1914–1918*, IV, *Nordsee*, p. 112; cited Corbett, II, p. 393n.
9. *The Times*, 10 May 1915.
10. See Chatterton, p. 229.
11. Seventy long-range boats against twenty in February 1915.
12. Corbett, II, p. 281.
13. 18 April 1916 note from Washington; Corbett, III, p. 286.

Chapter 15: Jutland, 1916 (Beatty)

1. Usborne, pp. 46–7.
2. Beesly, p. 152; Corbett, III, p. 324.
3. Campbell, p. 28; Fawcett and Hooper, 'Narrative of HMS *Galatea*', pp. 8–9.
4. Scheer, p. 141.
5. Signal sent 12.30, Beesly, p. 155; Corbett, III, p. 326.
6. A. Gordon, p. 55; Marder, *Dreadnought to Scapa Flow*, III, p. 56n.
7. See Jellicoe to Beatty, 18 Nov. 1915, and Beatty to Jellicoe, 21 Nov. 1915; Patterson, I, pp. 188–9; cited Brooks, pp. 226–7; and see N. A. Lambert, "Our Bloody Ships'", p. 42.
8. Beatty to Jellicoe, 15 Dec. 1915; Jellicoe Papers, Add. MSS 49008, f.78; cited Lambert, "'Our Bloody Ships'", p.42.
9. Beatty to Jellicoe, 7 May 1916; Beatty Papers, I, pp. 307–8; cited N. A. Lambert, "'Our Bloody Ships'", pp. 42–3.
10. A. Gordon, p. 82; Marder, *Dreadnought to Scapa Flow*, III, p. 53, writes: 'The best guess is Evan-Thomas turned on his own' – i.e. without receiving a signal.
11. Corbett, III, p. 331; Brooks, p. 233.
12. Campbell, p. 34. Most times, courses, ranges and hits in the gun action are taken from Campbell's meticulous researches.
13. Hipper's report, cited Brooks, p. 235.
14. Cited Chalmers, pp. 116–17.
15. This was in any case in the battle orders for a meeting with a numerically inferior squadron.
16. Chatfield, pp. 140–2.
17. Ranges from Campbell, p. 39; see also Brooks, pp. 235, 237.
18. Chalmers, p. 231.
19. Fawcett and Hooper, 'Narrative of the Gunnery Control Officer of HMS *Lion*', p. 107.
20. *Lion* hit six times; *Princess Royal* three; *Tiger* nine; *Queen Mary* one; *Indefatigable*

four certain and one possible; see Campbell, pp. 40–1.

21. See Fawcett and Hooper, 'Narrative from Officers of HMS *Princess Royal*', p. 19.
22. See Campbell, pp. 82–3.
23. See Campbell, pp.64–7; for the accepted account of Major Harvey giving the order to flood the magazine, see Fawcett and Hooper, 'The Effect of a Direct Hit on "Q" Turret HMS *Lion*', pp. 87–90; and Chalmers, p. 231.
24. Fawcett and Hooper, 'Narrative by the Navigating Officer of HMS *New Zealand*', pp. 28–9.
25. Corbett, III, p. 336.
26. Fawcett and Hooper, 'Loss of the *Indefatigable* and *Queen Mary*, as seen from the Conning Tower of HMS *Tiger*', p. 31.
27. Fawcett and Hooper, 'Narrative by the Navigating Officer of HMS *New Zealand*', p. 29.
28. Fawcett and Hooper, 'Narrative from the Officers of HMS *Princess Royal*', p. 20.
29. Campbell, p. 47.
30. Hase, p. 89.
31. Fawcett and Hooper, 'Loss of the *Indefatigable*', pp. 31–2.
32. Fawcett and Hooper, 'Narrative from HMS *Nicator*', p. 54.
33. Marder, *Dreadnought to Scapa Flow*, III, p. 60.
34. Churchill, III, p. 219; both Chatfield and Chalmers, who were, of course, on the bridge or compass platform at the time, cite this remark as coming after the loss of the *Queen Mary*.
35. Campbell, p. 52.
36. For detailed analysis of Beatty's signalling error, see A. Gordon, pp. 129ff; Campbell, p. 54. Campbell states that no German battleships opened fire on the 5th Battle Squadron before they had completed their turn north; Gordon, pp. 614ff, disputes this, citing eyewitness testimony, and suggesting that the German gunnery records were inadequate.

Chapter 16: Jutland, 1916 (Jellicoe)

1. Fawcett and Hooper, 'Narrative of a Midshipman Stationed in the Fore-Top of HMS *Neptune*', pp. 190–91.
2. See Sumida, 'Matter of Timing', p. 124.
3. 'A few notes on the determination of the most advantageous range at which the Grand Fleet should engage the High Seas Fleet', undated, probably after Oct. 1915; in DRYR 1/3; cited Brooks, p. 226.
4. Cited Marder, *Dreadnought to Scapa Flow*, III, p. 9; and see Sumida, 'Quest for Reach', p. 77.
5. Jellicoe to Jackson, 12 April 1916; Patterson, I, p. 232.
6. On Jellicoe's mental exhaustion, see R. Hall draft letter to Beatty, 1922; cited Anthony Pollen, p. 151.
7. Harper, p. 22.
8. Fawcett and Hooper, 'From a Turret Officer of HMS *Malaya*', p. 115.
9. See Hase, p. 103.
10. See Campbell, pp. 109, 135.

11. Marder, *Dreadnought to Scapa Flow*, III, p. 85.
12. R. K. Dickson, midshipman in HMS *Benbow* to starboard of *Iron Duke*; cited A. Gordon, p. 433.
13. Cited Massie, p. 555, with incorrect attribution.
14. Corbett, III, p. 361.
15. Dreyer, pp. 146–7.
16. See Campbell, p. 121.
17. In his memoirs he wrote that his first and natural impulse had been to deploy on his starboard wing column; Jellicoe, *The Grand Fleet, 1914–16*, p. 348; cited Corbett, III, p. 361.
18. Thirteen heavy shells and at least five 5.9-inch shells; Campbell, pp. 154, 173–9.
19. Ibid., p. 169.
20. Corbett, III, p. 367; Marder, *Dreadnought to Scapa Flow*, III, p. 99.
21. Scheer, p. 152.
22. Scheer, *Immediatbericht*, 4 June 1916; cited Marder, *Dreadnought to Scapa Flow*, III, p. 110; see also Scheer, pp. 155–6.
23. See Campbell, pp. 220–23.
24. Hase, p. 103.
25. See Campbell, p. 213.
26. See, for instance, A. Gordon, pp. 466–7; Stephen Roskill, 'The Role of Maritime Forces . . .', unpublished lecture; cited Marder, *Dreadnought to Scapa Flow*, III, p. 116.
27. Beesly, p. 161.
28. See Marder, *Dreadnought to Scapa Flow*, III, p. 138 n.11.
29. See Campbell, p. 275.
30. Hase, p. 125.
31. Paymaster Miller, HMS *Arethusa*; cited Thompson, p. 68.
32. Campbell, pp. 337–9.
33. N. A. Lambert, '"Our Bloody Ships"', p. 31.
34. Capt. Stephen Roskill to author, 18 Oct. 1969.
35. N. A. Lambert, '"Our Bloody Ships"', p. 55.
36. Ibid., p. 47.
37. Ibid., p. 32.
38. On the probability of this, see Campbell, pp. 368–9.
39. Ibid., p. 380.
40. Dr D. Jung to author, 10 May 1970; see Padfield, *Guns at Sea*, p. 278.
41. Capt. Stephen Roskill to author, 18 Oct. 1969.
42. Admiralty Staff, *Technical History and Index: Ammunition Supply and Handling*, Naval Library; cited Padfield, *Guns at Sea*, pp. 276–7; for loss of *Pommern*, see Campbell, pp. 378–9.
43. See, for instance, Captain Persius, in *Berliner Tageblatt*, 18 Nov. 1918: 'On 1 June 1916 it was clear to every thinking person that this battle must, and would be, the last one. Authoritative quarters [Wilhelm II and Scheer] said so openly'; cited Marder, *Dreadnought to Scapa Flow*, III, p. 206.
44. *Jutland Despatches*, p. 600; cited Marder, *Dreadnought to Scapa Flow*, III, p. 206; and see Scheer, p. 177.

Chapter 17: Unrestricted U-boat War, 1917

1. Cited Scheer, pp. 248–9.
2. Newbolt, IV, p. 323.
3. Marder, *Dreadnought to Scapa Flow*, IV, p. 71.
4. Mahan, *French Revolution*, II, p. 217.
5. See Operations Division, Admiralty War Staff, 'Remarks on Submarine Warfare, 1917'; Technical History Monograph TH 14 (1919), *The Atlantic Convoy System, 1917–1918*, p. 3; cited Marder, *Dreadnought to Scapa Flow*, IV. pp. 121–2.
6. Marder, *Dreadnought to Scapa Flow*, IV, p. 102.
7. Cited ibid., p. 97. For discussion of this institutional rigidity, see ibid., pp. 134ff. Marder blames excessive centralization at the Admiralty: the First Sea Lord and the Chief of War Staff had exclusive control of operations, and it was no one's business to think or plan ahead. Yet was not the Anti Submarine Division created for just that purpose?
8. Cecil and Liddle, p. 243.
9. See Lash, p. 45.
10. See Ferguson, *Pity of War*, pp. 328–9; and Strachan, p. 222.
11. See Beesly, p. 216.
12. See ibid., p. 223.
13. Cited Lash, p. 50.
14. See Patrick Quinn, 'The Experience of War in American Patriotic Literature', in Cecil and Liddle, pp. 757–9.
15. Arthur Guy Empney, *From the Fire Step: The Experiences of an American Soldier in the British Army*, Putnam, 1917 (US edn *Over the Top*), p. 7; cited ibid., p. 757.
16. See Lash, p. 48; and see Admiral Fullam's testimony in Cecil and Liddle, p. 43.
17. W. Sims, *The Victory at Sea*, Murray, 1920, p. 9; cited Marder, *Dreadnought to Scapa Flow*, IV, p. 148.
18. Newbolt, IV, pp. 379–80.
19. Cited ibid., V, p. 10.
20. Marder, *Dreadnought to Scapa Flow*, IV, pp. 150–52.
21. Newbolt, V, p. 19.
22. David Lloyd George, *War Memoirs*, Nicholson & Watson, 1933–36, III, pp. 1162–3; cited Marder, *Dreadnought to Scapa Flow*, IV, p. 161.
23. See, for instance Marder, *Dreadnought to Scapa Flow*, IV, pp. 186–7, 189–90.
24. Ibid., p. 182.
25. Ibid., pp. 263–4.
26. 394,115 tons; ibid., p. 277.
27. *Imperialism, the Highest Stage of Capitalism*, 1917; see *Encyclopaedia Britannica*, XXII, pp. 949, 952.
28. See Applebaum, pp. 3–5, 29ff.
29. Treaty of Bucharest, 7 May 1918.
30. See Strachan, p. 284.
31. Martin Kitchen, 'Ludendorff and Germany's Defeat', in Cecil and Liddle, p. 51.
32. Ibid., p. 52; and see Strachan, 'The Morale of the German Army, 1917–1918', in ibid., p. 386.

33. John Terraine, 'The Substance of War', in ibid., p. 10; Strachan, p. 312, states that 945,052 shells were fired in twenty-four hours to 29 September 1918.

34. Forty-two US divisions comprising some two million men by November 1918; Strachan, p. 302.

35. See Strachan, 'The Morale of the German Army, 1917–1918', in Cecil and Liddle, p. 395.

36. See Herwig, pp. 243–4.

37. Ibid., p. 264.

Chapter 18: The Baton Passes

1. In August, September and October 1918 over 300,000 German soldiers surrendered to the Allies; see Ferguson, *Pity*, pp. 368–70.

2. Macmillan, p. 171.

3. Cited ibid., p. 475.

4. Cited Marder, *Dreadnought to Scapa Flow*, V, p. 246.

5. See Macmillan, p. 484.

6. Burleigh, pp. 32–3, has 9 million war dead across Europe; and see Fisher, pp. 1156–7.

7. See Ferguson, *Pity*, p. 408; Macmillan, pp. 196, 490.

8. See Macmillan, p. 477.

9. Ferguson, *Pity*, p. 414; Macmillan, pp. 490–91.

10. It has been estimated that by 1932 Germany had paid between 19 and 22 billion gold marks, while receiving loans totalling 27 billion, on which she defaulted; see Ferguson, *Pity*, p. 417; Macmillan, p. 490.

11. Ferguson, *Pity*, pp. 421–2.

12. See Haffner, p. 47; Burleigh, pp. 57, 77–8, 80.

13. Haffner, pp. 41–2.

14. See Padfield, *Dönitz*, pp. 96, 102, 104, 111–12, 117–18; Macmillan, pp. 491–2.

15. The version accepted by British and German academics is that the Dutch communist youth, Marinus van der Lubbe, was the sole perpetrator. Comprehensive studies by the Internationales Komitee Luxemburg and Alexander Bahar and Wilfred Kugel, however, leave no doubt that the Reichstag fire was a carefully prepared pretext by the Nazis, probably devised by Hitler's propaganda chief, Joseph Goebbels, and carried out by a special paramilitary team which entered the building via an underground passage from the official residence of the Reichstag president, Hermann Göring, Prussian Minister of the Interior.

16. See Kershaw, I, p. 524; Padfield, *Himmler*, p. 160.

17. Britain had forty-two dreadnoughts, equal to the combined total of dreadnoughts in the fleets of the USA, France, Italy and Japan – excluding Germany's interned fleet.

18. See Kennedy, *Great Powers*, pp. 257–9; Kynaston, III, p. 59.

19. On 30 Dec 1918 the US Secretary of the Navy told the Naval Affairs Committee of Congress that the United States would need a navy 'bigger than any other in the world'; Marder, *Dreadnought to Scapa Flow*, V, pp. 225–6.

20. Cited ibid., p. 231.

21. First Lord of the Admiralty memorandum, 29 March 1919; Lloyd George MSS; cited ibid., p. 232.
22. Daniels to Capt. Dudley Knox, USN, 29 Jan. 1937; Benson Correspondence, US Navy Dept. MSS; cited ibid., p. 231.
23. See Macmillan, pp. 153–4.
24. See Kennedy, *Great Powers*, p. 386; Macmillan, p. 321.
25. See pp. 66–70 above.
26. See Ford, p. 283; and Honan, p. 63. Homer Lea's *The Valor of Ignorance*, NY, 1909, alerted the American public to Japan's dangerous ambitions in the Pacific in the same way as Erskine Childers' *Riddle of the Sands*, 1903, had alerted the British public to the threat posed by Germany.
27. Admiralty War Staff, 'Neutral Powers', 30 Dec. 1916; Beatty MSS; cited Marder, *Dreadnought to Scapa Flow*, V, p. 237.
28. see Padfield, *Battleship*, p. 250; O'Connor, pp. 4–5, 145.
29. This was Captain Allen Buchanan; Bergamini, pp. 406–7.
30. *Sea Power in the Pacific: A Study of the American–Japanese Naval Problem*, Constable, London/Houghton Mifflin, Boston and NY, 1921.
31. *The Great Pacific War: A History of the American–Japanese Campaign of 1931–33*, Constable, London/Houghton Mifflin, Boston and NY, 1925.
32. As recollected by Ichitaro Oshima, Yamamoto gave a lecture at the Navy Torpedo School soon after his return to Japan, stressing that the only chance of victory against the USA would be a pre-emptive strike against their fleet base; Compilation Committee, Government Documents, Japanese, vol. I, p. 278; cited Honan, pp. 187–8.
33. See Honan, pp. 179–80; Bergamini, p. 400.
34. O'Connor, pp. 81–2.
35. London Naval Treaty, Part IV, Art. 22 (2); cited O'Connor, p. 143.
36. Barnett, pp. 26–7
37. Kennedy, *Naval Mastery*, p. 285.
38. See Bix, pp. 23–57, 60–62; Bergamini, p. 312.
39. See Bergamini, p. 292; Bix, pp. 33ff.
40. See Reischauer, p. 156; Bergamini, pp. 396–7.
41. Bergamini, pp. 415–17.
42. Bix, pp. 228ff, gives a nuanced account suggesting that Hirohito was unprepared for the army's action, but endorsed it since it coincided with his aims.
43. See Bergamini, pp. 508ff.
44. John K. Emmerson, 'The Japanese Communist Party', in Livingston et al., p. 399.
45. Lord Lytton Commission Report; cited Bergamini, pp. 558–9.
46. Steinbach, p. 66.
47. See Kershaw, I, p. 408.
48. George Steiner, 'The Women Who Waited', review of Claudia Koonz, *Mothers in Fatherland*, Cape, 1987.
49. See Burleigh, pp. 229–32.
50. Steiner, 'The Women Who Waited'.

51. Hani Setsuko, *The Japanese Family System*, Tokyo, 1948, pp. 9–19, 26–8; cited Livingston et al., pp. 424ff.
52. See Bergamini, pp. 35–48.
53. See Padfield, *Himmler*, p. 270.

Chapter 19: Hitler's War, 1939

1. See Padfield, *Maritime Supremacy*, pp. 119–24, 127–8, 154–6, 168–9.
2. See Stafford, *Roosevelt and Churchill*, pp. 7–8.
3. Lash, pp. 25–6.
4. Cited Bailey and Ryan, p. 29.
5. Cited Lash, p.23.
6. See Dülffer, pp. 566–7; Kershaw, I, p. 554.
7. See pp. 60–1; and Padfield, *Hess*, p. 24.
8. *Raeder Akte: Gespräch mit dem Führer im Juni 1934*; Naval Library, PG 34004; see also Deist, p. 75.
9. See Naval Staff memo, 'Anglo-German Naval Discussion', PRO CAB 24/222; cited Haraszti, p. 103.
10. Montagu Norman, cited Kynaston, III, p. 433; see also Kershaw, I, p. 553.
11. The 'Hossbach Memorandum', 5 Nov. 1937; IMT Doc. 386-PS.
12. H. Heye, *Denkschrift, 'Seekriegsführung gegen England'*, 25 Oct. 1938; cited Salewski, III, p. 30.
13. See , for instance, Overy, *Interrogations*, pp. 221–4.
14. E. Raeder, '*Aufzeichnung*', 3 Sept. 1939; Naval Library, PG 32183, 1 Skl, Teil C VII.
15. Hansard, 5 Nov. 1937; and see Waters, p. 132.
16. Gretton, p. 20.
17. See H. P. Willmott, 'The Organisations: The Admiralty and the Western Approaches', in Howarth and Law, p. 180.
18. Ibid., p. 181; and see David Lyon, 'The British Order of Battle', in Howarth and Law, p. 267.
19. Interrogation of *UB 68* prisoners, NA ADM 137 3900.
20. *Beurteilung*, Nov. 1930; *P/Akte*, personal records of Grand Admiral Karl Dönitz, Naval Library, PG 31044.
21. *Beurteilung*, 1 Nov. 1936; ibid.
22. See K. Dönitz, *Die Verwendung von U-Booten im Rahmen des Flottenverbandes*, 23 Nov. 1937, Naval Library PG 33970.
23. K. Dönitz, *Bericht über FdU Kriegspiel*, 1939; Naval Library PG 33390.
24. Ibid.
25. See p. 209 above.
26. See *Gedanken über den Einsatz der deutschen U-bootswaffe, Anfang September 1939*; Naval Library PG 33970.
27. See Padfield, *Dönitz*, p. 104.
28. Shirer, p. 190.
29. Ibid., pp. 316, 319, 321, 334, 348–9.
30. IMT, vol. 13, Doc. C-191, p. 356.
31. Admiralty, Anti Submarine Reports, Nov. 1939, p. 65.

32. IMT, vol. 35, Doc. 642-D, p. 270.
33. Admiralty, Anti-Submarine Reports, Jan./Feb. 1940, p. 8.
34. Ibid., p. 12.
35. BdU KTB, 31 Oct. 1939.
36. Ibid., 21 Jan. 1940.
37. Sept. 1939 through Feb. 1940; Roskill, I, p. 615.
38. 4 June 1940; cited Gilbert, p. 468.
39. 'Declaration of Union'; cited David Thomson, 'The Proposal for Anglo-French Union in 1940', Zaharoff Lecture, Clarendon Press, Oxford, 1966, p. 28; see also Gilbert, pp. 550–51, 557–62; and see Colville, pp. 159–60.
40. Roskill, I, p. 229.
41. Milner, pp. 37–8.

Chapter 20: The Warlords

1. See Padfield, *Hess*, pp. 122–7.
2. Hansard, 18 June 1940, col. 61; cited Gilbert, pp. 570–71.
3. Ibid., p. 665.
4. See Eric Seal to John Colville, 25 June 1940; Colville, p. 170.
5. Sir James Marshall-Cornwall, Unpublished recollections, 26 July 1940,; cited Gilbert, pp. 683–4.
6. Speech notes, 20 June 1940; cited Gilbert, p. 579.
7. Churchill to Beaverbrook, 8 July 1940; cited Gilbert, pp. 655–6; and see John Keegan, 'Churchill's Strategy', in Blake and Louis, p. 341.
8. See R. V. Jones, *Most Secret War*, Hamish Hamilton, 1978, p. 45; cited Hastings, pp. 60–61; and Blackett, pp. 223–7; and John Keegan, 'Churchill's Strategy', in Blake and Louis, p. 342.
9. Cited Bailey and Ryan, p. 100.
10. Ibid., p. 101.
11. See Lord Lothian, British Ambassador to Washington, to Lady Astor, 20 May 1940: 'USA won't enter the war, unless and until its own vital interests are affected'; cited Lash, p. 132; and see Thorne, p. 93: a Gallup Poll of May 1941 showed 79 per cent of Americans heavily against entering the war.
12. See Thorne, p. 100.
13. Cited Warren F. Kimball, 'Churchill, Roosevelt and the Special Relationship', in Blake and Louis, p. 297; and see Robert Rhodes James, 'Churchill the Parliamentarian, Orator and Statesman', in ibid., p. 305.
14. See Lash, p. 194.
15. I. Berlin, *Personal Impressions*, NY, 1981, p. 13; cited Robert Rhodes James, 'Churchill, Roosevelt and the Special Relationship', in Blake and Louis, p. 508.
16. See Robin Edmonds, 'Churchill and Stalin', in Blake and Louis, p. 311.
17. 25 June 1940; cited Gilbert, p. 599.
18. See Padfield, *Hess*, pp. 135, 147–50, and revised edn, pp.xv–xx, xxiv.
19. 31 July 1940; Franz Halder, *Kriegstagebuch*, Stuttgart, 1963, II, p. 48; cited Padfield, *Hess*, p. 128.
20. Rayfield, p. 252.

21. Bergamini, p. 744.

22. See William Lockwood, 'Trade, Armament, Industrial Expansion, 1930–1938', in Livingston et al., p. 371; T. A. Bisson, 'Increase of Zaibatsu Predominance in Wartime Japan', in Livingston et al., p. 457.

23. Kennedy, *Great Powers*, pp. 391, 429, Table 31.

24. Ibid., p. 490.

25. See ibid., p. 430; Ienaga, pp. 139–40.

26. Bix, esp. p. 429, refers to Hirohito articulating fears for the imperial system of governance unless belligerent foreign policies were pursued; internal conflicts seemed to him more dangerous than escalating war – an echo of Kaiser Wilhelm II's concerns prior to the First World War.

Chapter 21: The Battle of the Atlantic, 1940–41

1. Padfield, *War beneath the Sea*, p. 89; Blair, *U-boat War*, p. 162, has 41,207 tons.

2. Padfield, *War beneath the Sea*, p. 89.

3. Blair, *U-boat War*, p. 169.

4. Roskill, I, p. 615.

5. Admiralty, Anti Submarine Reports, July and August 1940, p. 7.

6. Cited Bodo Herzog, 'Admiral Otto Kretschmer', in Howarth, p. 383.

7. Reduced by post-war research to six of 20,755 tons; Blair, *U-boat War*, p. 712.

8. See ibid., p. 178.

9. Cited Bodo Herzog, 'Admiral Otto Kretschmer', in Howarth, p. 387.

10. Admiralty, Anti Submarine Reports, Nov. 1940, p. 25; Blair, *U-boat War*, p. 199.

11. BdU KTB, 20 Oct. 1940; Admiralty, Anti Submarine Reports, Nov. 1940, p. 25; Blair, *U-boat War*, p. 200.

12. BdU KTB, 20 Oct. 1940.

13. Ibid.

14. Padfield, *War beneath the Sea*, p. 108.

15. Buchheim, *U-Boat War*, 'Storm' section.

16. Roskill, I, p. 616.

17. BdU KTB, 4 Dec. 1940.

18. Admiralty, Anti Submarine Reports, Nov. 1940, p. 113.

19. See P. Beesly, 'The Operational Intelligence Centre', p. 318; and for the success of evasive routing, see BdU KTB 18 April 1941.

20. Admiralty, Anti Submarine Reports, Nov. 1940, pp. 7–8.

21. See Blair, *U-boat War*, pp. 249–55; Dan van der Vat, 'Commander Günther Prien', in Howarth, p. 403.

22. See Padfield, *War beneath the Sea*, p. 115; Blair, *U-boat War*, p. 258.

23. Blair, *U-boat War*, p. 258n.

24. Hinsley et al., I, pp. 336–7.

25. Snr Officer 3rd Escort Group to Capt. (D), Greenock, 10 May 1941, in 'Capture of *U110*'; NA ADM 1/11133.

26. German authors believe he was shot in the water to prevent him reboarding his boat; it may be significant that there is no mention of his end in the British reports; see note 25 above.

27. Hinsley et al., I, p. 338.
28. J. Rohwer, 'The Wireless War', in Howarth and Law, pp. 411, 416.
29. See Milner, pp. 65, 77.
30. Ibid., p.77.
31. See Padfield, *Dönitz*, p. 195.
32. See Padfield, *Himmler*, pp. 331–2.
33. Ibid., pp. 324, 334.
34. See Kershaw, II, p. 311.
35. See Overy, *Russia's War*, pp. 71–2; Kershaw, II, p. 394; Padfield, *Himmler*, pp. 337–8.
36. Cited Lash, pp. 263–4.
37. See Thorne, p. 279.
38. 'ABC-1 Staff Agreement'; see Philip Lundeberg, 'Allied Co-operation', in Howarth and Law, p. 353.
39. See *Encyclopaedia Britannica*, I, p. 672.
40. Prange, p. 491.
41. Mrs John B. Earle to Gordon Prange, 1 Dec. 1963; cited ibid., p. 507.
42. See Kershaw, II, pp. 442–6.
43. See ibid., pp. 442ff; Lash, pp. 238–9.

Chapter 22: The Pacific, 1942

1. See pp. 209, 218 above.
2. See Roskill, I, pp. 555–6.
3. Received 0125 hours, 9 Dec. 1941; ADM 234/330 Appendix D(1), p. 31; cited Barnett, p. 411.
4. For the inadequacy of the Admiralty's High Angle Control System, see S. W. Roskill, *Naval Policy between the Wars*, Collins, 1981, II, pp. 333–4; cited Barnett, p. 47.
5. NA ADM 234/330, p. 17; cited Barnett, p. 420; and see Winton, pp. 164–72.
6. Hearings before the Joint Committee on the Investigation of the Pearl Harbor Attack, US Congress, 1946, Part 14, p. 1042; cited Prange, p. 31.
7. Ibid., p. 1044; cited Prange, p. 33.
8. See Padfield, *War beneath the Sea*, pp. 30–32, 185.
9. Ibid., pp. 191–2.
10. Roskill, II, p. 28.
11. Ibid., p. 5.
12. Bergamini, p. 945.
13. See George Hicks, *The Comfort Women*, Souvenir Press, 1995; review by Tunku Varadarajan, 'Female Spoils of War', in *The Times*, 25 March, 1995; see also Kozo Mizoguchi, 'We used sex slaves in war', *Daily Telegraph*, 5 Aug. 1993.
14. Ms Van der Ploeg; cited Barbara Smit, 'Victim of war who can never forgive', *Daily Telegraph*, 7 Feb. 1994.
15. Ienaga, p. 52.
16. See Hugo Gordon, 'Veteran of atrocity camp leads call for Tokyo to atone for past', *Daily Telegraph*, 21 Nov. 1994; Joanna Pitman, 'Findings deny tests on POWs', *The*

Times, 23 April 1992; Geoffrey Lee Martin, 'Wartime plot by Japanese to unleash "black death" ', *Daily Telegraph*, 18 Aug. 1993; Bix, pp. 362–3, states that bacteriological warfare experiments were sanctioned by Hirohito; see also internet Wikopedia.

17. See Padfield, *Himmler*, pp. 345, 357–9.
18. For this human experimentation see ibid., pp. 333, 373–4, 375–6, 438.
19. Morison, I, p. 115.
20. Ian Jacob diary, 14 Jan. 1943; cited Buell, p. 274.
21. E. J. King, 'Memorandum for the President', 5 March 1942; cited ibid., p. 532.
22. Ibid., cited Buell, p. 193.
23. Parshall and Tully, pp. 37, 43–5.
24. Ibid., p. 65.
25. Ibid., p. 66.

Chapter 23: Midway, 1942

1. Parshall and Tully, 'Japanese Order of Battle', pp. 450–61.
2. Cited John Wukowitz, 'Admiral Raymond A. Spruance', in Howarth, p. 161.
3. Parshall and Tully, p. 90.
4. See Padfield, *War beneath the Sea*, pp. 232–3.
5. Gordon W. Prange with Donald Goldstein and Katherine Dillon, *Miracle at Midway*, NY, 1982, pp. 185–6; cited Parshall and Tully, p. 110.
6. Parshall and Tully, p. 134.
7. Signal sent 0552 hours; ibid.
8. Ibid.
9. John Wukowitz, 'Admiral Raymond A. Spruance', in Howarth, p. 158.
10. Ibid., p. 160.
11. 0715 hours; Parshall and Tully, p. 156.
12. Ibid., pp. 157–8.
13. 0747 hours; ibid., p. 161.
14. Stephen, p. 169.
15. Ibid.
16. 0820 hours; Parshall and Tully, p. 183.
17. Ibid., p. 190.
18. See ibid.
19. Ibid., p. 217; and see Padfield, *War beneath the Sea*, pp. 236–7.
20. 'Reminiscences of Admiral Thach', Part 2, pp. 245–52; cited Spector, p. 201.
21. Ibid.
22. Ibid.
23. Parshall and Tully, p. 236.
24. Alvin Kernan, *Crossing the Line: A Bluejacket's World War II Odyssey*, US Naval Institute Press, Annapolis, 1994, pp. 54–5; cited Spector, pp. 201–2.
25. Parshall and Tully, p. 249.
26. See ibid., pp. 333–5, 342, 349–53.

Chapter 24: Allied Victory, 1943–45

1. Lundstrom, p. 92.
2. Professor Henry Tizard's mission to Washington; see Stafford, *Churchill and Secret Service*, p. 200; A. N. Wilson, *After the Victorians*, pp. 440–41.
3. See Spector, pp. 203–4, 219.
4. Kershaw, II, p. 549.
5. See Erickson, p. 43.
6. See Kershaw, II, p. 548.
7. See Padfield, *Himmler*, pp. 410–14.
8. See Overy, *Russia's War*, pp. 169–70.
9. Ibid., p. 198; see also pp. 194ff; and Erickson, pp. 83–4.
10. Marshal Zhukov in bugged conversation, 1963; cited Overy, *Russia's War*, p. 195. Overy also cites a taped interview in which Khrushchev quotes Stalin saying, 'if we had had to deal with Germany one to one we would not have been able to cope because we lost so much of our industry'; ibid.
11. Padfield, *War beneath the Sea*, p. 314.
12. See ibid., p. 328.
13. See Admiralty, Anti Submarine Reports, April 1943, p. 184.
14. BdU KTB, 23 May 1943, '*Schlussbetrachtung Geleitzug 42*' – Convoy HX 239.
15. Erickson, p. 214.
16. See Kennedy, *Great Powers*, pp. 455–8; Thorne, p. 138; Barnett, p. 880.
17. See Bergamini, pp. 1030–36.
18. Roskill, III, Part 2, p. 195; Spector, p. 281.
19. Hirohito's refusal to accept defeat although the loss of Saipan made it certain is documented in Bix, pp. 476–7.
20. See Bergamini, p. 1079.
21. Hanson W. Baldwin, *Battles Lost and Won*, Harper & Row, NY, 1966, p. 377; cited Spector, p. 311.
22. Spector, p. 313.
23. See IMT Doc.2878-PS, vol. 31, pp. 250–51.
24. Padfield, *War beneath the Sea*, p. 422; together with Roskill, III, Part 2, pp. 463–6.
25. Churchill was surprised and upset when Roosevelt first announced the Allied policy of unconditional surrender at the Casablanca Conference in January 1943; this was, however, because Roosevelt had not consulted him first. Professor Brian Bond, *Pursuit of Victory*, p. 159, states: 'the formula of "unconditional surrender" embodied Anglo-American determination to destroy German "militarism" (in Churchill's erroneous belief localized in "Prussia") . . . it seems clear that . . . the "unconditional surrender" formula represented not just the personal view of Roosevelt and Churchill . . . but also the trend of public opinion in their two countries'.
26. See Thorne, pp. 530–31.
27. Roosevelt told his son after Pearl Harbor, 'Don't think for a moment that Americans would be dying in the Pacific tonight, if it hadn't been for the greed of the French and the British and the Dutch'; Stafford, *Roosevelt and Churchill*, p. 249; and see Thorne, pp. 206–8.
28. See Thorne, pp. 714–15.

29. 12 Sept. 1941; Alanbrooke, p. 591.

30. See Robin Edmonds, 'Churchill and Stalin', in Blake and Louis, p. 318; and Erickson, pp. 156–7; Montefiore, p. 413.

31. Montefiore, p. 413.

32. Kennedy, *Great Powers*, p. 473; Barnett, p. 880; Thorne, p. 110.

33. See A. N. Wilson, *After the Victorians*, p. 442: Henry Morgenthau, Secretary to the US Treasury, could see that 'the faster the gold and dollar reserves ran out in London, the stronger Washington's position to bring about the financial ruin of Britain and the dismantlement of that British empire which he and Roosevelt so much detested'.

34. Padfield, *War beneath the Sea*, p. 461, citing latest figures from U-boat Archive, Cuxhaven.

35. Ibid. p. 448.

36. Interrogation Cdr T. Kuwahara, IJN, *US Strategic Bombing Survey, Pacific*, I, p. 216.

37. Potsdam Declaration, 26 July 1945; see Bix, pp. 499–501; Bergamini, p. 85.

38. For analysis of Hirohito's surrender and the condition that it should not compromise his imperial prerogatives, see Bix, pp. 503–30.

Chapter 25: The 'Cold War' – and After

1. Internet, http://messageinthewaves.com/facts.php; some 200,000 die each year, or 40 per cent.

2. Coleridge, p. 10.

3. Carson, p. 31.

4. Lovelock, p. 109.

5. Ibid., p. 146; and see p. 12.

6. E. O. Wilson, p. 29.

7. World Bank, *Mainstreaming the Environment*, p. 2.

8. P. B. Shelley, 'Ozymandias of Egypt'.

9. P. Johnson, reviewing J. Patterson, *Grand Expectations: The United States 1945–74*, in *Sunday Telegraph*, 23 June 1996; and Kennedy, *Great Powers*, pp. 461, 475.

10. Kynaston, III, pp. 502–3.

11. See Howe, p. 183; Frank Lynder to author, Nov. 1982.

12. See W. Rees-Mogg, 'Dollar millionaires on every block', *The Times*, 25 May 1998; and see Schmidt, pp. 131ff.

13. Cited Drescher, pp. 104, 134.

14. M. Fokken, *Beschryving der Wijdt-Vermaerde Koop-stadt Amstelredam*, cited Schama, p. 300.

15. W. Aglionby, cited Schama.

16. B. de Mandeville, cited Schama.

17. Over 14 million peasants alone fell victim to Stalin's policies, 1930–37; see 'How Stalin starved the Ukraine', excerpted from R. Conquest, *The Harvest of Sorrow*, Hutchinson, 1984, in *The Times*, 18 Aug. 1986; Overy, *Stalin's War*, gives Soviet military losses as 8,668,400.

18. O'Malley to FO, 30 April 1943, NA FO 371/40741A U2011/58/72; cited Aldrich, p. 51.

19. Cited Aldrich, p. 43.

20. Diary, 27 July 1944; Alanbrooke, p. 575.

21. OSS memo, 2 April 1945; Truman Papers, White House Central Files; cited Thorne, pp. 599–600.

22. See Thorne, pp. 714–15.

23. See p. 42 above.

24. Cited Reischauer, p. 215.

25. Ibid., p. 252.

26. See pp. 66–70 above, and p. 212.

27. See Hartscher, pp. 1–7, 251ff and *passim*.

28. See Fukuyama, pp. 130–33.

29. I. Buruma (author of *Inventing Japan*, Weidenfeld & Nicolson, 2003), 'Japan's no model for rebuilding Iraq', *Sunday Times*, 21 Sept. 2003.

30. See R. Guest, 'Japan's psyche chokes on the word "sorry"', *Sunday Telegraph*, 4 June 1995; J. Casey, 'Warriors without remorse', *Sunday Telegraph*, 13 Aug. 1995; J. Pitman, 'From Japan with apologies', *The Times*, 15 June 1995; Bix, pp. 559, 652; and Bix, pp. 556, 617–18 esp., argues that in absolving Hirohito from war guilt and propagating the myth that he, and by extension the Japanese people, had been deceived by 'military cliques', MacArthur's administration confused the Japanese acceptance of responsibility for the war.

31. Schmidt, p. 354.

32. Ibid., p. 357.

33. Ibid., p. 359.

34. Post, p. 30.

35. Ibid., p. 36.

36. Fisher, p. 1.

37. Schmidt, p. 129.

38. Cited H. Jackson, 'George Kennan', obituary, *Guardian*, 19 March 2005.

39. Ibid.

40. Cited Kennedy, *Great Powers*, p. 479.

41. See Montefiore, pp. 454–5, 461–2.

42. This has been disputed, but see Professor L. S. Pressnell (Official Historian, Cabinet Office Historical Section) to *Sunday Telegraph*, 1 June 1997; and see Winks, pp. 380ff.

43. Schmidt, p.122.

44. Reynolds, pp. 574–5.

45. Aldrich, pp. 401–3; N. Fielding, reviewing J. Bamford, *Body of Secrets*, Century, 2001, in *Sunday Times*, 13 May 2001.

46. Winks, pp. 426–7.

47. Cited Aldrich, p. 320.

48. See ibid., pp. 327–8.

49. See International Institute for Strategic Studies, *Military Balance*, 1971, pp. 1–2; see Kennedy, *Great Powers*, pp. 500–501.

50. It has been estimated that by the 1980s Soviet defence spending consumed 70 per cent of the national budget; R. Seitz reviewing D. Volkogonov (trans. Harold Shukman), *The Rise and Fall of the Soviet Empire*, Macmillan, 1998, in *Sunday Times*, 19 Apr. 1998.

51. Schmidt, p. 117.

52. See p. 228 above.

53. See Padfield, *Hess*, pp. 369–70 and *passim*.

54. See Kennedy, *Diplomacy*, pp. 317–18; Thorne, p. 504.

55. Thorne, p. 675n.

56. Louis and Robinson, p. 473; and see Winks, p. 381.

57. Kennedy, *Diplomacy*, p. 332.

58. Louis and Robinson, p. 495.

59. See Kennedy, *Diplomacy*, p. 341.

60. See Padfield, *Maritime Power*, pp. 108–9, 289.

61. A. Salter, *The United States of Europe*, Allen & Unwin, 1931, p. 92; cited Booker and North, pp. 20–21.

62. Preamble to Treaty of Rome; cited ibid., p. 105.

63. Aldrich, p. 343.

64. See ibid., p. 344.

65. Speech to Labour Party Conference, Oct. 1962; cited Booker and North, p. 144.

66. See Booker and North, pp. 146–8, 161–6.

67. NA FCO 30/789; cited ibid., p. 171.

68. *The United Kingdom and the European Communities*, Cmnd. 4715; cited Booker and North, p. 179.

69. Burke, p. 47.

70. E.g. wilderness, rainforest, water table, oil and strategic minerals such as antimony, hafnium, platinum, silver, tantalum, uranium, zinc; see Cohen.

Select Bibliography

Abbreviations

CUP	Cambridge University Press
HMSO	Her Majesty's Stationery Office, London
IWM	Imperial War Museum, London
JMH	*The Journal of Military History*
Mar.M	*Mariner's Mirror*
MM	*Militärgeschichtliche Mitteilungen*
MOD	Ministry of Defence, London
MZ	*Militärgeschichtliche Zeitschrift*
NA	National Archives (formerly the Public Record Office – PRO), Kew Gardens, London
NR	*Naval Review*
NRS	Navy Records Society, London
OUP	Oxford University Press
PRO	see National Archives

Official reports, histories and monographs

Admiralty, Anti Submarine Warfare Division Monthly Reports, Naval Library, MOD, now in NA

BdU KTB, War Diary, U-boat Command, Naval Library, MOD

IMT (International Military Tribunal), *Evidence and Documents presented at the Trials of the Major War Criminals*, Nuremberg, 1948

International Institute for Strategic Studies, *The Military Balance 1971–1972*, London, 1971

The Russo–Japanese War: Reports from Naval Attachés, Naval Library, MOD, Ca. 1263

United States Strategic Bombing Survey (Pacific), OPNAV-P-03-100, US Naval Analysis Division, Washington DC, 1946, vols 1 and 2

World Bank, *Mainstreaming the Environment*, Washington DC, 1995

Articles

Beesly, P., 'The Operational Intelligence Centre, Naval Intelligence Division', NR, Oct. 1975

Berghahn, V. R., 'Zu den Zielen des deutschen Flottenbaues unter Wilhelm II', *Historische Zeitschrift*, 210, 1970

Berghahn, V. R. and W. Deist, 'Kaiserliche Marine und Kriegsausbruch 1914. Neue Dokumente zur Juli-Krise', MM, 1, 1970

Cohen, D., 'Earth's natural wealth: an audit', *New Scientist*, 23 May 2007

Ford, D., 'US Naval Intelligence and the Imperial Japanese Fleet during the Washington Treaty Era, c.1922–36', Mar.M, 93 (3) (Aug. 2007)

Gardner, J., 'The Battle of the Atlantic, 1941 – the First Turning Point?', *Journal of Strategic Studies*, 17 (1) (March 1994)

Gretton, P. W., 'Why don't we learn from history?', NR, Jan. 1958

Grove, E., 'The battleship is dead; long live the battleship. HMS *Dreadnought* and the limits of technological innovation', Mar.M, 93 (4) (Nov. 2007)

Hiley, N., 'The Strategic Origins of Room 40', *Intelligence and National Security*, 22, 1987

Hopkins, R., 'A vision for food and farming in 2030', in *One Planet Agriculture: The Case for Action*, Soil Association, 2007

James, Admiral Sir W., 'Room 40', *University of Edinburgh Journal*, Spring 1965

Kennedy, P., 'Tirpitz, England and the second Navy Law of 1900: a strategical critique', MM, 2, 1970

—— 'German World Policy and the Alliance Negotiations with England, 1897-1900', *Journal of Modern History*, 45 (4) (Dec. 1973)

—— 'Mahan versus Mackinder: Two Interpretations of British Sea Power', MM, 2 ,1974

—— 'The development of German naval operations plans against England, 1896–1914', *English Historical Review*, LXXXIV (CCCL) (Jan. 1974)

—— 'The Operations Plans of the Great Powers, 1880–1914: Analysis of Recent Literature', MM, 19, 1976

Lambert, N.A., 'Admiral Sir John Fisher and the Concept of Flotilla Defence, 1904–1909', JMH, 59, Oct. 1995

—— '"Our Bloody Ships" or "Our Bloody System"? Jutland and the Loss of the Battle Cruisers, 1916', JMH, 62, Jan. 1998

—— 'Strategic Command and Control for Maneuver Warfare: Creation of the Royal Navy's "War Room" System, 1905–1915', JMH, 69, Apr. 2005

Louis, W. and R. Robinson, 'The Imperialism of Decolonisation', *Journal of Imperial and Commonwealth History*, XXII, (3) (Sept. 1994)

Pearson, Lord, 'What is the point of the European Union?', Memorandum to Opinion Formers, Oct. 2004

Röhl, J. G., 'Admiral von Müller and the approach of war, 1911–1914', *Historical Journal*, XII, Dec. 1969

Sumida, J. T., 'Sir John Fisher and the *Dreadnought*: The Sources of Naval Mythology', JMH, 59, Oct. 1995

—— 'The Quest for Reach: the Development of Long-Range Gunnery in the Royal Navy, 1901–1912', in Stephen D. Chiabotti (ed.), *Tooling for War: Military Transformation in the Industrial Age*, Chicago, 1996

—— 'Demythologising the Fisher Era: The Role of Change in Historical Method', MZ, 59, 2000

—— 'A Matter of Timing: The Royal Navy and the Tactics of Decisive Battle, 1912–1916', JMH, 67, Jan. 2003

—— 'Information Dominance and Maneuver Warfare at Sea in the early Twentieth Century . . .', Paper presented at 'Driving Strategic Change: The Admiral Sir John Fisher Centenary Conference', Joint Staff College, Shrivenham, Wiltshire, Sept. 2004

Terrell, C., 'Captain Bartholomew Sulivan and British Hydrography in the Baltic War of 1854–56', *Journal of the International Map Collectors' Society*, 68, Spring 1997

Thiesen, W. H., 'Construction of America's "New Navy" and the transfer of British Technology to the United States, 1870–1900', Mar.M, 85 (4) (Nov. 1999)

Waters, D. W., 'ASW: the First 40 Years', NR, Apr. 1986

Wright, C. C., 'Questions on the Effectiveness of US Navy Battleship Gunnery: Notes on the Origins of US Navy Gun Fire Control System Rangekeepers', *Warship International*, I, 2005

Books

(published in London unless otherwise stated)

Aldrich, R. J., *The Hidden Hand: Britain, America and Cold War Secret Intelligence*, John Murray, 2001

Alanbrooke, Lord, *War Diaries 1939–1945*, Weidenfeld & Nicolson, 2001

Applebaum, A., *Gulag: A History of the Soviet Camps*, Allen Lane, 2003

Arnold, M., *Essays in Criticism*, 1865 (reprinted George Routledge, ed.)

Bacon, R., *The Life of John Rushworth, Earl Jellicoe*, Cassell, 1936

—— *From 1900 Onwards*, Hutchinson, 1940

Bahar, A and W. Kugel, *Der Reichstagsbrand: Wie Geschichte gemacht wird*, Quintessenz Verlag, Berlin, 2001

Bailey, T. A. and P. B. Ryan, *Hitler vs Roosevelt: The Undeclared Naval War*, Free Press, NY, 1979

Balfour, M., *The Kaiser and His Times*, Cresset, 1964

Barnett, C., *Engage the Enemy More Closely: The Royal Navy in the Second World War*, Hodder & Stoughton, 1991

Batty, P. and P. J. Parish, *The Divided Union: A Concise History of the Civil War*, Tempus, 1999

Baxter, J. P., *The Introduction of the Ironclad Warship*, Harvard University Press, Cambridge, MA, 1933

Beesly, P., *Room 40: British Naval Intelligence 1914–1918*, OUP, 1982

Bergamini, D., *Japan's Imperial Conspiracy*, Morrow, NY, 1971

Berghahn, V. R., *Der Tirpitz Plan*, Droste, Düsseldorf, 1971

—— *Germany and the Approach of War in 1914*, Macmillan, 1973

Birkenhead, Lord, *Rudyard Kipling*, Weidenfeld & Nicolson, 1978

Bix, H. P., *Hirohito and the Making of Modern Japan*, HarperCollins, NY, 2000

Blackett, P. M. S., *Studies of War: Nuclear and Conventional*, Oliver & Boyd, 1962

Blair, C., *Silent Victory: The US Submarine War against Japan*, Lippincott, NY, 1975

—— *Hitler's U-boat War: The Hunters 1939–1942*, Weidenfeld & Nicolson, 1997

Blake, R. and R. Louis, (eds), *Churchill*, OUP, 1993

Bond, B., *The Pursuit of Victory: From Napoleon to Saddam Hussain*, OUP, 1996

Bonner-Smith, D. (ed.), *Russian War, 1855: Baltic: official correspondence*, NRS, 1944

Bonner-Smith, D. and A. C. Dewar, (eds), *Russian War, 1854 Baltic and Black Sea: Official correspondence*, NRS, 1943

Booker, C. and R. North, *The Great Deception: Can the European Union Survive?*, Continuum, 2003

Brett, M. V. (ed.), *Journals & Letters of Reginald Viscount Esher*, 4 vols, Nicholson & Watson, 1934

Brooks, J., *Dreadnought Gunnery and the Battle of Jutland: The Question of Fire Control*, Routledge, 2005

Buchheim, L-G., *The Boat*, Collins, 1974

—— *U-boat War*, Collins, 1978

—— *Zu Tode Gesiegt*, Bertelsmann, Munich, 1988

Buell, T. B., *Master of Sea Power: A Biography of Fleet Admiral Ernest J. King*, Little Brown, Boston, MA, 1980

Bülow, B. von, *Memoirs, 1897–1903*, Putnam, 1931

Burke, E., *Reflections on the Revolution in France*, ed. J. C. D. Clark, Stanford University Press, 2001

Burleigh, M., *The Third Reich: A New History*, Macmillan, 2000

Burrows, E. G. and M. Wallace, *Gotham: A History of New York City to 1898*, OUP, 1999

Cain, P. J. and A. G. Hopkins, *British Imperialism: Innovations and Expansion 1688–1914*, Longmans, 1993

Campbell, J., *Jutland: An Analysis of the Fighting*, Conway Maritime Press, 1986

Carson, R., *Silent Spring*, Hamish Hamilton, 1963

Cecil, H. and P. H. Liddle, (eds), *Facing Armageddon: The First World War Experienced*, Leo Cooper, 1996

Cecil, L., *Albert Ballin*, Princeton University Press, 1967

Chalmers, W. S., *The Life and Letters of David, Earl Beatty*, Hodder & Stoughton, 1951

Chatfield, Lord, *The Navy and Defence*, Heinemann, 1942

Chatterton, E. Keble, *The Big Blockade*, Hutchinson, ed.

Churchill, W. S., *The World Crisis*, 5 vols, Butterworth, 1923–31

Coleridge, S., *The Rime of the Ancient Mariner*, quotes from Arno Press edn., NY, 1979

Colomb, P. H., *Memoirs of Admiral Sir Astley Cooper Key*, Methuen, 1898

Colville, J., *The Fringes of Power: Downing Street Diaries, 1939–1955*, Hodder & Stoughton, 1985

Corbett, J., *Naval Operations*, vols I-III, Longmans Green, 1920–23

Crankshaw, E., *Bismarck*, Macmillan, 1981

David, S., *The Indian Mutiny 1857*, Viking, 2002

Deist, W., *The Wehrmacht and German Re-armament*, Macmillan, 1981

Dorpalen, A., *Heinrich von Treitschke*, Yale University Press, 1957

Drescher, S., *Tocqueville and England*, Harvard University Press, Cambridge, MA, 1964

Dreyer, F., *The Sea Heritage: A Study of Maritime Warfare*, Museum Press, 1955

Dülffer, J., *Weimar, Hitler und die Marine*, Droste, Düsseldorf, 1973

Erickson, J., *The Road to Berlin: Stalin's War with Germany*, vol. 2, Weidenfeld & Nicolson, 1983

Fawcett, H. W. and G. W. W. Hooper, *The Fighting at Jutland: The Personal Experiences of Sixty Officers and Men of the British Fleet*, Glasgow, 1921

Ferguson, N., *The Pity of War*, Allen Lane, 1998

—— *The World's Banker: The History of the House of Rothschild*, Weidenfeld & Nicolson, 1998

—— *The Cash Nexus: Money and Power in the Modern World, 1700–2000*, Allen Lane, 2001

—— *Empire: How Britain Made the Modern World*, Allen Lane, 2003

Fischer, F., *Germany's Aims in the First World War*, Chatto & Windus, 1967

Fisher, H. A. L., *A History of Europe*, Edward Arnold, 1936

Fox, C. E., *Lord of the Southern Isles*, Mowbray, 1958

Fukuyama, F., *The Great Disruption: Human Nature and the Reconstruction of the Social Order*, Profile Books, 1999

Gilbert, M., *Finest Hour: Winston S. Churchill 1939–1941*, Heinemann, 1983

Gordon, A., *The Rules of the Game: Jutland and British Naval Command*, John Murray, 1996

Gordon, J. S., *The Great Game: A History of Wall Street*, Orion Business Books, 1999

Graham, G. S., *The Politics of Naval Supremacy*, CUP, 1965

Grant, A. J. and H. Temperley, *Europe in the Nineteenth and Twentieth Centuries*, Longman (6th edn), 1952

Grey, E., *Twenty Five Years*, Hodder & Stoughton, 1925

Guedalla, P., *Palmerston*, Hodder & Stoughton, 1926

Haffner, S., *Defying Hitler: A Memoir*, trans. O. Pretzel, Weidenfeld & Nicolson, 2002

Haraszti, E., *Treaty Breakers or Realpolitikers?*, Boldt, Boppard am Rhein, 1974

Harper, J., *The Truth about Jutland*, John Murray, 1927

Hartscher, P., *The Ministry: The Inside Story of Japan's Ministry of Finance*, HarperCollins, 1998

Hase, G. von, *Kiel and Jutland*, Skeffington, 1921

Hastings, M., *Bomber Command*, Michael Joseph, 1979

Herwig, H., *The German Naval Officer Corps*, OUP, 1973

Hill, R., *War at Sea in the Ironclad Age*, Cassell, 2000

Hinsley, F. H. et al., *British Intelligence in the Second World War: Its Influence on Strategy and Operations*, 3 vols, HMSO, 1979–84

Hobsbawm, E., *The Age of Empire 1875–1914*, Weidenfeld & Nicolson, 1987

—— *Age of Extremes: The Short Twentieth Century 1914–1991*, Michael Joseph, 1994

Honan, W. H., *Bywater: The Man Who Invented the Pacific War*, Macdonald, 1990

Howarth, S. (ed.), *Men of War: Great Naval Leaders of World War II*, Weidenfeld & Nicolson, 1992

Howarth, S. and D. Law, (eds), *The Battle of the Atlantic*, Greenhill Books, 1994

Howe, E., *The Black Game*, Michael Joseph, 1982

Hughes, T., *Tom Brown's Schooldays*, 1857, Collins edn, 1904

Ienaga, S., *The Pacific War: World War II and the Japanese, 1931–1945*, Pantheon Books, NY, 1978

Internationales Kommittee Luxemburg, *Der Reichstagsbrand: Die Provokation des 20. Jahrhunderts*, Verlag der Freundeskreis, Luxemburg, 1978

James, L., *Raj: The Making and Unmaking of British India*, Little Brown, 1997

Jones, E. L., *Growth Recurring: Economic Change in World History*, OUP, 1998

Keegan, J., *The Battle for History: Re-fighting World War Two*, Hutchinson, 1995

Kemp, P. (ed.), *The Oxford Companion to Ships and the Sea*, OUP, 1976

Kennedy, P., *The Rise and Fall of British Naval Mastery*, Allen Lane, 1976

—— *The Rise of Anglo-German Antagonism 1860–1914*, Allen & Unwin, 1980

—— *The Realities behind Diplomacy: Background Influences on British External Policy, 1865–1980*, Fontana, 1981

—— *The Rise and Fall of the Great Powers: Economic Change and Military Conflict from 1500 to 2000*, Unwin Hyman, 1988

Kershaw, I., *Hitler*, 2 vols, Allen Lane, 1998–2000

Kynaston, D., *The City of London*, 3 vols, Chatto & Windus, 1994–99

Lambert, A., *The Crimean War: British Grand Strategy 1853–56*, Manchester University Press, 1990

Lambert, N. A., *Sir John Fisher's Naval Revolution*, University of South Carolina Press, 1999

Lash, J. P., *Roosevelt and Churchill 1939–1941: The Partnership that Saved the West*, Norton, NY, 1976

Lepsius, J. et al., *Die Grosse Politik der Europäischen Kabinette 1871–1914*, Berlin, 1922

Livingston, J. et al. (eds), *The Japan Reader*, vol I: *Imperial Japan 1800–1945*, Random House, 1973

Lovelock, J., *The Revenge of Gaia: Why the Earth Is Fighting Back – and How We Can Still Save Humanity*, Allen Lane, 2006

Lubbock, B., *The China Clippers*, Brown Son & Ferguson, Glasgow, 1946

Lundstrom, J. B., *First Team and the Guadalcanal Campaign: Naval Fighter Combat from August to November 1942*, US Naval Institute Press, Annapolis, 2005

Macauley, Lord, *Historical Essays*, OUP, 1913

Mackinder, H. J., *Britain and the British Seas*, Oxford, 1902 (quotes from 1930 edn)

—— *The Geographical Pivot of History*, 1904, reprinted Curwen Press, 1969

MacMillan, M., *Peacemakers: The Paris Conference of 1919 and the Attempt to End War*, John Murray, 2001

Magnus, P., *Gladstone: A Biography*, John Murray, 1954

Mahan, A. T., *The Influence of Sea Power upon History, 1660–1783*, 1890

—— *The Influence of Sea Power upon the French Revolution and Empire*, 2 vols, 1892

Marder, A., *British Naval Policy, 1880–1905*, Putnam, 1941

—— (ed.), *Fear God and Dread Nought: The Correspondence of Admiral of the Fleet Lord Fisher of Kilverstone*, 3 vols, Cape, 1952–9

—— *From the Dreadnought to Scapa Flow*, 5 vols, OUP, 1961–70

Massie, R. K., *Castles of Steel: Britain, Germany and the Winning of the Great War at Sea*, Cape, 2004

Milner, M., *Battle of the Atlantic*, Tempus, Stroud, 2005

Monger, G., *The End of Isolation*, Nelson, 1963

Montefiore, S. Sebag, *Stalin: The Court of the Red Tsar*, Weidenfeld & Nicolson, 2003

Morison, S. E., *History of United States Naval Operations in World War 2*, 15 vols, Little Brown, Boston, MA, 1947–62

Newbolt, H., *Naval Operations*, vols. IV–V, Longmans Green, 1928–31

Novikoff-Priboy, A., *Tsushima*, trans. E. & C. Paul, Allen & Unwin, 1936

O'Connor, R. G., *Perilous Equilibrium: The United States and the London Naval Conference of 1930*, University of Kansas Press, Lawrence, 1962

Ousby, I., *The Road to Verdun: France, Nationalism and the First World War*, Cape, 2002

Overy, R., *Russia's War*, Allen Lane, 1998

—— *Interrogations: The Nazi Elite in Allied Hands, 1945*, Allen Lane, 2001

Padfield, P., *Aim Straight: A Biography of Admiral Sir Percy Scott*, Hodder & Stoughton, 1966

—— *The Battleship Era*, Hart-Davis, 1972 (quotes from Birlinn edn, 2000)

—— *Guns at Sea: A History of Naval Gunnery*, Evelyn, 1973

—— *The Great Naval Race: The Anglo-German Naval Rivalry 1900–1914*, Hart-Davis, 1974

—— *Rule Britannia: The Victorian and Edwardian Navy*, Routledge & Kegan Paul, 1981

—— *Dönitz: The Last Führer*, Gollancz, 1984

—— *Salt and Steel*, Century, 1985

—— *Himmler: Reichsführer-SS*, Macmillan, 1990

—— *Hess: The Führer's Disciple*, Cassell, 2001

—— *War beneath the Sea: Submarine Conflict 1939–1945*, John Murray, 1995

—— *Maritime Supremacy and the Opening of the Western Mind*, John Murray, 1999

—— *Maritime Power and the Struggle for Freedom*, John Murray, 2003

Pakenham, T., *The Boer War*, Weidenfeld & Nicolson, 1979

Parshall, J. B. and A. P. Tully, *Shattered Sword: The Untold Story of the Battle of Midway*, Potomac Books, Washington, DC, 2005

Patterson, A. Temple (ed.), *The Jellicoe Papers*, 2 vols, NRS, 1966–8

Pollen, Anthony, *The Great Gunnery Scandal: The Mystery of Jutland*, Collins, 1980

Pollen, Arthur H., *The Navy in Battle*, Chatto & Windus, 1918

Post, L. van der, *The Night of the New Moon*, Hogarth Press, 1970 (quotes from Penguin edn, 1977)

Prange, G. W., *At Dawn We Slept: The Untold Story of Pearl Harbor*, Penguin, 1982

Rayfield, D., *Stalin and His Hangmen*, Viking, 2004

Reischauer, E. O., *Japan Past and Present*, Knopf, NY, 1945 (quotes from rev. edn, 1964)

Reynolds, C. G., *Command of the Sea: The History and Strategy of Maritime Empires*, Robert Hale, 1976

Richmond, H., *British Strategy Military & Economic*, CUP, 1941

Rintelen, Capt. von, *The Dark Invader: Wartime Reminiscences of a German Naval Intelligence Officer*, Lovat Dickson, 1933

Röhl, J. G. (ed.), *Delusion or Design?*, Elek, 1973

—— *The Kaiser and His Court: Wilhelm II and the Government of Germany*, CUP, 1994

Röhl, J. G. and N. Sombart, (eds.), *Kaiser Wilhelm II: New Interpretations*, CUP, 1982

Roosevelt, T., *The Strenuous Life: Essays and Addresses*, Nelson, 1902

Roskill, S. W., *The War at Sea 1939–1945*, 4 vols, HMSO, 1954–61

Salewski, M., *Die Seekriegsleitung, 1939–1945*, 3 vols, Bernard & Graefe, Munich, 1970–75

Schama, S., *The Embarrassment of Riches*, University of California Press, Berkeley, 1987

Scheer, Admiral, *Germany's High Seas Fleet in the World War*, Cassell, 1920

Schmallenbach, P., *Die Geschichte der deutschen Schiffsartillerie*, Koehlers Verlagsgesellschaft, Herford, 1968

Schmidt, H., *Men and Powers: A Political Retrospective*, trans. R. Hein, Cape, 1990

Schottelius, H. and W. Deist,, *Marine und Marinepolitik im kaiserlichen Deutschland, 1871–1914*, Droste Verlag, Düsseldorf, 1972

Scott, P., *Fifty Years in the Royal Navy*, John Murray, 1919

Shirer, W., *Berlin Diary*, Hamish Hamilton, 1941

Singer, P., *Animal Liberation: A New Ethics for Our Treatment of Animals*, Cape, 1976

Smith, A., *An Inquiry into the Nature and Causes of the Wealth of Nations*, 2 vols, 1776–78, reprinted J. M. Dent & Sons, 1910

Spector, R., *At War at Sea: Sailors and Naval Warfare in the Twentieth Century*, Allen Lane, 2001

Stafford, D., *Churchill and Secret Service*, John Murray, 1997

—— *Roosevelt and Churchill: Men of Secrets*, Little Brown, 1999

Steinbach, S., *Women in England, 1760–1914: A Social History*, Weidenfeld & Nicolson, 2004

Steinberg, J., *Yesterday's Deterrent*, Macdonald, 1965

Stephen, M., *Sea Battles in Close-up: World War 2*, ed. E. Grove, Ian Allen, 1988

Strachan, H., *The First World War*, Simon & Schuster, 2003

Strouse, J., *Morgan: American Financier*, Harvill Press, 1999

Sumida, J. T., *The Pollen Papers: The Privately Circulated Printed Works of Arthur Hungerford Pollen, 1901–1916*, Allen & Unwin for NRS, 1984

—— *In Defence of Naval Supremacy: Finance, Technology and British Naval Policy, 1889–1914*, Unwin Hyman, 1989

T-124, (Russell Grenfell), *Sea Power*, Cape, 1940

Thomas, H., *The Slave Trade: The History of the Atlantic Slave Trade: 1440–1870*, Simon & Schuster, NY, 1997

Thompson, J., *The War at Sea 1914–1918*, Sidgwick & Jackson/Imperial War Museum, 2005

Thorne, C., *Allies of a Kind: The United States, Britain and the war against Japan, 1941–1945*, OUP, 1978

Thornton, R. H., *British Shipping*, CUP, 1945

Tirpitz, A. von, *My Memoirs*, 2 vols, Hurst & Blackett, 1919

Tocqueville, A. de, *Democracy in America*, trans. H.Reeve, 2 vols, Schocken Books, NY, 1961

Usborne, C. V., *Blast and Counterblast*, John Murray, 1935

Warner, R. F., *Imperial Cricket*, London, 1912

Werner, H. A., *Iron Coffins: A Personal Account of the German U-boat Battles of World War II*, Arthur Barker, 1970

Willmott, H. P., *The Barrier and the Javelin: Japanese and Allied Pacific Strategies February–June 1942*, US Naval Institute Press, 1983

Wilson, A. N., *The Victorians*, Hutchinson, 2002

—— *After the Victorians*, Hutchinson, 2005

Wilson, E. O., *The Creation: An Appeal to Save Life on Earth*, Norton, NY, 2006

Wilson, H. W., *Ironclads in Action*, 2 vols, London, 1896

Winks, R., *Cloak and Gown: Scholars in America's Secret War*, Collins Harvill, 1987

Winton, J., *The War at Sea, 1939–1945*, Hutchinson, 1967 (Vintage edn, 2007)

Woodham-Smith, C., *Florence Nightingale 1820–1910*, Constable, 1950

Woodman, R., *The Arctic Convoys 1941–1945*, John Murray, 1994

Index

Index